Bartók, Hungary, and
the Renewal of Tradition

CALIFORNIA STUDIES IN 20TH-CENTURY MUSIC

Richard Taruskin, General Editor

Bartók, Hungary, and the Renewal of Tradition

*Case Studies in the Intersection
of Modernity and Nationality*

DAVID E. SCHNEIDER

University of California Press

BERKELEY   LOS ANGELES   LONDON

The publisher gratefully acknowledges the generous
contribution to this book provided by the Ahmanson
Foundation Humanities Endowment Fund of the
University of California Press Foundation.

University of California Press, one of the most distinguished
university presses in the United States, enriches lives around the
world by advancing scholarship in the humanities, social sciences,
and natural sciences. Its activities are supported by the UC Press
Foundation and by philanthropic contributions from individuals
and institutions. For more information, visit www.ucpress.edu.

University of California Press
Berkeley and Los Angeles, California

University of California Press, Ltd.
London, England

Library of Congress Cataloging-in-Publication Data

Schneider, David E., 1963–
    Bartók, Hungary, and the renewal of tradition : case studies in the
intersection of modernity and nationality / David E. Schneider.
        p.   cm. — (California studies in 20th-century music ; 5)
    Includes bibliographical references (p.   ) and index.
    ISBN-13: 978-0-520-24503-7 (cloth : alk. paper)
    ISBN-10: 0-520-24503-2 (cloth : alk. paper)
        1. Bartók, Béla, 1881–1945—Criticism and interpretation.
    2. Composers—Hungary—Biography.   3. Music—Hungary—
    20th century—History and criticism.   I. Title.   II. Series.
    ML410.B26S36   2006
    780.92—dc22

                                                        2006040262

Manufactured in the United States of America

15   14   13   12   11   10   09   08   07   06
10   9   8   7   6   5   4   3   2   1

This book is printed on New Leaf EcoBook 50, a 100% recycled fiber of
which 50% is de-inked post-consumer waste, processed chlorine-free.
EcoBook 50 is acid-free and meets the minimum requirements of
ANSI/ASTM D5634–01 (Permanence of Paper).

In memoriam
Sándor Móricz and Jeffrey Alan Willick

Contents

Acknowledgments

My interest in Bartók dates back to my days as a professional clarinetist and predates my musicological studies. In those days Bartók's *Contrasts* for clarinet, violin, and piano held a special place in my repertoire, and his Violin Concerto (1938), which first captivated me at the Aspen Music Festival in 1983 when it was the required audition piece for the violin concerto competition, was for many years my favorite symphonic composition. Both works struck me as near-perfect combinations of sweet and sour: immediately accessible, but multilayered and complicated enough not to wear thin even after repeated hearings. László Somfai rekindled my interest in these two works in 1989 when he visited UC Berkeley as Bloch Lecturer at the beginning of my graduate studies there. At Somfai's lectures I was intrigued to learn of a connection between the first movement of *Contrasts*, entitled *"Verbunkos,"* and the first movement of the Violin Concerto, which Bartók had designated "tempo di verbunkos" in an early manuscript version of the solo violin part. Much of the present book has grown out of my attempt to understand Bartók's relationship to *verbunkos,* a slippery term with several interrelated meanings that I have gradually come to realize are all intimately bound to nineteenth-century Hungarian musical traditions.

It gives me great pleasure to recognize and thank the individuals who have supported this project. To László Somfai, director of the Budapest Bartók Archives, I owe nothing less than the initial spark for fusing my interests as a performer to those of a scholar. I am also indebted to him for allowing me access to the materials of the Budapest Bartók Archives, for his frank and detailed criticism of my work, and for his scholarly example—especially the brilliantly eclectic set of analyses collected in *Tizennyolc Bartók-Tanulmány* (Eighteen Bartók Studies) that have inspired many of my own interpretations. Other members of the Hungarian Musicological

Institute whose work has influenced my own and who have provided a sounding board for some of my ideas include Tibor Tallián and László Vikárius. Folk-music specialists László Kelemen, István Pávai, Bálint Sárosi, Ferenc Sebő, and Lujza Tari have generously responded to my ideas about the relationship between accompanimental patterns in Bartók's work and Hungarian instrumental folk music. Ágnes Papp provided valuable criticism of chapter 1, and Éva Gurmai was a resourceful research assistant while I was working on chapter 3. Adrienne Gombocz of the Budapest Bartók Archives, Zsuzsa Szepesi, head of the library of the Hungarian Institute for Musicology, and Katalin Szerző, director of the Music Division of the National Széchenyi Library, have all provided valuable assistance in the use of their collections. Csaba Nagy generously provided me with a photograph of a modern *tárogató*.

Iván Waldbauer gave valuable encouragement at an early stage of this project. Peter Laki has been a generous critic, and, as editor of *Bartók and His World*, he provided a useful forum for some of the material that is now chapter 4. Judit Frigyesi's work on the development of Bartók's political ideas at the turn of the century has influenced my own understanding of Hungarian nationalism; I am grateful to her for encouragement and for detailed comments on an early draft of material for chapter 4. I am thankful to Danielle Fosler-Lussier and Beth Levy for friendship, scholarly example, and editing—especially their work as editors of *repercussions*, in which much of what is the sixth chapter of this book first appeared. Lynn Hooker has been generous in sharing her own work on Bartók and nineteenth-century Hungarian music. Other scholars to whom I owe a debt include Elliott Antokoletz, Amanda Bayley, Michael Beckerman, Jonathan Bellman, Malcolm Gillies, János Kárpáti, and Derek Katz.

I am thankful to Peter Bartók, the composer's younger son, for granting me permission to publish a portion of Bartók's manuscript to the Violin Concerto, and for providing me with facsimiles of manuscripts that contributed to my interpretation of the First Piano Concerto and Orchestral Suite No. 2. He also generously shared with me his reflections on his and his older brother's decision to return their father's body to Budapest in 1988.

I thank Mary Francis of UC Press for her sage guidance and support in the publishing process, Kalicia Pivirotto for her help in preparing the manuscript for submission, Rose Vekony and David Anderson for editorial guidance, and Ernie Mansfield for his expert preparation of musical examples.

I am pleased to be able to acknowledge the organizations that have provided support for my work. At the early stages of this project I received financial support from the International Research and Exchanges Board, the

American Musicological Society (AMS 50 Fellowship), and the American Council of Learned Societies. Later stages of my work have been generously supported by a grant from the Amherst College Faculty Research Award Program, as funded by the H. Axel Schupf '57 Fund for Intellectual Life.

Words cannot do justice to my debt to Richard Taruskin. His own work on neoclassicism and Russian traditions in Stravinsky's music bears directly on the present study. His mentorship, vision, and virtuoso editorial hand have repeatedly helped me to clarify my understanding of my material. Errors that remain are mine alone.

My greatest thanks go to my wife, Klára Móricz, herself a leading Bartókian and scholar of Jewish nationalism in music. She has been a constant, patient sounding board, insightful editor, partner in translation, and generous and honest critic. Those who know me will recognize that I do not engage in hyperbole when I say that she has provided me with the best possible model, inspiration, and support.

Introduction

All profound changes in consciousness, by their very
nature, bring with them characteristic amnesias.

BENEDICT ANDERSON

At the beginning of the twentieth century there was
a turning point in the history of modern music. The
excesses of the Romantics began to be unbearable for
many. There were composers who felt: "This road does
not lead us anywhere; there is no other solution but
a complete break with the nineteenth century."

BÉLA BARTÓK, 1931

In the first decade of the twentieth century the sense that the forging of a
new road in composition demanded a break with the traditions of the nineteenth century was a sentiment shared by many of the greatest musicians.
Loudly declared detachment from the past was part and parcel of a modernist aesthetics. But, for all the new directions championed by Debussy,
Janáček, Schoenberg, and Stravinsky, few if any composers so professed to
disdain their predecessors in their respective national schools of composition
as did the Hungarian Béla Bartók. Debussy praised Offenbach and idolized
Rameau. Janáček proudly considered himself part of a national lineage that
included Dvořák.[1] Schoenberg touted a connection to Brahms. Stravinsky,
however carefully he concealed his debts, made a show of idolizing Chaikovsky and never entirely repudiated Rimsky-Korsakov. Bartók, by contrast,
traced his lineage exclusively to non-Hungarians—Debussy, Beethoven,
and Bach—and had few kind words for earlier Hungarian composers. When
he did praise Ernő Dohnányi and Ferenc (Franz) Liszt, it was for their compositional skill, not the Hungarian qualities of their works. In Bartók's
telling of Hungarian music history, he (with Zoltán Kodály) was not simply
the first modern Hungarian composer, but the first composer to write what
could legitimately be considered Hungarian national music, because, in his
view, he was the first to base his works on a legitimate national source,

authentic Hungarian folk music. Thus, in Hungary, the turn to musical modernism went hand in hand not only with a break from the past, but also with the repudiation of earlier notions of what constituted the Hungarian style.

Bartók's view of his role in the creation of Hungarian national music exemplifies a change of consciousness so profound as to produce the amnesia that Benedict Anderson has asserted as necessary for narratives describing the history of a nation.[2] In the narrative of Bartók's artistic development, his personal life story had been told in conjunction with the history of the nation, and hence the break with the past—necessary for both the modernist and national tales—opened up an even bigger gap with the immediate past. What has variously been forgotten, overlooked, underestimated, and misunderstood in his life is the composer's continued debt to the very nineteenth-century Hungarian inheritance he professed to disavow. The purpose of this study is to explore aspects of Bartók's oeuvre that exemplify connections to these earlier traditions of Hungarian art music, to examine the strength of his creative involvement of these traditions in his early works, and to demonstrate how thoroughly and productively he transformed them in his mature compositions. By viewing Bartók's work from an angle that sheds light on its past, I hope to illuminate the richness of that past and at the same time to deepen our appreciation of his innovations. In this study I reexamine long-held beliefs not only about Bartók's relationship to his past, but also about the relationship of authentic folk music to Hungarian popular music. As has been the case with national histories, amnesia served an important function. It allowed Bartók to forge his own musical identity. But, as productive as amnesia may have been for him, the historian's job is to fill the memory hole.

As an introduction to the particulars of my argument, it may be instructive to take a small detour to recall Bartók's reburial in Hungary some forty-three years after his death in New York City. Observing how the composer was unwittingly made part of a Hungarian tradition of repatriation after his death serves as a telling symbol of how profoundly Hungarian national customs affected him during his lifetime.

In 1988 Béla Bartók's remains were exhumed from Ferncliff Cemetery north of New York City and returned to Budapest for reburial. Repatriation was not requested in his will, and, according to the composer's younger son, Peter, the decision to have Bartók transported to his native land was not an easy one.[3] Still, because post-mortem repatriation of national heroes has been a recurrent theme in Hungarian history, Bartók's return has the appearance of inevitability. It reflects his literal embodiment of Hungarian traditions that, while frequently resisted by the composer, ultimately tied him to Hungarian soil.

Like a number of the traditions I discuss in this book, post-mortem repatriation is not unique to Hungary. Its status as a Hungarian tradition stems from historical circumstances that have repeatedly allowed the return of well-known artists and political figures for burial to play an important role in the formation of Hungarian national consciousness. The practice was especially prominent in Bartók's youth and early maturity, a time of fervent nationalist sentiment fueled by the sense of indignity caused by Hungary's second-class position vis-à-vis Austria in the Austro-Hungarian monarchy. At this stage, Hungarian nationalism largely fit what Hans Kohn has described as "Eastern nationalism," which "grew in protest against and in conflict with the existing state pattern."[4] In this context, (re)burial of politically and culturally significant figures functioned to strengthen the myth of common national ancestry as a basis for political self-determination.[5]

The body of Lajos Kossuth (1802–94), leader of the Hungarian revolution of 1848–49 and the subject of Bartók's first completed symphonic composition, was returned to Budapest for burial upon his death in Turin after some forty-five years in exile. Six years later, in 1900, the body of Mihály Munkácsy (1844–1900), the most successful Hungarian painter of the nineteenth century, was brought back to Budapest for a massive public funeral from Paris, where he had lived for most of his adult life. In 1906 the nation once again focused its attention on the return of a hero when the ashes of Prince Ferenc Rákóczi II (1676–1735), leader of the early-eighteenth-century War of Independence (1703–11), were transported to Hungary from Turkey, where he had died in exile more than a century and a half before. All the returns were elaborate, much publicized affairs. The return of Rákóczi's ashes to his hometown, for instance, followed a three-week-long tour of the country. Pompous funereal processions greeted the entourage at every stop.[6]

Leaders in a small nation frequently dominated by foreign powers, Kossuth and Rákóczi, Hungary's two most important revolutionaries, had escaped into exile after the failure of their causes. Munkácsy left for Munich and continued on to Düsseldorf and Paris to seek artistic opportunities unavailable in his native land. Bartók's decision to leave Budapest for New York in 1940 combined the traditions of artistic relocation and political exile. The significant number of prominent Hungarians forced into exile since Rákóczi's day—in the last hundred years, of the fourteen Nobel prizes awarded to men of Hungarian birth, only two were residents of Hungary at the time of their awards—signals the repeated failure of Hungary to live up to the expectations and ideals of its greatest sons.[7] The imposing processions, lavish press coverage, and atmosphere of national mourning that accompanied the post-mortem returns of prominent Hungarians established in Hungary a practice of recycling examples of national failure as symbols of national pride.

Bartók too was part of this tradition, but what makes his belated return especially poignant is that the nation, which by the time of his reburial had long accepted him as its greatest composer, had regarded him and his works with great suspicion during his lifetime. Because Bartók's approach to composition had challenged long-held beliefs about the function and style of national music in Hungary, his work had raised objections on both social and aesthetic grounds.

Although even some of Bartók's early works combine "national" and "progressive" elements, the national markers in his first large-scale compositions, written before his discovery of peasant music, were displayed within a tonal language conventional enough to convey a sense of continuity with earlier, nineteenth-century Romantic notions of Hungarian music. Bartók's mature style, which he began to develop in earnest after his first folk-music collecting expedition to Transylvania (1907), seemed to fly in the face of those notions. Although from a Germanic nineteenth-century perspective Bartók's interest in Hungarian folk music would seem to be a continuation of a Herderian desire to locate the essence of the nation in its *Volk*, from the perspective of early-twentieth-century Hungary, Bartók's belief in the oppressed peasantry as the true guardian of national ethos was radical, even revolutionary. In Hungary it was not the peasantry but the nobility and those with noble pretensions who had been considered to embody the national spirit ever since the emergence of the concept of Hungary as a nation in the early nineteenth century. In the Hungarian context *Volk* referred not to the peasantry but to the lower nobility.[8]

Bartók's rejection of the popular music cherished by the gentry in favor of the older, rougher-hewn music of the peasantry was thus unacceptable to a large segment of Hungarian society. A further offense was his acceptance of the peasant music of non-Magyar peoples as a creative resource, especially peoples (e.g., Romanians, Slovaks) who, especially following the partition of Hungary after World War I, were often in politically antagonistic relationships with the Magyars. Bartók's incorporation of non-Magyar folk music in his own works may be seen as a refusal to endorse Hungary's hostile postwar stance toward its neighbors. At the same time, however, a work such as *Dance Suite* (1923), in which the Hungarian-style theme of the ritornello binds together dances evocative of several non-Magyar peoples, suggests that even after the war Bartók's ideal remained a Hungarian-led, multiethnic state, what he called a "brotherhood of peoples."[9] These political overtones notwithstanding, it would be a mistake to regard his compositions written after 1905 as a reflection of mainstream Hungarian nationalism.[10] After an initial infatuation with aggressive nationalism in the first half-decade of the twentieth century, only rarely did Bartók align his music with specific political movements. His mature work betrays none of the chauvinism, stemming from a sense of collective inadequacy or failure, that marred nationalist movements in East Central Europe and reached a peak of intensity in Hungary between the millennial celebrations of 1896 and the end of the Second World War—almost exactly the period, in other words, of Bartók's career.[11]

Bartók's insistence on the authenticity of his folk material, and his location of authenticity in peasant lore, is not the only point of difference between him and earlier generations of composers. He also sought in genuine peasant music the basis and justification of a radically new musical language. Bartók's modernism made his music more difficult to understand than any previous musical embodiment of the Hungarian national impulse. His call for its acceptance as national music despite its difficulty and its modernity might seem to corroborate Ernest Gellner's view that nationalism frequently consists of the imposition of high culture in the name of a putative folk culture.[12] And yet Gellner's insight fails to make allowance for the perverse twist peculiar to Hungarian musical culture, whereby the aristocracy's concept of national music was the one accepted by all classes, including peasants, who were quick to adopt the aristocracy's favorite popular songs. Thus Bartók's use of peasant music was, in contrast to the folk-inflected styles of Dvořák, Grieg, or Liszt, far more elitist than populist. His reliance on peasant artifacts has much in common with the Russian neonationalist movement in art that inspired Igor Stravinsky's stylistic appropriations from folk tunes in his "Russian period."[13] But unlike Stravinsky, who after emigrating to the West deemphasized his Russian background and sought recognition as a cosmopolitan modernist, Bartók was viewed abroad too emphatically as a Hungarian composer and (despite the controversy surrounding his work) was too prominent a figure in Hungarian cultural life to disassociate himself from his Hungarian roots. That Bartók's reputation in Western Europe and the United States as the greatest living Hungarian composer played a crucial role in his domestic reception is symptomatic of Hungary's sense of cultural inferiority toward what Hungarians refer to as "the West."

For Bartók, as for the relatively small number of propagators of his music during his lifetime, the authenticity of his peasant sources served to justify both the aesthetic value of his modernist style and his claim that he was writing national music. The desire to replace a widely accepted, generally conservative national style with a modernist one led Bartók and his Hungarian apologists to discredit the national credentials of earlier composers who had written their Hungarian music on the basis of popular music (often misleadingly termed "Gypsy") rather than peasant music.

The opposition between what Bartók presented as new "authentic" and what he dismissed as older "corrupt" approaches to Hungarian national music became such a fundamental component of the composer's legacy that it went virtually unquestioned for some five decades after his death.[14] "From pure springs only," a quote from Bartók's *Cantata Profana*, has been repeated so frequently in Hungary as to become a mantra symbolizing the uncritical acceptance of the composer's claim to have discovered the "true" path toward the creation of Hungarian music.[15] Until recently his status as a national hero has inhibited recognition of his lifelong debt to nineteenth-century Hungarian music. Implicit in this scholarly omission was anxiety lest acknowledgment of such debt compromise the foundation of Bartók's reputation, weakening both the modernist cachet of his work, central to his prestige outside of Hungary, and the claim of authenticity, the cornerstone of his status at home.

To establish Bartók's intimate knowledge of nineteenth-century Hungarian musical traditions and the continuities between his "old" and "new" approaches to Hungarian music, I devote significant attention to three of Bartók's works composed before 1907: *Kossuth* (1903), the Rhapsody for Piano, op. 1 (1904), and the Andante of the Suite for Orchestra No. 2 (1905). These early works provide an important bridge between Bartók's later works and earlier traditions of Hungarian art music. Similarly, focusing on genres and works designed to appeal to large audiences—ballets, concertos, rhapsodies, an orchestral suite, and an oft-played character piece for piano—allows me to emphasize an aspect of Bartók's compositional voice that has sometimes been overshadowed by the more prestigious and gritty works of chamber music that were aimed at a more elite and international audience of modern-music connoisseurs. Extending three and a half decades from *Kossuth* to the Violin Concerto (1938), the penultimate work completed in Europe, the compositions discussed here offer an overview of Bartók's changing position vis-à-vis his own country before his last years in the United States.

Because my primary aim in musical analysis has been neither to develop an analytic theory nor to provide a comprehensive guide to Bartók's music, my musical discussions focus on single movements and passages that provide evidence for my historical argument. I maintain that although all attempts to characterize the sound of music as nationalist must identify particular stylistic traits as national, it is the historically determined confluence of such gestures rather than their individual character that produces national specificity. For one conspicuous example, the front-accented *short-long* rhythm that signals Hungarianness in much of the music discussed in these pages is anything but uniquely Hungarian—it is equally characteristic of Scottish and Czech music and regularly appears in music lacking a distinctive national character. What gives it denotative power is the context, both stylistic and historical, in which it occurs. This book seeks to define such contexts.

Despite my emphasis on nineteenth-century traditions in Bartók's music, my aim is not to expose him as a Romantic or a chauvinist in spite of himself. Rather, by reading Bartók's life and works with eye and ear attuned to precisely those aspects that are often written out of modernist biography, I hope to highlight and more accurately characterize the stylistic change that emerged from Bartók's engagement with his national inheritance. At the same time I hope to call into question the habit of sharply dichotomizing modernism and Romanticism, or nationalism and universalism. Precisely insofar as Bartók's life and work resist such categorization, they hold crucial lessons for music history.

ONE

Tradition Rejected

*Bartók's Polemics and the Nineteenth-Century
Hungarian Musical Inheritance*

Naturally a composer will be most influenced by the music he
hears the most—the music of his home.

BARTÓK, 1921

Attempting to answer the question "What is Hungarian?" has been a preoccupation of educated Hungarians since the rise of national consciousness
in the early nineteenth century. The question "What is Hungarian in
music?" that lies behind so many of Bartók's essays is itself part of a
national debate that had been going on for decades before his compositions
and folk-music research redefined and intensified it.[1] Despite the rigidity of
some who have striven to define it, Hungarianness *(magyarság)* has never
been a static concept. On one level Bartók, like all Hungarian composers,
redefined it with every piece he wrote. Certain generalizations can be made,
however, in relation to various historical contexts. In the decade before the
First World War, *magyarság* was most often defined in opposition to
Austria, the dominant partner in the Austro-Hungarian monarchy. After
1918, when Hungary gained its independence but lost two-thirds of its territory to its neighbors, *magyarság* was often associated with a desire to
regain the "glories" of Hungary's imperial past. Another, interrelated set of
meanings emerged in the 1930s in connection with the rising influence of
National Socialist Germany.

In this third phase, historian Gyula Szekfű (1883–1955) brought the
question of Hungarian identity to the front lines of scholarly debate by
asking a group of Hungary's leading intellectuals to address it for each of
their respective fields. The result was a collection of essays published in
1939 as *Mi a magyar?* (What Is Hungarian?).[2] The collection contained an
extensive article entitled "Magyarság a zenében" (Hungarianness in Music)
by Bartók's closest friend and colleague, the composer and folklorist Zoltán

Kodály (1882–1967).[3] His inclusion in Szekfű's volume is testimony to the centrality of music in the discourse about Hungarian identity. Kodály's essay, like so many of his and Bartók's writings, detached musical *magyarság* from the set of musical topics that had come to symbolize the nation with the rise of nationalism in the first half of the nineteenth century. Because Hungarian folk music, like the Finno-Ugric Hungarian language, was distinct from the music of its Indo-European neighbors, Kodály argued that it should replace the nineteenth-century Hungarian style as the building block of a national musical culture. Folk music, Kodály believed, could reinforce an image of the nation proud to set itself apart from the rest of Europe because of its Asiatic roots. Emphasizing Hungary's unique position between East and West, he brought his essay to a close with a pair of leading questions: "One of our hands holds the hand of the Nogay-Tartars, the Votyaks and Cheremiss, the other that of Bach and Palestrina. Can we bring these two distant worlds together? Can we be not only a ferryboat shuttling between the cultures of Europe and Asia, but a bridge—perhaps even dry ground that is an integral part of both?"[4] The image of Hungary as a synthesizer of Eastern traditions and Western high culture bespeaks an inclusive, liberal vision of the nation. In this formulation, Hungarian music is defined by its openness to both the "primitivism" of its own past and the "refinement" of European high culture. But because what Kodály accepted as Hungary's past was confined to the country's folk music, his version of *magyarság* in music also represented a modernist, neonationalist stance that secured its authenticity by authenticating its national sources.

The idea of synthesizing foreign and native traditions into a national style was hardly Bartók's or Kodály's invention. It was the usual presumption of nationalist composers. To mention only one example, in the mid-nineteenth century Glinka expressed a Russian national ideal by mixing and matching the best of two Western European traditions—Italian bel canto melody and German contrapuntal technique—with Russian folk music. Bartók and Kodály's approach, like Glinka's, stemmed in part from a sense of cultural inferiority, but turned the relative lack of a distinctively native high culture into a source of opportunity and pride. In some respects their technique was not new in Hungary at the beginning of the twentieth century. Mixing of foreign and native musical styles was just what nationally minded Hungarian composers had practiced throughout the nineteenth century. Bartók and Kodály's image of synthesis, however, implied more. In Hungary, East and West were not just international destinations, but ciphers for the two disparate worlds within Hungary's own borders: the Hungarian village and the Hungarian city.

The suggestion of a Hungarian musical unification of the "East" (rural culture) with the "West" (urban culture) touched a raw political nerve and thereby engaged Bartók and Kodály in a domestic social debate. The combination of the culture of peasants and that of the bourgeoisie was, at least through the first several decades of the twentieth century, anathema to the majority of educated Hungarians. In Hungarian the word "peasant" (*paraszt*, from the Slavic *prost*, i.e., simpleton) was no mere neutral descriptive term. It was an insult, in historian Andrew Janos's words, "a term of disparagement conveying a sense of callous simplicity that made [it] nearly unfit for use in polite society."[5]

Another layer of rural society, the landowners known as the gentry or petty nobility, even more stridently opposed the idea that the peasantry held something of cultural value in their music. Their opposition derived from their specific social status. Throughout the nineteenth century, increasing numbers of the gentry had fallen victim to the dual blows dealt by the inefficient, out-of-date means of agricultural production on their small estates and their own sense that they were above the lowly work of capitalist enterprise. They found some material recompense for the steady decline in their economic status by entering the civil service. More significantly for music history, they tended to compensate for their loss of political power by claiming themselves as the sole proprietors of the ancient Hungarian national spirit. Their favored music was the fare typically played in cafés and country inns by so-called Gypsy ensembles. To suggest to members of this class that the music of the peasants—the people over whom the gentry wielded their bureaucratic power most vindictively—held the key to authentic Hungarian identity was at least as unsettling for its social as for its artistic implications.

And yet that was precisely what Bartók and Kodály claimed in the spirit of their modernist aesthetics. It was the gentry's popular musical culture, which was part of both men's backgrounds, that these composers tried to write out of their musical heritage. For in their judgment, that music was at once more artificial than the traditional music of the peasants, and less artful than art music.

Discovery and Mission

A crucial catalyst for Bartók's rejection of the musical style long regarded as representative of the spirit of the nation was his discovery of what he would come to call "old-style" Hungarian folk songs during his first folk-song collecting expedition to Transylvania in summer 1907.[6] The "old-style" melodies bore little resemblance to the Hungarian style as it had been previously conceived, and the strangeness of these songs would become one of the strongest inspirations for Bartók's modernist style. Precisely because these were not tunes with which he had grown up, they triggered his musical imagination. Integrating the characteristics of these "old-style" melodies and of other folk repertoires—"new-style" songs, instrumental music, the peasant music of non-Hungarians—into a modern musical style was the artistic project that sustained Bartók for the rest of his life.

A parallel lifelong mission was winning for peasant music due recognition as a Hungarian national treasure. It bore fruit in articles, lectures, and longer studies—some aimed at specialists, some at the general public—in which Bartók sought to articulate the differences between Hungarian peasant music, especially the "old-style" pentatonic folk songs that he believed to have been brought to the Carpathian Basin a thousand years before by the Asiatic Magyar tribes, and the newer elements that had come to define the Hungarian style in the popular and concert music of the late-eighteenth and nineteenth centuries.

In his writings intended for the general public, Bartók often exaggerated the difference between peasant music (not all of which was ancient) and more popular Hungarian musical traditions. Although he made more nuanced analyses of the interrelationships between various types of peasant music and Hungarian popular music in several of his scholarly writings, the stark distinctions Bartók drew in his more popular essays have rarely been questioned. The sources of his own music have been interpreted along similarly simplified lines. Despite Bartók's professed rejection of Hungarian music that was based on the popular notions of the Hungarian style, the composer's own synthesis of folk music and contemporary art music was not as different from earlier attempts to create a national style as he implied. The most characteristic categories of the nineteenth-century Hungarian music—the instrumental dance music known as *verbunkos* and the sentimental popular song called *magyar nóta*, both disseminated by Gypsy bands and hence called "Gypsy music"—were not unrelated to folk traditions. Their incorporation into national art music stemmed initially from the same aspirations as Bartók's. Nor was the composer's own music completely devoid of traditionally accepted elements of the Hungarian style. To assess Bartók's position in the history of the creation of a specifically Hungarian art music we need first to investigate the roots of the nineteenth-century Hungarian style and his reasons for rejecting it.

The Polemics of a Convert

Typical of Bartók's polemical writings for nonspecialists was a 1911 essay entitled "A magyar zenéről" (On Hungarian Music).[7] Written some seven years after he had made his first notation of a Hungarian peasant song, but only four years since he had recognized pentatonicism as a crucial structural element of "old-style" melodies, Bartók's essay included a scathing assessment of all previous attempts to create a Hungarian style in music. Writing with a convert's zeal, he effectively removed himself from the traditional lineage of Hungarian music. This view was quickly accepted as an accurate description of Bartók's unique place in Hungarian music history and has only recently come under scholarly scrutiny.[8] As a prelude to an overdue critique, his words are worth quoting at some length:

> According to the natural order of things, practice comes before theory. We see the opposite with Hungarian national music: scientific works were already published years ago dealing with the characteristic features of Hungarian music, an attempt to define something nonexistent at the time.[9]
> [Until a few years ago] there was no valuable, distinctive, and characteristically Hungarian art music. The music of Bihari, Lavotta, and a few foreigners—Csermák, Rózsavölgyi, Pecsenyánszki, etc.—that is to say, nothing but more or less dilettante musicians all under the influence of Gypsy music and unworthy of the admiration of people of good taste, cannot be taken as a basis [for Hungarian art music].[10] Only dilettante musicologists can discuss these dilettante works in a serious tone of voice. Moreover, all of this is not even national music, because it is surely not Hungarian but Gypsy. That is, its characteristics are the melodic distortions of a foreign people, of the Gypsies.
> On the other hand, the endeavors of our serious-minded musicians were also sterile, because, while several of them servilely imitated foreign styles, others, for instance, Ferenc Erkel, tried to solve the task by wedging one or two Gypsy-style tunes or *csárdás* between musical items of Italian character. The mixture of such heterogeneous elements does not produce a Hungarian style, merely a conglomerate lacking any style.[11]

The haughty, at times xenophobic tone of Bartók's essay is reminiscent of his letters around the time of his symphonic poem *Kossuth* (1903). Such nationalist zeal was not, however, typical of *Auróra* (Dawn), the journal of progressive art and literature in which "On Hungarian Music" appeared. *Auróra*, which ceased publication in 1912 after seventeen slim issues, had caught the notice of Budapest's intelligentsia for its high-brow modern literary offerings and coverage of contemporary art.[12] The magazine covered subjects ranging from Hungarian folk art to the latest artistic trends in

Western Europe, including the Paris seasons of Diaghilev's Ballets Russes, and the redesigning of Budapest's public spaces on the model of other great European cities. As its title implies, the goal of the magazine seems to have been to herald the dawn of a new age in Hungarian art and culture. The scope of its coverage suggested that the renovation of Hungarian high art depended both on staying up to date with the latest European trends and on awareness of Hungarian peasant culture. Thus, despite the unusual stridency of Bartók's tone, his call for the renewal of Hungarian music through folk music well fit *Auróra*'s implicit mission. Reprinted thirteen times in seven languages,[13] Bartók's essay, or rather its rhetoric, has encouraged the understanding of Hungarian music in terms of categorical oppositions: Gypsies versus Hungarians (read: peasants); nineteenth- versus twentieth-century music (i.e., Bartók's and Kodály's compositions); amateur versus professional musicians; and original composers versus epigones. Yet as soon as one confronts the messy world of actual musical practice, Bartók's categories begin to unravel.

Distinctively Hungarian music has existed in a continuous tradition since the end of the eighteenth century. Although in "On Hungarian Music" he dismissed all claims to authenticity in Hungarian art music previous to his own, in fact the very nationalism that inspired Bartók to reject his predecessors was a continuation of the fervor of nineteenth-century Hungarian nationalism. Even the music that represented this earlier Romantic nationalism, although not based on the same self-conscious and scientifically rigorous relationship to folk music that he began advocating around 1906, nevertheless relied on a set of conventions that had roots in folk music. This common heritage of folk music explains why a number of melodic and accompanimental patterns typical of the Hungarian style can be found both in Bartók's music and in that of his Hungarian predecessors, who were unaware of peasant music. Bartók's assertion of the superiority of his and Kodály's approach to Hungarian national music was based on an unprecedented knowledge of Hungarian folk music, but the categorical distinctions he made in his article "On Hungarian Music" are not scientific. Rather, they seem to be the fruit of frustration, likely fueled by criticism Bartók had received both for his modernist style and for his radical assertion that only music informed by first-hand experience with folk culture deserved to be accepted as representative of the Hungarian nation. An effective piece of journalism given the atmosphere of jingoistic nationalism in Hungary at the time, "On Hungarian Music" was a polemic undeserving of credence on a par with Bartók's more scholarly work.

The Mixed Origins of the Hungarian Style

The emergence of a distinctly Hungarian musical style in the late eighteenth century seems to have been the result of mixing elements of Hungarian folk music with the common-practice harmony of classical music. Although this markedly national style developed gradually and at the hands of countless anonymous practitioners, the process was not unlike Bartók's own combination of Hungarian folk music with more modern idioms of European art music. Its origins have been traced to a type of melody that began to appear in Hungarian manuscripts in the late seventeenth century.[14] These new melodies, which are believed to have belonged to an earlier oral tradition, were distinguished from dance tunes in earlier Hungarian manuscripts by several new features, most crucially by their use of a characteristic scale. This scale can be described as a Phrygian scale with the second and third scale degrees raised when ascending, or, because the ear naturally reinterpreted the Phrygian as minor when the melodies were harmonized, as a melodic minor scale starting on the fifth scale degree (example 1). Melodies with this particular scale were common not only in Hungarian, but also Polish and Slovakian, manuscripts of instrumental music.[15] Bartók recognized the ethnically mixed origin of this melody type and believed it to be related to Persian-Arab melodies.[16] Yet as he pointed out, despite its unclear national affinities the melody became representative of a particularly Hungarian style. Because in the eighteenth century a song of this type used words referring to the Transylvanian prince Ferenc Rákóczi II (1676–1735), the leader of an anti-Habsburg war of independence (1703–11), these melodies have come to be known as the Rákóczi-melody type *(Rákóczi-nóta dallamkör)* (example 2). From the seventeenth century on, this type of melody existed in both folk-music and popular dance-music repertories. Whereas in the nineteenth century it became the basis for the new national dance music, in the early twentieth century it was preserved as part of the repertoire collected from Hungarian peasants. Thus although not only "racially" mixed, as Bartók pointed out, but also impure in terms of its mixed popular and folk roots, this melody type came to constitute an important part of the repertoire of Hungarian folk song. The popular song "Szép vagy, gyönyörű vagy Magyarország" (Hungary, You Are Beautiful) from Zsigmond Vincze's 1926 operetta *A hamburgi menyasszony* (The Bride from Hamburg)—a tune now famous for Bartók's adaptation of it in the fourth movement of his Concerto for Orchestra—is a latter-day example of a piece that takes its Hungarian quality from the Rákóczi-melody type (example 3).[17]

EXAMPLE 1. Characteristic "Phrygian" scale

EXAMPLE 2. "Rákóczi, Bezerényi" (László Dobszay, *Magyar zenetörténet*, 2nd exp. ed. [Budapest: Planétás Kiadó, 1998], 185)

EXAMPLE 3. Zsigmond Vincze, "Szép vagy, gyönyörû vagy Magyarország" (Hungary, You Are Beautiful), from the operetta *A hamburgi menyasszony* (The Bride from Hamburg; 1926)

The development of the rhythmically loose Rákóczi-melody type into the rhythmically more regular Hungarian style of dance music known as *verbunkos* in the late eighteenth century seems to have been the result of cross-fertilization with another type of folk songs known as swineherd melodies *(kanász-nóták).* Like the Rákóczi melodies, the swineherd melodies owe their name to the text of a well-known example of the type, "Megismerni a kanászt" (One can recognize the swineherd . . .) (example 4). The most typical characteristic of this type of dance tune is a thirteen-syllable rhythmic pattern ♪♪♪♪|♪♪♪|♪♪♪♪|♩♩|, which is thought to have been applied to some melodies of the Rákóczi type. Tunes that combine the melodic characteristics of the Rákóczi-melody type with the rhythmic outline of the swineherd type became popular in instrumental music in the eighteenth century. Although the process of transformation cannot be traced in detail, scholars believe that a gradual slowing down of the tempo of these tunes and a concomitant introduction of dotted rhythms common in slow dances of the period resulted in a new type of instrumental music,

EXAMPLE 4. "Megismerni a kanászt" (One Can Recognize the Swineherd), the melody from which the "swineherd-melody type" takes its name

EXAMPLE 5. Derivation of the *verbunkos* rhythmic pattern from the "swineherd" rhythm (Dobszay, *Magyar zenetörténet*, 190)

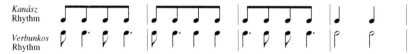

EXAMPLE 6. Late-eighteenth-century Hungarian dance melody *(verbunkos), 34 pesti magyar tánc* (34 Hungarian Dances from Pest) (Dobszay, *Magyar zenetörténet*, 268)

often referred to as *verbunkos* (example 5). Bartók himself traced the origin of *verbunkos* to the combination of these two types of melodies.[18]

During the last quarter of the eighteenth century an explosion of manuscripts and publications featuring dances combining the rhythmic characteristics of swineherd songs, the melodic formulas typical of the Rákóczi-melody type, the harmonic vocabulary of Viennese classicism, virtuoso embellishments typical of Hungarian Gypsy performers, and phrase structure common to both classical periodic structure and Hungarian folk songs testifies to the establishment and popularity of *verbunkos* dances (example 6).[19] Nowhere were the distinctions Bartók would often invoke between rural and urban, Gypsy and peasant, Hungarian and Western European styles more blurred than in this repertoire.

Verbunkos

Verbunkos, from the German *Werbung* (recruitment), takes its name from the practice of recruiting Hungarian peasants for the Habsburg army. Although recruitment had occurred sporadically in Hungarian lands earlier, the practice began in earnest in 1715 with the formation of a permanent militia and officially ended in 1849 when, after the failed Hungarian War of Independence (1848–49), universal conscription made the practice obsolete.[20] Ironically, although the style of music associated with recruitment came to embody Hungary's aspirations for independence from Austria beginning in about 1820, *verbunkos* owes its name to a practice born of Habsburg domination.

In today's parlance the term *verbunkos* is used in a variety of different, if interrelated, ways. Most specifically, *verbunkos* refers to a large group of men's folk dances usually identified by the inclusion of the term in their titles: *Vasvári verbunk* (*Verbunkos* from Vasvár), *Magyar verbunk* (Hungarian *verbunkos*), *Szóló verbunk* (Solo *verbunkos*), to name just a few.[21] The term becomes less specific when applied to music. Not only is it used to describe the music for dances specifically referred to as *verbunkos*, it also encompasses the music for a number of other folk dances, including men's dances such as the *legényes* (young man's dance) and *botoló* (stick dance), as well as the couple's dance known as the *csárdás* (from *csárda*, country inn).[22] *Verbunkos* is also used to refer collectively to a suite of instrumental pieces, arranged in order of increasing tempo and frequently consisting of the following three parts:[23]

> 1. A slow (*lassú*), free introductory section sometimes without a steady beat. Since the middle of the nineteenth century this has been commonly

referred to as *hallgató* (literally: "listening," best understood as music for listening as opposed to dancing).

2. A dance of medium tempo with a steady beat, sometimes referred to as *közép gyors* (medium fast) or *figura* (figure), which may consist of several dances strung together. Together parts 1 and 2 make up the *lassú* (slow) first section of the series of dances and are not always distinct from each other.

3. A fast dance (*friss*) or series of increasingly fast dances, sometimes referred to as *trio*.

In art music, nationally inspired Hungarian rhapsodies (à la Liszt) take their slow-fast structure directly from this folk/Gypsy practice. In some contexts, the slow dance is also specifically referred to as *verbunkos*, much as "minuet" refers both to a section and to the whole of the dance sequence minuet-trio-minuet.

In the context of art music, *verbunkos* designates a large body of late-eighteenth- and nineteenth-century virtuoso instrumental music in duple meter either based on or influenced by the tunes used to accompany folk dances. Because of an outpouring of compositions in this style by virtuoso violinists such as János Bihari, Anton Csermák, János Lavotta, and Márk Rózsavölgyi, historians of Hungarian music commonly refer to the first half of the nineteenth century as "the golden age of *verbunkos*."[24] Notations of these dance tunes are sometimes identified as *verbunkos* by some variation of the word (*Werbung, verbunk, barbunc*) or by *toborzó*, another Hungarian word for recruitment.[25] More often pieces in the *verbunkos* style simply carry titles that suggest the Hungarian or "Gypsy" style—*Ungarishe, Magyar, Zingaresca*—and/or a Hungarian tempo marking such as *lassú* (slow), *lassan* or *lassacskán* (slowly), or *friss* (sometimes *friska*, fast). Most generally *verbunkos* is used to describe the style of all characteristically Hungarian instrumental music of the late eighteenth and nineteenth centuries. In this case its meaning is no more specific than what is known internationally as the *style hongrois* or Hungarian style.[26]

FUNCTION AND STRUCTURE

The function of music in recruitment was to accompany the dancing that was part and parcel of festivities intended to break down potential recruits' resistance to joining the army with an abundance of wine and soldierly posturing designed to glorify military life. Both the music—originally often performed by a peasant bagpiper, later more often by small Gypsy ensembles of strings and hammered dulcimer (cimbalom)—and the dances used in recruitment are believed to have overlapped with the folk music and dances of the region. The musicians, whether a peasant bagpiper or members of a Gypsy band, are thought to have been hired locally rather than imported by the military. It is presumed, therefore, that they would not have been expected or able to play a new or unusual repertoire specifically for recruitment. Similarly, because one intention seems to have been to encourage young men of the village to join in the dancing, it is likely that the dances were already known to them, although the recruiters tried to impress them with new levels of virtuosity. The most detailed description of recruitment in nineteenth-century Hungary is by the Benedictine monk and scholar Gergely Czuczor (1800–1866) from 1843:

> We stand in the market square of a small town in which peasants from the surrounding country gather. From among the various noises the harsh music of the Turkish pipe *(tárogató)* strikes our ears. The bobbing guardians of the peace come into sight, and then, behold, there come the soldiers accompanied by a crowd, mostly village youngsters. First comes the sergeant, who with military demeanor steps with most manly seriousness. He doesn't lope, jump, click his heels, or shout, but his every step marks the rhythm of the music— and he lifts his cane to it. . . . Three or four steps behind him come a recruiting company among whom the corporal stands out straight away with his bearing, even if we were not to consider his hazel stick and the gold trimming on his hat. An official facial expression colored with some sauciness and a measured light step are his conspicuous features. He is less serious than the sergeant but of more moderate humor than the young lads, he moves his feet pointedly and stands as something of an example before the young men, because normally he is the master directing the group of dancers, and for this reason his every movement is simple but characteristic, while the young lads surround him with dashing lightness, clicking their ankles and clapping, ornamenting and sharpening their steps. They move round the market like this until the sergeant stops at a suitable place and, leaning on his cane, gives a sign. Then the young men stand round in a circle with the corporal in the center, and with the Gypsy band, usually in uniform, playing a new song, the recruiting begins. While the first verse is being played we do not see any dance steps; but the men either remain in their place clicking their heels or they walk round in a circle and in this way learn the turns and rhythm of the song, and adjust themselves to the dance. Then follows a largely determined series of slow figures—but if not, the corporal announces it, the dancers' eyes watching him while everyone watches his opposite partner. It is characteristic of this part of the dance that it is made up only of systematic and less ornamental steps, so that if the song is eight bars, two bars to the right, one to the left, once more two to the right and one to the left, which is then finished off by two corresponding bars to drop back into place. After they have danced five or six slow verses like this, it is time for something more showy, which is faster and more fiery than what precedes it because now they are moving here

and there and bobbing about, to which the rattling of the swinging swords and the hesitant swaying of the bags contribute and evoke a picture of the true heroic dance. But this, just like the more passionate emotion which it depicts, does not last long, and the music, and with it, the movement, return to the earlier slow and dignified mood. This goes on, alternating two or three times, until at a sign from the sergeant the merry group draws apart.[27]

The orderly sequence of events in Czuczor's account may represent a somewhat idealized version of what is often likely to have been a drunken revelry. Several aspects of the description do, however, correspond to features found in contemporaneous notated sources of *verbunkos* music and to the Transylvanian instrumental music that is thought to have preserved early-nineteenth-century Hungarian folk music relatively intact. Among these are the embellished repetitions of eight-bar phrases and the progression from the *hallgató* section (in which the recruiters stand or walk and click their heels) to increasingly fast dances. The particular slow-fast-slow *(lassú-friss-lassú)* pattern Czuczor describes, although not a typical arrangement for folk dances preserved in Transylvania today, does conform to an arrangement *(lassú-*trio*-lassú)* sometimes found in notations of Hungarian dances from the early nineteenth century.[28]

MUSICAL CHARACTERISTICS

Like the vast majority of peasant and Gypsy performers in Hungary until after World War II, the musicians who took part in recruitment were, with few exceptions, musically illiterate. The notation of *verbunkos* therefore already points to urban influence. In notated sources *verbunkos* accompaniments largely conform to common-practice functional harmony, while the melodies preserve some Phrygian elements inherited from the Rákóczi-type tunes. Augmented seconds are a particular hallmark of the style. The characteristic scale that sometimes results from these augmented seconds is commonly known as the Hungarian or Gypsy scale, which may be thought of as an ascending harmonic minor scale with a raised fourth degree and thus contains augmented seconds both between the third and fourth and between the sixth and seventh scale degrees. Other typical aspects of *verbunkos* tunes include regular four-bar phrases in $\frac{2}{4}$ time (often notated in $\frac{4}{8}$ for the *lassú*), which frequently betray the influence of the characteristic rhythm of the swineherd song; dotted rhythms, often presented in a series embellished by grace notes and turns; decorative triplet figures; occasional pairs of accented quarter notes (long-long); and *short*-long rhythms in which the short first note comes on the metrically stronger part of the beat or bar.[29] Three common rhythmic patterns exhibit this last feature: the so-called dotted rhythm or *iambus* ♩ ♩ or ♪♩ or ♫, which I refer to simply as a *short*-long to avoid confusion with other dotted figures; a syncopation sometimes referred to as *alla zoppa* ♩♩ ♩ or ♪♩♪; and the so-called Hungarian choriamb ♩♪♪♩. These rhythms are also typical of Hungarian folk songs; the Hungarian penchant for them may stem from the way in which such rhythms mimic patterns of accentuation typical of the Hungarian language. The *short*-long pattern occurs when the first syllable of a word (always accented in Hungarian) is followed by an unaccented syllable of double duration (e.g., the rhythmic notation of Bartók: ♪♩ over Bartók, the diacritical mark over the second syllable (ó) indicating doubled length, not emphasis). A variety of stock *verbunkos* figures are illustrated in example 7, which is taken from a collection of pieces originally written for violin, but arranged for piano and published between 1823 and 1832 by the Musical Society of Veszprém County in western Hungary.

An aspect of the traditional *verbunkos* style that is difficult to capture in arrangements for instruments other than strings is the nearly ubiquitous accompanimental figures known as *dűvő* and *esztam*. *Dűvő* (sometimes *dűva*) is taken to be a Hungarianization of the Romany (Gypsy) expression *dui var*, which has the common Indo-European meaning "two times." This refers to a manner of playing an accompanimental string instrument with two articulated chords for each *portato* bow stroke (notated: ♩♩ or ♫). That is, each pair of notes is played alternately by upward or downward strokes of the bow; the articulation under the slur is the result of stopping the bow and then continuing in the same direction, not from changing the direction of the bow. The word *dűvő*, with its unusual arrangement of two consecutive long vowels, is also onomatopoetic—the slightly different intonations of the *ű* and *ő* imitate the contrasting quality of the first and second articulations in the sets of chords. *Dűvő* provides yet more evidence for the strong relationship between art music and folk music in *verbunkos*, for it is a nearly ubiquitous accompanimental pattern in late-eighteenth- and early-nineteenth-century Hungarian dances for strings by composers such as Bihari, Csermák, Lavotta, and Márk Rózsavölgyi, as well as a common improvised accompaniment among traditional ensembles. The transcription of *dűvő* given in example 8d likely demonstrates the way the accompanimental figures in the composed examples 8a–c were supposed to have been played. (At slow tempi, *dűvő* is often performed with the second note of the pair slightly longer than the first.)

Esztam is thought to have developed in the course of the nineteenth century as a natural solution to the fashion for playing at tempos faster than were easily sustainable with the portato bowing characteristic of *dűvő*. A

EXAMPLE 7. Ignatz Ruzitska, *Magyar Nóták Veszprém Vármegyéből*, "Cholera Verbung"

a. Mm. 1–8 (AS = augmented second; DT = decorative triplet)

b. Mm. 21–30 (SL = *short*-long; HS = Hungarian syncopation; DT = decorative triplet)

EXAMPLE 8. *Dűvő* as composed (a–c) and improvised (d)

a. János Bihari, continuous *dűvő* in the second violin part of 15 *Ungarishe Tänze für 2 Violinen* (1811): Dance No. 1, mm. 1–8; Dance No. 2, mm. 1–10

b. Anton Csermák, Six Hungarian Dances for String Quartet, No. 3 (1810?), mm. 1–4

c. Márk Rózsavölgyi, Csárdás Serkentő (Stirring Tune) with *dűvő* accompaniment (1846), part 2, mm. 1–4

EXAMPLE 8 *(continued)*

d. *Düvő* in accompaniment as played by a three-member central-Transylvanian village band in 1971 (Bálint Sárosi, *Hangszerek a magyar néphagyományban* [Budapest: Planétás kiadó, 1998], 202)

variation on *düvő, esztam* breaks up the two notes under a slur into an "oompah" figure in which a bass or cello plays the first of the pair and a viola *(brácsa)* or accompanying violin *(kontra)* plays the second ♪♪♪ (example 9). Although the etymology of *esztam* is less clear than that of *düvő* (it may have roots in the Romany language or be derived from the Medieval Provençal dance the *estampida*), the two short vowels of *esztam* imitate the quick interchange between the two accompanying instruments.

In a traditional ensemble of four players, the first violinist *(prímás)* plays an embellished melody, and a second violin *(kontra)* or a three-stringed viola with a flat bridge *(brácsa)* plays a *düvő* pattern in double or triple stops (as in example 9). A bass *(bőgő)* either joins the *düvő* at the speed of the *kontra* or *brácsa* or plays half that speed. Alternately, and especially at very fast tempi, these instruments may play *esztam*. A cimbalom may double or embellish the melody, join in the rhythm of the other accompanying instruments, or fill in chords with arpeggios. (When one or two instruments in an ensemble play *düvő* while others play *esztam*, the overall effect is considered to be *esztam*.) Because both *düvő* and *esztam* tend to emphasize the second or metrically weaker notes of each pair, these accompaniments make for an effective counterpoint to Hungarian-style melodic figures, which often have accents in metrically strong positions.

Magyar nóta

The vocal counterpart of *verbunkos* is the *magyar nóta* (literally: Hungarian tune), a term that was used interchangeably with *verbunkos* in the

EXAMPLE 9. Márk Rózsavölgyi, Csárdás Serkentő with *esztam* accompaniment (1846), part 3, mm. 1–4

first half of the nineteenth century. In its more recent usage it refers to the folk-song imitations that constituted the bulk of Hungarian popular songs in the nineteenth century. Since Bartók introduced the distinction between what he considered the spontaneous creations of the peasants and the "composed" music of the more educated classes, terms such as *népies dal* (folksy song) and *népies műdal* (folksy art song) have been used to distinguish the *magyar nóta* from peasant music. In practice, however, there is no sharp distinction between *magyar nóta* and folk song, although the melody of the former generally conforms more easily to functional harmony, often has longer text lines, and sometimes contains more "difficult" intervals. Like *verbunkos*, the *magyar nóta* grew out of a combination of elements from both art and folk music: eighteenth-century collections of songs for use in schools, *verbunkos* melodies themselves, and Hungarian folk songs.[30] Disseminated by traveling companies of actors who sang them in *népszínművek* (folksy plays), by "Gypsy" ensembles that performed them in often highly embellished instrumental renditions, and in sheet-music publications, *magyar nóták* were known to virtually all segments of rural and urban Hungarian society. As with *verbunkos*, composers often used or imitated these popular tunes in concert works in the Hungarian style.

"Gypsy Music"

Having officially gained the right to enter Hungarian towns in 1765, by the last two decades of the eighteenth century ethnic Romanies made up the bulk of the professional performers of music for dance and light entertainment in Hungary.[31] Therefore although composers of all stripes—professionals, amateurs, Hungarian Romanies, Hungarian nobles, and foreigners—composed *verbunkos* and *magyar nóta*, in common parlance both were considered "Gypsy music." "Gypsy music" is an overly broad category, a misnomer and a term potentially offensive to those aware of the historical oppression of the Roma or Romany people in East Central Europe. Yet because it was used universally in Hungary in the time period under consideration, it would be misleading to avoid it when describing Bartók's musical environment. The inherent contradictions and ambiguities of both the term and the music associated with it are emblematic of the contradictions and ambiguities of defining Hungarian music.

As Bartók was fond of pointing out, the term "Gypsy music" has never been understood to describe music composed by professional Romany musicians—although such compositions are occasionally included in the category for reasons of musical style. Nor has the term been used to describe the folk music that amateur Romany musicians perform among themselves, a repertoire commonly labeled "Gypsy folk music."[32] Instead, in common parlance "Gypsy music" refers to the popular music often performed in cafés or restaurants in regions historically belonging to Hungary by professional musicians who are frequently ethnic Romanies. The ethnicity of the performer has never been a wholly accurate gauge of the musical style: Márk Rózsavölgyi, a Hungarian Jew, Anton Csermák, of Bohemian origin, and János Lavotta, a Hungarian of noble extraction, all mastered the virtuosic "Gypsy" style made famous by János Bihari, a Hungarian Romany and the most famous "Gypsy violinist" of his day. Furthermore, "Gypsy" ensembles did not play exclusively *verbunkos* or improvisations on *magyar nóta:* elite bands like Bihari's played all manner of European ballroom dances in addition to the Hungarian repertoire for which they were most renowned, while the ethnic Romany musicians in villages assimilated into the musical culture of the peasants.

Bartók was not the first to resent the role "Gypsy music" and Gypsy musicians played in Hungarian musical life. The history of this resentment goes back at least as far as the debates sparked by Liszt's *Des Bohémiens et de leur musique en Hongrie* (Of the Gypsies and Their Music in Hungary, 1859, published in Hungarian in 1861), which propagated the idea that Gypsies rather than Hungarians were the creative spirit behind the Hungarian style. Although Liszt's view was immediately criticized by Hungarian musicians, it was accepted by many in Hungary well into the twentieth century. Liszt's implication that Gypsies created Hungarian music, rather than simply performed or preserved it, was offensive to those who believed that Hungarian music is the expression of the Magyar soul, and thus should stem from ethnically Hungarian musicians.[33] Bartók was aware that the controversy over "Gypsy music" dated back to Liszt, as is clear from the following passage from his 1931 article "Gypsy Music or Hungarian Music?": "When Franz Liszt's well-known book on Gypsy music appeared it created strong indignation at home. But why? Simply because Liszt dared to affirm in his book that what the Hungarians call Gypsy music *is really Gypsy music!* It seems that Liszt fell an innocent victim of this loose terminology. He must have reasoned that, since the Hungarians themselves call this music 'Gypsy' and not 'Hungarian,' it cannot conceivably be Hungarian music. A century later the situation has not changed fundamentally."[34] For Bartók, clarifying the Hungarian claim to "Gypsy music" was of secondary importance. More offensive to him was that "Gypsy music" occupied a position in Hungarian culture that he believed rightly belonged to Hungarian peasant music.

Although Bartók claimed in 1931 to have resigned himself to the fact that what he called the "shallow taste" of the "half-educated multitude of urban and semirural populations" would continue to favor "Gypsy music" over his own music and over folk music for the foreseeable future, he was never resigned to the reluctance of educated Hungarians to embrace his favorite cause. In his words: "It is disconcerting . . . to observe how musical artists and writers in high positions endeavor to endow this popular music [Gypsy music] with the attributes of a serious and superior art. In so doing they value it—either because of inherently bad taste or bad intentions— above really serious Hungarian music of a higher order."[35] Lest anyone read the last phrase as praise for his own compositions, he added, "We refer to Hungarian peasant music." But, given Bartók's dissatisfaction with the Hungarian reception of his own music at the time, it is likely that he was frustrated with the privileged position of Gypsy music in Hungarian society, seeing it as an insult and a hindrance to the acceptance of his own scholarly and creative work.[36]

Bartók did recognize that not all the music performed by Romanies was "Gypsy music." He acknowledged that, in addition to the "Gypsy music" played by professional Romany musicians, Romanies also played "Gypsy folk music," as well as instrumental folk music in "a genuine peasant style." The "Gypsy music" of common parlance designated only what Bartók described as "music that is nowadays played 'for money' by urban Gypsy bands."[37] The composer's definition of Gypsy music was thus dependent not on ethnicity, but on musical style as largely determined by the urban or rural environment in which the music was made. Still, although the urban-rural dichotomy defined categories that differed in important ways, setting them up as mutually exclusive is once again misleading.

The traditional music of the Hungarian village and the popular commercial music of the Hungarian city are best conceived not as entirely separate categories, but as different points on a continuum. The differences between rural and urban styles are clear only at the outer boundaries of this continuum: the ancient stratum of pentatonically based vocal music (what Bartók called "old-style" Hungarian folk song) at one extreme, and, at the other, the *instrumental* improvisations on *magyar nóta* that constituted a significant part of the "Gypsy" repertoire. Bartók's reduction of rural and urban musics to these extremes occasionally allowed him to focus on a crude and misleading difference between folk song and "Gypsy music," namely, the presence or absence of text:[38] "In folk song, text and music are an inseparable unity. Gypsy performance destroys this unity because without exception it transforms texted folklike art songs into instrumental music.[39] This in itself suffices to prove the lack of authenticity in Gypsy performance, even with regard to popular art music. If someone were forced to reconstruct our folklike art music only on the basis of the performances of Gypsy bands, he would be incapable of fulfilling the task, because half of the material needed for reconstruction—the text—goes down the drain in the hands of the Gypsy."[40]

Bartók's reasoning here is forced and surprisingly hostile. In his polemical effort to discredit the authenticity of "Gypsy music" he denies what he knew from experience: namely, that the simple act of rendering folk songs on instruments was not sufficient grounds for distinguishing "Gypsy" performances from the performance of instrumental music by Hungarian peasants. Bartók himself reported that he found no "specifically instrumental music among the Hungarians" that was not based on folk songs: in other words, what Hungarian peasants played on instruments were embellished renditions of texted folk songs.[41] This is not to say that there were no differences between the songs the "Gypsies" and Hungarian peasants chose to adapt to their instruments (*magyar nóta* versus Hungarian folk song) or that different styles of embellishment were not typical of each group, but that the differences could not be fairly reduced to the absence of text in "Gypsy" performance. In short, instrumental folk music in Hungary was a hybrid practice that did not represent the degree of purity that Bartók found so attractive in the "old-style" melodies. *Verbunkos* and *magyar nóta*, which together achieved the dominant role in defining the characteristics of distinctively Hungarian music at the same time that Romany musicians came to dominate popular instrumental music in Hungary, sit squarely on the blurry boundaries between folk music and art music, on the one hand, and peasant music and "Gypsy music," on the other.

The Status of the Hungarian Style

Why, then, did Bartók choose to dismiss the music of the likes of Bihari, Csermák, and Lavotta, when he could have legitimately argued that their *verbunkos*-inspired compositions represented an early-nineteenth-century form of the synthesis between folk music and art music that he himself was striving for in the context of twentieth-century modernism? The answer is complex and must take into consideration a number of possible factors, personal as well as artistic. Acknowledging the legitimacy of his Hungarian predecessors might have compromised Bartók's own claims of originality. He may have deemed the discrediting of what had formerly been considered folk music necessary to establish the credentials of the ancient folk melodies, unknown to urban musicians until he and Kodály identified them. Moreover, the association of nineteenth-century Hungarian popular music with Gypsy musicians and the petty nobility had social and political associations from which Bartók was eager to distance his own work.[42] More pertinent to the present study, however, was his exacting sense of musical quality. As he stated in the 1911 polemic in which he dismissed them, he considered the composers of *verbunkos* "dilettante musicians," and the music they composed, regardless of its authenticity, "not fit to delight people of good taste."[43] As an academically trained composer, Bartók valued learned compositional techniques such as motivic integration, contrapuntal subtlety, and harmonic complexity. Bihari, who was musically illiterate and had his compositions written down by others, was no Beethoven. (Beethoven did, however, reportedly marvel at Bihari's playing.)[44] Yet a lack of academic composerly technique is a poor basis for dismissing Bihari's contribution to the development of a Hungarian national style.

Bartók's rejection of the first generation of *verbunkos* composers was based in part on a narrow emphasis on these musicians as composers rather than virtuoso performers. But if the creation of high-art music was not a primary concern of Bihari, Csermák, and Lavotta's generation, their descendants—Ferenc Erkel (1810–93), Mihály Mosonyi (1815–70), Franz Doppler (1821–83), and Liszt as well as composers of the generation that directly preceded and overlapped with Bartók such as Géza Allaga (1841–1913), Kálmán Chován (1852–1928), Ernő Dohnányi (1877–1960), Jenő Hubay (1858–1937), Árpád Szendy (1863–1922), and Géza Zichy (1849–1924)—

did aim to integrate the *verbunkos* style into the major genres of the concert hall and opera house. If none of these composers save Liszt were among the most harmonically daring of their generation, all were sophisticated musicians, professional composers, and representatives of a tradition that, Bartók's denials notwithstanding, did have a lasting impact on his development. His condemnation of Erkel's operatic music as "a conglomerate lacking any style" because it mixed Hungarian and Italian styles was especially ungenerous. Erkel's choice of different musical styles at different points in his operas arose in part from the dramatic demands of his plots, not, as Bartók implied, simply from compositional ineptitude.

Still, despite the impressive achievements of some of Bartók's Hungarian predecessors and contemporaries in Hungarian opera (Erkel's *Hunyadi László* [1844] and *Bánk bán* [1861]; Mosonyi's *Szép Ilonka* [1861]; Hubay's *A falu rossza* [1896]; and Zichy's *Rákóczi Trilogy* [1905–12]), oratorio (Liszt's *The Legend of St. Elisabeth* [1862]), and symphony (Dohnányi's Symphony in D Minor [1901]), the Hungarian style was admittedly more prevalent in lighter compositions. In addition to the ever popular *magyar nóta*, the most common genres at the turn of the century included light character pieces (salon music), virtuosic show pieces (rhapsodies and fantasies) based on popular tunes, and symphonic suites—all genres that tended to limit thematic development and thus had little prestige among the German-trained musicians like János Koessler (1853–1926) and Ödön Mihalovich (1842–1929) who dominated the atmosphere at the Music Academy.[45] As a critic writing for the *Esti Újság* (Evening News) observed in 1903:

> [At the Music Academy] nobody inspires the students to become Hungarian. Occasionally Ödön Mihalovich composes a *kuruc* song. Koessler, always practical, tells his students, "so be it, go ahead and try writing something in the Hungarian style." With brilliant erudition, Géza Molnár holds forth about the construction of Hungarian melodies. Some professors, among them the excellent Béla Szabados [1867–1936] and László Kun [1869–1939], are deeply committed Hungarian artists in their own limited spheres. But the general spirit at the Academy, no matter how they try to cover it up, is German. Brahms is their idol, and the young musicians are taught to worship him.[46]

Kodály, like Bartók a student of Koessler's, confirmed the opinion of this anonymous reviewer in his recollection that their teacher disapproved of using any style other than a Germanic one for more than an occasional splash of color. Kodály further remembered that Koessler responded in German to Debussy's *Pelleás et Mélisande* with the comment "Mann kann nicht einen ganzen Abend im Dialekt sprechen."[47]

Bartók did not share Koessler's prejudice against the sustained use of Hungarian elements in serious concert music and incorporated them liberally in several of the pieces he wrote under his tutelage. But, despite their different orientations and the young composer's distress at Koessler's apparently harsh criticism of his compositions, Bartók did apparently agree with his teacher's highbrow attitude toward musical quality. As he reported in a tone of deep indignation to his mother at the beginning of his final year at the Music Academy:

> When I registered for composition, the secretary sez [asszongya]: well, then you'd better write some music now. I referred to my symphony. He sez: yes, but compose—he sez—something Hungarian. At that I started to laugh. To this he sez: aha, you see! you're all that way. If we sez you should compose something Hungarian, you start laughing. Hearing this the director came over to me and suggested [János] Arany's [poem] "Rodostó."[48] He sez one could compose something on that and work in the strains of the Rákóczi March.—What a notion, I really must congratulate myself![49]

Bartók appears to have been congratulating himself on disdaining both the secretary, who, he implies, had the small-mindedness to believe that a work in the Hungarian style (implying a lighter genre) would be more worthwhile than his symphony, and the director, whose idea of what would make a work Hungarian was the mere incorporation of the most hackneyed musical symbol of Hungarianness. His contempt of the existing Hungarian style would be hard to distinguish from Koessler's.

The same documents also indicate that outside of elite circles in which Bartók moved there was indeed significant interest in fostering Hungarian music in Budapest. That he was aware of this interest is clear not only from the account of his exchange with the secretary of the Music Academy, but also from his attention to articles in the press. Already before reading the article in *Esti Újság* that criticized the Germanic orientation of the Music Academy,[50] Bartók had reported that Aurél Kern, music critic of the jingoistic *Budapesti Hírlap* (Budapest News), had gone so far as to recommend closing of the Music Academy because of the non-Hungarian orientation of the faculty.[51] His reaction to Kern's stridently nationalistic stance shows that despite his own nationalist sentiments, he was unwilling to compromise artistic quality in the pursuit of his political ideals:

> What do you say to Aurél Kern's outburst on Sunday! To his proposal to shut down the Music Academy!!! *There is some truth to what he says.* But don't pick on the Music Academy! What does he want?! Is there even just one Hungarian [who is a great] cellist?[52] Or is there a Hungarian composer who could replace Koessler? (and who would undertake the professorship?) . . . Let

them struggle against the tyranny of the Austrian army. Nobody is forced to go to the Music Academy. In contrast, everyone is forced into the Austrian army, and they issue commands in German. That is an affront! That should be, must be changed! But who can help it if, for example, we have no cellist! At least it's better to study music here at home in Hungarian, with the exception of a few subjects, than to study every subject abroad![53]

By the middle of his last semester at the academy (spring 1903), Bartók himself would express his aggressively anti-Austrian sentiments in music when he began composing his symphonic poem *Kossuth*. In so doing, however, he did not abandon his elitist stance. He intensified it by integrating traditional musical markers of Hungarianness into the most complex, modern musical style known in Hungary at the time.

Although the traditional markers of the Hungarian style would be strongest in *Kossuth* and the other works preceding Bartók's discovery of "old-style" folk songs, these markers would never be entirely banished. The Hungarian style was too complex, too much infused with elements that derived from Hungarian peasant music, and too deeply ingrained in his compositional assumptions to be excluded wholesale from his own music. In short, Bartók the polemicist could reject his Hungarian past much more easily than could Bartók the composer. Justifiably proud of his music's unprecedented and intricate relationship to genuine peasant music, Bartók's genius as a musician also lay in his unique ability to reinterpret and transform—which is to say, to develop and continue—the nineteenth-century Hungarian inheritance he so vigorously professed to reject.

TWO

Tradition Maintained

Nationalism, Verbunkos, Kossuth, *and the Rhapsody, Op. 1*

Everyone, on reaching maturity, has to set himself a goal and must direct all his work and actions toward this. For my own part, all my life, in every sphere, always and in every way, I shall have one objective: the good of Hungary and the Hungarian nation.

BARTÓK to his mother, 8 September 1903

Declarations of maturity are often a sign of adolescence. This is true of Bartók's fervent outburst of patriotic enthusiasm, which he made some three years before he would seriously take up the cause of folk music and begin to reevaluate the nationalist beliefs with which he was so preoccupied in 1903. Despite its naiveté, this oft-quoted pronouncement serves as an important point of entry into Bartók's world at a crucial time in his development. His words reverberate with the idealistic sentiments of Hungarian Romantic poets like Sándor Petőfi (1823–49) and Mihály Vörösmarty (1800–1855) whose writings had spurred their countrymen into a patriotic fervor ever since first appearing some half century before Bartók's own infatuation with nationalism. The music he wrote between his final term at the Music Academy in 1903 and his first attempts to integrate peasant music into his original compositions in 1907 is indispensable for understanding the scope and subtlety of his engagement with Hungarian Romantic traditions. Most important, for all its conservatism when viewed from the perspective of his later style, this music reveals characteristics of Bartók's compositional method that would remain in place throughout his career—just as his commitment to serving his country remained constant even when his national sentiments became more subtle.

In this early period Bartók faced the problem of reconciling two passions: one for elite, rhetorically complex music, another for a national cause most often associated with rhetorically simpler music based on popular melodies. The desire to bring sophistication and weight to the national style was not new in 1903, but it was especially pressing for Bartók. Among the students at the Music Academy, only he was so intensely caught up in the movement for Hungarian independence that he found a way to express overtly anti-Austrian sentiments in his music. Only he seems to have been searching so passionately for direction and purpose that he would embrace the "good of Hungary and the Hungarian nation" as a lifelong goal. Since the death of Liszt in 1886, Hungary had lacked a composer of instrumental music who was both a master of the Hungarian style and highly respected abroad. An astute reader of the daily press in Budapest would have noticed that there was a contingent of critics ready to endorse a composer willing to write music at once Hungarian and stylistically elevated. By addressing this challenge a young composer might launch his career.

Bartók's symphonic poem *Kossuth* (1903) and his Rhapsody for Piano, op. 1 (1904), represent two contrasting approaches to bridging the gap between Hungarian idioms and learned compositional techniques. In *Kossuth*, Bartók incorporated Hungarian elements into the symphonic poem, a genre of considerable international prestige. In the Rhapsody for Piano, he took the nearly opposite approach by infusing the rhapsody, a traditionally light, nationally inflected showpiece, with the weighty rhetoric more closely associated with foreign (read: Germanic) forms. The contrasting receptions of these two works at their Hungarian premieres suggest that each approach carried with it assumptions about the expressive limitations of national music.

Hungarian Nationalism and the Cult of Kossuth

Lajos Kossuth (1802–94), the subject of the symphonic poem Bartók completed three weeks before his above-quoted declaration of maturity, was the leader of the Hungarian Revolution of 1848–49. Having presided over the government during Hungary's short-lived independence from Habsburg Austria during the revolution, Kossuth was a national hero and the most important symbol of Hungarian self-determination in the nineteenth century. Like the previous series of Hungarian uprisings against the Habsburgs (1703–11), those of 1848–49 were ultimately defeated. Despite several Hungarian victories, some of them seemingly decisive, the Austrian army overwhelmed the majority of the Hungarian forces in the summer of 1849. Kossuth fled the country and lived in exile the rest of his life.

Although the Austrians initially instituted a police state and oversaw bloody reprisals—including the infamous execution of thirteen Hungarian generals at Arad—conditions steadily improved over the course of the 1850s and '60s.[1] In 1867, weakened by defeat at the hands of Bismarck's Prussia in 1866, Austria agreed to many of the demands for autonomy originally sought by Hungary in 1848. This compromise *(Ausgleich)* made Hungary the junior partner in what would now be called the Austro-Hungarian Empire. In this new dual monarchy the Hungarian kingdom was given autonomy in most of its internal affairs. Three of the most important ministries—defense, foreign affairs, and finance—were, however, shared jointly with Austria and convened in Vienna. Although Austrian domination of the army would eventually become a lightning rod for Hungarian nationalism, the compromise began a period of political stability and economic growth in Hungary that lasted until the early 1890s. It is hardly surprising that during this period Hungarian artists and composers produced few significant works on the subject of Hungarian independence.

In the 1890s the aggressive anti-Austrian sentiments that had lain largely dormant for more than twenty years began to resurface in both politics and the arts. There are five commonly cited reasons for the reawakening of strident nationalism: economic stagnation in the 1890s; a new requirement that even officers serving in specifically Hungarian regiments use German;[2] the openly anti-Hungarian stance of the emperor/king's nephew Franz Ferdinand, the heir apparent; the increased pressure on the Magyars to share power with other ethnic groups living in the territory assigned to Hungary in the *Ausgleich* (principally Croats, Romanians, Serbs, and Slovaks); and the observation in 1896 of the millennial anniversary of Magyar settlement in the Carpathian Basin.[3]

The revitalization of the independence movement in the 1890s had a significant effect on Hungarian cultural life. In the fine arts, some of Hungary's best painters turned to subjects associated with the War of Independence. The most famous of these works include János Thorma's *The Martyrs of Arad* (1893–96), a shockingly realistic depiction of Austria's vindictive execution of the thirteen revolutionary generals in 1849, and *Rise Up, Hungarian!* (begun 1898), which portrays the first uprising in 1848 (figure 1); István Réti's *Burial of a Hungarian Soldier* (1899), a dark elegy for the passing of the generation that had fought for independence; and Simon Hollósy's *The Troubles of the Country* (1893) and *The Rákóczi March* (1899), the latter strongly reminiscent of Eugène Delacroix's well-known canvas *Liberty Leading the People*.[4]

A concomitant change in emphasis can be seen in Hungary's musical life when the Philharmonic Society dramatically increased the performance of

FIGURE 1. János Thorma, *Talpra Magyar! (Rise Up, Hungarian!)*, 1898–1937. (Used by kind permission of the János Thorma Museum, Kiskunhalas, Hungary)

Hungarian works in the 1890s. The forty-three concerts of the Philharmonic in the 1870s had contained a mere ten Hungarian works, whereas sixty-eight concerts in the following decade had included just a dozen, an even lower percentage of the total works performed. But from among the eighty concerts in the 1890s, thirty-three works were Hungarian, which indicates that works of Hungarian composers were being programmed at over twice the rate they had been in the previous decade. The increased presence of Hungarian music on the concerts of the Philharmonic signifies both the growing professionalism of Hungarian composers and an intensification of nationalist sentiment. In fact, the percentage of Hungarian works programmed by the Philharmonic in the 1890s represented a return to the nationalist atmosphere of the 1860s. The percentage of Hungarian pieces performed by the Philharmonic continued to increase through at least the first decade of the twentieth century (table 1).[5]

Kossuth, never entirely absent from the Hungarian national consciousness during his forty-six years in exile, also played an important role in rekindling the Hungarian independence movement in the 1890s. Because he had not set foot in Hungary for forty years, Kossuth's citizenship officially lapsed in 1889. Whether to extend his citizenship by a special act of Parliament became a hotly debated issue in the winter of 1889–90. Although his citizenship was not officially extended, several Hungarian cities voiced their opposition to the Austrian-endorsed government party by making Kossuth an honorary citizen. Upon his death in Turin in 1894, Kossuth's body was returned to Budapest for an elaborate public funeral that became an occasion for the display of revolutionary sentiment. Although the emperor/king Franz Josef refused to recognize the funeral as a state occasion, the city of Budapest demonstrated its independence from the national government by declaring three days of mourning.[6]

After his death, Hungarian musicians, artists, and writers commemorated Kossuth in their work. Composer Emanuel Moór honored him in his heroic Symphony No. 2 in C Major, which was performed by the Philharmonic soon after its completion in 1895. Painter József Rippl-Rónai captured the nostalgia for the revolution in his portrait of an aged soldier entitled "Uncle Rippl, the Kossuth Enthusiast" (1897). In the background of this portrait is a rendition of a well-known lithograph of Kossuth that often adorned Hungarian parlors—another sign of the revolutionary's pervasive presence in Hungary at the turn of the century.[7] Sculptor Alajos Stróbl was commissioned to design the monumental "Kossuth Mausoleum" (1901–9) in Budapest's most prestigious cemetery. In his poem "Est" (Evening), lines of which Bartók quoted in his own *Kossuth* Symphony, writer Kálmán

TABLE 1. Hungarian Works Performed by the Philharmonic
(1860–1905)

Based on lists of programs presented by the Philharmonic Society in Béla Csuka, *Kilenc évtized a magyar zeneművészet szolgálatában: a filharmóniai társaság emlékkönyve 90 éves jubileuma alkalmából* (Nine Decades in the Service of Hungarian Musical Art: Memorial Album of the Philharmonic Society on the Occasion of Its Ninetieth Anniversary) (Budapest: Filharmónia Társaság, 1943), 109–18 and 159–207.

1860s: Twenty-nine concerts total included fourteen works by seven Hungarian composers. Eight of these pieces are likely to have been in the Hungarian style.

Mihály Mosonyi: *Gyászhangok Széchenyi István halálára* (Funeral Music on the Death of István Széchenyi), 16 Dec. 1860

Ferenc Erkel: Aria from *Erzsébet*, 16 Dec. 1860

Ferenc Erkel: Finale from *Bánk bán*, 6 Jan. 1861

Mihály Mosonyi: *Magyar ünnepi nyitány* (Hungarian Festival Overture), 6 Jan. 1861

Mihály Mosonyi: Quartet and Finale from the 2nd act of *Szép Ilonka* (Fair Ilona), 25 March 1862

Ferenc Erkel: Overture to *Sarolta*, 30 March 1862

Leó Festetich: Ave Maria, 1 March 1863

Ferenc Erkel: Introduction, bass solo, and march from *Dózsa György*, 18 Dec. 1864

Ágoston Adelburg: Overture to the opera *Zrínyi*, 11 March 1866

Ferenc Bräuer: *Ünnepi nyitány* (Festival Overture), 11 March 1866

Bódog Orczy: Overture to *A renegát* (The Renegade), 15 Dec. 1867

Gusztáv Böhm: "A dalnok átka" (The Bard's Curse), 5 Jan. 1868

Mihály Mosonyi: *Gyászhangok Széchenyi István halálára*, 30 Dec. 1868

Ferenc Liszt: *Hungaria*, 30 April 1869 (Only works by Liszt in the Hungarian style are included in this enumeration)

1870s: Forty-three concerts total included ten works by five Hungarian composers. Six of these pieces are likely to have been in the Hungarian style.

Sándor Bertha: *Nászinduló* (Wedding March), 5 April 1871

Ferenc Liszt: *Hunok harca* (Battle of the Huns), 8 Nov. 1871

Ferenc Liszt: Hungarian Rhapsody No. 1, 26 March 1871

Bódog Orczy: Overture to *A renegát*, 5 April 1871

Ferenc Erkel: *Dózsa György* (solo scene), 26 March 1871

Ferenc Erkel: *Himnusz* (National Anthem) arranged for chorus and orchestra by Liszt, 19 March 1873

László Zimay: *Honvédek csatadala* (Battle Song of the National Guard), 16 Dec. 1874

Ferenc Liszt: *Hunok harca*, 27 Feb. 1876

Ferenc Liszt: Hungarian Rhapsody No. 2 (arranged by Müller-Berhaus), 2 Jan. 1876

Ferenc Erkel: Romance from *Brankovics György,* 14 Nov. 1877

1880s: Sixty-eight concerts total included twelve works by ten Hungarian composers. Four of these pieces are likely to have been in the Hungarian style.

Ferenc Liszt: *Hunok harca* (Battle of the Huns), 5 March 1884

József Joachim: Violin Concerto in the Hungarian style, 27 Feb. 1885

Ödön Mihalovich: Symphony No. 1 in D Minor, 20 March 1885

Jenő Hubay: Violin Concerto No. 1, 17 March 1886

Jenő Hubay: *Magyar dallam Szentirmay E. után* (Hungarian Melody after Elemér Szentirmay), 17 March 1886

István Stocker: Violin Concerto in D Minor, 4 April 1887

Ármin Angyal: "Alkony" (Twilight), song to a text of Petőfi, 15 Feb. 1888

Jenő Hubay: Symphony in B♭ Major, 15 Feb. 1888

Gyula Major: Concert symphonique for piano, 15 Feb. 1888

Lajos Steiger: "Nádas-dalok" (Schilflieder, by Lenau), 15 Feb. 1888

Ferenc X. Szabó: *Rondeau capricieux et sentimental* in D Minor, 15 Feb. 1888

Mór Vavrinecz: Overture to *Abydosi menyasszony* (The Bride of Abydos), 15 Feb. 1888

1890s: Eighty concerts total included thirty-three works by eighteen Hungarian composers. Seventeen of these works are likely to have been in the Hungarian style.

Jenő Hubay: *3 jellemdarab a "Virágrege" cyclusból* (Three Character Pieces from the Cycle "Flower Tale"), op. 30, 19 Nov. 1890

Ferenc Erkel: Mixed Quartet with Chorus, 7 Nov. 1890

Ferenc Erkel: Overture to *Bátori Mária,* 7 Nov. 1890

Ferenc Liszt: *Hunok harca,* 5 March 1890

Ferenc Erkel: *Dózsa György* ("The Poet's Songs," "Rose's Farewell," and first act, final scene), 7 Nov. 1890

Gyula Beliczay: Symphony in D Minor, op. 45, 18 Nov. 1891

Géza Zichy: Love scene from the opera *Alár,* 16 Dec. 1891

Ede Bartay: Symphonic poem, 23 Nov. 1892

Ferenc Liszt: *Szent Erzsébet legendája* (The Legend of St. Elisabeth), 13 Jan. 1892

Tivadar Nachéz: Violin Concerto, 9 Nov. 1892

Ödön Mihalovich: Symphony No. 2 in B Minor, 11 Jan. 1893

Ferenc Erkel: *Ünnepi nyitány,* 8 Nov. 1893

Ferenc Liszt: Rákóczi March, 26 Jan. 1894

Ferenc Liszt: Hungarian Fantasy for Piano and Orchestra, 14 Feb. 1894

Gyula Mannheimer: Serenade No. 2 for Orchestra, op. 6, 19 Dec. 1894

(continued)

TABLE 1 *(continued)*

Viktor Herzfeld: *Nyitány Grillparzer "Megálmodott élet" (Der Traum ein Leben) c. drámai regéjéhez* (Overture to Grillparzer's Dramatic Tale "Life Is a Dream"), 18 Dec. 1895

Manó (Emanuel) Moór: Symphony No. 2 in C Major (to the memory of Lajos Kossuth), 20 Nov. 1895

József Bloch: Suite in D Major for String Orchestra, 4 March 1896

László Kun: Scherzo for Orchestra, 9 Dec. 1896

Ferenc Liszt: Hungarian Rhapsody No. 1, 22 Jan. 1896

Gyula Mannheimer: Rákóczi Overture, 8 Jan. 1896

József Bloch: Second Suite for String Orchestra, 24 March 1897

Ákos Buttykay: *Ábránd zongorára zenekarral* (Fantasy for Piano and Orchestra), 7 April 1897

Viktor Herzfeld: *Tavaszi idyll* (Spring Idyll), 1 Dec. 1897

Gyula Erkel: *Suite de ballet* in Hungarian style, 17 Nov. 1897

Ákos Buttykay: Scherzo, 21 Dec. 1898

Mihály Mosonyi: *Gyászhangok Széchenyi István halálára*, 16 March 1898

Ferenc Erkel: *Ünnepi nyitány*, 12 Jan. 1898

József Bloch: Hungarian Overture, 22 Feb. 1899

Ernő Dohnányi: Piano Concerto in E Minor, 11 Jan. 1899

Gyula Major: *Suite romantique*, 8 Feb. 1899

Ödön Mihalovich: *Gyászhangok Erzsébet királyné emlékére* (Funeral Music in Memory of Queen Elisabeth), 25 Jan. 1899

Ferenc Erkel: Overture to *Bátori Mária*, 27 March 1899

1900–1905: Sixty-three concerts total included thirty-seven works by Hungarian composers. Sixteen of these pieces are likely to have been in the Hungarian style.

József Bloch: Hungarian Rhapsody, 5 Dec. 1900

Ákos Buttykay: Symphony in C♯ Minor, 10 Jan. 1900

Ákos Buttykay: *Szvit magyar stilben* (Suite in Hungarian Style), 21 Nov. 1900

Ferenc Liszt: Hungarian Rhapsody No. 1, 21 Feb. 1900

Gyula Major: Serenade for Strings, op. 24, 19 Dec. 1900

Alfréd Rieger: Serenade, op. 16, 7 Feb. 1900

Gusztáv Schmidt (Szerémi): *A szabadban* (Out of Doors), 12 March 1900

Ferenc Erkel: *Ünnepi nyitány*, 7 Nov. 1900

Szidor Bátor: Overture, 6 March 1901

Péter König: Hungarian Symphony in D Minor, 18 Dec. 1901

Viktor Herzfeld: Serenade for Strings, 16 Jan. 1901

Ferenc Liszt: *Hunok harca*, 23 Oct. 1901

Ödön Mihalovich: Symphony No. 3 ("Pathetique"), 30 Jan. 1901
N. Pischinger: *Suite de ballet* (excerpts), 4 Dec. 1901
Nándor Rékai: Suite, 6 Nov. 1901
Károly Szabados: *Romeo and Juliet* Overture, 20 March 1901
Emil Ábrányi: Symphony in C Minor, 22 Jan. 1902
Ákos Buttykay: Second Symphony ("Salambo"), 17 Nov. 1902
Ernő Dohnányi: Symphony No. 2 in D Minor, 7 Jan. 1903
Ferenc Liszt: Hungarian Fantasy for Piano and Orchestra, 4 May 1903
Gusztáv Szerémi: Serenade for Strings, 4 Nov. 1903
Ödön Farkas: *Hangulatok* (Moods), 11 March 1903
Jenő Hubay: Idyll and Gavotte for Violin, 4 May 1903
Ödön Mihalovich: Symphony in C Minor, 18 Feb. 1903; 4 May 1903
Nándor Rékai: *Kuruc* Overture, 18 Nov. 1903
Ferenc Erkel: *Ünnepi nyitány*, 4 May 1903
Ferenc Erkel: "Elvennélek" (I Would Marry You) for Chorus, 3 May 1903
Béla Bartók: *Kossuth*, 13 Jan. 1904
Viktor Herzfeld: *Meseképek* (Fairy-Tale Pictures), 17 Feb. 1904
Béla Bartók: Scherzo for Large Orchestra, 15 March 1905
Károly Aggházy: *Gyászhangok Rákóczi Ferenc emlékére* (Funeral Music in Memory of Ferenc Rákóczi), 15 March 1905
Ákos Buttykay: *Ünneprontók* (Party Crashers), symphonic poem, 25 Jan. 1905
Ödön Farkas: *Szondy két apródja* (Szondy's Two Pages), 11 Jan. 1905
Attila Horváth: Overture to *Zrínyi Ilona*, 20 Dec. 1905
Jenő Hubay: Violin Concerto No. 2, 1 March 1905
Albert Siklós: *Rákóczi* Overture, 22 Nov. 1905
Ferenc Erkel: *Ünnepi nyitány*, 15 March 1905

Harsányi treated Kossuth's death as metaphor for the failure of the revolution.[8] In short, Kossuth could not have been a more timely or popular subject for Bartók's first complete large-scale orchestral composition.

Bartók's *Kossuth*

Like much of the Hungarian public, Bartók entertained a passion for nationalist subjects around the turn of the century. A more specific musical catalyst for his composition of *Kossuth*, however, seems to have been the Budapest reception of Dohnányi's D-Minor Symphony (1901), a work

Bartók had performed on the piano before its formal Hungarian premiere. Following its first performance in Manchester in 1902, the Philharmonic introduced Dohnányi's symphony to the Hungarian public on 7 January 1903. The next major composition Bartók embarked on was *Kossuth*, which he began less than three months later on 2 April 1903.[9] Among the reviews of Dohnányi's symphony was a detailed article that occupied almost the entire front page of the *Esti Újság* the day following the concert (8 Janurary 1903).[10] The reviewer was Aurél Kern (1871–1928), introduced in chapter 1, a vocal proponent of modern Hungarian music who opposed the Germanic bent of the Music Academy. In a letter written to his mother two days after the concert, Bartók reacted both to Dohnányi's new work and to its reception: "The Dohnányi symphony sounds great. He conducted it himself exceptionally well. They even gave it a big ovation. In Thursday's *Esti Újság* the lead article was published with the following headline: Ernő Dohnányi. Aurél Kern is behind it. The good gentleman is, however, very much mistaken that Dohnányi is creating Hungarian art music. He has not the slightest intention of this. Only the second movement of his symphony is Hungarian, the first has only a hint of [Hungarian flavor], and the last three movements none at all."[11]

Bartók's slightly irritated reference to Kern's review suggests that the reviewer had touched a nerve. Although intended as a description of Dohnányi's achievement, parts of Kern's review can be read as prescriptions for the future of Hungarian music, a future in which Bartók was eager to play a leading role. In fact, Kern's review of Dohnányi's symphony fits Bartók's *Kossuth* more closely than the reviewed work, suggesting that Kern's opinions may have inspired Bartók to claim the laurels somewhat awkwardly thrust on Dohnányi.

Four years Bartók's senior, Ernő Dohnányi had been the younger composer's friend and occasional advisor in musical matters since their student days in Pozsony (present-day Bratislava). It was Dohnányi who had persuaded Bartók to follow in his footsteps by attending Budapest's Music Academy rather than accept a scholarship in Vienna, and it was Dohnányi to whom Bartók would turn for piano lessons upon graduation from the Academy. More than anyone else in the years before Bartók began collaborating with Kodály on collecting folk music in 1905, Dohnányi personified Bartók's own ambitions. Dohnányi was the most successful student of István Thomán (1862–1940), who was also Bartók's piano teacher. By the end of 1900 Dohnányi had established an international reputation as a pianist of the first rank, a goal that Bartók would not achieve until the 1920s. Likewise, Dohnányi's international status as a composer was firmly in place long before Bartók's: in 1895 his Piano Quintet in C Minor, op. 1, was championed by Johannes Brahms, and in 1899 Dohnányi won the Bösendörfer Prize for his Piano Concerto in E Minor, op. 5. With his Symphony in D Minor, Dohnányi seemed to have also established his reputation as a composer of Hungarian national music. As Bartók's comment about Kern's review suggests, this was one area in which the younger composer felt he could surpass his friend and mentor.

In the fall of 1902 Bartók was particularly interested in Dohnányi's recently completed symphony.[12] He was then beginning his final year as a student at the Academy of Music and concentrating on developing his symphonic technique in a Symphony in E♭, his first large-scale orchestral work. In October Bartók obtained a copy of the score of Dohnányi's symphony. During the following month he performed parts of it on the piano on no fewer than three occasions and in the process memorized much of the work.[13]

Members of the press shared Bartók's enthusiasm at the first Hungarian performance of Dohnányi's symphony. A source of pride for the critics—and surely for the audience members, who gave the composer an ovation after each of the work's five movements—was that Dohnányi was not only Hungarian by birth, but had received his training in Hungary. His success was seen both as an individual achievement and, more crucially, as a triumph for the nation and its Music Academy. Here was proof that Hungarian culture had risen to what Hungarians commonly refer to as a "European" standard. There was good reason to celebrate. Dohnányi was the first internationally acclaimed graduate of the academy, an institution founded in 1875 in hopes of bringing Hungarian state support of music to a level comparable to that of Prussia and France, and with the express purpose of keeping native talent at home.[14] In the words of the reviewer of *Pesti Napló:*

> Let us bow our head before the first true symphonist to be created in Hungary, and whom we got to know in Ernő Dohnányi's Second Symphony [in D minor]. . . . Especially in its development and orchestration, only [the works of] Brahms and Chaikovsky can be compared to this symphony. . . . This evening was quite an event: the unfolding of a world-class Hungarian talent in front of a Hungarian audience. . . . Hungary had a right to be proud at this evening's concert [because] this great talent was raised on her soil. The Music Academy can take pride in having brought him to maturity for the benefit of Hungarian musical art.[15]

Although "Hungarian musical art" is a potentially ambiguous expression that could ostensibly have meant any composition produced by a Hungarian, in this context it also implied music in a specifically Hungarian style. Kern explicitly addresses the characteristically Hungarian qualities of Dohnányi's symphony:

> Particularly interesting from a Hungarian point of view are the Hungarian features of the themes, which are free of Gypsyness. Immediately the first movement's main theme and the finale's monumental fugue are interesting, Hungarian, and moreover entirely symphonic inventions. The second movement, the Adagio, is not only Hungarian in its themes, but the crying-rejoicing of the Hungarian soul pervades its entire mood, especially in the development of the theme, when the woodwinds weave impetuous, flittering, sometimes almost Gypsy-like embellishments around the main melody.[16]

Applauding Dohnányi for avoiding the "Gypsy" style in his themes and at the same time praising him for the employment of "Gypsy-like embellishments" exposes a contradiction typical of Hungarian criticism of the day.

The reason for Kern's inconsistency appears to stem from the discrepancy between his abstract ideal of Hungarian music and the actual musical style of Dohnányi's symphony. Aside from the symphony's second movement, which accounts for less than a quarter of the entire work, nothing except the first theme of the first movement could be considered characteristically Hungarian. In his enthusiasm for promoting Dohnányi as the creator of Hungarian symphonic music, Kern seems to have painted himself into a rhetorical corner. On the one hand, he is forced to praise the second movement, which contains music that in its debt to the "Gypsy" style of performance fails to fit his prescription. On the other, Kern implies that the entire symphony exudes a Hungarian quality. Thus, while arguing for the specifically Hungarian quality of Dohnányi's music, the critic could only resort to the vague clichés of nationalist rhetoric when it came to defining the quality he was touting:

> We recognized, we felt: here stands before us the much awaited great composer, who speaks to us in Hungarian, in whose art beats a Hungarian heart, who will create Hungarian symphonic music. A God-inspired genius had to come to give birth to it. Hungarianness in music is just like [Hungarianness] in the other arts: it can hardly be tied to rules, it occurs spontaneously, in the blood, a quality rooted in feeling. Music, more than any other art, is the product of feeling. Only he who truly feels Hungarian can create Hungarian music.[17]

Kern admitted that he had long been waiting for a composer whom he could applaud as the creator of Hungarian symphonic music. That strong desire led him to hear Dohnányi's symphony as above all Hungarian. It is, however, less a spontaneous outpouring of "Hungarian feelings" than a virtuoso display of academic credentials by a recent conservatory graduate. It includes a first movement in sonata form, a scherzo with a trio, and a finale that includes a theme and variations and a fugue. Dohnányi's symphony is in effect a tour de force of "foreign" forms. Even the exuberant "Gypsy-like" flourishes in the middle section of the work's second movement could have been inspired by a foreign model—just this type of music (in an analogous formal position) is the topic of the middle section of the second movement of Brahms's Clarinet Quintet.

Thus Kern's evaluation of Dohnányi's symphony was based on a Romantic, metaphysical view of Hungarianness that could be conveyed with few concrete musical markers of nationality. Bartók's observation that Kern was mistaken in believing that Dohnányi was establishing a specifically Hungarian symphonic idiom reflected a more modern notion of Hungarianness in music as something that could be measured by more objective standards. The young composer criticized Kern's review both because he shared the critic's desire for the establishment of a uniquely Hungarian approach to symphonic music and because he had his own ideas about how to realize it.

NATIONAL IN CONTENT

It is well known that in writing *Kossuth* Bartók was inspired by the music of Richard Strauss, particularly *Ein Heldenleben* and *Also sprach Zarathustra*.[18] Bartók's debt to Dohnányi's D-Minor Symphony in *Kossuth* is more complicated because the older composer seems to have served Bartók both as an inspiration and as a negative example.[19] The reception of Dohnányi's symphony shows how enthusiastically the Budapest audience could greet a serious work that incorporated Hungarian elements. A comparison of the first themes of Dohnányi's symphony and Bartók's *Kossuth*, and a consideration of the relationship of these themes to the works as a whole, demonstrates how Bartók asserted his national identity both more aggressively and more pervasively than had Dohnányi.

The similarities between the initial bars of Dohnányi's symphony and Bartók's *Kossuth* are striking (example 10a–b). Both are in minor keys, begin with moderately fast tempi (*Allegro non troppo* and *Allegro moderato*), and open softly with pedal tones in the bassoon and contrabassoon. In both, the sustained tones in the bassoons are complemented by repeated figures in the low strings that touch on the root and fifth of the tonic chord. In both, after two bars of introductory accompaniment, the horn and another wind instrument of similar tone color (trumpet and bassoon, respectively) enter on the downbeat with the main theme. Both themes begin on the

EXAMPLE 10. Dohnányi as a model for Bartók's *Kossuth*

a. Dohnányi, Symphony in D Minor, movement 1, mm. 1–9

tonic minor chord and use pitches of the so-called Hungarian or "Gypsy" scale, the most characteristic interval of which is the augmented second between scale degrees 3 and 4. The themes also share two typically Hungarian rhythmic patterns: a dotted figure (*short*-long) and a syncopated pattern (short-long-short).[20]

Bartók's opening, a representation of Kossuth, has a more marked and pervasively Hungarian character than Dohnányi's, especially in its rhythmic profile and accompaniment. In Dohnányi's introduction triplet arpeg-

EXAMPLE 10. *(continued)*

b. *Kossuth*, section 1, mm. 1–5

gios in the violas and cellos create an energetic but rhythmically vague and nationally unspecific texture. In Bartók's introduction the low strings artic-ulate their open-fifth, drone bass with a *short*-long dotted figure ♫. . The marked quality of the articulation of the beat suggests the first *tempo giusto* dance from a series of *verbunkos*. Bartók reinforces the Hungarian topic with the alternation of the drone fifths an octave apart in the basses and celli, a texture that recalls the peculiar organ-grinding effect of *düvő*, the traditional accompanimental pattern of *verbunkos*.

The difference in the degree of national coloring also extends to the opening melodies. Dohnányi's gradually assumes a Hungarian hue as it tra-verses the augmented intervals of the "Gypsy"-minor scale (mm. 5–6). The seventh bar contains a gently syncopated rhythm ♫♩ ♩, which adds to the pastel Hungarian coloring of the theme. Bartók forcefully begins his melody in the Hungarian style with a dotted figure that, like its retrograde in the accompaniment, is strongly associated with *verbunkos* in a medium tempo. Whereas Dohnányi uses Hungarian-style syncopation only once in his melody (m. 7), Bartók uses it twice initially (mm. 3–4), and owing to the motivic importance of these two bars, it emerges as the central rhythm of his theme. Moreover, by folding the dotted figure into the first beat of the syncopation, Bartók expresses Hungarianness on two layers simultaneously. Because the two Hungarian rhythmic figures in the melody are combined with two Hungarian effects in the bass, the result is the simultaneous presentation of four distinct layers of Hungarian rhythm: the dotted rhythms folded into syncopations in the melody, and the *short*-long and *dűvő*-like alternation of open fifths in the accompaniment. The somewhat martial topical reference to *verbunkos* resonates with Kossuth's historical reputation as the leader who most effectively recruited his countrymen to the cause of Hungarian independence.

According to its program, Bartók's symphonic poem illustrates events relating to the Hungarian War of Independence (1848–49) in ten sections, depicting Kossuth, his meditations prior to entering into battle, the battle between the Hungarians and Austrians, and the mourning following the Hungarian defeat. In the outline given below, the programmatic titles in the score are coupled with brief amplifications derived from Bartók's own program note to the first performance:

1. "Kossuth." (A portrait of the hero.)
2. "What sorrow lies so heavily on thy heart?" (Kossuth's wife worries about her husband's sad condition.)
3. "Danger threatens the fatherland." (Kossuth loses himself in sorrowful recollections of the bygone glories of the nation.)
4. "A better fate was ours then." (A continuation of Kossuth's memory of bygone days.)
5. "Yet this short-lived happiness soon disappeared." (Kossuth remembers how the Austrians' tyranny proved fateful for Hungary.)
6. "To the battlefield." (Kossuth tears himself away from his meditations and determines to take up arms.)
7. "Come, oh come, ye haughty warriors, ye valiant heroes!" (Kossuth summons Hungarians to battle; they gather and swear an oath to persevere unto death.)
8. "......" (Depicts the approach of the Austrian troops, identified by a distortion of the Austrian national anthem; battle and defeat.)
9. "All is finished." (Mourning [a funeral march].)
10. "Everything is silent . . ." (The country is silent because after the Hungarian defeat the Austrian oppression is so great that even mourning is forbidden.)[21]

EXAMPLE 11. *Kossuth,* section 6, mm. 123–26

EXAMPLE 12. Dohnányi, Symphony in D Minor, movement 1, mm. 117–19

As would be expected of a symphonic poem, the ten sections feature a combination of thematic repetition and transformation. Each of the first eight sections has a characteristic theme or themes, and the last two return to the music of the first section, slowed to the tempo of a funeral march.[22] The work is most obviously unified by numerous modified repetitions of the opening ("Kossuth") theme, which appears in every section of the work save the fifth. Most incarnations of the Kossuth theme are clear enough to require little explanation. An exception is the theme of section six, a somewhat disguised transformation of the first bar of the Kossuth theme that retains its melodic contour and the syncopated underpinning, but is played at approximately twice the speed of its first appearance and without the characteristic dotted figure on the first beat (example 11). Subtler from an analytic point of view is Bartók's use of short-long-short syncopated figures, which unites sections of divergent character

The use of the short-long-short figure as a unifying device is another overlap between *Kossuth* and Dohnányi's Symphony in D Minor. Dohnányi uses the rhythm not only in the opening theme of the first movement, but also as the head motive of a new theme at the beginning of the development section (example 12). On this appearance Dohnányi's syncopated figure folds a dotted rhythm into its first beat and has a character very similar to

EXAMPLE 13. *Kossuth, hallgató*-like embellishments in section 9, m. 463

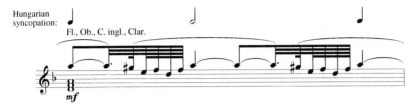

EXAMPLE 14. *Kossuth,* syncopations in section 7, mm. 205–13

EXAMPLE 15. *Kossuth,* syncopations in section 5, mm. 90–91

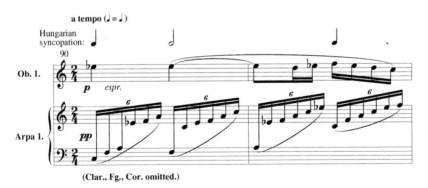

EXAMPLE 16. *Kossuth,* syncopations in section 2, mm. 29–34

the transformed version of the theme Bartók uses in the sixth section of *Kossuth*. In section nine of *Kossuth* syncopation provides a Hungarian background rhythm to several bars in which the more obvious "surface" Hungarian characteristics are elaborate, *hallgató*-like lamenting figures (example 13). In section seven the *alla zoppa*–like syncopation makes two unembellished appearances as a cadential tag to the winds' rendition of the theme, here serving, as it might in a folk dance, to articulate the end of a four-bar phrase (example 14). In section five Bartók again makes the opening gesture an elaboration of a short-long-short syncopation (example 15). Hungarian-style syncopations are used similarly in section two (example 16), where they occur on several different metric levels, some obscured by ties.

HUNGARIAN IN THEORY

Bartók's reliance on the short-long-short figure closely corresponds to one of the most influential contemporaneous theoretical descriptions of Hungarian music. Géza Molnár (1870–1933) was Bartók's professor in a course on Hungarian music, which he taught at the Music Academy from 1900 until the year of his death.[23] In May 1903 Molnár worked the lectures for this class into a book entitled *A magyar zene elmélete* (The Theory of Hungarian Music), published the next year. As Lynn Hooker has demonstrated, Molnár's analysis was the most intricately detailed contribution to a longstanding discourse on the nature of Hungarian music, which we have already glimpsed in less technical terms in the criticism of Aurél Kern.[24]

The most important aspect of Molnár's work for the present discussion is his well-nigh exhaustive treatment of Hungarian rhythm, which includes numerous tables demonstrating how complex patterns may be generated from and related to a few simple and commonly accepted Hungarian elements. Taken prescriptively, as it seems they were intended to be, Molnár's tables provide an impressively detailed method for ensuring the presence of a Hungarian essence in rhythms a good deal more complex and abstract than the *style hongrois* clichés on which they are based. In short, Molnár, like Bartók, was preoccupied with the question of how to elevate the Hungarian style without abandoning its national specificity.

A table that begins with the short-long-short rhythm first demonstrates how both this figure and the *short*-long dotted rhythm are variations on the same principle of elongation through adding or tying eighth notes together following an initial, metrically emphasized *short*. The example then goes on to spell out five longer patterns that use the same principle of elongation, each of which supposedly maintains something of the fundamentally Hungarian character of the initial rhythm. In Molnár's words:

> The dotted [*short*-long] and syncopated [short-long-short] rhythms—as we have already observed—are the result of tying together [notes of equal value]. Here [by extending this principle] we have ample opportunity to achieve Hungarian effects:
>
>
> This table, which could be extended at length, clarifies the origin of numerous Hungarian rhythms.[25]

Although the longer syncopated patterns Molnár lists do not duplicate the rhythms Bartók uses in the second section of *Kossuth*, he and Bartók do share the technique of extending and abstracting syncopations by tying the last short of the short-long-short pattern to the first short of the next.

Another intersection between Bartók's rhythmic constructions and Molnár's theory is the generative importance of the *short*-long. Molnár describes the *short*-long (which he refers to as an iamb) as the fundamental Hungarian rhythm out of which all others grow. Since the *short*-long is the first rhythm to be heard in *Kossuth*, it is easy enough to derive (or to imagine Bartók "generating") nearly all the Hungarian rhythms in the work from this basic motive. Its relationship to the next two Hungarian rhythms in Molnár's book is obvious: the dotted rhythm of the melody is the rhythmic retrograde of the *short*-long; and the syncopation is a *short*-long in which a three-unit long is, to adopt Molnár's way of thinking, "untied" into a two-unit long plus a one-unit short.

Overlaps between Bartók's compositional practice and Molnár's theory hardly prove that Molnár influenced Bartók. What the overlap shows is that complex or abstract ways of thinking about or working with Hungarian motives need not be seen as simply applying a "foreign" method to native materials. Molnár's work demonstrates that even before Bartók's first large-scale essay in Hungarian music, the potential for breaking the *style hongrois* into its constituent elements and then using those elements to generate more elaborate and less explicitly Hungarian structures had been recognized. Bartók could as easily have gleaned his sophisticated methods for manipulating elements of the Hungarian national inheritance from studying the works of Brahms as he could have from studying Molnár's theories. Bartók was the most successful composer to attempt the elevation of the national style to a level of "European" sophistication, but, as Molnár's work demonstrates, he was not the first Hungarian to understand that a Hungarian work could be constructed "organically" from elements that at once guaranteed coherence and expressed nationality on multiple levels.

NATIONAL IN FORM

Kern's assertion that the true Hungarian spirit in art is reflected in spontaneous expression applies more easily to the symphonic poem, a genre with few a priori formal conventions, than it does to the symphony, formally one of the most tradition-bound genres. Liszt's symphonic poems *The Battle of the Huns* and *Hungaria* had set a precedent for the symphonic poem as a genre suited to Hungarian expression, but there were no Hungarian works of comparable prestige that had succeeded in making the symphony a similarly accepted genre for music in the Hungarian style.[26] Chaikovsky and Dvořák notwithstanding, Hungarians considered the symphony quintessentially German. Thus, a symphonic poem such as Bartók's *Kossuth*, despite its debt to Richard Strauss, could be heard more easily as continuing a Hungarian tradition than could Dohnányi's symphony.

Reviewing *Kossuth* after its premiere in Budapest on 13 January 1904 (a year and six days after the Hungarian premiere of Dohnányi's Symphony in D Minor), Kern again emphasized spontaneity as an essential component of true Hungarian expression. This time, however, he acknowledged that Bartók's approach to form better fulfilled this requirement than had Dohnányi's: "[I]n Bartók there is something deliberate and willful that springs from the depths of artistic conviction. Dohnányi proceeds in the footsteps and forms of the German masters Beethoven and Brahms, in these he produces perhaps a more refined and mature art, but [Bartók] creates form according to Hungarian feeling: wild, luxuriant, rhapsodic, not so sober and symmetrical that it requires the rules of the German symphony."[27] Here Kern uses the term "rhapsodic" to convey a sense of *Kossuth* as a work of youthful, specifically Hungarian, exuberance. The critic could have strengthened his point had he noticed that in fact Bartók seems to have derived his approach to form in *Kossuth* at least as much from the formal conventions of Hungarian rhapsodies as he had from the symphonic poem à la Strauss.

Hungarian rhapsodies are intimately tied to the *verbunkos* tradition. Liszt's Hungarian rhapsodies, the most famous examples, are virtuosic renditions of *verbunkos* tunes he heard played by Hungarian Gypsy bands in the middle of the nineteenth century. It is therefore plausible that in a work so indebted to other aspects of *verbunkos*, Bartók may have been influenced by the customary formal arrangement of *verbunkos* tunes. The structure of Hungarian rhapsodies imitates the typical order of *verbunkos* tunes in performance, whether by commercial "Gypsy" ensembles or folk musicians, with its progression from slow *(lassú)* to fast *(friss)*, each part containing an indeterminate number of sections. A detail important to the present discussion is that the *lassú* often begins with a highly embellished section *(hallgató)* that segues into somewhat faster, *tempo giusto* dances. Furthermore, in addition to the general difference in tempo between the *lassú* and *friss*, there can be a significant difference in the rhythmic character of the two sections. Whereas the dances of the *lassú* typically feature intricate dotted rhythms and embellishments, the dances of the *friss* tend to be less rhythmically ornate and sometimes consist almost entirely of long strings of virtuosic sixteenth notes.

The ten sections that make up *Kossuth* can be divided into three parts according to the type of action they depict. Part A, sections one through five, depicts static images: Kossuth in various modes of contemplation. Part B, sections six through eight, depicts action: the call to war, the swearing of an oath, and battle. Part C, sections nine and ten, combines aspects of action and contemplation: the return of music from part A transformed into a funeral march. Judit Frigyesi has aptly observed that parts A and B of *Kossuth* are analogous to the two main parts of a rhapsody. Like the *lassú*, part A has a high proportion of dotted rhythms and moderate tempi. Like the *friss*, part B has generally faster tempi and a relative paucity of dotted rhythms.[28] The pause that separates parts A and B and the dramatic shift in mood and tempo that occurs at the beginning of part B reinforce the notion that the form of *Kossuth* owes a debt to the slow-fast structure of Hungarian rhapsodies.

The funeral march that constitutes part C of *Kossuth* would seem to contradict the rhapsody as a formal model.[29] The rhapsody paradigm, however, need not be abandoned entirely in part C, for it is precisely here that for the first time in the work we encounter a truly slow tempo, that is, the tempo that by rights should appear at the beginning. The slow tempo filled out with the elaborate embellishments typical of Hungarian funeral marches provides something of the character of the *hallgató*, the part of the *lassú* "omitted" from the work's opening. Therefore, the form of *Kossuth* may be considered a rhapsody modified by the unconventional placement of what would have traditionally been its first section, the *hallgató*. (As will be discussed below, Bartók also ends his Rhapsody, op. 1, with a slow section.)

Bartók's approach to form in his symphonic poem thus uncovered a potential similarity between two genres from disparate traditions. Such an affinity between the symphonic poem, a sequence of sections governed in theory only by a program, and the Hungarian rhapsody, a sectional medley of nationally inflected tunes presented in order of increasing tempo, had rarely, if ever, been recognized previously.[30] Well versed in the Hungarian style and a passionate student of Strauss's symphonic poems, Bartók was in a position to understand how the formal elements of the two genres could be combined. This realization seems to have been crucial to his success in creating a symphonic style that was both elevated and Hungarian throughout. The rhapsody form was the logical frame for his *verbunkos*-inflected themes and supported the work with a Hungarian backbone, but a Hungarian rhapsody in the traditional sense would have lacked an ending of the requisite profundity. With its tradition of thematic transformation and narrative thrust, the symphonic poem brought to Bartók's work the cohesion and rhetorical weight necessary to rise to Kern's and Dohnányi's challenge.

NATIONAL IN NARRATIVE

In addition to *Kossuth*'s form, content, and subject, its narrative, ending in mourning for the defeat of the revolution, also has national roots. The last section of the work takes its subtitle "Csöndes minden, csöndes . . ." ("All is silent, silent . . .") from the first line of "Est" (Evening), a poem by Kálmán Harsányi (1876–1929), written between 1896 and 1899 when the return of Kossuth's body to Hungary for burial in 1894 was still a memory shared by virtually the entire country. Besides alluding to "Est" in *Kossuth*, Bartók also composed two settings of the entire poem. The fact that all three works were composed in 1903 suggests that Bartók knew Harsányi's poem from a collection published that year.[31] The connection between the evening of the title and Kossuth is clarified in the poem's last line:

Csöndes minden, csöndes,	All is silent, silent,
Hallgatnak a lombok,	Quiet are the leafy heaps,
Meghalt a nap;—ott a vérfolt,	The sun has died; there's the bloodstain
Ahol összeomlott.	Where it collapsed.
Gyász van; mély, sötét gyászt	There is mourning; in deep, dark mourning
Ölt a táj magára,	Has the landscape dressed itself,
Harmatot sír a mezőnek	Dew is wept by the meadow's
Minden szál virága.	Each and every flower.
És susogják halkan:	And they whisper softly:
"Sose látjuk többé?	"Not to see it ever?
Nem lehet az, hogy éj legyen,	It cannot be that night
Most már mindörökké."	Will now be forever."
S várják, visszavárják,	And they wait, they await its return,
Míg a láthatáron	Until on the horizon
Fölmerül a hold korongja	The disk of the moon arises
Halotthalományon.	Glowing deathly ashen.
Kísértetes fénytől	Bathed in ghostly light
Sápad az ég alja.	The horizon is pallid.
Megborzongnak a virágok:	Together the flowers shudder:
"Visszatért, de—halva!"[32]	"It/he has returned, but—it/he is dead!"

On one level the moon is the lifeless specter of the sun. On another level, however, given the date of the poem and the depth of the mourning Harsányi depicts, the sun and the moon, the "it" or "he" of the last line, stand for Kossuth. Bartók strongly reinforces this interpretation by making reference to the poem's title in his symphonic poem. Evening, the time just after the last glimmer of hope has slipped below the horizon, is a metaphor for Kossuth's death and the loss of the hope for independence that he embodied.

Harsányi's "Est" belongs to a long tradition of poetry in which death and/or defeat are metaphors for the Hungarian condition. Its first line ("All is silent, silent") recalls the phrase "Europe is silent, silent again" ("Európa csendes, újra csendes"), the well-known first line of a dark poem by Sándor Petőfi, Hungary's most popular Romantic poet.[33] Petőfi's poem is about the failure of the European revolutions of 1848, a failure that at the time of the writing of the poem still awaited the last of them, the Hungarian.

The sense of defeat as a central element of Hungarian national identity had been deeply embedded in the national consciousness even before the revolution. This is hardly surprising in a country that had been under foreign domination since the sixteenth century. In Mihály Vörösmarty's 1836 poem "Szózat," the so-called second national anthem, set to music by Béni Egressy in 1839, the poet captures the spirit of defeat that continues to characterize the Hungarian mind-set even today despite the end of the last occupation, that of the Red Army, in 1989. The "Szózat" does have bright passages, but it ends darkly. Patriotic citizens are implored to remain in the country and accept their fate. The concluding verses trace a progression from optimism to morbid acceptance:

Még jőni kell, még jőni fog	A better time has to come,
Egy jobb kor, melly után	It will come, and for it
Buzgó imádság epedez	Ardent prayer yearns
Száz ezrek ajakán.	On the lips of a hundred thousand.
Vagy jőni fog, ha jőni kell,	Or magnificent death will come,
A nagyszerű halál,	If come it must,
Hol a temetkezés fölött	Where above the burial
Egy ország vérben áll.	A country stands in blood.
S a sírt, hol nemzet sülyed el,	And the grave in which a nation sinks
Népek veszik körül,	Is surrounded by other nations,
S a népek millióinak szemében	And the eyes of the millions of nations
gyászköny ül.	Are filled with tears of mourning.
Légy híve rendületlenűl	Be steadfastly faithful
Hazádnak, oh magyar,	To your homeland, oh, Hungarian,
Ez éltetőd s ha elbukál,	It is your life force, and if you fail,
Hantjával ez takar.	It will cover you with clods of earth.
A nagy világon e kívül	The whole world over
Nincsen számodra hely;	There is no place for you;
Áldjon vagy verjen sors keze,	Should the hand of fate bless you or beat you down,
Itt élned, halnod kell.	Here must you live, here must you die.

With its several victories ending in crushing defeat, the War of Independence that is the subject of *Kossuth* offers an objective correlative to the fatalism—the sense of transience of success and inevitability of failure—that has long dominated Hungarian national sentiment. Thus the programmatic aspect of *Kossuth* that motivates the break with traditional rhapsody form is itself traditionally Hungarian. The funeral march, with its own tradition of *verbunkos*-like embellished dotted rhythms, added a further layer—a stylistic one—to the formal and narrative elements that infused Bartók's work with Hungarian national expression.[34]

Rhapsody, Op. 1

Kossuth is unique in Bartók's instrumental music for the explicitness of its program. Still, traces of the Hungarian Romantic narrative toward inevitable despair can also be found in some of the composer's more mature works—most obviously in *A Kékszakállú herceg vára* (Duke Bluebeard's Castle) and the Sixth String Quartet. More broadly, however, the deep-seated Hungarian suspicion that triumphs are illusory may lurk behind what László Somfai has identified as Bartók's lifelong difficulty with writing conclusions that are at once uplifting and free of banality.[35] The problem of creating moments of arrival that are not undermined by their own potentially false optimism was a recurrent problem for Bartók.

The Rhapsody for Piano, op. 1, composed as a showpiece to launch Bartók's career as a virtuoso pianist in the year following *Kossuth*, allows us to explore the notion of triumph undermined as opposed to defeat.[36] Like *Kossuth*, the Rhapsody is not a fully mature work. Like *Kossuth*, it serves as an example of Bartók's early attempt to be explicitly national and yet sophisticated, elevating the genre of the rhapsody through motivic transformation and repetition. Like *Kossuth*, the Rhapsody has a concluding section that begins with a slightly transformed recapitulation of the main theme of the work and ends in a mood of somber reflection. In *Kossuth*, however, the quasi recapitulation of the main theme in the final section of the Rhapsody begins as a triumphant arrival, not as a funeral dirge. The Rhapsody therefore serves as both a companion work to *Kossuth* and as an important counterweight to the symphonic poem for understanding the relationship of Bartók's music to Hungarian nationalism prior to the composer's awareness of peasant music.

TRIUMPH AS CULMINATION POINT

Formal similarities between the Rhapsody and *Kossuth* lend further support to the notion that Bartók used the Hungarian rhapsody as a model when composing his symphonic poem. As in *Kossuth*, the Rhapsody's two main sections are related by thematic transformation (example 17). As in *Kossuth*, a slow coda that also performs a somewhat recapitulatory function ends the Rhapsody in a somber tone. In the Rhapsody, however, rather than pausing between the end of the second, fast section and the slow coda as in *Kossuth*, Bartók elides them. At the end of the second section he generates tension over a dominant pedal that forcefully drives the music into the coda (see example 19 below). The buildup literally rings with the dominant, A, sounded *fortissimo* in six octaves including the lowest pitch on most

EXAMPLE 17. Rhapsody, op. 1, thematic transformation of main theme

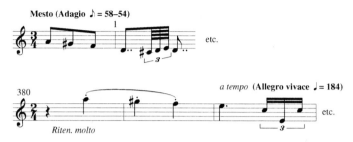

pianos.[37] The *fortississimo* resolution to a D-major chord brings with it a slightly altered version of the main theme from the slow first half of the Rhapsody (section A), introduced by an elongated version of the three-note pickup to the main theme in the last three bars of the dominant preparation. The bombastic effect of the passage is reflected in Bartók's daunting notation: the theme in octaves supported by a sea of black figuration spread over three staves. This is the earliest example in Bartók's oeuvre of what László Somfai has dubbed the "characteristically Hungarian culmination point" (mm. 561–63).[38]

The Rhapsody's culmination point exhibits at least three qualities that recur at analogous points in many of Bartók's large instrumental compositions: there is a climactic reprise of music that has been heard before in a somewhat different form; the climactic passage occurs near the end of the movement but does not actually end it; and, most important, this most exuberantly expressive passage of the work is densely packed with characteristically Hungarian markers.

The main theme of the Rhapsody is made up of a series of typically Hungarian gestures (example 18). The first part of the melody has three typically Hungarian features: the augmented second between G♯ and F (scale degrees 3 and 4 in D minor) in the three-note pickup to bar 1 (implying the "Gypsy scale"); the dotted rhythms embellished with turns on beats 1 and 2 (*verbunkos* figures); and the final bouncing between the upper tonic (D) and the lower dominant (A)—so-called *kuruc* fourths typical of Rákóczi-style songs. The second part of the theme, beginning on the second eighth of bar 2, continues the dotted rhythms and the "Gypsy"-inflected scale (namely, B♭ and G♯, m. 2) of the first part of the theme. In the accompaniment, a consistent accent on the second eighth in each beat in bars 1 and 2 maintains a mild trace of *düvő* or *esztam*.

In spite of Bartók's saturation of the theme with Hungarian rhythmic,

EXAMPLE 18. Rhapsody, op. 1, main theme, mm. 1–4

ornamental, and melodic formulas, there is one figure that seems to be missing from the melody: the *short*-long. Its apparent omission is odd in a theme so obviously reliant on the stereotypical emblems of Hungarian music. A reason for the apparent omission in the initial version of the theme emerges, however, if we compare the first version of the theme with its later incarnations, especially the climactic version of the theme in the culmination point (example 19).

The main theme of the Rhapsody begins with two contrasting phrases. The first phrase, ending on the first eighth of bar 2, consists of four Ds, one on each beat of the phrase following the pickup, each connected by embellishments typical of a *lassú*. The first two decorative turns (*verbunkos* triplets) lead to progressively more intense iterations of D. The point of highest dissonance and tension in the phrase occurs on the third beat of bar 1 with a half-diminished ii^7 chord. In contrast, the open sound of the final *kuruc* fourth helps dissipate the tension of beat 3. On the downbeat of bar 2, an unaccompanied D rounds off the phrase and returns the music to the *piano dolce* fragility of the unaccompanied pickups to bar 1. Bartók further articulates the division between the two phrases with the phrase marks and by beginning a new chordal accompaniment and a *crescendo molto espressivo* after a rest in the left hand on beat 1. The change in register in the right hand further complements the sense of starting anew at this point. In sum, the least emphasized characteristic of the main theme in its first incarnation

EXAMPLE 19. Rhapsody, op. 1, climactic return to main theme, mm. 556–63

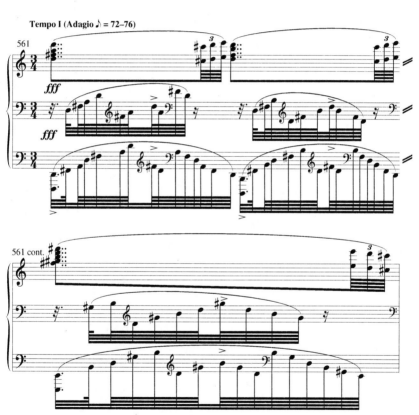

(continued)

EXAMPLE 19 *(continued)*

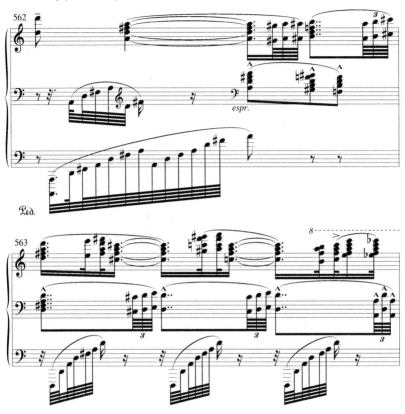

is the leap of a fourth between the D that concludes the first phrase and the A that begins the second.

In some later occurrences of the theme, including that of the culmination point, Bartók changes a few of its details in a way that creates more of an elision between the two phrases (see example 19). Significantly, he adds a *tenuto* mark to the fourth D, suggesting it should be emphasized and sustained rather than tapered.[39] In this phrasing, the role of D changes dramatically. Instead of rounding off the phrase, the D on the first eighth of the second bar of the theme becomes a climactic note—storing within it the energy of the preceding triplets, which it releases as it resolves down a fourth to A. The connection between D and A now becomes the focus of the passage, revealing D as the accented first note in a *short*-long pair. Bartók emphasizes the *short*-long figure at the culmination point in four additional ways: increased speed ($\flat$ = 72–76 versus $\flat$ = 58–54 of the opening), which helps elide the two phrases; extension of the A by an eighth note, which exaggerates the "long" of the *short*-long; replacement of the third D with an F♯, which emphasizes the transformation of the theme to major and saves the D from overuse; and, finally, substitution of a descending scalar figure in place of the *kuruc* fourths, thereby driving energy into the final D.

Several later renditions of the main theme derive power from tapping the energy of the *short*-long figure latent in the opening phrase. The culminating statement of the theme outdoes all previous incarnations with its increased dynamic, tempo, figurations, and octave doublings. Bartók seems to revel in the Hungarianness of the moment by adding a new layer of Hungarian rhythms (choriambs: ♪♪♪) in the third bar (m. 563).

Although capping off a minor-mode composition with a climactic major-mode return to the main theme is hardly a rarity in nineteenth-century music, this is one of the few aspects of Bartók's Rhapsody that does not have a precedent in either the *verbunkos* tradition or Liszt's Hungarian Rhapsodies proper.[40] There is, however, precedent for something analogous to Bartók's culmination point in Liszt's *Hungarian Fantasy*, an expanded version of his Hungarian Rhapsody No. 14 arranged for piano and orchestra that Bartók heard Dohnányi play with the Philharmonic in May 1903.[41] Like Bartók, Liszt lends symphonic weight to his *Hungarian Fantasy* by including a striking return to the opening theme near the end of the work (example 20).[42] Although the main theme of the *Hungarian Fantasy* is a popular *magyar nóta* "Magasan repül a daru" ("High Flies the Crane"), and Bartók's theme is of his own invention, these culminating moments are both equally and explicitly Hungarian.

The climactic arrival in Bartók's Rhapsody generally fits Somfai's description of the "characteristically Hungarian culmination point."[43] It differs from the examples he discusses, however, in that the culmination point of the Rhapsody is not followed by the *Entfremdungsprozess* that in later works serves as a cool antidote to the bombastic effect of the overtly expressive culminations. Unlike Liszt who concludes with a brief, virtuosic race to the finish in the spirit of the fast dance that had preceded the heroic return of the main theme, Bartók eschews a traditional virtuosic ending. The Rhapsody ends with a long, slow peroration that concludes with a series of gentle chords in which Bartók embeds the opening notes of the main theme (example 21). Furthermore, whereas Liszt uses his climactic music to interrupt the F-major music of the *friss* with an abrupt and jarring harmonic move from a C dominant 7th chord to E major, Bartók's technique is to lead smoothly to the culmination point, which arrives as the harmonic resolution of the preceding

EXAMPLE 20. Franz Liszt, *Hungarian Fantasy*, return to the opening theme,
3 after reh. K, mm. 441–57

EXAMPLE 21. Rhapsody, op. 1, closing bars, mm. 588–92 (diamond noteheads indicate main theme)

buildup. Bartók's integration of the culmination point into the essential fabric of the Rhapsody and the slow coda with which it ends brings to the work a formal elegance, solemnity, and rhetorical weight uncommon for the genre. Like *Kossuth*, the Rhapsody can be heard as ending with death, but unlike *Kossuth* this is an end not of emptiness and despair, but rather one of transcendence, the last chords rising like a halo around the final recollection of the theme. As Bartók softly embeds the theme in the final chords of the Rhapsody, so does he seem to confirm its nationalistic message. Despite their contrasting narratives and their impressive craftsmanship, both *Kossuth* and the Rhapsody for Piano reflect Bartók's youthful acceptance of *verbunkos* as the appropriate vessel for national sentiment.

NATIONALIST INSPIRATION

Whereas for Liszt *verbunkos* was primarily a local color and a medium for his impetuous virtuosity, for Bartók in 1903–4 the nationalistic implications of the Hungarian style held a personal imperative. Around the time he was composing *Kossuth* and the Rhapsody, Bartók expressed his nationalist sympathies in every aspect of behavior, from dressing in a traditional Hungarian suit to calling his sister Böske, the Hungarian equivalent of her Germanic given name, Elza.[44] Although Bartók greatly admired Dohnányi's musicianship, he was frustrated by the latter's lack of nationalist passion. Writing to his mother on 23 September 1903 from Gmunden where he had gone to study piano with Dohnányi, Bartók reported: "You are quite wrong about Dohnányi. I think very highly of him both as a man and an artist. There is not a trace of malice in him. As an artist, he is too severe on his fellow artists; but that's not such a very great fault. His much worse and unforgivable sin is his lack of patriotism. This excludes the possibility that there might ever be a 'better relationship' between us."[45]

Bartók reserved his strongest censure for his family, the members of which were unable to meet the unreasonable standards he set in his naively moralistic zeal for the Hungarian national cause. The sheer length and stridency of a fervently nationalistic passage in a letter to his mother on 8 September 1903 demonstrates the vehemence of Bartók's views:

I have no news at the moment. The most I can send you is a social-political dissertation to the effect that the ruin of the Hungarians will not be caused by [Germanic influence in the army], because—as Dohnányi asserts—[sooner or later] the language and spirit of our army will be Hungarian. Indeed, the ruin of the Hungarians will be caused much more by the fact that the individual members of the Hungarian nation, with insignificant exceptions, are so distressingly indifferent to everything Hungarian. Not in high politics, where there is plenty of enthusiasm for national ideals, but in everyday life where we incessantly commit wrongs against the Hungarian nation in all sorts of seemingly unimportant trifles. "It's all the same to us whether and how anybody speaks our unique and peerless language, instead we ourselves speak everybody else's language; we deride people who speak only Hungarian as uneducated, no matter how much they know; our girls, the mothers of future generations, we ruin at a tender age with foreign education . . ." This is what Jenő Rákosi says in one of his fine speeches. He is right. This is how Hungarians act when really they ought to do all they can to foster the use of their mother tongue. Only thus can it become strong, at least within our own boundaries. But of course we don't mind, Hungarian speech or German (we even take pride in this), Hungarian goods or Austrian. . . . Unfortunately there are in this respect many things in my own home which need correcting. The last time we were together, I noticed with sorrow that both you and Böske, whether from negligence or forgetfulness, committed the very errors I have mentioned. I don't deny that if there's a row somewhere over Gotterhalte [the Austrian national anthem], it causes a great uproar. But this does the Hungarians no good; at the most there might be some government legislation to put that right. But as not everyone can be prime minister, those whom fortune has spared should work quietly and unobtrusively in their everyday life for everything that is Hungarian. Spread and propagate the Hungarian language, with work and deed, and with speech! Speak Hungarian between yourselves!!! How ashamed of myself I should be if for instance in Pozsony or perhaps later in Budapest an acquaintance who knows my way of thinking visited me and by chance heard that you speak German between yourselves and perhaps even to me. He would think me a hypocrite.—You bring up in defense that you have got used to speaking German with Aunt Irma. This is an acceptable excuse, but at the same time the outcome of a neglect that can never be made good. Why didn't you get used to speaking Hungarian when you were young? Aunt Irma, after all, spent quite a long time in Békés County; there she learned our language to some extent, and you could have done the rest. If, much later, you got used to speaking German to us so that we should learn the German language, you could in the same manner have got used to speaking Hungarian with Aunt Irma in order that she should learn Hungarian.

But what am I talking about? For in Hungary knowing German is obligatory and necessary; it does no harm if, in addition, they speak Hungarian too (a little)!

Hear now the thesis addressed to every Hungarian:

Speak in a foreign language only when absolutely necessary! That is, I wish that, even if you speak in another language with Aunt Irma, you should, with Böske, whether at home or elsewhere, whether I'm at home or not, speak in Hungarian without fail. If "it's difficult to get used to it," then one must take pains; the Hungarian language deserves it.

As for you addressing me in German—well, not even as a joke do I want this. . . . [W]hat I am writing about in this letter, what I am asking, you must do.[46]

Bartók's conviction appears to have been as heartfelt as it was rigid and impractical. But, like his compositions from the same time, his writing style was far from wholly original. The man he quotes, Jenő Rákosi, was the owner and editor-in-chief of the *Budapesti Hírlap,* the same paper in which Aurél Kern had written in support of Hungarian music in 1902 and an important forum for nationalist views. Bartók's own overblown rhetoric owed much to the expressions of nationalism found in the Hungarian press.[47]

During Bartók's infatuation with Hungarian nationalism, he viewed his social awkwardness in Budapest's bourgeois society through a nationalistic lens. By birth, Bartók was a member of the provincial middle class. His father, the director of a provincial agricultural school, had pretensions to noble rank and was a community leader in cultural affairs.[48] This segment of Hungarian society was small and concentrated in leadership positions in rural towns. Members of this "gentry" middle class strongly supported nationalism and the music associated with it—*verbunkos, magyar nóta,* and the "Gypsy music" with which these categories were intertwined.

Bartók's move to Budapest and his studies at the Music Academy brought him into the midst of what was for him a foreign culture, the musical and intellectual circles of the metropolis. This community was dominated by bourgeois Germans and Jews, who were more affluent than Bartók's family, and who had a different, less nationalistic cultural and political orientation than his own. Although Bartók enjoyed many of the social gatherings he attended with these people, depended on their patronage, and was accepted in these circles, he also frequently seems to have felt like an outsider. In reference to a party given by the violin-playing Arányi sisters,

Bartók wrote to his mother on 25 November 1902 about his surprise at feeling comfortable at a purely social gathering with members of this class: "A month ago I would have laughed at someone who said that I would go voluntarily to the type of party I attended on Sunday. Indeed! because they completely banished music from this gathering; in its place were—parlor games. . . . Jews and Germans shared the same fate as music."[49]

In fact, the Arányis were themselves Jewish (elsewhere Bartók describes them as "anti-Semitic" Jews), but unlike most Jews in Budapest they spoke French instead of German. Apparently, for Bartók, Catholic by birth but atheist by conviction, the Budapest Jews' most disturbing trait was not their ethnicity or religion, but their lack of nationalist devotion.

Writing in 1905 from Paris, where he had gone to compete in the Rubinstein Competition with the Rhapsody, Bartók inveighed even more vehemently against urban cosmopolitanism: "Real Hungarian music can originate only if there is a real *Hungarian* gentry. This is why the Budapest public is so absolutely hopeless. The place has attracted a haphazardly heterogeneous, rootless group of Germans and Jews; they make up the majority of Budapest's population. It's a waste of time trying to educate them in a national spirit."[50] It should be borne in mind that Bartók's target here was the city, not the Jews or Germans who happened to make their homes there. He maintained friendly relations with a number of individual Jews—among those most important to him were his piano teacher István Thomán (a pupil of Liszt's), Emma Gruber (later Mrs. Kodály), an enthusiastic supporter of Bartók's work and the highly cultured host of a Sunday musical salon, and József Lukács (father of philosopher György Lukács), a banker who provided Bartók with a rent-free apartment for two years in the early 1920s.[51] Bartók's exasperation bespoke conflict between the culture of the provincial towns in which he had been raised and the sophisticated, ethnically heterogeneous bourgeois circles in which he found himself in Budapest.

Zoltán Kodály, who like Bartók had come to Budapest from a provincial town to pursue his higher education, seems to have shared Bartók's disappointment. Speaking about the musical life of Budapest around the turn of the century, Kodály said:

> [Y]ou must recall what the world was like here in Pest in our young days. At
> that time the Wagner cult was at its climax here. If it had not been for the fact
> that the program was in Hungarian, the music played at concerts would have
> made one think that one was in a small German town; besides, it was only a
> few years ago that the German text was omitted from the back page of the
> Philharmonic concert programs. . . . [T]he majority of professional musicians
> did not know Hungarian, and even the lovers of finer music—not the opera-

goers, but those who practiced music at home, the performers of classical chamber music—preferred speaking German to [speaking] Hungarian. No wonder that in this great German world we were overcome by a terrific longing for the real Hungary, which could not be found anywhere in Pest, for here German was virtually the official language of music. We were amazed at this for Budapest had been (at least in the newspapers from which we had known it until then) the focal point of Hungarian life reflected in the glory of the millennium. We were unable to reconcile ourselves to this great disappointment.[52]

Kodály's disenchantment with the musical culture of Budapest was a reflection of a larger disillusionment with the false image of a unified Hungarian nation fostered by the print media. It took Bartók several years to see through the bloated nationalistic rhetoric of the newspapers and form his own subtler opinions. Ever since the compromise of 1867, Hungarian domestic policy had included a program of forced assimilation of non-Magyars. Embracing popular nationalism, Bartók also embraced its chauvinism. Before discovering the richness of the folk music of the peoples of the outlying regions, he was as quick to lump minorities with the enemies of the nation as he would later be to defend of their cultures. Using the rhetoric of nationalist newspapers, he remarked in a letter of 18 June 1903: "It is really an untenable situation that we are ordered about in our own army by foreigners, to the shame of the Hungarian nation, and the joy of the minorities and our enemies."[53]

In turn-of-the-century Hungary, a chauvinistic stance toward Romanians, Slovaks, Croats, Serbs, and other peoples living within the nation's borders was an essential component of Hungarian nationalism. Jenő Rákosi, the propagandist Bartók greatly admired at this time, in 1900 had called for "a total Hungarianness, when every man in Hungary will feel in his innermost soul that he has become a Magyar chauvinist."[54] Whereas the heyday of nineteenth-century national music had corresponded to a liberal phase in Hungarian nationalism, by the turn of the century much the same musical style had been associated with an intolerant, backward view of the nation. We have seen that Bartók shared this view at the time of *Kossuth* and the Rhapsody. Within only a few years, however, he would repudiate it.

OPERATIC PARALLELS

Although Bartók's Rhapsody continued a Lisztian pianistic tradition, together with *Kossuth* it was even more closely akin to the midcentury operas of Ferenc Erkel (1810–93). Erkel's operas had captured the spirit of the independence movement in the years surrounding the Revolution of

1848–49 and set a standard for high artistic quality combined with political engagement in Hungarian national music. This standard would not be matched until Bartók's *Kossuth*, a work that represents a similar confluence of outstanding individual talent and a newly revitalized, politically charged intellectual atmosphere.

Erkel, the composer of the Hungarian national anthem, was the most celebrated composer of Hungarian opera in the nineteenth century. His two most successful works, *Hunyadi László* (1844) and *Bánk bán* (premiered 1861), have remained in the repertory of the Hungarian Opera almost continuously since their first performances. A gauge of the status of *Bánk bán* in 1904 is the role it played in the composer and critic Pongrác Kacsóh's review of *Kossuth* for *Zenevilág* (World of Music): "What we Hungarian musicians only suspected that we desired, [Bartók] saw with prophetic eyes; what we had hoped for, he realized. The Kossuth Symphony is the greatest cultural achievement in the history of Hungarian music since the premiere of *Bánk bán*. What Ferenc Erkel did in opera is now being done by Bartók in the form of the symphonic poem, which is being raised to even greater heights than it was by Liszt in *Hungaria* and *The Battle of the Huns*."[55] Following *Bánk bán* by nearly half a century, *Kossuth* and the Rhapsody were connected to Erkel's opera by their reliance on the *verbunkos* style to convey nationalist sentiment.[56] Although the same might be said of any music in the Hungarian style beginning with the national awakening in the early nineteenth century, there was a particularly strong connection between the sentiments of the middle of the nineteenth century and the first years of the twentieth. These periods shared an intensity of emotion and rhetoric largely missing from the politically more stable time following the Compromise of 1867.

Zoltán Kodály pointed out the connection between the spirit of mid-nineteenth-century and turn-of-the-century Hungary in a recollection of Bartók from 1946:

> For our generation the horrible memory of 1849 was still a living reality. Old gentlemen with Kossuth-beards, who had seen the War of Independence with their own eyes, were to be met with every day. Bartók, too, may have met such men. "The witness of great times—thus the newspapers indicated in their obituaries the death of a warrior of 1848. I myself lived in a house with "cannon balls" [damage from the War of Independence]. When I was a secondary-school pupil [1890s] a decree was issued that, instead of March 15th [the day of the initial uprising in 1848], April 11th [the day of the emperor's first concession to the demands of the revolutionaries] was to be celebrated. . . . The young people marched to the Hungarian soldiers' monument

at night, for daytime demonstration had been prohibited. At night Emil Ábrányi's poems for March 15th were recited. As far as I can remember, this happened all over the country. That was the soil from which the *Kossuth Symphony* had sprung.[57]

Based on a historical incident in thirteenth-century Hungary, Erkel's *Bánk bán*, after the play of the same name by József Katona, was written as a thinly veiled call for liberation from Austrian domination. In the opera a queen of Austrian birth and her brother Ottó run the country to ruin while the Hungarian king is fighting abroad. In the opera's second act the metaphoric rape of the country is mirrored by Ottó's literal rape of Melinda, the innocent wife of Bánk, the patriotic Palatine (*bán*) of Hungary.

Erkel's primary musico-dramatic device in *Bánk bán* is contrast between identifiably Hungarian music and the Italianate international operatic style of the time. The *verbunkos* style defines the positive characters Bánk and his wife Melinda. The nationally unspecific music of the Austrian-born queen, Gertrud, and her conspirator brother, Ottó, reflects their lack of virtue.

Erkel ensures that a melody sung several times by Melinda will be the most-remembered tune of the opera by making it appear in three distinct sections in the score: the orchestral prelude, the first finale to act 1, and the duet between Melinda and Bánk in act 2.[58] The melody is a full-blown eight-bar period that is sung in its entirety twice in both of its dramatic appearances. In both the first finale to act 1 and Melinda and Bánk's duet in act 2, Melinda is the first to sing the melody, which she repeats immediately, now emphatically doubled by all the soloists in her company. At the end of the first finale to act 1 (example 22), having sensed the lascivious intentions of Ottó, Melinda sings her theme while directing her thoughts to her husband, who is absent from the royal court. Her words are a prayer that Bánk rescue her and take her to the safety of his own castle:

MELINDA: *Édes Bánkom végy karodba*
Vígy magaddal csend lakodba,
Ott nem árad ennyi pompa fény,
Ah, de Bánkom szíved enyém.

My sweet Bánk take me in your arms,
Take me with you to your tranquil castle,
There the light does not shine so brilliantly,
Oh, but Bánk, there your heart is mine.

During Melinda's first, gentle rendition of her signature tune, Gertrud, Ottó, Petur (a sympathetic Hungarian nobleman), and a chorus of courtiers

EXAMPLE 22. Ferenc Erkel, *Bánk bán*, act 1 first finale, Melinda's theme

EXAMPLE 22 *(continued)*

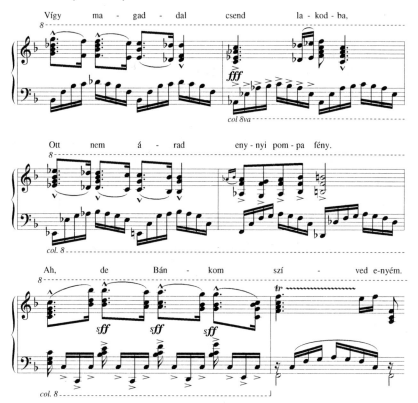

accompany Melinda with texts reflecting their own states of mind and music of little melodic interest:

GERTRUD: *Hódol nékem vendég koszorú,*
A hatalomnak érc karja véd,
Csillagomra nem szállhat ború,
Fénye örökre ég.

OTTÓ: *Szép Melinda ne légy szomorú,*
Bajnokodnak erős kara véd,
Homlokodról oszoljon a bú,
Láng szerelmem tiéd.

PETUR: *Szép Melinda ne légy szomorú,*
E haza minden bajnoka véd
Homlokodról oszoljon a bú,
Bánkod szíve tiéd.

GERTRUD: All the guests pay homage to me,
    The iron arm of power protects me,
    My star cannot fall,
    Its light burns forever.

OTTÓ: Beautiful Melinda, don't be sad,
    The strong arm of your champion protects you,
    Chase away the sadness from your forehead,
    My fiery love is yours.

PETUR: Beautiful Melinda, don't be sad,
    All champions of this country are protecting you,
    Chase away the sadness from your forehead,
    The heart of your Bánk is yours.

Melinda's melody, however, proves irresistible. When she repeats it, the three other soloists join her in a full-throated unison rendition.

In act 2 Melinda's theme functions similarly, this time to bring Bánk into Melinda's musical realm. After having been drugged and abused by Ottó, Melinda appears before Bánk, who in his frustration curses their infant son. Full of remorse, Melinda begs her husband to kill her but withdraw his curse. When Bánk recants, Melinda thanks heaven with her patriotic tune. Upon its repeat Bánk joins her at the octave, and they both sing the melody in an impassioned *fortissimo* very near the top of their ranges (example 23). This final rendition of Melinda's tune is the most cathartic moment in the opera:

MELINDA: *Égi szózat, Bánk nem átkoz*
    Drága fiam! Nem átkoz atyád,
    Nem édes fiam!

BÁNK: *Édes nőm, megáld a férjed;*
    Drága fiam, megálda atyád.

MELINDA: Heaven speaks, Bánk does not curse you,
    My dear son! Your father does not curse you,
    He does not [curse you] my sweet son!

BÁNK: My sweet wife, your husband blesses you,
    My dear son, your father blesses you.

The emotional power of Bánk and Melinda's singing Melinda's tune together notwithstanding, much of the force of the scene derives from our knowledge that this moment of optimism must be short-lived. Melinda cannot recover from Ottó's abuse, just as the Hungarian nation she represents cannot extricate itself from destructive foreign domination. Despite Bánk's forgiveness, in the next act Melinda takes her own life in a fit of demented

EXAMPLE 23. Erkel, *Bánk bán*, act 2, Melinda's theme sung by Melinda and Bánk

(continued)

EXAMPLE 23 *(continued)*

despair. In the final minutes of the opera, the news of Melinda's death destroys Bánk. Like *Kossuth*, the work ends in mourning for a hero whose life represented the hope of a better future for the nation.

Although they recount a historical incident in thirteenth-century Hungary, both *Bánk bán* the opera and the stage play by József Katona on which it is based were thinly veiled critiques of nineteenth-century Austrian domination. Although the play seems to have been completed as early as 1815, its subject was long unacceptable to the censor, and it reached the Hungarian stage only in 1838.[59] Likewise the opera, which may have been largely complete as early as 1852, could not be performed in the tense political climate directly following the revolution. It was performed for the first time in 1861.

Because of the parody of the Austrian national anthem in *Kossuth*, Bartók's symphonic poem encountered similar obstacles. The orchestra of the Music Academy, a state institution, could not perform it. The Philharmonic Society, which counted a number of Austrians among its members, was also resistant to the work. Indeed, it is unlikely the Philharmonic would have performed *Kossuth* had the Wagnerian conductor (and Hungarian native) Hans Richter not scheduled the work with his Hallé Orchestra in Manchester. In Budapest, protests during the Philharmonic's rehearsals and sick-outs by five Austrian musicians at the concert nearly sabotaged the first performance.[60] Still, for all Bartók's incendiary bluster, by focusing on the Hungarian independence movement in his first publicly performed orchestral work, the young composer had in fact adopted what Katona and Erkel had already shown to be a tried and true formula for artistic success in Hungary.

Although the Rhapsody for Piano does not share the despairing narrative or explicit revolutionary message of *Bánk bán,* there is a musical similarity worth noting between Melinda's theme and the culmination point of the Rhapsody. As might be expected from two passages so indebted to the *verbunkos* tradition, they both employ dotted rhythms and the augmented seconds of the "Gypsy scale." More significantly, however, the emotional core of both themes comes when the dotted rhythms lead to a climactic *short*-long figure over a descending perfect fourth in a broader rhythm than the dotted figures preceding it. Erkel and Bartók not only worked in the same Hungarian tradition, but in this instance they both tapped the expressive potential of its rhythmic and melodic formulas in very similar ways.

Erkel's and Bartók's climactic themes also share a dramatic function. In *Bánk bán* Melinda's tune gradually recruits all who surround her on stage as it is designed to recruit the audience to the cause of Hungarian independence. In Bartók's Rhapsody the culminating version of the main theme drives home the work's nationalistic message with a force that may well strike listeners today as exaggerated. Whom, one may wonder, was Bartók (at age twenty-three still searching for artistic direction) trying to convince of the strength or validity of his nationalist style? Emma Gruber, to whom the Rhapsody is dedicated? Foreign audiences that he hoped to conquer in the wake of Dohnányi? Or himself, who in 1903 so forcefully proclaimed that his most important objective will always be "the good of Hungary and the Hungarian nation"?[61] Just as the Rhapsody and *Kossuth* rely on *verbunkos* formulas that had become clichés by the early twentieth century, Bartók's proclamation seems to borrow its bombastic style from the jargon of the nationalistic press.

Still, for all their bluster, both the Rhapsody's naively optimistic and bombastic culmination point and Bartók's equally naive and bombastic declaration of maturity carry a palpable emotional punch, in part attributable to the raw boldness of the gestures. As Bartók's ideas became more truly his own, he would express them with greater caution and economy. So too, as his compositions would become more original, the relationship between the culmination point and the rest of the work would acquire greater subtlety. Rather than simply embodying a more extreme expression of the overriding sentiment in a work, these moments came to shine as beacons of Hungarianness in less overtly or exclusively Hungarian contexts. The cooler music that seems to question the validity of the culmination points' expressivity in later works reflects an ironic self-consciousness typical of the twentieth century. Throughout Bartók's career, however, these culmination points continued to embody a remnant of *verbunkos*, and, with it, the composer's youthful, characteristically Hungarian desire to recruit us to his cause.

The National Implications of Reception

From the perspective of Bartók's maturity *Kossuth* and the Rhapsody, op. 1, look like conservative extensions of nineteenth-century traditions rather than radical forays into a new world of twentieth-century music. At the time of the Hungarian premieres of these works, however, Bartók's often Straussian use of dissonance was treated by many Hungarian critics as audacious. Strauss's own music was less controversial in Hungary than the criticism Bartók's Straussian works received might lead one to believe. On the contrary, the Philharmonic Society's programming of Strauss and other modern composers conformed to another Hungarian tradition: staying abreast of the latest European trends in art. The relative ease with which Hungarian critics either accepted Strauss or made light of his modernism while resisting the Straussian side of Bartók suggests that Hungarian composers, especially those writing in identifiably Hungarian styles, were held to different standards than foreigners.[62] What was either accepted as daring or dismissed as banal in Strauss was often criticized more aggressively in Bartók. For Hungarian critics Strauss's music was a foreign novelty that presented little threat to their national self-image. By contrast, Bartók's music implicitly challenged the comfortable familiarity of the national style.

At the premiere of *Kossuth*, the nationalist subject of the work (especially the parody of the Austrian national anthem) aroused such strong nationalist support for the work as to overshadow the occasionally harsh criticism of its modern style.[63] Contrariwise, at the first Hungarian performances of the Rhapsody (Pozsony, 1906, and Budapest, 1909) critics seem to have ignored Bartók's national aspirations to emphasize the modernity of the work. Although the reviews of the first two performances of the Rhapsody in Hungary are too brief and insubstantial to be placed on an equal footing with the voluminous criticism of *Kossuth*'s premiere, the difference in the initial reception of the two works does suggest that their genres carried different expectations. Why did the Rhapsody, a work in the most traditional of all Hungarian genres, meet with more resistance than *Kossuth*, a work written under the strong influence of one of the most radical composers of the day? A provisional answer might be that the critics heard *Kossuth* as the Hungarianization of a foreign style, whereas it seems that the Rhapsody may have been heard as the corruption of a noble Hungarian genre by modern, cosmopolitan influences.

The dominant Hungarian national ideology of the time would have supported such an interpretation.[64] Almost any inhabitant of Hungary could be considered a good Hungarian if he or she adopted Hungarian customs. By contrast, as Bartók's hectoring letters to his mother demonstrate, even native Hungarians might be regarded as unpatriotic if they spoke foreign languages or held themselves apart from Hungarian culture. *Kossuth*, for all its debt to Strauss, was easily heard as a work of assimilation, for with it Bartók put a Hungarian stamp on nearly every feature he imported. The Rhapsody, despite its debt to the traditions of *verbunkos* and Bartók's nationalist sentiments at the time of its composition, seems to have been heard initially as a work in which the composer held himself too much apart from the accepted notion of Hungarian national music. In the opinion of a critic at the work's Budapest premiere, the Rhapsody's Hungarianness was "rather ambiguous,"[65] while a critic in Pozsony criticized Bartók's "hypermodern passion" and called for a return to Liszt.[66] The clichés of *verbunkos* were not enough in themselves to win Bartók the support of his countrymen.

It would become much harder for Bartók to find acceptance at home outside of small, intellectual, and artistic circles when, in place of *verbunkos*, he would combine a modern style with elements of peasant music. Historically *verbunkos* was associated with the nobility and gentry and, like these privileged classes, was believed to embody the soul of the nation.[67] In contrast, peasant music, like the peasants themselves, played no part in the traditional Hungarian national consciousness. Bartók's project of turning peasant music, a native product, into the basis for a new type of modernity in his music grew out of national pride, but was far removed from the naive Romantic nationalism of his younger self. By using peasant music as a source for his modernity Bartók would eventually try to turn the tide. Instead of following in the footsteps of foreign innovators, he would lead in an arena in which modernity was defined by a new concept of Hungarianness.

Such a transformation did not occur overnight, and was still unimagined at the time of *Kossuth* and the Rhapsody, op. 1. But already in these works

Bartók demonstrated the ability to analyze, to break apart, and to reconfigure elements of the Hungarian tradition in a style that vied with the most modern idiom he knew. What remained was to apply these extraordinary analytic skills to a repertoire with which Bartók himself was as yet unfamiliar. Still, it would be a mistake to give peasant music quite as much credit for Bartók's entry into the world of twentieth-century modernism as the composer himself did. As we shall see in the following chapter, Dohnányi's example and nineteenth-century Hungarian musical traditions not only inspired much of *Kossuth*, but also provided part of the inspiration for one of the most critical moments of the development of Bartók's modern style.

Tradition Transformed

"The Night's Music" and the Pastoral Roots of a Modern Style

On 8 December 1926 Bartók gave a recital of his own works at the Academy of Music in Budapest that included the premieres of four pieces: *Falun* (Village Scenes, 1924) for voice and piano, the Sonata for Piano (1926), seven short movements from *Nine Little Piano Pieces* (1926), and the first and fourth movements from the suite for piano *Szabadban* (Out of Doors, 1926).[1] Of all the pieces on the program, critics seem to have been most taken by the fourth movement, "Az éjszaka zenéje" (literally: "Music of the Night" or "The Night's Music" as it is translated in the published score).[2] Soon Bartók began including "Az éjszaka zenéje" in his recitals with a frequency that indicates it had become one of his more popular works.[3]

The apparent popularity of "Az éjszaka zenéje" even among the conservative Hungarian audiences of Bartók's day is perhaps surprising for a work that would come to be seen as the locus classicus of a uniquely Bartókian contribution to the language of musical modernism. Its dual status as both a crowd pleaser and a landmark in the development of twentieth-century music stems from Bartók's ability to harness a musical language characterized by sudden, unpredictable, and dissonant gestures to programmatic effect. The composer uses a highly dissonant but very soft tone cluster made up of five adjacent semitones ($E\sharp/F–F\sharp–G–A\flat–A/B\flat\flat$) as a static background throughout most of the work (example 24). Continual changes in the order of the presentation of the pitches of the cluster (indicated by grace notes begun on the beat) animate its static harmony. The night of the work's title might suggest that this cluster serves as a musical analogue for the peculiar sense of space created by the distant background noise in the still darkness of a summer evening. The rapid interjections that Bartók places at irregular intervals and often in widely disparate ranges might be heard as imitations of the sounds of nocturnal animals: crickets, insects, frogs.

EXAMPLE 24. *Szabadban* (Out of Doors), "Az éjszaka zenéje" (The Night's Music), mm. 1–5

Confining each interjecting motive to its own fixed register, he shows himself to be a keen observer of the natural world in which each species communicates in its own characteristic way. Two melodies that appear in the second half of the piece suggest the addition of a human element. The first, a stark, chorale-like melody, evokes a mournful song or lonely meditation (example 25). Its eerie doubling at the triple octave is one of several effects evocative of open spaces that contribute to the sense of loneliness that pervades the work. The second, a light dance tune, grows out of the sounds of nature and recalls a *furulya* (peasant flute) (example 26). By thus combining night with nature and a human presence, Bartók calls upon fundamen-

EXAMPLE 25. "Az éjszaka zenéje," chorale-like melody, mm. 17–25

EXAMPLE 26. "Az éjszaka zenéje," dance tune reminiscent of a peasant flute, mm. 37–39

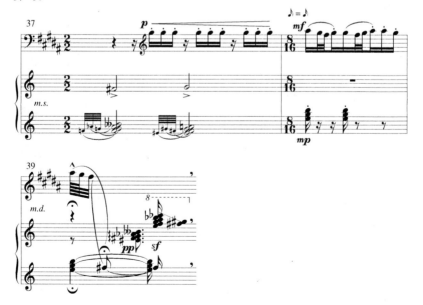

tal mythical symbols to construct a modernist image of human loneliness and isolation—a mythical and existential loneliness he had explored quite differently some fifteen years earlier in the oppressive confines of Bluebeard's eternally closed castle.[4]

"Night Music": From Title to Topic

Almost all of the reviewers at the Hungarian premiere of "Az éjszaka zenéje" captured the spirit of the work's nocturnal imagery. Aladár Tóth (1898–1968), the most important writer about music for Budapest's daily press between the two world wars, also considered Bartók's new piece a signal contribution to a specifically Hungarian tradition of poetic representations of the night. In his words:

> In these strains one can hear everything imaginable—a kind of crying, vague, distant music, bird-music, star-music, then the tranquil sounding of the transcendental melody of the night's sublime hymn. Without the notes attempting to be crickets, birds, or stars, they truly capture the unearthly picture of the night—of Bartók's night—in front of your eyes. This is one of the most wonderful masterpieces of Hungarian nature-poetry. This grandiose picture of the "Night" is, together with Kodály's "Hegyi éjszakák" [Mountain Nights], worthy of the verses of the greatest Hungarian poets, and [let us not forget that] Petőfi and Vörösmarty also wrote poetry about the stars![5]

By invoking Sándor Petőfi, a poet whose verses inspired revolutionaries in the Hungarian War of Independence, and Mihály Vörösmarty, a leading Romantic poet and ardent patriot, Tóth emphasized what was for most Hungarians an unassailable tradition of Romantic Hungarian nationalism over the technical innovations of musical modernism. In Tóth's review, "Az éjszaka zenéje" emerged as a bright new star, but one securely situated in the constellation of Hungarian nocturnal evocations.

At the premiere of "Az éjszaka zenéje," Tóth could not have predicted that Bartók would continue to rely on similar effects—eerie dissonances providing a backdrop to sounds of nature and lonely melodies—for the rest of his life. The following list gives the most notable examples:

Five Songs, op. 15: "Itt lent a völgyben" (In the Valley, 1916, published posthumously)

Out of Doors, Suite for Piano: mvt. 4, "The Night's Music" (1926)

String Quartet No. 3: (mm. 35–42) (1927)

String Quartet No. 4: mvt. 3 (mm. 34–54, 64–71) (1928)

Piano Concerto No. 2: mvt. 2 (mm. 23–29, 39–53, 62–63, 85–120, 209–17) (1931)

String Quartet No. 5: mvt. 2 (mm. 1–9, 26–35, 50–56) and mvt. 4 (mm. 1–22, 90–101) (1934)

Music for Strings, Percussion, and Celesta: mvt. 3 (mm. 1–13, 20–30, 75–82) (1936)

Sonata for Two Pianos and Percussion: mvt. 2 (mm. 28–47) (1937)

Concerto for Orchestra: mvt. 3, "Elegia" (mm. 10–18, 106–11, 118–28)

Piano Concerto No. 3: mvt. 2 (mm. 58–88) (1945)

Viola Concerto: mvt. 2 (mm. 30–39) (1945)

As these effects emerged as characteristically Bartókian modes of expression, Tóth joined other critics in emphasizing their novelty over the features that linked them to a Hungarian national tradition. "Night music" now came to be regarded as a topos unique to Bartók that owed nothing to a past beyond its first published appearance in "Az éjszaka zenéje." We can observe Tóth transforming Bartók's musical depiction of the night into a musical topic of "night music" in his review of the Fourth String Quartet (1928). Commenting on the third movement (Adagio) of the quartet at its Hungarian premiere on 20 March 1929, Tóth observed:

> And now the slow movement rings out. . . . [N]ature's vast empire opens with the secret magic of the night; and in it sounds the song of a man awake: a monumental cello monologue, the arioso recitative of which springs from its heroic melancholy and for a minute reminds us of Kodály—but the way the monologue is followed by the enigmatic, sublime night's music *[éjszaka muzsikája]* involuntarily makes us think of a Beethovenian moment in which a lonely man stands face to face with the starry universe. But all of this is only superficial association. Because a *completely unique enchantment* pervades this sublime Adagio, *an enchantment related exclusively to that found in other works of Bartók's, above all in the piece for piano entitled "[Az] éjszaka zenéje,"* which may be seen as a preliminary study for the mystical notturno sections of this movement of the quartet. Bartók's genius has never before combined the hot fire of human emotion with the secretive murmurs of cool, starry, demonic Night in such a staggering vision.[6]

As he did when reviewing "Az éjszaka zenéje," Tóth mentions Kodály. But, in contrast to the earlier review in which he had presented Kodály as Bartók's equal in the Hungarian tradition of nocturnal depiction, Tóth dismisses similarities between the two composers as superficial. Although Beethoven's presence in the review communicates the sublime profundity Tóth heard in Bartók's quartet and was likely an attempt to elevate the work to the status of a classic, the reviewer ultimately dismisses even Beethoven as an important precedent for Bartókian "night music." Thus, in Tóth's review of Bartók's Fourth Quartet, "Az éjszaka zenéje" emerges as a watershed: initially hailed as a continuation of a Hungarian national tradition, it comes to be taken as the progenitor of a new topic of modernist expression peculiar to Bartók. Yet, as Tóth had recognized initially, "Az éjszaka zenéje," and by extension many passages of "night music" in Bartók's oeuvre, are indeed related to a Hungarian national tradition. What Tóth failed to mention is that this tradition consisted not only of Hungarian "poetry about the stars," but also of Hungarian musical depictions of nature and the night. Examining this tradition allows us to recognize connections between works by composers as diverse as Ferenc Erkel, Mihály Mosonyi (1815–70), Árpád Szendy, Ernő Dohnányi, Leó Weiner (1885–1960), and Bartók. More important, it exposes the Romantic Hungarian roots of what has been taken as one of Bartók's most modern, and least markedly national, modes of musical expression.

Hungary's Symbolic Center: The *Puszta* and Its Nineteenth-Century Musical Representation

Bartók's first wife, Márta Ziegler, his two sons, and other relatives who spent summers with the Bartók family in the 1920s all agreed that the inspiration for "Az éjszaka zenéje" came from Bartók's impressions of the croaking of frogs and other nocturnal sounds of nature in Szőllős-puszta.[7] Szőllős-puszta, an estate managed by Bartók's brother-in-law beginning in 1921, lies in Békés County on the Great Hungarian Plain (Nagy Magyar Alföld). Impressions of the country's natural phenomena in general, and of the Great Hungarian Plain in particular, have a long history in nineteenth-century Hungarian literature, painting, and music. This region, commonly referred to as the *puszta* (literally: desert, but best understood as "deserted place"), is a large plain that lies to either side of the Tisza River in east central Hungary. The *puszta* looms large in the Hungarian national consciousness in a manner somewhat analogous to that of the American West in the United States. Unlike the American West, however, which has often been associated with the bright future waiting for those who conquer the frontier, the Hungarian *puszta* is more often associated with the darker hues of its country's past.[8] In nineteenth- and early-twentieth-century Hungarian art and literature, the *puszta*, with its great expanses inhabited by nomadic cowherds and horsemen, was frequently used as a backdrop to the lonely struggles and hardships of Hungarian life. Located roughly in the geographic center of pre-Trianon Hungary, the *puszta* was considered the country's heartland, heir to the mythical spirit of the ancient Magyars, themselves nomadic horsemen. Lines from Petőfi's poem "Az Alföld" (1844), taught to all Hungarian school children, capture the importance of this region to the nation:

Lenn az Alföld tengersík vidékin	Down on the Alföld flat as the sea
Ott vagyok honn, ott az én világom;	There am I home, there is my world;
Börtönéből szabadúlt sas lelkem,	My soul is like an eagle freed from its prison
Ha a rónák végtelenjét látom.[9]	When I see the endless open country.

Considering the significance of the *puszta* as a symbol of Hungary, it is not surprising that references to it in the titles of musical pieces is a common indication of works in the Hungarian style (table 2).

Many of the works that include references to the *puszta* in their titles are virtually indistinguishable from the *verbunkos*-inspired rhapsodies and fantasies that form the bulk of the nineteenth-century Hungarian repertoire. But a significant subset—including works now regarded as historically the most significant—use a portion of the slow section *(lassú)* of the form to introduce a specifically Hungarian pastoral tone. Although not the earliest example, the locus classicus of the pastoral *lassú* is the opening section of Mihály Mosonyi's Hungarian fantasy for piano *Pusztai élet* (*Puszta Life*, 1857), his first work wholly in the Hungarian style. Evidence of the work's importance in its day was its inclusion in a special album produced by the Hungarian music publisher Rózsavölgyi in honor of the 1857 visit to Pest of Empress Elisabeth, much beloved by Hungarians for her sympathy to their national aspirations.[10]

In keeping with the Hungarian style of the work, Mosonyi begins the fantasy with an elaborate and rhythmically free *hallgató* section (example 27). What makes this *hallgató* unusual as an introduction to a fantasy for piano is that it consists only of a right-hand melody without accompaniment and that the melody imitates the figuration of a *furulya* or shepherd's flute as opposed to an instrument traditionally associated with a "Gypsy" band such as a cimbalom or violin. Mosonyi's choice of key (D minor) and range (a^1–a^3) as well as the almost hypnotic repetition of short scalar flourishes are all characteristic of the instrument and immediately suggest a pastoral tone appropriate to the work's title.[11] The so-called Gypsy scale (harmonic minor with a raised fourth degree) lends geographic specificity to the pastoral evocations of the peasant pipe and the loneliness of the unaccom-

TABLE 2. Chronological List of Works with *Puszta* as Subject

Franz Doppler: *Bojtár a pusztán* (Herdsman on the *Puszta*), for piano (c. 1850)

Béni Egressy: "Télen nyáron pusztán az én lakásom" (In Winter and Summer My Home Is on the *Puszta*), for voice and piano (*magyar nóta*) (c. 1850)

Louis Köhler: "In der Puszta," from *Zwölf ungarishe Volkslieder für das Pianoforte* (c. 1850)

Imre Székely: "A pusztán" (On the *Puszta*), from *Hungarian Idylls*, for piano (c. 1855)

Imre Székely: *A pusztán születtem* (I Was Born on the *Puszta*), for piano (c. 1855)

Imre Székely: *A puszta viszontlátásnál* (Upon Seeing the *Puszta* Again), for piano (c. 1855)

Imre Székely: *Tisza partján* (On the Banks of the Tisza), for piano (c. 1855)

Mihály Mosonyi: *Pusztai élet* (Life on the *Puszta*), fantasy for piano (1857)

Béla Kéler: *Alföldi búcsúhangok* (Farewell Music of the Great Plain), for piano (c. 1859) (The *Alföld* (literally lowlands) is another name for the Great Hungarian Plain.)

Géza Allaga: "Télen-nyáron pusztán az én lakásom" (In Winter and Summer My Home Is on the *Puszta*), fantasy for piano based on Béni Egressy's *Magyar nóta* of the same name (see above) (c. 1860)

Ferenc Erkel: *Bánk bán:* act 3, scene on the banks of the Tisza (1861)

Friedrich Nietzsche: *Im Mondschein auf der Puszta*, for piano (c. 1870)

Heinrich Hoffmann: "In der Puszta," from *Ungarische Suite für grosses Orchester*, op. 16 (1873)

Joachim Raff: "Auf der Puszta," from Suite for Orchestra No. 2 in F, "in ungarischer Weise" (1875)

Károly Aggházy: *Puszta-Klänge*, op. 7, dramatic sonata for violin and piano, written in collaboration with Jenő Hubay (1880)

Ferenc Liszt: *Puszta-Wehmut/A Puszta keserve* (Sorrow of the *Puszta*), for piano (c. 1881)

Béla Kéler: "Puszták fia" (Son of the Plains), from *Three Hungarian Idylls*, for violin and piano) (before 1882)

Gyula Nádor: "Pusztai élet" (*Puszta* Life), for voice and piano? (c. 1885)

László Zimay: "Pusztai élet" (*Puszta* Life), for male chorus (c. 1885)

Antal Siposs: *Pusztai hangok* (Sounds of the *Puszta*), for piano (1892)

Jenő Hubay: *Impressions de la Puszta*, for violin and piano (1894)

Jenő Hubay: *Pusztai hangok* (Sounds of the *Puszta*), op. 57, for violin and piano (c. 1895)

Jenő Hubay: *Impression de la Puszta*, op. 50, for orchestra (also used as a prelude to *A falu rossza*, act 3) (1896)

Kornél Ábrányi: *Pusztai csendélet zenekép* (Musical Still Life of the *Puszta*), for piano? (n.d.)

TABLE 2 *(continued)*

Alajos Tarnay: *Alkony a Tisza partján* (Twilight on the Banks of the Tisza), for piano (n.d)

László Kun: "Szerenád a Tiszaház előtt" (Serenade in Front of the House on the Tisza), from *Az Ocskay brigadéros,* for voice and piano (1892?)

Kálmán Chován: "Pusztai kép" (Picture of the *Puszta*), op. 35, series 2, no. 4, for piano (1900?)

Emil Hoffmeister: *Puszta*-Scene, for violin and piano (1900)

Ernő Dohnányi: Symphony in D Minor, 2nd movement (Molto adagio) (1901)

Ede Poldini: "Gipsies on the Puszta," from *Impressions for Piano,* op. 34 (1903)

Béla Bartók: Suite for Orchestra No. 2, Andante (1905), arranged for two pianos as "Scena della Puszta"(1940)

Kálmán Chován: *Magyar alföldi kép* (Hungarian Picture of the Great Hungarian Plain), op. 49, for piano (1905?)

Árpád Szendy: "Tárogató hangzik . . ." (Song of the *tárogató* . . .), from *Hat magyar zeneköltemény* (Six Hungarian Tone Poems), for piano (1905?), orchestrated 1909

Albert Hetényi: *Petőfi a Hortobágyon* (Petőfi on the Hortobágy), melodrama for speaker, violin, cimbalom, and piano (n.d.) (The Hortobágy is a somewhat elevated plain that forms part of the *puszta* east of Debrecen.)

László Kun: *Petőfi a Hortobágyon,* melodrama for speaker, violin, cimbalom, and piano (1906)

Johann Hummel: *Zigeuner-Flucht auf der Puszta,* op. 374, for piano (1909)

Michael Krausz: *Puszta-Liebchen,* operetta (1925)

Béla Bartók: "Az éjszaka zenéje" (The Night's Music), from Suite for Piano (*Out of Doors*) (1926)

Tibor Kazacsay: "Este a pusztán" (Evening on the *Puszta*), from *Falusi képek* (Village Pictures), for orchestra? (1944)

Tibor Polgár: *A puszta,* suite for orchestra (1960)

László Lajtha: *Hortobágy,* op. 21, for orchestra (1965)

Jan Van der Roost: *Puszta,* for symphonic band (1988)

panied melody. The remainder of the work continues in the Hungarian manner, but Mosony most clearly captures the *puszta* of the work's title in the introduction.

Mosonyi's friend Ferenc Erkel, who was similarly striving to create a Hungarian national idiom in art music, continued the tradition of the pastoral *lassú* in the prelude to the third act of his opera *Bánk bán.* The act opens on the *puszta* at night with Melinda cradling her infant son in her

EXAMPLE 27. Mihály Mosonyi, *Pusztai élet* (Puszta Life), m. 1

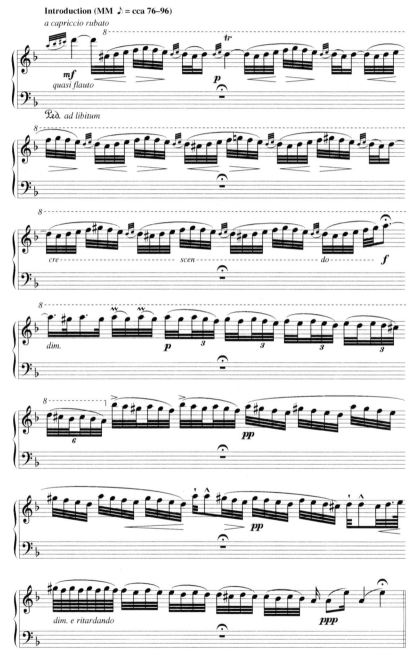

arms while standing on the western bank of the Tisza. As midnight approaches, she waits for a boat to help her cross to the safety of her husband's castle. Ever more distraught and delusional, she eventually leaps, delirious, into the river, drowning herself and her child.

Before the curtain rises on the third act, Erkel sets the tone of the *puszta* at night with an orchestral prelude in the form of a three-part *verbunkos*. The first part (example 28) contains many typical features of a *lassú:* minor key including intervals of an augmented second (mm. 10, 13, and 15), dotted rhythms, equal-length repeated notes at the end of phrases (mm. 2 and 4), an accompaniment that emphasizes the second and fourth beats of the bar (mm. 1–8), and notation in $\frac{4}{8}$. In spite of the plethora of Hungarian features, this is no ordinary *lassú*. The fragility of the music is exceptional in a genre usually associated with the robust playing of a virtuoso violinist. This fragility captures the nocturnal setting of the scene and Melinda's lonely, vulnerable condition.

The second part of the introduction continues the fragile, lonely atmosphere of the first while specifically emphasizing the pastoral setting with an eighteen-bar duet for flute and piccolo accompanied by soft chords in the strings and the faint tremolo of a cimbalom (example 29).[12] Like Mosonyi before him, Erkel imitates a shepherd's flute by constructing the flute and piccolo's lines from relatively short, repeated scalar motives in the traditional flute key of D. Like Mosonyi, Erkel also uses the "Gyspy scale" to add national flavor to the pastoral scene. The inclusion of a cimbalom in the accompaniment both reinforces the Hungarian topic and adds an eerie quality to Erkel's depiction of the *puszta* at night. (Erkel's inclusion of the cimbalom may well be another example of his debt to Mosonyi, who, in his 1860 arrangement of Liszt's symphonic poem *Hungaria*, was the first to write for the instrument as a member of the symphony orchestra.)[13] The high, distant sound of the shepherd's flute(s) communicates the pastoral setting and, by implying a far-off human presence, emphasizes Melinda's isolation.

The prelude to the third act of *Bánk bán* shows its national colors not only in the musical gestures of the two-part *lassú* with which it begins, but also in the brief fast section *(friss)* with which it ends. But whereas the two parts of the *lassú* have a clear relationship to the drama of the opera, this miniature *friss* fulfils only a formal obligation of *verbunkos;* it has no dramatic justification in the tragedy of the opera's third and final act. Pomp, glitter, and gaiety have nothing to do with Erkel's vision of the darkened condition of an oppressed nation.

EXAMPLE 28. Erkel, *Bánk bán*, prelude to act 3 (part 1), scene on the banks of the Tisza

EXAMPLE 29. *Bánk bán*, prelude to act 3 (part 2), continues example 28

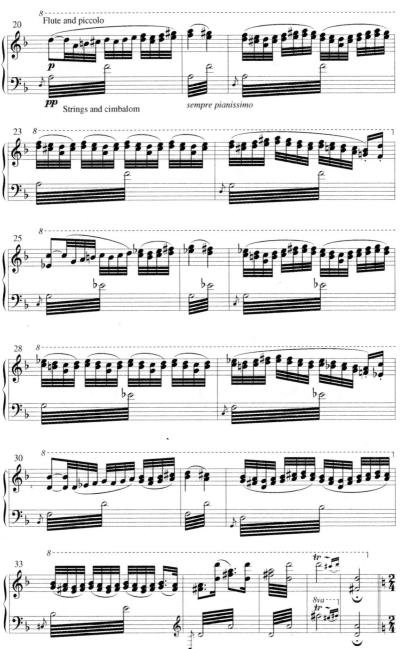

Like so much Hungarian instrumental music, the Hungarian pastorale has it roots in *verbunkos*. It was only a matter of time before composers working in the Hungarian style would free themselves from the formal conventions of *verbunkos* and allow the pastoral *lassú* to stand alone. By the time Dohnányi and Bartók took up the tradition, some four decades after Mosonyi and Erkel had written their seminal works, this transformation had already taken place.

Bartók's "Scena della puszta"

The third movement (Andante) of Bartók's Second Suite for small orchestra (1905) is a pivotal work in the history of the Hungarian pastorale. Written more than twenty years before "night music" became a catchword for Bartók's modernistic style, the Andante serves to bridge the gap between Romantic depictions of the *puszta* by Bartók's Hungarian predecessors and the modernism of "Az éjszaka zenéje."

Bartók himself suggested a strong connection between the Andante of the Second Suite and the Hungarian pastoral tradition by giving the movement the descriptive title "Scena della Puszta" when he arranged the work for two pianos in 1940. He made the arrangement to expand his and his wife's repertoire for concertizing as duo pianists during their years of self-imposed exile in the United States. In Hungary at the time of the premiere of the original version of the work (22 November 1909) the topic of the movement was clear to the Hungarian critics even without a descriptive title. A critic for the German-language *Pester Lloyd* observed that Bartók's Andante had the "gloomy atmosphere of the *puszta*," while the critic for *Magyarország* remarked that the "genuine atmosphere of the *puszta* reaches down to the deepest tones with the characteristic 'solo of a bass clarinet.'" The movement, he added, emanated "pure Hungarian air."[14] Indeed, the long, pensive solo for unaccompanied bass clarinet with which Bartók opens the movement suggests a far-off lone voice in the wilderness much in the tradition of the shepherd's flutes of Mosonyi and Erkel.

Like his Hungarian predecessors, Bartók relied on widely recognized Hungarian features to lend geographic specificity to the pastoral topic of the solo wind instrument (example 30). The most prominent of these are the *short*-long dotted rhythms that mark the climax of the solo (m. 30) and articulate its main cadences (mm. 15, 34, and 36) and the syncopated (short-long-short) figure that will emerge as the main theme of the movement (mm. 17 and 21). Other Hungarian features include the two equally

EXAMPLE 30. Suite No. 2 for Orchestra, movement 3, mm. 1–40

weighted notes that mark the ends of the first two subphrases (mm. 3 and 6)—much slower versions of the two notes that often accompany the heavy stomping at the ends of phrases in Hungarian dances; a pronounced emphasis on perfect fourths; the augmented second (m. 8); and the so-called *verbunkos* triplet (m. 35), which Bartók renders unusually slowly but places in a conventional position as the pickup to a cadence.

One does not have to look exclusively to nineteenth-century Hungarian music to find a precedent for this contemplative initial solo. The profound and meditative tone of Bartók's music for unaccompanied bass clarinet—a result of its often tonally ambiguous chromaticism, dark timbre, and extreme length—also points to the influence of the extended English-horn solo from the beginning of the third act of Wagner's *Tristan und Isolde.* Although the English-horn solo in *Tristan* does not take place at night, it does have dark overtones: *Tristan,* near death and seemingly abandoned by Isolde, lies in a feverish sleep in the overgrown garden of a dilapidated, ancient castle on the edge of the sea. Bartók's choice of key in the Andante of the Second Suite has even more literal nocturnal implications. F♯ minor, the key of the movement and the key he would later choose to symbolize darkness in his opera *Bluebeard's Castle* (1911), may also be indebted to Wagner—specifically to the nocturnal scene in F♯ minor that opens the second act of *Lohengrin.* The dark implications of the key are intensified by the low range and mysterious tone of the bass clarinet, an instrument associated with sepulchers and death in nineteenth-century opera.[15] Lurking behind Bartók's choice of the bass clarinet, however, was more than its gloomy topical associations. Given the date of composition and the movement's Hungarian features, the bass clarinet was clearly a stand-in for the *tárogató,* a peculiarly Hungarian wind instrument that was undergoing a renaissance precisely at the time Bartók was composing the Second Suite.

The *Tárogató* and Hungarian Nationalism

The original instrument to go by the name of *tárogató* in Hungary was a short, high-pitched folk oboe with a penetrating tone (figure 2). Also referred to by Hungarians as the *török síp* (Turkish pipe), it is of ancient Middle Eastern origin and remains well known both there and in the Balkans.[16] Although a version of the instrument may have existed in Hungarian lands earlier, the appellation *török síp* indicates a strong association with the Ottoman Turks who conquered much of Hungary in 1526 and remained in power for approximately the next 150 years. Despite its identification with the Turkish occupiers, the *tárogató* became a symbol for Hungarian independence around 1700. By this time the Turks had already been expelled from Hungary as a result of their decisive defeat by Habsburg armies in 1687. Having liberated Hungary from Turkish rule, the Habsburgs assumed control of most of the country and thereby came to be regarded by many as the next oppressive foreign force. The association of the *tárogató* with Hungarian independence stems from its popularity among *kuruc* soldiers, members of a militia led by the Prince Ferenc Rákóczi II in his unsuccessful war against the Habsburgs (1703–11).

The method of playing the *kuruc tárogató* involved placing the entire length of its short reed inside the performer's mouth. Instead of cushioning the reed, as is the practice with the oboe, the lips press against a metal disk at its base. The inability of the player to modify the vibrations of the reed with the lips results in a loud, raucous tone that made the *tárogató* well suited for conveying military signals in the field.

Although the *tárogató* was also popular among the Habsburg soldiers *(labanc)* against whom Rákóczi's troops were fighting, the instrument's association with the *kuruc* was reputedly strong enough to inspire Habsburg authorities to attempt to ban it after Rákóczi's defeat. Accounts mentioning the instrument from the late eighteenth century suggest that the ban was not highly effective, although the popularity of the instrument in Hungary does appear to have fallen off significantly after 1711.[17] Although the instrument is mentioned in Gergely Czuczor's 1843 account of recruiting (see chapter 1) and an oboist in the orchestra of the Hungarian National Theater made an attempt to resurrect it in the 1860s, the nineteenth century found the *tárogató* on the brink of extinction. It survived mainly as a curiosity in a few museums and in the memories of a few enthusiasts for whom it was a nostalgic reminder of "great times of yore" (régi nagy idők).[18]

Only in 1888 did the renowned Budapest instrument maker Wenzel Josef Schunda (1845–1923) begin the experiments that would lead to the reinvention of the instrument in 1896.[19] Schunda, best known for modernizing the cimbalom in the 1870s, was convinced to undertake a similar task with the *tárogató* by Gyula Káldy (1838–1901), a professor of music history at the Music Academy who specialized in the *kuruc* period. The latter-day *tárogató* manufactured by Schunda and his competitors János Stowasser and Károly A. Wágner was no longer a high-pitched, raucous member of the oboe family used for communication over long distances, but a mellow hybrid of the clarinet and saxophone suitable for genteel drawing rooms (figure 3).[20] The strident double reed of the *kuruc tárogató* was replaced with a clarinet-style mouthpiece and a single reed that made the new *tárogató* much easier to blow than the original. Its commercial production resulted in a fad for the *tárogató* in Hungary that lasted at least until the middle of the First World War. Produced in several sizes, all of which were lower in pitch than the original version, its muffled tone blended well with other instruments, although it seems to have been used most frequently by amateurs to play unaccompanied *kuruc* melodies.[21]

The first appearance of Schunda's *tárogató* (1896) coincided with the Millennium Exhibition, a celebration of the thousand-year anniversary of the conquest of the Carpathian Basin by Magyar tribes. This event was a

Un Fiffre de Theis.

Le Fiffre de Theis en marche, en campagne, et quartier,
Par le son de sa flute donne envie de danser,
Les joues comme son ventre fait tout de même enfler,
Et n'oublie pas les coups, à l'art d'un guerrier.

Mart. Engelbrecht excud. A. V.

FIGURE 2. Martin Engelbrecht, engraving of a *tárogató* player from the first half of the eighteenth century. (Used by kind permission of the Hungarian National Museum, Budapest)

FIGURE 3. The type of *tárogató* developed by W. J. Schunda in the late
nineteenth century. (Used by kind permission of Csaba Nagy)

catalyst for a new wave of Hungarian national display: monuments and paintings depicting the conquerors were commissioned, and it became fashionable to wear Hungarian uniforms inspired by the suits worn by the seventeenth- and eighteenth-century Hungarian nobility.[22] The mood of historical nostalgia was exploited by manufacturers of the *tárogató*, all of whom advertised playing the instrument as a wholesome and patriotic enterprise. In his 1915 introduction to an instruction book for the instrument, *tárogató* manufacturer Károly A. Wágner proudly declared: "The *tárogató* is the favorite instrument of the Hungarian people; and no wonder. Is it possible to imagine the most valuable treasures of the Hungarian nation, the *kuruc nóták* [*kuruc* tunes], on any other instrument besides the *tárogató*? . . . [T]oday there hardly remains a region of our homeland where one cannot hear—especially now in the middle of the burning enthusiasm of the days of war—a few melancholy Hungarian songs or fiery warrior tunes played on the sweet-voiced *kuruc-tárogató*—from the great times of yore."[23]

The fashion for the *tárogató* extended beyond patriotic amateurs. Beginning in 1902 it was regularly used at the Hungarian Opera in place of the English horn for the on-stage solos in *Tristan*. In fact, it is conceivable that the Hungarian conductor Hans (János) Richter, who employed the *tárogató* in a London production of *Tristan* in 1904, could have piqued Bartók's interest in the instrument when they worked together on the January 1904 Manchester performance of *Kossuth*.[24] The modern *tárogató* made its appearance as a full-fledged member of the opera orchestra no later than the 1905 premiere of Géza Zichy's *Nemo*, part of a trilogy of operas about Ferenc Rákóczi II in which Schunda's version of the instrument was used to lend historical "authenticity" to the music, in keeping with the subject matter.[25] By 1908 the *tárogató* had become a regular enough part of the Hungarian symphonic tradition to warrant a substantial entry in Albert Siklós's textbook on orchestration.[26] In addition to writing specifically for the *tárogató*, Hungarian composers also imitated it with various combinations of clarinet and English horn—a practical necessity for performances outside of Hungary.

As we have seen in chapter 2, Bartók was caught up in the fashion for the nostalgic expression of national sentiment most intensely in 1903, the year of his symphonic poem *Kossuth*. While the Second Suite was not as explicitly nationalistic a work as *Kossuth*, the bass clarinet–cum–*tárogató* solo in its third movement signals Bartók's continued reliance on popular nationalist tropes. It also betrays his debt to turn-of-the-century fashions in Hungarian art music, Ferenc Rákóczi II, the historical figure most closely associated with the instrument, being perhaps the most fashionable subject for Hungarian composers in the years 1905–6. The preoccupation with Rákóczi at this time was not only a result of the general turn-of-the-century Hungarian preoccupation with independence; it was also specifically related to the fact that, 170 years after his death in Turkish exile, Rákóczi's ashes were returned to Hungary on 28 October 1906. In addition to Zichy's opera *Nemo*, works with Rákóczi as their subject composed at this time include *Gyászhangok II. Rákóczi Ferenc fejedelem emlékére* (Funeral Music in Memory of Prince Ferenc Rákóczi II, 1905) and the cantata *Rákóczi* (1905) by Károly Agghazy (1855–1918); the operetta *Rákóczi* (1906) by Pongrác Kacsóh (1873–1923); and the *Rákóczy Symphony* (1903) and the opera *Kurucvilág* (World of the *kuruc*, 1906) by Ödön Farkas (1851–1912).

Dohnányi's D-Minor Symphony, the "Rákóczi Nóta," and Bartók's "Contradiction of the Commonplace"

The "*tárogató* solo" in the Second Suite was not only the result of Bartók's elevating elements of Budapest's latest musical fashion to Wagnerian heights. It was also very likely another of Bartók's responses to the imposing challenge of Dohnányi's Symphony in D Minor. A similarity between the slow second movement (Adagio) of Dohnányi's symphony and Bartók's Andante is immediately apparent in their shared pastoral subject, which Dohnányi establishes with a long, initially unaccompanied solo for English horn, a more common substitute for the *tárogató* than Bartók's bass clarinet (example 31). As would later be the case with Bartók's Andante, Hungarian critics needed no descriptive title to recognize Dohnányi's Adagio as a nostalgic portrait of the *puszta*. The critic of *Pesti Hírlap* (Pest News) singled out one of the most striking geographical features of the *puszta* when he called the English horn's opening tune a "theme of sorrowful Hungarian character . . . that arouses in us the authentic image of the banks of the Tisza."[27] Connected to the evocation of a Hungarian landscape was the recollection of the imagined glory of Hungary's distant past. As the critic of the *Magyar Nemzet* (Hungarian Nation) declared: "The distinguished composer's Hungarian temperament is also evident in this movement. It is just as if the *tárogató* of the *good old days of yore* would play some of the motives—in fact with a little imagination the melancholy runs of the wind instruments could be taken as a musical painting of Rákóczi's time."[28] As the critic implied, not only did the tone color of the English horn (and other woodwinds) recall the *tárogató*, but the specific motives Dohnányi used were also typical of the instrument.

EXAMPLE 31. Dohnányi, Symphony in D Minor, movement 2, mm. 1–18

EXAMPLE 31 *(continued)*

Comparison of the theme of Dohnányi's Adagio with the popular *kuruc* melody most frequently associated with the *tárogató* and Árpád Szendy's "Tárogató hangzik . . ." (The *tárogató* resounds . . .) reveals the melodic gestures most characteristic of the instrument. Recognizing these gestures can help clarify the ways in which Bartók was simultaneously continuing and contradicting tradition in the bass clarinet solo of the Second Suite.

The "Rákóczi nóta" (Rákóczi melody/song), not to be confused with the later Rákóczi March, was one of the most popular *kuruc* melodies.[29] Although its roots reach back to the seventeenth century when it belonged to the group of melodies later designated as the "Rákóczi type," the tune is most strongly associated with Ferenc Rákóczi's war of independence. In addition to many stock Hungarian melodic characteristics, the "Rákóczi nóta" also makes conspicuous use of motives reminiscent of military signals. Of all the *kuruc* melodies, the "Rákóczi nóta" was the one most consistently associated with the *tárogató*. No method book or collection of pieces for the instrument was complete without the so-called "original" version of the tune based on the version Gyula Káldy published in his 1895 collection of old Hungarian melodies with the authenticating phrase "as it was played on the *tárogató* in Rákóczi's time."[30] This version of the "Rákóczi nóta" was the most important source of musical gestures used to

EXAMPLE 32. "Rákóczi nóta" ("original" version) as arranged by Gyula Káldy (1895)

EXAMPLE 32 (continued)

evoke the *tárogató* (example 32). The first two bars of the tune present its
two most characteristic motives: the so-called *kuruc* fourth, a repeated figure that bounces between the dominant and the upper tonic (m. 1), and a
held note that gives way to a gentle roulade (m. 2). The extent to which
these two motives were associated with the *tárogató* is demonstrated by
Árpád Szendy's evocation of the instrument in his character piece for piano
"Tárogató hangzik . . .".

Szendy, a virtuoso pianist and Bartók's senior colleague on the piano faculty of the Music Academy, was a respected composer of works in the
Hungarian style.[31] "Tárogató hangzik . . ." is the first piece of *Hat magyar
zeneköltemény* (Six Hungarian Tone Poems), a set of character pieces for
piano roughly contemporaneous with Bartók's Second Suite.[32] Reports in
the press surrounding the March 1909 premiere of Szendy's orchestration
of the work (renamed *Magyar poémák* [Hungarian Poems]) reinforce three
points about the *tárogató:* the strong association of the instrument with
Rákóczi's time, the practice of imitating it with English horn and clarinet,

and, of particular importance for understanding the bass clarinet solo of Bartók's Second Suite as a predecessor of the nocturnal subject of "Az éjszaka zenéje," a connection between the *tárogató,* the *puszta,* and the night.

A listener's guide to *Magyar poémák* in *Zeneközlöny* (Music Gazette) published in advance of the premiere states: "[In 'Tárogató hangzik . . .'] the composer recalls the memory of the times of the *kuruc* of old. He paints that painful, desperate atmosphere, in which the Hungarian people grieved over Rákóczi's defeat and the sorrowful, dismal fate that resulted from it. The sound of the *tárogató,* an instrument that is difficult to handle and is rarely found in the orchestra, is artificially suggested by the combined declamation of the English horn and clarinet."[33] The critic of *Pesti Hírlap* summarized the movement similarly, reporting, " '[T]árogató hangzik . . .' is the kind of melancholy *tárogató* paraphrase that laments the glory of bygone times."[34] Instead of historical reverberations, the critic of *Zenelap* (Music Journal) associated the melancholy mood of "Tárogató hangzik . . ." with the *puszta* at night, reporting: "The first movement [of Six Hungarian Poems] could have the title: 'Night on the *Puszta* (the *tárogató* resounds enchantingly).' "[35] Thus the sad sound of the *tárogató* seems to have sufficed to recall a nocturnal image of the *puszta.*

Szendy's Italian performance indication for "Tárogató hangzik . . ." "poco lento e malinconico" (a bit slow and melancholy) suggests a mood similar to the marking *siralmasan* (lamentingly) traditionally applied to the first eight bars of the "Rákóczi nóta" (cf. examples 32 and 33). More important, Szendy also echoes the two main motives of the "Rákóczi nóta" in his work. He opens the melody with a held note followed by a gentle roulade (mm. 1–3) and begins the accompaniment with a repeated ascending perfect fourth (mm. 1–2). These two gestures are also prominent in Dohnányi's Adagio, which begins with an ascending perfect fourth (E–A) leading into a held tone (G), which in turn gives way to a gentle roulade of sixteenth-note triplets, the shape of which (first descending, then returning) relates it to the analogous passages in Szendy's "Tárogató hangzik . . ." and the "Rákóczi nóta" (cf. examples 31 and 32).

Bartók, like Szendy and Dohnányi in their *tárogató* imitations, uses gestures typically associated with the instrument in the bass clarinet solo in the Andante of his Second Suite, but he does so in the context of a more modern style. Although Bartók begins his melody with the traditional ascending fourth, the triplet that follows is only a faint shadow of the customary roulade (see example 30). In place of the harmonically straightforward opening two-bar phrases of the "Rákóczi nóta" (and Dohnányi's Adagio),

EXAMPLE 33. Árpád Szendy, "Tárogató hangzik . . . ," mm. 1–4

Bartók begins with two three-bar phrases, the harmonic implications of which are more complex, especially in bar 5 with the introduction of the flat second and fifth scale degrees. The chromatic meandering first hinted at in bar 5—decidedly not characteristic of Szendy or Dohnányi's *tárogató* imitations—becomes even more harmonically complex in bars 10–14. As in bar 5, Bartók initiates this second longer harmonic departure from the key with a sustained written B♭ (concert G), the flat second scale degree. The B♭ is perhaps best understood as a deceptive cadence, which avoids the expected tonic pitch (written A). The chromatic move to B♭ gives the melody a seemingly endless quality by extending the phrase an additional six bars, which includes a harmonically obscure descending sequence. This passage might be seen as a combination of Wagnerian chromaticism with the descending sequence from bars 17–18 of the "Rákóczi nóta"—a portion of the tune not recalled in the *tárogató* imitations of Dohnányi or Szendy (see example 32). The emphasis on the flat second scale degree may hark back to the Phrygian-inflected flat second degree generally characteristic of Rákóczi-type melodies and found in measures 13 and 25 of the "Rákóczi nóta."

Bartók thus referred sufficiently to the Hungarian pastoral tradition for his bass clarinet solo to be recognizable as an emblem of the *puszta*. At the same time he avoided cliché by obscuring the most stereotypical *tárogató* gestures and using a more chromatic idiom than was conventional in the style. Bartók seems to have recognized his relationship to tradition accurately when he wrote in a letter to Frederick Delius on 23 April 1910 that he had intended parts of his Second Suite as a "contradiction of the commonplace."[36] This description is certainly apt for the bass clarinet solo, for the richness of the passage stems precisely from Bartók's ability to work against the clichés of the Hungarian style. The brilliance of his approach in this instance is that he did not simply abandon Hungarian tradition, but expanded it by exploiting aspects of it that had been overlooked by others. It is typical of this approach that the flat second degree that plays such a prominent role in the chromaticism of his solo for bass clarinet is both a sign of the work's modernity and a recollection of one of the most exotic and ancient features of *kuruc* melodies. In other words, even before he began to research peasant music there is evidence that Bartók sought to exploit precisely those aspects of the Hungarian tradition that overlapped with European musical modernism. As Bartók became more experienced with peasant music, he would consistently exploit just such intersections between folk music and the modern style.

Dohnányi and the Pastoral Origins of Bartók's Modern Style

The importance of the Andante as a link between longstanding Hungarian Romantic traditions and the modernism of "Az éjszaka zenéje" also extends to one of the most important aspects of musical modernism: the emancipation of dissonance. Looking back on the movement in 1928, Bartók singled out its final chord as the first example of unresolved dissonance in his work. Although he had not yet begun the serious study of folk music in 1905 when he wrote the piece, and would not recognize pentatonicism as a defining feature of the oldest layer of Hungarian folk song until his trip to Transylvania in the summer of 1907, he nevertheless asserted in retrospect that the idea for the ending had come from his analysis of pentatonic Hungarian folk songs:

> Because of the equal importance of the [third, fifth, and seventh] degrees of the pentatonic scale [in some Hungarian folk songs], it follows that in pentatonic melodies the minor seventh takes on the character of a consonant interval. This fact, as early as 1905, led me to end a composition in F♯ minor with the chord: F♯ A C♯ E. Hence in the closing chord the seventh figures as a consonant interval. At that time a close of this kind was something quite out of the ordinary. (Only in works by Debussy of approximately the same period could a parallel case be found, namely the following closing chord: A C♯ E F♯.) . . . When the consonant form of the seventh was established, the ice was broken: from that moment the seventh could be applied as a consonance even without a necessarily logical preparation.[37]

It is indeed likely that Bartók arrived at the "consonant seventh" without benefit of Debussy, with whose music he was probably unfamiliar until Kodály brought him several scores in 1907; but otherwise much of what Bartók suggests in this passage appears to be evidence of faulty memory, at least.[38] The fact is, ending a movement with a minor-seventh chord was not unprecedented in Hungarian art music by 1905. The slow movement of Dohnány's D-Minor Symphony, already cited as a precedent for the Hungarian pastoral

EXAMPLE 34. Dohnányi, Symphony in D Minor, movement 2, conclusion, mm. 174–78

topic, ends similarly. Bartók's intimate knowledge of Dohnányi's score rules out the possibility of coincidence.

In other ways, too, the two endings accord. Both are approached *pianissimo* with wind instruments passing off fragments of the main theme. In both the last rendition of the motive returns to the instrument of the opening solo (English horn or bass clarinet) and leads to a final chordal progression. In Dohnányi's Adagio the English horn ends on a G that elides with the final chord, which the composer presents in three stages (example 34). First, the tympani enters under the English horn to create an exposed minor seventh (A–G) implying an A-minor-seventh chord. Then the woodwinds and horns enter on the pitches of an A-minor chord, which, combined with the G of the English horn, completes the A-minor seventh. Finally, the English horn fades out, leaving only the A-minor chord in the winds reinforced by a pizzicato of the tonic pitch in the low strings. Thus, although the final sonority is a simple minor triad, the seventh is present until the final seconds of the chord, when, rather than resolving, it simply evaporates.

Bartók takes Dohnányi's idea one step further (example 35). The motive played by the solo winds leading to the conclusion of Bartók's Andante does not, as is the case in the Dohnányi, overlap with the final chord. Instead, the motive is subtly repeated in slow motion as the bass underneath the final sequence of chords, the last of which is a minor-seventh chord on F♯. Bartók holds the F♯-minor-seventh chord—itself a vertical presentation of the movement's main motive—without resolution to the end of the movement. The difference between Bartók's and Dohnányi's handling of the minor-seventh dissonance may have been small (Bartók merely holding it for a few seconds more than Dohnányi), but its ramifications were profound. Not only was the concluding F♯-minor-seventh chord the "icebreaker" for Bartók's modernist use of dissonance, as he declared in 1928, but it suggests that this

EXAMPLE 35. Suite No. 2 for Orchestra, movement 3, conclusion, mm. 105–9

crucial step in his development was in part born out of a desire to compete with an older Hungarian contemporary both literally and figuratively on Hungarian turf: that is, within the Hungarian tradition of the pastorale.

Despite its reflections of contemporaneous fashions in Hungarian music, the Andante of the Second Suite shows that even before his life-changing discovery of peasant music Bartók was a maximalist who sought to transform the gentle Hungarian pastorale into a medium for modernist expression. Thus the Andante of the Second Suite may be seen as an important precursor to "Az éjszaka zenéje" not only because it depicts a lonely, nocturnal image of the *puszta,* but because in it Bartók laid the groundwork for the use of dissonance that would eventually turn his "night music" trope into a modernist icon.

Musical Landscape and the *Klangfläche:* Rheingold, The Wooden Prince, and Weiner's "Night"

Wagner's influence was not limited to the pastoral English horn solos of *Tristan;* it also extended to the tradition of natural depiction involving what

EXAMPLE 36. *The Wooden Prince,* mm. 1–36 (condensation)

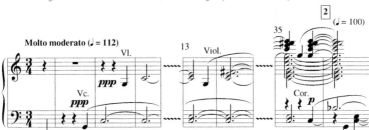

Carl Dahlhaus has appropriately dubbed a *Klangfläche* or "sheet of sound." *Klangfläche* describes an extended pedal point or harmony "outwardly static, but inwardly in constant motion" used to depict nature, whether a thunderstorm (prelude to act 1 of *Die Walküre*) or an idyll (development section of the first movement of Beethoven's Sixth Symphony).[39] The most explicitly Wagnerian *Klangfläche* in Bartók's oeuvre occurs in yet another darkly colored nature scene: the opening seventy-seven bars of his ballet *A fából faragott királyfi* (The Wooden Prince, 1914–16), a depiction of the forest at dawn (example 36). Like the 138-bar E♭ pedal that opens *Das Rheingold, The Wooden Prince* begins with a deep pedal tone that gradually blossoms into a major chord. Although the model is clear, Bartók goes beyond Wagner by adding a modernist coloring to the static harmony—first the sharp fourth degree (F♯), then the flat seventh (B♭) join the C-major triad, which results in a dissonant chord of five pitches. (This is an example of the so-called acoustic scale, a major scale with sharp-fourth and flat-seventh degrees, often associated with nature in Bartók's work.)[40]

The tone cluster that forms the background ostinato in "Az éjszaka zenéje," itself "inwardly in constant motion" because of the continual alteration in the order of the presentation of its pitches, is similarly a *Klangfläche* of five pitches, but one in which dissonance has been maximalized. A crucial difference between the five-note chord in *The Wooden Prince* and the five-note tone cluster in "Az éjszaka zenéje" is of spacing. Whereas the *Klangfläche* of *The Wooden Prince* grows to spread expansively over five octaves, that of "Az éjszaka zenéje" is confined to five adjacent half steps—the most compressed, and hence most dissonant possible, presentation of five distinct pitches in the Western musical system. The different spacings correspond to different moods. The wide distribution of the chord in *The Wooden Prince* captures the sublime grandeur of the forest, an effect Bartók heightens with expansive sweeps of a minor seventh in the horn, an instrument long associated with woodland scenes. In contrast, the compression of the tone cluster in "Az éjszaka zenéje" reflects a different relationship to nature: in place of a scene that overwhelms the listener with its sheer size, Bartók presents sounds of nature in a setting that encourages the listener to focus on the small details of the nocturnal world. The technique Bartók used in both instances is remarkably similar; what distinguishes them may be largely boiled down to the higher degree of dissonance in the later work—a sine qua non of musical modernism.

Although the *Klangfläche* of "Az éjszaka zenéje" can be traced back to Wagner through *The Wooden Prince*, an important Hungarian precedent for the explicit combination of night and nature in Bartók's work is Leó Weiner's "Éj" (Night). Four years Bartók's junior, Leó Weiner was, like Dohnányi, a composer with whom Bartók was in friendly competition in the early years of his career. Weiner wrote "Night" in 1913 as part of what has come to be regarded as his best score, the incidental music to the Hungarian Romantic poet and playwright Mihály Vörösmarty's play *Csongor és Tünde* (Csongor and Tünde, 1833). Specifically "Night" was meant to follow the "monologue of the night," the play's best-known passage, the associations of which were strong enough to have been recalled by Aladár Tóth in his review of the premiere of "Az éjszaka zenéje." The play begins with the separation of the young hero Csongor, a mortal, and his beloved Tünde, a fairy; it ends with their reunification made possible by Tünde's renunciation of the immortality of the fairy world. In the "monologue of the night," the Mistress of the Night reacts to Tünde's decision to join the world of mortals with a long soliloquy in which she ruminates on the meaninglessness of human life, which begins and ends in dust. Weiner depicts this depressing vision with desolate nature music: the second violins play a stark, fragile high E pedal as an eerie harmonic, while the first violins and harp repeat a four-note ostinato (example 37). Again, this is a *Klangfläche*: "outwardly static, but inwardly in constant motion." In contrast to Wagner's and Bartók's treatment of the *Klangflächen* in *Rheingold* and *The Wooden Prince*, in "Night" Weiner does not build up the "sheet of sound" from low to high and thereby mimic the dawn of a new day. Instead he captures eternal night by beginning with a high pedal as ethereal as dust itself. It is thus tempting to hear Bartók's opening to *The Wooden Prince* not only as a paraphrase of *Rheingold*, but also as a loose inversion of Weiner's "Night" first performed just two months before Bartók began work on his ballet.[41]

EXAMPLE 37. Leó Weiner, *Csongor és Tünde*, "Éj" (Night), mm. 1–7

Foggy Valley, Clear Night

The association of tone clusters composed of adjacent half steps with a dark, lonely landscape occurs for the first time in Bartók's oeuvre some ten years before "Az éjszaka zenéje" in the song "Itt lent a völgyben" (In the Valley). Written in a single day on 6 February 1916, two months before Bartók resumed work on *The Wooden Prince* after shelving it in the fall of 1914, "In the Valley" is the fifth of his Five Songs, op. 15.[42] In the song the composer uses rolled three-note clusters of half steps to capture the desolate, dark tone of a poem that uses the image of a cold, foggy valley in autumn to create a sense of human isolation in nature (example 38). Despite the fact that in both works Bartók uses half-step tone clusters to create dark images of nature and a sense of loneliness, the relationships between the human world and the natural world that emerges from "Az éjszaka zenéje" and "In the Valley" have crucial differences.

The text of "In the Valley," by the precocious (if not yet subtle) fifteen-year-old Klára Gombossy with whom Bartók was infatuated, relies on common autumnal images of death and loneliness:

Itt lent a völgyben már gyilkol az ősz,	Here down in the valley autumn already kills,
Sápadt virágok sorsukat várják.	Pale flowers await their fate.
A földet fázva, szomorún nézem,	Freezing, sadly I gaze at the earth,
Mint jeges vízbe süllyedő gályát.	Like a galley sinking in icy water.
A hangos erdő már néma halott,	The noisy forest is already mute,
Könnyek csillognak minden göröngyön.	Tears shine on every clump of earth.
A ködben járva azt hiszem,	Walking in the fog I believe
Hogy már egyedül csak én élek a földön.	That I alone am alive upon the earth.

The obscure quality of the tone clusters of "In the Valley"—all the muddier for the low range and *forte* dynamic of their initial presentation—seems to reflect the fog in which the protagonist wanders. Bartók further emphasizes the protagonist's isolation from her surroundings by strictly separating the musical material of the vocal line from that of the piano. The piano postlude, which occupies more than a third of the total work, seems to represent the envelopment of nature (example 39). To recall the imagery of the poem, the human element disappears into nature's icy grip as the tone cluster becomes a frozen "sheet of sound" in the final six bars of the work. The proclamation

EXAMPLE 38. "Öt dal" (Five Songs), op. 15, No. 5, "Itt lent a völgyben" (In the Valley), mm. 1–4

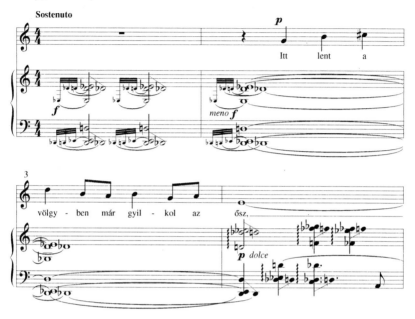

of a single living being upon the earth in the last line of text emphasizes the sense of loneliness and death that dominates the song.

By contrast, the night of "Az éjszaka zenéje" is no hackneyed Romantic metaphor for death, but a lively nocturnal world. Here, in the absence of light, Bartók imitates sounds of nature rather than "painting" a landscape. In this context the *pianissimo* tone clusters do not seem to imply a physical or psychological fog. Instead of obscuring the perception of nature, they provide a backdrop against which the sounds of the night stand out with clarity. This clarity captures the seeming proximity of distant sounds on a still night when the band of cool air hugging the earth's surface allows sounds to be conveyed over great distances without dissipating. The analogy to a scientifically verifiable phenomenon is apt because one aspect that distinguishes "Az éjszaka zenéje" from so many earlier Hungarian pastorales is that Bartók eschews hazy images of Romantic nostalgia—the *tárogató* reminiscent of the "great times of yore," for example—in favor of imitations of specific natural sounds.

One way in which Bartók does nod to the tradition of the Hungarian pas-

EXAMPLE 39. "Itt lent a völgyben," postlude, mm. 33–38

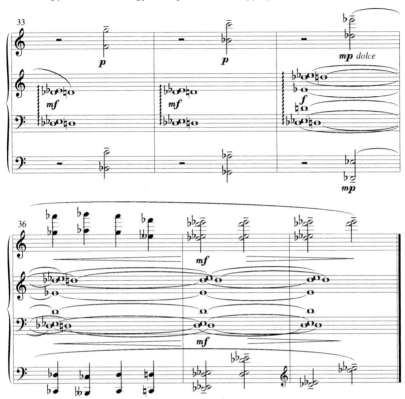

torale in "Az éjszaka zenéje" is with the imitation of a peasant flute (see example 26, p. 83). Still, unlike the forlorn depictions of far-off shepherds by Erkel and Mosonyi or the melancholy recollections of the *kuruc* in the earlier *tárogató* imitations by Dohnányi, Szendy, and Bartók himself, the *furulya*-like melody of "Az éjszaka zenéje" recalls a spirited peasant dance. Rather than a lonely human presence in a vast wilderness, Bartók suggests that the dance tune is one with nature by allowing the repeated G♯'s with which it begins to gradually emerge from the myriad of other natural sounds. He further implies the unity of nature and the folk dance by transforming it back into the nature sounds from which it sprang at the end of the piece. Bartók seems to be suggesting musically the old Romantic organicist idea that peasant music is a natural phenomenon, a view he expressed in writing on several occasions.[43]

However much "Az éjszaka zenéje" teems with life, Bartók did not completely abandon the melancholy atmosphere often associated with the Hungarian pastorale. He expressed this with music Aladár Tóth described as "the transcendental melody of the night's majestic hymn," and which I would suggest captures the loneliness and alienation Bartók believed was the dominant human condition in a world removed from the natural state of peasant society (see example 25, p. 83). The steady plodding of this chorale-like tune contrasts sharply with the impetuous interjections of the nature sounds and the lithe dance of the peasant *furulya*. Although Bartók combines the "chorale melody" and the "peasant dance" in the penultimate section of the piece, he resists the complete synthesis of the elements of the movement by excluding the chorale from the work's final section. In the spirit of Vörösmarty, Bartók seems to capture the transience of human existence in contrast to eternal nature. Although the abstractness of the work allows for multiple layers of interpretation at once subjective and integral to its meaning, the elements of the interpretation offered here overlap both with the tradition of Hungarian poetic representations of the night and with Bartók's personal artistic convictions.

. . .

Nineteenth-century Hungarian traditions were not the only ones that exerted an influence on "Az éjszaka zenéje." Its stark, unsentimental depiction of the night may also reflect something of the "objective" aesthetics of the 1920s. But, in contrast to the often ironical tone of Stravinsky's neoclassical style with which he sought to challenge Romantic notions of profundity, in "Az éjszaka zenéje" Bartók sought to remain on the cutting edge of musical modernity while addressing a profound and quintessentially Romantic subject: the relationship of man and nature. (Not for nothing did Aladár Tóth recall Beethoven in his review of the "night-music" episode in Bartók's Fourth Quartet.) The Romantic profundity of Bartók's treatment was exceptional not only in the context of the fashion for objectivity. It was also unusual in the context of the Hungarian pastorale. When Bartók and Dohnányi's composition teacher János Koessler, a devoted Brahmsian, criticized the Adagio of Dohnányi's Symphony in D Minor, he cited its lack of emotional depth, for which he believed Dohnányi (and Bartók) lacked the requisite life experience.[44] This criticism could have been leveled at the Hungarian pastoral tradition itself, the roots of which can be traced to the light *verbunkos*-inspired genres of the Hungarian rhapsody and Hungarian fantasy. (The emotional punch of Erkel's scene on the banks of the Tisza, like that of Verdi's "La donna è mobile" in *Rigoletto*, was born of its juxtaposition with the onstage drama rather than the intrinsic weight of its musical material.) Bartók had already begun to break away from the shallowness of the Hungarian pastoral tradition when he borrowed from Wagner to add a note of profundity to the "tárogató" solo in the Second Suite.

Although a number of Hungarian composers—Dohnányi and Weiner among them—had begun to follow Bartók and Kodály's lead by incorporating peasant music into their compositions, by the 1920s Bartók's modernism was unique in Hungary. For the most part, Hungarian musical traditions survived the upheavals of World War I with their naive nostalgia intact. Comparison of "Az éjszaka zenéje" with a nearly contemporary pastoral work like Dohnányi's *Ruralia hungarica*, op. 32b (1924), in which the first movement opens with a telltale meandering solo for unaccompanied oboe, demonstrates just how radically Bartók had steered his music from the nostalgic Romanticism of even his most musically sophisticated countrymen.[45] The fact that in the 1920s the aristocratic Kisfaludy Society passed over Bartók's works in favor of those of Szendy and Dohnányi for the prestigious Greguss Prize suggests that influential members of Hungarian society were not prepared to relinquish the status quo.[46]

The importance of Hungarian precedents for the depiction of nature (and specifically of the *puszta*) and night in "Az éjszaka zenéje" need not imply that Bartók consciously modeled his work on that of his predecessors, or that he consciously reinterpreted the Hungarian pastoral tradition. Rather, like the tone clusters in "Az éjszaka zenéje," these works form a backdrop to Bartók's "night music" that helps clarify his role as both the greatest heir to the Hungarian national tradition and its most radical critic. The powerful new mode of expression that he achieved in 1926 and never abandoned would not have taken the form it did without a strong tradition of Hungarian art music. But neither would it have come into being without Bartók's extraordinary ability to reimagine the very foundations of that tradition. Although one of the "insects" in "Az éjszaka zenéje" chirps in *short*-long Hungarian rhythms (see example 24, p. 82), Bartók's subject, like the mythic symbols of which it is composed, addresses questions more universal than national. Still, as Tóth sensed at the premiere of "Az éjszaka zenéje," one of Bartók's most abstract, evocative, and influential contributions to the vocabulary of twentieth-century music had its roots in a characteristically Hungarian Romantic tradition of using nocturnal nature to symbolize the nation.

FOUR

Tradition Challenged

Confronting Stravinsky

Interpreting works like *Kossuth*, the Rhapsody, op. 1, and the Second Suite for Orchestra as reflections of Bartók's national identity is a relatively straightforward task. Both the Hungarian national movement Bartók endorsed while composing these works and the musical style he used to signify his allegiance to it are clearly defined and were recognized by Hungarian audiences of the day. His compositions of this period were impressive technically, but their style signaled sympathy for an intolerant patriotism that celebrated a heroic, pompous vision of the nation.

Bartók's arrogant nationalism and exclusive devotion to Hungarian culture soon gave way to a more tolerant and enlightened stance. The precise reasons for his change in attitude are not well understood, but they seem in part to have grown out of his folk-music research. What began as an informal project to collect folk songs from the Hungarian peasantry in 1905 soon led to a rigorous scholarly study of peasant music of several ethnic groups living within the territory ruled by Hungary in the years before the First World War. Bartók's research suggested that there had been a productive cultural exchange between peasants of the Carpathian Basin for hundreds of years. He thus came to regard the political tensions between the Hungarians and the various different ethnicities living under Austro-Hungarian rule before World War I and then as citizens of bordering countries after the war as an artificial product of questionable political propaganda. His interest in the music of these peoples and his willingness to incorporate their music into his own work, combined with his implicitly cosmopolitan dedication to modernism, made Bartók's music a powerful symbol of a nuanced, tolerant notion of *magyarság*. This view differed significantly from the mainstream, especially when Hungarian nationalism entered its most desperate revanchist phase after World War I.

The vindictive terms of peace imposed on Hungary following the war set in motion the official agenda for the next two decades. The defeat of Germany and Austria-Hungary in the war weakened Austria and gave Hungary its independence. But it also weakened Hungary and allowed for the secession of other nationalities from the empire, including Croats, Slovaks, and Ruthenians who had significant populations on the periphery of prewar Hungary.[1] The peace treaty signed at the Grand Trianon palace in Versailles on 4 July 1920 officially stripped Hungary of more than two-thirds of its prewar territory by redrawing its borders with Austria, Croatia, Romania, Slovakia, and the Ukraine. Interwar Hungarian nationalism was therefore dominated by the irredentist desire to resurrect "greater Hungary" by reclaiming lost territory. The pledge repeated every day by school children in Hungary between the world wars captures the spirit of a nation that no longer considered itself whole:

> I believe in one God.
> I believe in one homeland.
> I believe in one divine eternal truth.
> I believe in the resurrection of one Hungary.
> A mutilated Hungary is no country.
> A whole Hungary is heaven.[2]

Romanians, Ukrainians, Slovaks, and southern Slavs who had constituted minority populations in Hungary before the war now joined majority populations in countries from which Hungary was eager to recapture its territory. Bartók, like virtually all Hungarians and most historians, believed that the conditions of Trianon were unjust, but he did not endorse mainstream nationalism. In the context of post-Trianon Hungary, Bartók's openness both to the modernist influence of European high culture and to the peasant traditions of neighboring countries with which Hungary had strained relations made him appear to be almost the antithesis of a national composer. Still, his stance continued to be rooted in a Hungarian tradition of viewing the Carpathian Basin as a multiethnic territory in which Hungarians were culturally dominant. More crucially, he continued to believe that music had a leading role in defining the nation.

A Progressive View of the Nation

Whether the rather loosely and at times oddly interwoven constellation of ideas propagated by progressive Hungarian writers, artists, musicians, and critics in the interwar period constituted a national movement is open to debate. The vision of Hungary with which Bartók and his music were associated was never highly popular and never came close to being realized. The progressive ideals of the interwar period never garnered sufficient support to dampen in any significant measure the popular irredentist nationalism that became one of the main incentives for Hungary's alliance with the Axis powers in the Second World War. Still, in the 1920s a shared dedication to changing and redefining their country united Bartók, Kodály, and a number of intellectuals including music critics such as Aladár Tóth and Antal Molnár (1890–1983)—all nationalists, but of a radically progressive bent. However international his reputation, however much he relied on non-Hungarian folk material, Bartók always saw his music as Hungarian. Yet with his strong modernist stance he lost the undivided popular support he had enjoyed at the time of *Kossuth's* premiere. Furthermore, the frequently uneasy reception of his work "at home" was almost always tied to the challenge his work posed to Hungarians' notion of themselves.

Whereas the influence of Hungarian peasant music on Bartók's original compositions was considered suspicious by those for whom only the clichés of *magyar nóta* and *verbunkos* could constitute national music, progressive critics had always taken his interest in Hungarian folklore to be a legitimate expression of the composer's patriotism. But Bartók's reliance on Hungarian peasant music was by no means the only factor critics like Tóth and Molnár saw as Hungarian in his work. They also considered his borrowings from other folk traditions and from the latest trends in European music as integral to his Hungarian identity. In Bartók's international reputation as a leading modernist they saw a model for Hungary as a modern nation capable of holding its own among the great European cultures. In Bartók's use of folk music as the basis for his modern style they saw an opportunity for Hungarian music to embody an ideal synthesis of East and West, old and new. Thanks in part to the sophisticated interpretations of Bartók's work put forward by his apologists, in some circles his music came to be seen as an embodiment of Hungary's claim to a leadership position in European culture. This interpretation relied on the fact that by virtue of the supposedly Asiatic customs preserved by its peasantry, Hungary had ties to both a European and an Asian cultural heritage. Hungary therefore was in a unique position to lead Europe in the cultural sphere by demonstrating how modernity could be reconciled with tradition. In other words, Bartók's music represented a neonationalist belief that new forms of high art could be derived from and combined with ancient peasant culture, a culture that was the exclusive treasure of Central and Eastern European countries that had been historically considered backward. In this view of modernism, the medieval conditions of the Hungarian peasantry could be transformed from a liability to an asset, from a source of embarrassment to a source of pride.

The conception of Hungary as uniquely suited to assuming a leading role in European culture became particularly relevant in the interwar period. When the brutal terms of the Treaty of Trianon left Hungary one of the politically and economically weakest European nations, its cultural resources became all the more important. With the country's having little hope of assuming a leadership position in politics, Bartók's music was important as a symbol of Hungary's ability to excel in the cultural sphere. But although it inspired a new generation of progressive artists and intellectuals, his work also threatened those who held the traditional view that the upper classes defined the nation. The sense of urgency and profundity that characterized much Hungarian music criticism of the interwar years suggests that discussions of Hungarian music, especially Bartók's music, were an integral part of the discourse of redefining the Hungarian nation and its constituent society in its newly emerging role in European culture.

Nowhere was the rhetoric surrounding Bartók more impassioned than in the Hungarian criticism of Igor Stravinsky. In a country that longed for cultural equality (if not superiority) with Western Europe (referred to by Hungarians alternately as "Europe" and "the West") Stravinsky was a natural choice for comparison with Hungary's most progressive composer. Critics like Aladár Tóth considered it an obligation to work against provincialism by introducing Stravinsky to Hungarian audiences. They found it still more imperative to demonstrate how Bartók's music represented the most profound, or at least most appropriate, approach to modernity in a Hungarian context.

Stravinsky's influence on Bartók had four distinct phases. Already from the late teens through 1920 Stravinsky seems to have been an important inspiration for Bartók. From 1921 through early 1926 Bartók appears to have been troubled by the mood of Stravinsky's latest compositions and his shift away from folk music. In 1926 the Hungarian premiere of Stravinsky's Concerto for Piano and Winds triggered a reaction from Bartók to what at the time he felt to be an irreconcilable difference between Stravinsky's "objective" style and his own desire for music expressive of human emotion. Bartók's first major response to this new Stravinskyan challenge was his First Piano Concerto (1926). With the Second Piano Concerto (1932), which betrays Stravinsky's influence still more overtly, Bartók seemed to come to terms with Stravinsky's neoclassical style. At the same time he found a way to reconcile his own reliance on folk music with the rhetoric of objectivity. The combination had political significance. It corresponded with a vision of Hungary open to the modernism of the West but deeply rooted in its own Eastern past.

TÓTH'S MISSION

Aladár Tóth was the most erudite and influential writer on music in Hungary in the two decades following World War I. More than any other critic of the time he articulated a consistent vision of music's role in Hungarian culture. The author of a dissertation on the aesthetics of Mozart's operas, he was associated with the progressive press throughout his career, beginning in 1920 as a staff writer at *Új Nemzedék* (New Generation) and a contributor to *Pesti Napló* (Pest Journal) and *Nyugat* (West). In 1923 he became staff critic both for *Pesti Napló*, the daily with the most extensive coverage of the arts, and for *Nyugat,* the biweekly journal that was the leading Hungarian forum for progressive literature and criticism in the years 1908–41. Tóth remained in these positions until 1939, leaving Hungary in 1940 with his wife, the pianist and Dohnányi protégé Annie Fischer, to spend the war years in Sweden. In 1946 he returned to assume the directorship of the Hungarian Opera.[3]

Tóth was a man with a mission: to cultivate a high-quality, uniquely Hungarian musical life in his nation's capital. In part because Bartók seems to have been Tóth's ideal Hungarian musician, and in part because Tóth's views may have affected Bartók's outlook, Tóth's criticism gave verbal expression to the progressive nationalism embodied in Bartók's compositions.[4] From his bully pulpits at *Nyugat* and *Pesti Napló,* Tóth acted the part of the nation's musical conscience, insistently demanding that Hungary's leading musical organizations pursue a repertory that would distinguish them from foreign institutions. Tóth's prescription for reaching this goal assigned the highest priority to the programming of modern Hungarian works, but he also advocated foreign contemporary works along with what he regarded as "classics"—works of Bach, Beethoven, Handel, Haydn, and Mozart.

Tóth asserted his standards especially forcefully in annual appraisals of the Hungarian Opera and the Philharmonic Society. In an essay written to coincide with the beginning of the 1921–22 concert season Tóth attacked the Opera for trying to compete directly with foreign companies in performances of French, German, and Italian works that required productions more spectacular and singers more celebrated than the company could afford. The limited financial resources of Hungary's musical organizations in the interwar years led the critic to adopt what might be described as a

Hungarian neoclassical stance. Fighting against the popular appeal of Romantic music, Tóth advocated the performance of eighteenth- and twentieth-century works. After acknowledging that "naturally Mozart stands at the center of classical opera," he declared that "the Opera's most pressing obligation is the revival of Bartók's two one-acters [*Bluebeard's Castle* and *The Wooden Prince*]."[5]

In his review of the Philharmonic Society's 1922–23 season, Tóth placed another slate of Central European "classics" at the head of his prescription for Hungarian musical life, complaining that "among the great classicists only Beethoven got his rightful place" on the Philharmonic programs. "Bach and Handel," he continued, "were not played. Mozart's G-minor concerto [*sic*] appeared on the program only as a last-minute substitution. Haydn was represented only by a single symphony." Dismissing Chaikovsky and the "technically proficient epigones" Riccardo Zandonai (1883–1944) and Ottorino Respighi (1879–1936), Tóth warned: "As long as Schoenberg, the greatest German pioneer of modern music, remains unknown in Budapest, it is sinful for our Philharmonic to waste even a minute on second-rate, post-Romantic composers. Nor does Igor Stravinsky, the most eminent figure of foreign modern music, enjoy the favor of our Philharmonic."[6]

Worst of all was the Philharmonic Society's treatment of Bartók and what the critic regarded as its general failure to promote Hungarian culture. In sum, Tóth demanded that the Philharmonic Society "not serve 'popular taste' in its work, but educate and direct its public." His criticism of Hungary's most prestigious musical organizations reflected an idealistic vision of Hungarian society—modern, open to the West, proudly supportive of its most progressive members. In his self-righteous nationalist fervor Tóth scolded the Hungarian public for preferring imported foreign fluff like Vienna State Opera star Alfred Piccaver (1884–1958) singing Italian *verismo* arias over the Hungarian contralto Mária Basilides (1886–1946) in a recital of Bartók and Kodály's folk-song arrangements.[7] Attacking the taste of bourgeois society, Tóth took a stand for music as moral instruction. Through exposure to the music of Schoenberg and Stravinsky he hoped the Budapest public would escape its provincialism; through performances of Bartók's music he hoped they would be educated in what it meant to be a modern Hungarian.

Over the course of the 1920s some of what Tóth fought for came to pass. In the 1928–29 season the Hungarian Opera produced the Hungarian premieres of Stravinsky's *Oedipus Rex*, Manuel de Falla's *El sombrero de tres picos*, Paul Hindemith's *Hin und zurück*, and Dohnányi's *Der Tenor*. That season also included continued performances of *Petrushka*, first given at the Opera in 1926,[8] and the Hungarian premieres of Bartók's First Piano

Concerto and *The Miraculous Mandarin* Suite. Although Hungarian musical institutions were becoming somewhat more adventurous in their programming, the Hungarian audience remained resistant to Bartók's music, even as it welcomed Stravinsky, a glamorous foreign celebrity.

For Bartók himself, the main attraction of Stravinsky was that, like Bartók, he used folk music in a neonationalist fashion, most notably in the trio of ballets (*L'oiseau de feu*, *Petrushka*, and *Le sacre du printemps*) that established his international reputation. The Russian composer who had made good in Paris was thus potentially a vindication, as well as a model and a competitor, for Bartók, who was trying to achieve a similar success from his more provincial home base in Budapest. His relationship to Stravinsky therefore had to be ambivalent, especially in the 1920s when Stravinsky abandoned folk music for neoclassicism. Stravinsky crystallized the dilemma that Bartók faced, torn as he was between the conflicting demands of musical fashion and national tradition. Investigating the tensions surrounding Stravinsky's Budapest reception will sharpen the focus on the relationship between Hungarian musical modernism and progressive nationalism in the 1920s.

Stravinsky's Challenge

"I never liked his music anyway"[9]—Stravinsky's private response to news of Bartók's death should probably be charitably ignored. Another statement, however, one made for publication, is hardly less dismissive: "I met [Bartók] at least twice in my life, once in London, in the nineteen-twenties and later in New York in the early forties, but I had no opportunity to approach him closer either time. I know the most important musician he was, I had heard wonders about the sensitivity of his ear, and I bowed deeply to his religiosity. However, I never could share his lifelong gusto for his native folklore. This devotion was certainly real and touching, but I couldn't help regretting it in the great musician."[10]

Stravinsky's erroneous reference to the atheist Bartók's "religiosity" suggests he knew little about the Hungarian composer. Even if one considers his condescending dismissal of Bartók's "gusto" for folk music as intended to deflect attention from his own debt to Russian folk music,[11] his assumptions about Bartók sound like information garnered from a popular magazine.[12] The single meeting Stravinsky mentions "in London in the nineteen-twenties" actually took place in Paris, and consisted of two encounters, both in April 1922. The first occasion was a private performance Bartók gave of his First Sonata for Violin and Piano with Jelly d'Arányi

(1895–1966) at the home of Henry Prunières (1886–1942), editor of *La Revue musicale;* the other was at the offices of the Pleyel piano company.[13] These factual errors notwithstanding, the chief implication of Stravinsky's recollection rings true: there is little reason to think that Stravinsky was significantly affected by his contact with Bartók. But even a cursory comparison of the two composers' catalogs suggests that Bartók was less immune to Stravinsky's influence. The following list includes a few examples of a curiously consistent trend: Bartók's compositions often appear only a few years later than Stravinsky's essays in the same genres.

STRAVINSKY	COMPARABLE WORK BY BARTÓK
The Firebird (1909)	*The Wooden Prince* (1914–17)
Petrushka (1911)	
The Rite of Spring (1913)	*The Miraculous Mandarin* (1918–19) (riots greeted both premieres)
Le rossignol (1914)	
Les noces (1922)	*Village Scenes* (1924; orchestrated 1926)
Sonata for Piano (1924)	Sonata for Piano (1926)
Concerto for Piano and Winds (1924)	First Piano Concerto (1926)
	Second Piano Concerto (1931)

Bartók's tendency to echo Stravinsky was in part a manifestation of the notion that for Hungarian culture to be taken seriously on the greater European stage, it could not, in Tóth's words, "shut the windows facing West."[14] Although Stravinsky, operating from the cultural capitals of Western Europe, could easily dismiss Bartók as a poor "country cousin" whose greatness was simply the result of a natural gift, Bartók could not afford an equally cavalier dismissal of his most successful contemporary. By the early 1920s Stravinsky's name so dominated European music journals that there was no doubt who was *the* modern composer Hungarians would have to know if they were to stay up to date.

Setting the Stage with Ballet:
The Firebird and *The Wooden Prince*

As early as 1913 Géza Vilmos Zágon (1890–1918), an expatriate Hungarian composer living in Paris, predicted that music history would eventually pair

Bartók and Stravinsky.[15] Because Bartók did not become widely known outside of Hungary until his tours to Western Europe after World War I, the pairing of the two names became commonplace only in what English critic Cecil Gray dubbed the "Noah's ark" tradition of music-historical couplings in the 1920s.[16] Typically, however, Stravinsky was invoked to help describe Bartók's style. Outside of discussions of Bartók, the emblematic modernist pairing remained Schoenberg and Stravinsky.

Through nearly the end of the First World War, Bartók, frequently preoccupied with folk-music research, was often isolated from developments in other parts of Europe. Although he knew a few of Stravinsky's compositions, most notably *The Rite of Spring*, Stravinsky does not appear to have had a significant influence on Bartók's musical style until after the war. Similarly, neither Stravinsky's music nor reputation was a significant force in Hungarian musical life until the latter part of the 1910s. Still, Bartók's ballet *The Wooden Prince* owes its existence, if indirectly, to Stravinsky.

The seasons 1912–13 and 1913–14 were a time of great innovation at the Royal Opera under the leadership of Count Miklós Bánffy (1874–1950), who assumed the directorship in February 1912. Bánffy's charge was to bring the Opera out of a crisis brought on by the opening of a second, competing opera house, the Népopera (Volksoper) in Budapest in 1911.[17] The success of Diaghilev's Ballets Russes in Paris and an invitation from the Népopera to the Ballets Russes for a guest appearance inspired Bánffy to put his mark on the Royal Opera by initiating it into the field of modern ballet. Despite Bánffy's reluctance to stage *Bluebeard's Castle* because of its supposed lack of theatricality, he believed that Bartók was the composer best suited to establish a new tradition in Hungarian ballet. Shortly after a second residency of the Ballets Russes in Budapest (this one sponsored by the Royal Opera, December–January 1912–13), which included two performances of *The Firebird*, Bartók accepted Bánffy's commission for *The Wooden Prince*.[18] Although there is no evidence of direct contact, Bartók's first essay in the genre does have some notable similarities to Stravinsky's first ballet for Diaghilev.

The precise date of Bartók's first acquaintance with Stravinsky's music is unclear. The first work of Stravinsky's to be performed publicly in Hungary was *Feu d'artifice* (Fireworks), conducted by László Kun in Budapest on 3 December 1911, but we have no record of Bartók's being aware of the concert. Similarly, he seems to have shown no particular interest when the Ballets Russes performed *The Firebird* in Budapest on 30 December 1912 and 4 January 1913.[19] On a folk-song collecting expedition until 31 December, Bartók could not have attended the December performance of

The Firebird and seems to have missed the January performance of it as well.[20] The fact that the Hungarian reviews of *The Firebird* covered only the dance to the exclusion of the music suggests that Stravinsky's star had not yet risen in Budapest's musical community by the winter of 1912–13.[21] Thus we have no reason to doubt Bartók's statement from 1920 in which he omits *The Firebird* from the list of Stravinsky's works he knew before the end of the war.[22]

Béla Balázs (1884–1949), the author of the text of *Bluebeard's Castle* and the scenario of *The Wooden Prince*, spent seven months abroad in 1911–12 (Paris, October–February, and Berlin, April–May) and thus may have been more au courant than Bartók with artistic developments in Western Europe. He would also have had the opportunity to read about the Ballets Russes in the Hungarian press.[23] It is therefore possible that the fairy-tale subject of *The Wooden Prince* was in part inspired by the mixture of Russian folk tales in *The Firebird*. It remains an open question whether Balázs's publication of *The Wooden Prince* in *Nyugat* in December 1912, just in advance of the Ballets Russes' arrival in Hungary, was only a lucky coincidence or a calculated effort to take advantage of the increased interest in ballet the Russian performances were sure to inspire.

That the scenario of *The Wooden Prince* shares several superficial features with *The Firebird* as well as with *Petrushka* and *Le rossignol* is primarily a result of their common debt to fairy-tale archetypes. As the magical King Kashchey initially blocks the union of the Princess and the Tsarevitch in *The Firebird*, so the fairy in *The Wooden Prince* initially foils the union of the Princess with the human Prince. As in *Petrushka*, the title character of *The Wooden Prince* is an animated puppet. In both *The Wooden Prince* and *Le rossignol*, mechanical doubles—the imitation prince and the toy nightingale—are, for a time, unjustly favored over the living originals. Without strong evidence of a specific connection, such correspondences can be regarded as coincidental, as can Bartók's and Stravinsky's exploitation of folk music in their folk-inspired scenarios. A comparison of roughly analogous sections of *The Wooden Prince* and *The Firebird* reveals significant differences in the two composers' treatment of folk song, differences rooted in Russia's and Hungary's divergent nineteenth-century musical legacies.

In a tradition that originated with Glinka and was embalmed by Rimsky-Korsakov, nineteenth-century Russian opera composers followed the practice of representing supernatural figures with music characterized by chromaticism or exotic scales (often octatonic or whole tone) in contrast to the simpler folk or folklike diatonic themes associated with human characters. Stravinsky adopted this technique directly in *The Firebird* with diatonic music for the Tsarevitch and Princess and chromatic music for the magical Firebird and the sorcerer King Kashchey.[24] In contrast, Ferenc Erkel, Hungary's leading nineteenth-century opera composer, gave a more specifically political edge to such juxtapositions. As noted in chapter 2, in *Bánk bán*, Erkel contrasted musical styles representing pure Hungarians and corrupt foreigners. The former displayed their noble patriotism by singing in the heroic Hungarian style of the *verbunkos*, whereas the latter voiced their impure desires in a generically foreign (but basically Italianate) operatic idiom.

As we have seen, Bartók drew directly on the *verbunkos* tradition to lend a Hungarian character to the works of his early nationalist period and specifically contrasted Hungarian and Austrian musical topics to depict the battle scene in *Kossuth*. In his first two stage works, however, he transformed the old paradigm of pitting Hungarian and foreign musical styles against each other into an opposition of two types of Hungarian music. He contrasted what he had come to regard as "authentic" Hungarian peasant music, strong enough to maintain the pentatonic backbone of its ancient Asiatic heritage even when surrounded by diatonic influences, with what he regarded as the ersatz folk music of the Gypsy-gentry *verbunkos*, which according to his analysis preserved no trace of the "old-style" Hungarian folk song in its underlying structure. Thus ironically Bartók now employed the style that had been taken to represent the nation by Erkel and others (including the young Bartók) as the corrupt element. Still, the underlying opposition between "pure" and "corrupt" musical styles in his music remained.[25] And indeed the latter was corrupt, for by the late 1910s the composer rightly associated the popular clichés of the Hungarian national style with an ideologically naive and politically dangerous form of nationalism. The shift of positive and negative poles of musical style thus signaled both a change in Bartók's notion of authenticity in Hungarian music and a shift in his political views.

Although, like Stravinsky, Bartók uses chromatic music to depict the supernatural (the fairy) in his ballet, it is the contrast of "authentic" and "corrupt" Hungarian styles that provides *The Wooden Prince* with its primary musical dramaturgy. Bartók communicates the Princess's shallowness in the odd mixture of musical topics that characterize her opening dance (example 40). The clarinet, an instrument strongly associated with the commercial music of Gypsy ensembles, plays an aimless melody, the embellishments of which suggest *verbunkos*.[26] Unlike *verbunkos*, however, which is in duple meter, this dance is in $\frac{3}{4}$ time, which makes it something of an amorphous hybrid of *verbunkos* gestures fit into the meter and mood of a

EXAMPLE 40. *The Wooden Prince,* dance of the Princess in the forest, reh. no. 11

EXAMPLE 41. *The Wooden Prince,* entrance of the Prince, reh. no. 19

waltz, a decadent symbol of Viennese kitsch. (Although the main rhythmic pattern of the Princess's dance ♩.♫♫♪ is typical of the polonaise, the music projects nothing of the martial nobility that characterizes that dance.) With this "inauthentic," foreign-influenced mixture of musical styles Bartók's music epitomizes the Princess's superficiality and sets the stage for her misguided attraction to the wooden puppet. In contrast, Bartók immediately shows the Prince as a deeply sympathetic character by accompanying his entrance with a robust, unaccompanied melody in the low strings and harp. This monophonic music in D Mixolydian and $\frac{4}{4}$ time *(espressivo sonore)* is emblematic of "authentic" Hungarian folk song. With it Bartók marks the Prince's heroic sincerity (example 41).

Both Bartók and Stravinsky depict the resolution of the dramatic conflict of their ballets with a climax clearly indebted to folk song. Borrowing his melody virtually verbatim from Rimsky-Korsakov's collection *100 Folk Songs* (St. Petersburg, 1878), Stravinsky reaches a climactic close with a scene of thanksgiving built on twelve complete repetitions of the Dorian *khorovod* tune "U vorot sosna raskachalasya" (By the Gate a Pine Tree Was Swaying To and Fro) (example 42).[27] The scene begins *Lento maestoso* with the melody played expressively by the horn *(piano dolce, cantabile)* and maintains the original flowing rhythms of the folk song throughout the first six renditions. From the seventh rendition (beginning at the *Allegro non troppo*), at which point interpolations of incomplete statements of the tune start to appear, Stravinsky strips the melody of its humanly expressive quality by flattening out its varied rhythms into a stream of pounding quarter notes in asymmetrical $\frac{7}{4}$ time.

EXAMPLE 42. *Khorovod* tune "U vorot sosna raskachalasya" (By the Gate a Pine Tree Was Swaying To and Fro) from Rimsky-Korsakov's collection *100 Folk Songs* (St. Petersburg, 1878)

EXAMPLE 43. *The Wooden Prince*, the union of the Prince and Princess, reh. no. 183

Unlike Stravinsky, Bartók does not rely on a specific folk song to celebrate the union of the Prince and Princess. Instead he accompanies the lovers' passionate embrace with a four-note motive that is a subset of the pentatonic scale emblematic of "old-style" Hungarian folk song (example 43). The descending perfect fifths that dominate the passage belong to a *leitmotiv* introduced at the Prince's first profession of love for the Princess (*Poco lento,* six bars before 21) and associated with the expression of deep emotion throughout the ballet. In these fifths and in the Tristanesque accompaniment of an ascending chromatic line in a lower middle voice we sense the expression of human desire. The abstracted folk music at the core of this passage lends it a mythic quality that serves to temper its sentimentality. In both *The Firebird* and *The Wooden Prince* the apotheosis of folk song celebrates a human union. But whereas Stravinsky statically repeats his tune over and over at increasingly high dynamic levels until the ballet's final curtain, Bartók allows the passion of his culmination point gradually to subside; the human outpouring of emotion dissolves into a cleansing C-major chord.

Just as Wagner brought back the music from the opening of *Das Rheingold* to depict the Rhine overflowing its banks as nature reclaims control of the world at the end of *Götterdämmerung*, Bartók restores nature to its original state at the conclusion of *The Wooden Prince*. The similarity between Bartók's presentation of the awakening of nature over a long C pedal and Wagner's famous 138 bars of E♭ at the beginning of *Rheingold* shows that the comparison between Bartók's hour-long one-act ballet and Wagner's seventeen-hour operatic tetralogy is not exaggerated (see example 36, p. 111). As with Wagner, Bartók's introduction symbolically reenacts the process of creation by gradually building a distinct shape from amorphous material. "Creation" openings play an important role in Bartók's oeuvre and belong to a topos commonly associated with large-scale works of the nineteenth century—a tradition that reaches back at least as far as the overture to Haydn's *The Creation* and includes the opening of Beethoven's Ninth Symphony.[28] Stravinsky also begins *The Firebird* with quiet, amorphous music. Rather than using an opening pedal, however, Stravinsky opens the work with a sinuous, chromatically inflected basso ostinato that serves as a premonition of fantastic magical forces, not as the first rustlings of nature. By evoking the creation metaphor in *The Wooden Prince*, Bartók shows not only a musical debt to Wagner and Beethoven, but also a spiritual kinship to their common Central European Romantic heritage, which considered the expression of the profundity of human emotion and the sublimity of nature to be music's noblest calling.

By analogy to the opening of the ballet, the "white-note" purity of the C-major chord that concludes *The Wooden Prince* provides a clue to another difference between Bartók's and Stravinsky's use of folk song in these works. In *The Firebird*, folk song articulates the diatonic extreme in the dichotomy between supernatural chromaticism and human diatonicism. In *The Wooden Prince*, folk song represents an expressive, human middle ground between a different set of opposites: *verbunkos*-inflected sentimental gestures and the purifying force of nature.

Apparently because the Ballets Russes' performances of *The Firebird* in Budapest had preceded *The Wooden Prince* at the Opera by some four-and-a-half years, critic János Hammerschlag (1885–1954) felt justified in referring to Stravinsky to explain Bartók's music to his countrymen. Reviewing the premiere of *The Wooden Prince* for *Pester Lloyd*, he commented: "[Bartók's] music, which is understandable even to the layman, best displays a relationship with the music of Igor Stravinsky, whose works have been played here several times."[29] The comparison of the two composers is clearly meant to flatter Bartók, as would have been any positive mention of a native son in connection with a foreign celebrity. But pointing out similarities between Stravinsky and Bartók might also be seen as a threat to the latter's reputation as an innovator—presumably an issue more important to progressive artists and intellectuals than to the general German-speaking bourgeois readership of *Pester Lloyd*. Writing for the artistically sophisticated audience of *Zenei Szemle* (Music Review), Antal Molnár proactively defended Bartók's originality in his review of *The Wooden Prince:* "Bartók altogether spontaneously discovered numerous methods that similarly occurred to other outstanding composers without knowing about each other. This is the point where the original creator differs from the epigone. Consequently the mutual influence can only be healthy; it is extremely natural that Bartók studied, for example, Stravinsky with pleasure."[30] Molnár's view was typical of progressive Hungarians of the day in its combination of a cosmopolitan stance and national pride.

Bánffy's gamble on *The Wooden Prince* paid off at the ballet's premiere on 12 May 1917.[31] This was Bartók's first truly popular success as a composer since the Philharmonic's performance of *Kossuth* more than a dozen years before. After his years of withdrawal from the concert life of Budapest following the failure of the New Hungarian Music Society (*Új Magyar Zene-Egyesület* or UMZE) in 1912, *The Wooden Prince* made him a star of Hungary's cultural life virtually overnight. As Bartók had hoped, the brightly colored ballet paved the way for a production of *Bluebeard's Castle*, which had its premiere on a double bill with *The Wooden Prince* on 24 May 1918. Sándor Bródy (1863–1924), perhaps the most celebrated Hungarian playwright of the day, wrote an ecstatic review of *Bluebeard's Castle* for the theater magazine *Színházi Élet* (Theater Life), which further solidified Bartók's reputation in artistic circles.[32]

Confident in his newly gained reputation, Bartók behaved toward Stravinsky in a manner that was for the moment anything but defensive or territorial. Sándor Bródy and Bartók's first wife, Márta Ziegler, both recalled that Bartók attended the rehearsals of *Bluebeard's Castle* at the Opera carrying the four-hand piano score of *The Rite of Spring* with the intention of playing it for Bánffy and convincing him to stage the ballet.[33] Although a production of *The Rite of Spring* appears to have been planned by Egisto Tango (1873–1951), the conductor responsible for the success of *The Wooden Prince*, his dismissal in 1919 left no one at the Opera interested in pursuing the project.[34] A similar fate would befall Bartók's pantomime, *A csodálatos mandarin* (The Miraculous Mandarin).

Barbaric Redemption

Three days after the premiere of *Bluebeard's Castle*, Bródy accepted a commission from the Opera to write a new ballet scenario for Bartók. The Opera expected Bródy to construct a work based on "Anna Molnár," a Hungarian ballad that is a folk prototype of the Bluebeard legend. After accepting the commission, it seems that Bródy switched to another Hungarian topic, *Vitéz László* (László the Knight). Neither of these subjects appears to have attracted Bartók, who seems to have been positively relieved when Bródy did not fulfill his contract.[35] Even before Bródy missed the deadline, Bartók had been drawn to *The Miraculous Mandarin*, a pantomime by Menyhért (Melchior) Lengyel (1880–1974) that had been published in *Nyugat* on 1 January 1917.[36] The work may have been originally offered to Dohnányi, who had already scored a success in the genre of pantomime with his *Der Schleier der Pierrette* (The Veil of Pierrette, 1909), but Dohnányi reputedly thought that the subject was better suited to Bartók's musical style.[37] Like *Bluebeard's Castle* and *The Wooden Prince*, *The Miraculous Mandarin* was not a specifically Hungarian subject, but Bartók's setting reflected a characteristically Hungarian interpretation of the tale. But what kind of tale was it, then? Bartók's description captures the grim naturalism of Lengyel's story. "Just listen how *miraculously beautiful* it is," he told his interlocutor in 1919:

> In a thug's hideout, three thugs force a beautiful young girl to seduce men to come up to the room where they rob them.—The first is a poor young man [*sic*], the second isn't anything special either, but the third is a rich Chinese man.[38] The catch is good, the Girl entertains him with a dance, and awakens desire in the Mandarin, in whom love violently flares up; such love, however, repels the Girl.—The thugs attack him, rob him, suffocate him in the bedding, stab him with a sword; all in vain, they are no match for the Mandarin. He keeps looking at the Girl with love and desire in his eyes.—Womanly intervention comes to the rescue; the Girl satisfies the Mandarin's desire, at which he falls to the floor dead.[39]

Beautiful? Bartók's comment, though taken at face value by previous commentators, was a cocky jest born of the same consciousness that he could now call the shots that led him to choose Menyhért Lengyel's disturbing "pantomime grotesque" as a subject to begin with. A letter from

Bartók's wife to his mother at the time he was completing *The Miraculous Mandarin* suggests the extent of his self-confidence: "B[éla] is just about completely finished with the pantomime, perhaps he'll begin to orchestrate it soon. [Elza] Galafrés and Dohnányi are already very curious about it, because Elza (who, as you perhaps know, has become the pantomimiste of the Opera) wants to dance the Girl. Now he'll play it for them sometime—well, *they* won't *like* it, that's for sure—but because the name of Bartók has recently been associated with *success*, this perhaps makes the bitter pill tempting. You see how sarcastic I've become!"[40] In addition to all the encouragement Bartók was getting on the home front, he also received a generous contract from the prestigious Viennese music publisher Universal Edition, which he officially accepted on 4 June 1918.[41] He had every reason to believe that his next work for the stage would be produced by the Opera in short order.

The gritty setting of *The Miraculous Mandarin* in a tenement of an anonymous metropolis was a rarity in Hungarian art and literature of the time. When Budapest appeared in literature the focus tended to be on idyllic corners of the city, not its sordid side. Hungarian artists tended to shun the city as too cosmopolitan and corrupt to serve as a symbol of the nation.[42] Indeed, Bartók's own attempt to live a life of peasant-like simplicity outside Budapest in Rákoskeresztur, where he moved in 1911, was his own protest against the city. As a composer at once dedicated to the "simplicity" of peasant culture and to the cutting edge of modernism, Bartók's attraction to Lengyel's scenario is therefore easy to understand. On the one hand, Lengyel's story conformed to the recent European fashion for violently erotic subjects (e.g., *Cavalleria rusticana, Pagliacci, Salome*). More important, the Mandarin's power to evoke sympathy from the prostitute suggests the power of the "primitive" East to redeem the corruption of the modern West. The tale thus embodies a central tenet of Bartók's belief in the purifying value of primitive culture—a belief that is likely to have also attracted him to *The Rite of Spring*.

It is a commonplace in Bartók literature to mention a connection between Bartók's *Miraculous Mandarin* and Stravinsky's neoprimitivist ballet. The comparison, though, rarely goes beyond pointing out the "barbaric" nature of both scores. Although close examination reveals a number of similarities, most of the passages in *The Miraculous Mandarin* reminiscent of *The Rite of Spring* rely on techniques Bartók had already used in his music before he knew Stravinsky. Thus it is primarily the increased levels of rhythmic complexity and dissonance that suggest Stravinsky's influence.

Although Bartók had already exploited ostinati to primitive effect in pre-

EXAMPLE 44. Rhythmic layering in Bartók and Stravinsky

a. *The Miraculous Mandarin,* rhythmic layering (one measure before reh. no. 3)

b. *The Rite of Spring,* rhythmic layering (twelve measures before "The Augurs of Spring")

vious works such as *Allegro barbaro* (1911), the cacophonous layering of noncomplementary subdivisions of the beat around the opening ostinato pattern in *The Miraculous Mandarin* is particularly reminiscent of Stravinsky. Compare Bartók's simultaneous subdivision of the dotted-quarter note into three, four, and seven parts in the introduction to *The Miraculous Mandarin* (1 before reh. no. 3) with Stravinsky's division of the quarter note

EXAMPLE 45. *The Miraculous Mandarin*, parallel tritones, reh. no. 34

into three, five, and eight parts in an analogous position in the introduction to *The Rite of Spring* (12 bars before "The Augurs of Spring") (example 44a and b). Similarly, Bartók had harmonized folk or folklike tunes with parallel dissonance long before encountering *The Rite of Spring*. In earlier works, however, the parallel dissonant interval had been the relatively tame minor seventh (e.g., *Fourteen Bagatelles* nos. 4 and 11). In *The Miraculous Mandarin* he harmonizes a pentatonic melody with more bitingly dissonant major sevenths, minor ninths, and parallel tritones (example 45).[43] The inspiration for treating a folklike melody in this manner could well have come from the parallel major sevenths in "The Mystic Circle of the Young Girls" (example 46). Other effects in *The Miraculous Mandarin* that suggest the influence of *The Rite of Spring* include the jagged accents in $\frac{6}{8}$ time that Bartók uses to depict the thugs attacking the seduced men (reh. nos. 21, 29, 76), which bear a resemblance to the similarly violent accents with the

EXAMPLE 46. *The Rite of Spring,* parallel major sevenths ("The Mystic Circle of the Young Girls"), reh. no. 94

compound meter of the "Jeu du rapt," and the music depicting the Girl's struggle to escape from the Mandarin (2 before reh. no. 60), which bears a similarity to Stravinsky's treatment of a folk tune in the "Ritual of the Two Rival Tribes" (3 after reh. no. 57).

The music in *The Miraculous Mandarin* that displays the greatest debt to *The Rite of Spring* is the passage depicting the rising tension in the thugs' den as the first victim approaches (example 47). Bartók's unpredictable distribution of a continuous flow of eighth notes between single notes and chords in different registers generates a complex pattern of accents that has no significant precedent in his oeuvre. It does, however, clearly recall the final section of "The Sacrificial Dance" (example 48). Although Bartók notates his passage in a deceptively simple $\frac{4}{4}$, its irregular groupings mimic the effect of Stravinsky's constantly changing meters. Both composers work with a steady stream of notes articulating a quick, subtactile pulse (eighth notes in *The Miraculous Mandarin,* sixteenth notes in *The Rite of Spring*). Both composers unpredictably alternate fragments of a bass line that consists of two alternating notes a minor third apart (with occasional octave displacements) and chordal interjections. Elisions between the bass notes and the chords further add to the unpredictability of the patterns of alternation. Although Bartók's chords differ from Stravinsky's, the two composers' common restriction of all melodic motion to minor thirds and half steps makes Bartók's debt to Stravinsky all the more explicit.

Although not all the "Stravinskyan" effects in *The Miraculous Mandarin* are specific instances of the Russian composer's influence, the number of similarities between *The Rite of Spring* and *The Miraculous Mandarin* clearly demonstrates that Bartók had Stravinsky in his ear (and fingers)

EXAMPLE 47. *The Miraculous Mandarin*, rising tension as the Old Gallant approaches the thugs' garret, reh. no. 16

[The girl sees a man] coming up the stairs.
aki már jön is fel a lépcsőn.

EXAMPLE 48. *The Rite of Spring,* beginning of the final section of "The Sacrificial Dance," reh. no. 186

while composing his pantomime. Despite a significant debt to Stravinsky, one area in which Bartók was less susceptible (perhaps even impervious) to Stravinsky's influence in *The Miraculous Mandarin* was the dramaturgy of musical form.

Among Stravinsky's most radical innovations in *The Rite of Spring* was his virtual abandonment of the Germanic symphonic ideal of unity built on the recapitulation, development, and transformation of themes.[44] Instead, Stravinsky juxtaposes often violently contrasting blocks of music virtually without transition. He uses repetition, layering, and alternation of musical elements to accumulate inertial force and build tension within individual dances, which are cut off abruptly by the next dance or the end of one of the ballet's two parts. Although the final three bars of *The Rite of Spring* do nod in the direction of a traditional cadential gesture, it is far less powerful than the abrupt halt of motion that precedes it. Ending in music generally implies a process that leads to a conclusion, not simply cessation. Stravinsky's bold new technique abandoned the notion of ending as a process, frequently leaving tensions built up in the score unreleased. The result is inhuman, a form that does not breathe. Nothing could have captured the barbaric, ritualistic aspect of Stravinsky's subject more effectively; nothing would have been more antithetical to Bartók's message in *The Miraculous Mandarin*.

Bartók's approach to formal cohesion in *The Miraculous Mandarin* is nearly the opposite of Stravinsky's in *The Rite of Spring*. In fact, although a comparison of Stravinsky's sketches with the final score demonstrates an attempt to cover up a few traditional interrelationships between themes, manuscript sources for *The Miraculous Mandarin* demonstrate that Bartók sought to enhance the degree of thematic cohesion as he refined his score.[45] Stravinsky does occasionally recall music first heard a minute or two previously (e.g., the famous opening bassoon solo, which reappears near the end of the Introduction), but no themes unify the whole work. In contrast, Bartók relies on *leitmotivs* to bind *The Miraculous Mandarin* together with "organic" thematic and motivic recall and transformation. To cite only the most obvious example, whereas Stravinsky abandons the music of the Introduction as soon as the dancing begins, Bartók uses his opening music to impose something of a rondo form on the ballet—bringing it back, transformed but clearly recognizable, four times in the course of its unfolding (reh. nos. 21, 29, 76, and 1 after 87). Bartók is capable of the Stravinskyan sudden stop, but he does not employ it as a principle of musical construction. In *The Miraculous Mandarin* Bartók uses the effect only once, serving a specific stage action, the Mandarin's stumble during his frantic pursuit of the Girl (immediately before reh. no. 71). Admitting the ebb and flow of tension and release, Bartók's form lends the work a human quality. This approach, although conservative in its observance of traditional techniques of achieving unity, ultimately conveys a message no less disturbing than Stravinsky's.

In *The Miraculous Mandarin* Bartók uses a number of musico-dramatic devices analogous to those of *The Wooden Prince*. Just as in the earlier ballet a dramaturgical conflict was built on contrasting musical representations of the Princess and the Prince set against the backdrop of nature, in *The Miraculous Mandarin* the contrast between the Girl and the Mandarin is set against the backdrop of the metropolis. In both works the union of male and female is initially prevented by outsiders: in *The Wooden Prince* by the fairy, in *The Miraculous Mandarin* by the three thugs. In both works Bartók follows formula in depicting the cathartic union of the protagonists with the most climactic passage in the score. But whereas the characterization of the

EXAMPLE 49. *The Miraculous Mandarin*, entrance of the Girl, reh. no. 11

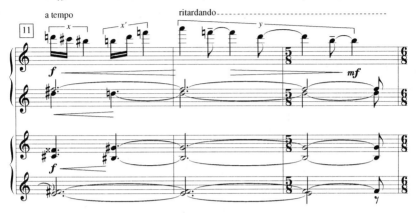

Princess in *The Wooden Prince* is one-dimensional, Bartók's musical representation of the Girl is complex.

Bartók introduces the Girl with a passage consisting of two main gestures: a measure containing two varied statements of a vigorous motive (X), followed by a two-bar languorous descending arpeggiation of a half-diminished-seventh chord (Y) (example 49). Each gesture can be interpreted as having a specific meaning that goes beyond the stage action of the Girl's pantomime. The first statement of motive X is a three-note descending chromatic figure originally associated with the thugs, suggesting that the Girl belongs to their world. Motive Y, in contrast, belongs to a family of arpeggiated seventh chords (major, minor, and half-diminished) that Bartók frequently associates with the feminine; it prefigures the softer, more sympathetic side of the Girl's character. (Later Bartók also uses this figure to suggest the effeminate innocence of the young student, the thugs' second victim.) Motive X' provides an adroit transition between the two sides of the Girl by maintaining the rhythm of motive X while introducing the pitch content of motive Y. Thus, in the short space of three measures, Bartók establishes both the Girl's connection to the thugs and the compassion she will eventually show toward the Mandarin. The first brushstrokes of Bartók's portrait of the Girl, incomplete as they are, lend her a psychological depth and veracity greater than any of the other characters of the pantomime and completely foreign to Stravinsky's antipsychological approach to characterization in *The Rite of Spring*.

A crucial part of the complexity Bartók lends to his depiction of the Girl is the strong motivic relationship between her music and that of the

EXAMPLE 50. *The Miraculous Mandarin*, thematically significant descending minor thirds in the Girl's opening pantomime, 3 after reh. no. 12

Mandarin. Although the music Bartók writes for the Girl tends to be in a higher range than that for the Mandarin, he does not define the Girl as the polar opposite of a male character as he did in earlier works for the stage. Instead he unites the Girl and the Mandarin by strongly associating both with a descending minor third. Bartók first introduces the interval as thematically significant in the course of the Girl's opening pantomime, distilling it from the top two notes of one of her "feminine" arpeggios of a minor-seventh chord and stating it five times in succession (example 50). Accompanying the Girl's reluctant decision to seduce men for the thugs, the motive acquires an association with sexual allure.

In contrast to his multifaceted depiction of the Girl, Bartók makes a stereotypically one-dimensional characterization of the Mandarin throughout most of the score. He evokes the primitive exoticism of the East by confining the Mandarin's music even more than the Girl's to the descending minor third, a motive sometimes notated as an augmented second (reh. no. 36), sometimes held as a dyad (4 before reh. no. 37 to 4 after 39), and frequently filled in with a sensuous descending glissando. Bartók connects the interval with the Mandarin *sotto voce*, *tranquillo* already when he first appears (reh. no. 34) and solidifies the association with heavy-handed *fortissimo sforzando* reiterations when the Mandarin enters the thugs' garret (reh. no. 36).[46]

As Bartók knew from his study of peasant music, the association of the minor third with a primitive quality is supported by numerous children's songs, in which the interval serves as a fundamental building block. He also may have related it to pentatonic "old-style" melodies that rely on the frequent use of the same interval. In fact, the melody that Bartók first uses to introduce the Mandarin begins with several iterations of a minor third and quickly progresses to encompass a full pentatonic scale. The stripped-down, elemental quality of the descending minor third, which even lacks a strongly articulated rhythmic profile, makes it perfectly suited to represent the Mandarin, who functions in the pantomime as a symbol of man reduced to his raw sexual instinct.

The prominence of the descending minor third in Bartók's characterization of both the Girl and the Mandarin serves to create an important bond between them. It suggests that the Mandarin's desire is not only a product of his exotic, Eastern primitivism, but also inhabits the Western, urban Girl. As the only character in the pantomime with the capacity for compassion, the Girl is the only one whose actions display a real human quality.[47] To admit that she is human, however, is also to acknowledge that the Mandarin's desire lives in us all. The erotic union of the Girl and the Mandarin, illustrated with tense, trilling tone clusters spanning the minor third of desire and jagged, upward thrusting gestures that certainly qualify as pornophony, also achieves the reconciliation of the urbanized, alienated Girl with her own primitive instinct (reh. nos. 108–10). Since the Girl's understanding of the Mandarin's primal passion redeems the man, his death, following his consummating "duet" with the Girl, can be seen as a modern, albeit inverted, *Liebestod*.[48] Only the Girl's acceptance of the human quality of the Mandarin's primitive desire could make the Mandarin's brutal death redemptive. As the blood begins to flow from the Mandarin's wounds, an expressive melodic fragment in the orchestra signals that we are witnessing a human tragedy (circled in example 51). The irregularly repeated chords that dominate the final six bars of the score accompany the Mandarin's final convulsions. This is not an exotic death, but an all too human one. Abandoning the miraculous exoticism that had provided a comforting separation between the Mandarin and us spectators, Bartók turns the Mandarin into a fellow human being in death. *The Rite of Spring* is profoundly disturbing for its depiction of human sacrifice and the dehumanizing effects of its brutal rhythms and dissonances. But the primitive world Stravinsky creates in his "Scenes of Pagan Russia" is clearly distinct from our own modern world. What makes *The Miraculous Mandarin* so unsettling is that in it Bartók denies the separation between the primitive and modern urban life.

In its dramatic thrust *The Miraculous Mandarin* is in several respects a conventional love narrative driven by the concept of transformation: man redeems a fallen woman by bringing out her capacity for compassion, while the woman redeems the man by blessing him with understanding. The

EXAMPLE 51. *The Miraculous Mandarin*, death of the Mandarin, reh. no. 110 to end

The Mandarin's desire satisfied, his wounds begin to bleed, he becomes weaker and weaker
Vágyát immár kielégítette a mandarin, sebei elkezdenek vérezni, egyre jobban gyengül - - - - - - - -

(continued)

EXAMPLE 51 *(continued)*

redemptive death of the Mandarin is a process that brings the pantomime to an excruciating denouement in the tradition of Romantic opera. In *The Rite of Spring*, by contrast, the death of the sacrificial virgin abruptly cuts off the progress of the work; it is the quintessential Stravinskyan stop. One moment she is dancing, the next moment dead. No transition, no transformation, no redemption. Although Bartók borrowed some brutal effects from *The Rite of Spring*, he could not assimilate Stravinsky's approach to form, which contradicted his belief in the importance of organic construction, his inheritance from the Central European Romantic tradition. Beyond that, without its organically integrated thematic transformations, *The Miraculous Mandarin* could never have so fully embodied Bartók's radical belief in the power of primitive culture to transform, humanize, and redeem modern society. Even as European musical fashion came to be dominated by the rhetoric of objectivity associated with Stravinsky's later "neoclassical" compositions, Bartók would not abandon an approach to composition in which peasant music played a humanizing role, as Herder had envisioned it more than a century before.

Stravinsky and Bartók circa 1920

As Hungary emerged from the relative isolation of the war years and the domestic turmoil associated with the rise and fall of the Hungarian communist regime that held power for five months in 1919, Bartók was keen to catch up with developments in modern music from abroad. He discussed his interest in modern composers and his reaction to Stravinsky's works in several exchanges with Philip Heseltine (penname Peter Warlock, 1894–1930), editor of the short-lived and controversial English music journal *The Sackbut*. Responding to Heseltine on 24 November 1920, Bartók observed:

> I see by your letter and by the issues of your *Sackbut* that you are making a campaign against the fierce partisans of Stravinsky and of Debussy etc. It is possible that in England there is a great deal of exaggeration in this regard that justifies the war declared by the *Sackbut* against the blind worshippers of the composers mentioned above. But I must confess: I admire Debussy very much. . . .
>
> Regarding Stravinsky, I only know his piano arrangement of the "Rite of Spring" and of the "Nightingale" and the score of his "Three Japanese Songs." But these three works have made a great impression on me. It is true, I also see in him the traces of some mannerisms that are too often repeated and the lack of a grand conception; but so far these faults are not very significant. I

would like very much to know how he has developed since 1914, but—alas—in our situation we cannot buy foreign books or scores.[49]

In his 1921 essay for *The Sackbut,* "The Relation of Folk Song to the Development of the Art Music of Our Time," Bartók enlarges on these sentiments:

Stravinsky's *Sacre du printemps* is one of the best examples of the intensive permeation of art music by genuine peasant music. The work, in spite of its extraordinary verve and power, fails to be completely satisfying. Under the influence of the short-winded structure of the Russian peasant melodies, Stravinsky did not escape the danger of yielding to a broken mosaic-like construction which is sometimes disturbing and of which the effect is enhanced by his particular technique, monotonous as it becomes by repetition and by its practice of as it were automatically superimposing several chord-sequences of varying length, in constant repetition, without regard to their consonances. It is not the Russian peasant music that we must blame for this, but the composer's lack of grasp and power of organization.[50]

The "lack of a grand conception" of which Bartók complained to Heseltine seems in part a reference to the paucity of motivic development in Stravinsky's work. Although, as Bartók says, this did not prevent him from greatly admiring *The Rite of Spring,* a work that is serious in affect, grand in scale, and indebted to folk music,[51] Stravinsky's lack of grandeur troubled him more in some of Stravinsky's later works. As Bartók wrote in his next letter to Heseltine on 7 February 1921:

Lately I had the opportunity to see several new publications of Stravinsky, and I must tell you: I am quite disappointed. The only works I like of all these are the "4 Chants Russes" and the "Pribaoutki"; even these are "miniature art" only. His "Piano Rag Music" is curious, but somewhat dry and empty. But the other works: his Rag Time for 11 instruments, his pieces for piano "à 4 mains" etc. are not even curious. I had expected *something of real grandness,* of a real development; and I am really very sad for not finding at all what I imagined.

Bartók's favorable reaction to the *Four Russian Songs* and *Pribaoutki* implies that even when he found Stravinsky's music lacking he approved of its debt to folk music. The remainder of the letter shows just how eager Bartók was to learn new music and how hard he was to please:

I have the same disappointment when seeing the works of other modern composers. Some works of Malipiero, Goosens, Piz[z]etti arrived in Budapest in the last days; but I can't find any value in them. Now all my hope is in van Dieren! How can I get his works? What did he compose?[52]

Some two months later, Bartók did his part to bring Stravinsky's music before the Hungarian public by including *Piano-Rag-Music, Four Russian Songs,* and *Three Tales for Children* in a recital he gave at the Academy of Music on 23 April 1921.[53] Although couched in praise, Bartók's report of the concert suggests that he found it difficult to appreciate Stravinsky's lighter side:

> [I]n spite of their bizarre form and novelty [Stravinsky's songs] were a decided success, and one of them, the "Chanson pour compter," had to be repeated. But as a matter of fact the public failed in the true valuation of these songs, all of which bear evidence of Stravinsky's musical breathlessness. By far the most valuable is the "chant dissident" which is a gem of its kind, at times reaching depths of spiritual inspiration totally different in character to the musical extravaganzas [sic] and quips in which Stravinsky so often indulges.[54]

Despite differences in their musical temperaments, Bartók saw Stravinsky as his most important ally in the integration of folk music into a modern musical idiom, explicitly claiming him as such in a 1920 article for *Melos.* Using Kodály, as he often did, as a substitute for himself, Bartók declared:

> The works of Debussy and Ravel should be considered the first ones on which the folk music of Eastern Europe and Eastern Asia exerted a permanent and, to some extent, leading influence. This influence is still more decisive in the works of the Russian Stravinsky and the Hungarian Kodály: the oeuvre of both composers develops from the pure folk music of their country to such an extent that the former can be considered almost an apotheosis of the latter (as, for instance, Stravinsky's *Sacre du Printemps*). . . .
> How is this influence of the completely tonal folk music compatible with the atonal trend? Reference to one, especially characteristic example is suffi-cient: Stravinsky's *Pribaoutki.*[55]

Bartók goes on to devote the last third of his article to an analysis of the last song of *Pribaoutki* to demonstrate how the tonal orientation of a folk or folklike melody is not disturbed by atonal accompaniment. The same ana-lytic observation could have easily been made with reference to any num-ber of Bartók's own compositions.[56] By using Stravinsky as his example Bartók was both being modest and following a rhetorical ploy he had already used in the Hungarian press—implicitly justifying and elevating his own music by analogy to Stravinsky's. The Russian composer's aban-donment of folk music in the early 1920s meant the loss of Bartók's most prestigious, if unwitting, supporter.

The Turn to Objectivity

If in 1921 Bartók had suspected that Stravinsky was turning away from folk music, Stravinsky confirmed it when the two composers met for the first time one year later in Paris. Although the meeting appears to have made little impression on Stravinsky, Bartók wrote about it proudly in letters to his family.[57] Upon his return to Budapest Bartók also gave Aladár Tóth a detailed account of Stravinsky's musical pronouncements, which Tóth then passed on to the readers of *Nyugat:*

> Stravinsky naturally expounded to Bartók that his [Stravinsky's] music is the most objective absolute music, it does not depict, does not symbolize, does not express anything, it has nothing to do with emotional life, it is just line, harmony, and rhythm. This "objective" theory of music is spreading dangerously although its principles are not clear. . . . In the midst of their conversation in Paris, Bartók mentioned [his admiration of *The Rite of Spring*] to Stravinsky. Although Stravinsky did not renounce his earlier work, he assured Bartók that *Le rossignol* was the last in this style; after that he already turned to "completely objective" music.[58]

In his account of Bartók's Parisian sojourn Tóth balances two demands. On the one hand, he emphasizes Bartók's fashionable cosmopolitanism by stressing his success with an illustrious set of composers—Stravinsky, Ravel, Szymanowski, Roussel, and members of *Les Six*—who had come to hear Bartók play his first Sonata for Violin and Piano with Jelly d'Arányi at a salon hosted by Henry Prunières. On the other hand, Tóth was quick to disassociate Bartók from Stravinsky's rhetoric of objectivity by assuring his readers that Bartók "by no means identifies himself with Stravinsky's theories."

Indeed, Bartók was also at pains to distance his music from the postwar "objective" trend. In a letter regarding a preconcert lecture for a 1924 production of *The Wooden Prince* and *Bluebeard's Castle* in Weimar, Bartók asks the theater director to emphasize that "my music is absolutely tonal, and has nothing to do with 'objective' and 'impersonal' tendencies," continuing with a parenthetical dig at Stravinsky's growing monopoly on the aesthetics of modernism that "[my music] is not at all 'modern'!"[59]

Although Bartók was happy to rebel along with Stravinsky against the "hyper"-expression of Wagner and Strauss, he maintained a traditional Romantic allegiance to human expression even after the First World War and regarded the radical concept of music devoid of expression as an oxymoron. In May 1925 in response to progressive Hungarian writer Dezső Kosztolányi's statement that "every art is human by necessity," Bartók replied: "This is natural. Otherwise music would turn into machine music." He continued with an example surely inspired by the neoclassical argument that with their new "objective" stance composers were returning to the aesthetics of J. S. Bach: "Bach also expresses something, a few moments of life. We can see that he tries to express this in his compositions with text. If I write a low note and then a higher one, that is rising; if I strike a high note and then a lower one, that is sinking: the one undoubtedly merriment, the other despair. I must admit, however, that there are certain advantages to this turnaround, because the outgrowth of musical Romanticism with Wagner and Strauss had become unbearable."[60]

Another aspect of Stravinsky's credo that Bartók could not accept was the denigration of Beethoven as a "Romanticist." Asked about the direction of new music in 1925, Bartók again made it clear that he wanted to distance himself from Stravinsky's pronouncements:

> One of the slogans is: away from Romanticism! The other: neoclassicism! They even consider Beethoven Romantic. The tendency began already with Debussy and is reaching its peak with Stravinsky, who proclaims that Beethoven might have been a great person, an outstanding personality, but on the other hand was absolutely not—a musician. Naturally I don't agree. Maybe it's possible to assert that he doesn't orchestrate like Mozart, but I enjoy the *Eroica* as much today as I ever did. . . . With regard to Stravinsky, I was enthusiastic about his previous works. I feel, however, that his latest works are dry; they don't warm me up.[61]

Bartók's surprise that Beethoven, *the* standard for profundity in music and a "classicist" in the Hungarian canon, should be denigrated as Romantic accords with his expectation that music of the highest quality should be "grand," "emotional," and "free of jests." Bartók's incorporation of peasant music into a modern musical idiom was taken (and touted) as a radical rebellion against his conservative, Brahms-oriented education at the Academy of Music. But he never abandoned the fundamentally Hungarian (and Central European) outlook that at once burdened and privileged art music with a weighty ethical obligation.

New Classicism à la Molnár

Even the Hungarian music critics most sympathetic to Stravinsky echoed Bartók's ambivalent reaction to Stravinsky's compositions of the 1920s and the rhetoric that accompanied them. These critics responded to the challenge of what was for them an alien and contradictory notion of "musical objectivity" by making explicit their hitherto unspoken assumptions about art's expressive and serious nature. The debate came to a head in 1926 following an all-Stravinsky concert in Budapest with the composer as piano soloist. In addition to Aladár Tóth, Antal Molnár also came to the defense of progressive Hungarian musical values against the Stravinskyan threat. Molnár's contribution was a small book with a long title that expressed a characteristically Hungarian belief in the centrality of ethics to modern music: *Az új zene: A zeneművészet legujabb irányának ismertetése kultúretikai megvilágításban* (The New Music: A Review of Music's Newest Directions in the Light of the Ethics of Culture). Molnár, whose association with Bartók had begun at least as early as 1910 when he had joined Bartók in the collection of Hungarian folk music, was entrusted by the composer with providing an analysis of his First Piano Concerto for the Universal Edition pocket score (1927). This trust surely owed something to Molnár's vigorous defense of Bartók the year before.

Molnár's principal criterion for judging composers was the extent to which their work demonstrated "ethical responsibility." On this view, a work exhibits this ethical quality if it has both "social content" and "expresses the personal feelings of the composer."[62] For Molnár, folk music was a "human universal," which justified its use in modern composition. The use of folk music guaranteed the "social content" of modern music and tied it to the Beethovenian tradition, presumably to works like the Ninth Symphony, the "social content" of which was the notion of universal brotherhood expressed by Schiller's "Ode to Joy." This reasoning served to place Stravinsky's Russian works as well as the music of Bartók and Kodály above the music of Schoenberg, which in Molnár's formulation lacked "social content" because it had no basis in folk music. Molnár used his requirement that music embodying ethical responsibility should "express the personal feelings of the composer" to counter the notion of "objectivity" and the music of Stravinsky. Having silently shuffled Kodály out of consideration, Molnár's argument gave an easy victory to Bartók, the true representative of "new classicism," Molnár's highest category for modern art: "New classicism cannot be 'objective,' properly formulated: to compose with an indifferent spirit; indeed we find objectivity in Bach's music, but this is objectivity of belief in God, which is beyond every individual subjectivity, not the objectivity of neutrality. For just this reason Bach's music—in spite of all its objectivity—pours heat waves of emotion, eternal music is not 'inhuman'. . . . [Stravinsky] is the battering ram of new classicism, the blind strength, but not the spirit of new classicism."[63]

For Molnár and Bartók, as for many musicians, classicism had two primary and interrelated meanings. In one sense it referred to Viennese classicism: Haydn, Mozart, and, most crucially, Beethoven, the composer considered to epitomize the profound, ethical side of music so central to the aesthetics of Bartók and Hungarian critics. In the other sense, classical was used to describe any art thought to have eternal value. In this usage classic was the opposite of fashionable, an adjective perennially paired with Stravinsky in the 1920s. Thus when in 1926 the Hungarian critic László Fábian opened an extensive article on Stravinsky in *Zenei Szemle* (Music Review) by calling him "today's most fashionable composer," he was in fact denying his claim to classic status.[64] Implicit in Molnár's discussion of Hungarian "new classicism" is a line from Beethoven to Bartók that bypassed Stravinskyan neoclassicism.

Bartók took Molnár's distinction one step further. In his formulation the difference between Kodály's (read: Bartók's) and Stravinsky's relationships to the past constituted a veritable antithesis:

> In general two opposite [approaches to new music] crystallize in practice: one (for example, Stravinsky) is revolutionary, that is, on the one hand, it shows a sudden break with the music of yesterday, and on the other, it throws the whole range of dazzling novelties and new departures into the music of today. The other type seems rather to be comprehensive: a summation of all the elements available up to now. It is thus not a revolutionary break with yesterday, for it even rescues everything it can use from Romanticism . . . that is, whatever has vitality. The most characteristic representative of this is the Hungarian Kodály. Which of the two will better withstand the test of time, the innovators or the summarizers, remains to be decided in the future. If, however, we think of parallels in music history, we would be inclined to rule in favor of the great comprehensive art.[65]

This passage, part of a draft the composer seems to have intended for use in a preconcert lecture in 1928 or '29, reveals a competitive streak in Bartók's relationship to his more successful contemporary better than anything he wrote for publication.

Stravinsky's Challenge: The Concerto for Piano and Winds in Hungary

If Stravinsky's renown in Hungary by 1925 had challenged Bartók's position of dominance enough to provoke Molnár's reformulation of neoclassicism in the composer's defense, Stravinsky's personal appearance in Budapest on 15 March 1926 turned abstract threat into palpable reality. By devoting an entire evening to his works—*The Song of the Nightingale,*

Concerto for Piano and Winds, and *Petrushka*—the Philharmonic Society, Hungary's finest orchestra, honored Stravinsky as no Hungarian orchestra had ever honored Bartók. To add insult to injury, the Philharmonic had already performed Stravinsky's *Pulcinella* that season, and publicity had just been released for the upcoming production of *Petrushka* by the Hungarian Opera, which had last performed a work by Bartók in January 1919. Perhaps even more significant, Stravinsky, in his role as piano soloist in his own freshly minted piano concerto, was now encroaching on yet another of Bartók's domains. Bartók began to compose his First Piano Concerto a few months after Stravinsky's Budapest engagement; it was complete by November of that year.

Stravinsky's 1926 appearance in Budapest was much anticipated by progressive Hungarians intent on keeping their nation's capital in step with modern European trends. *Nyugat* paved the way for his sympathetic reception by publishing in translation an extensive celebratory article on Stravinsky by François Gachot, and both *Pesti Napló* and *Pesti Hírlap* published interviews with the composer on the day before his concert.[66] This concert was literally a dream come true for Aladár Tóth. Not only had he long been using his position as music critic of *Nyugat* and *Pesti Napló* to call for performances of Stravinsky, but his appetite had also recently been whetted by the first Hungarian performance of *Pulcinella* four months before.[67] Tóth saw the fact that a Hungarian orchestra had not only performed Stravinsky's music but performed it well as a source of national pride: "Today's Stravinsky concert is the glory of Hungarian music culture. Our Philharmonic orchestra created a true miracle with two rehearsals. It brings joy to our heart, our soul, that this fine orchestra, destined for greatness, realized its calling so well."[68]

At the same time as Tóth saw the performance of Stravinsky's music as a Hungarian triumph, he also feared the degree to which Stravinsky's great success with the Budapest audience, unanimously reported by all reviewers, might threaten Bartók's status as culturally superior to foreign musical modernists. It had been nearly a decade since the premiere of *The Wooden Prince*, the last occasion at which Bartók's music had achieved a degree of success with the Hungarian public comparable to Stravinsky's in 1926. In his review of Stravinsky's concert, Tóth took the opportunity to dig in his heels and fight for Hungary's own composer/pianist and the moral superiority of the values Tóth believed he represented. In reference to Stravinsky's pianism in his Concerto for Piano and Winds Tóth comments:

> We know well the power of barbaric, wild rhythms, for here among us lives the greatest master of them: Béla Bartók. But Stravinsky's rhythm is something entirely different: it resembles Bartók's only in its demonic verve. Bartók's

rhythm is always deeply poetic, born in a high spiritual sphere from which it is transformed with convincing strength into the world of gestures of ancient man. Bartók rises when he plays the piano, Stravinsky remains earthbound.

Later in the review Tóth disguises his jibes as praise for *Petrushka*, again finding a way to display Bartók as Beethoven's heir:

> One praises Stravinsky's sense of form—he really wrote this music for ballet. Ballet music, easy, characteristically pantomime dance music, not in the sense that Beethoven's *Prometheus* or Bartók's *Wooden Prince* attempt to reform ballet into a genre equal to opera and symphony, but in the sense that Lully or Delibes writes ballet music.[69]

Yet even Bartók emerged from the concert with a new appreciation of Stravinsky's latest style. In an interview five weeks after Stravinsky's Budapest appearance Bartók called Stravinsky's concert the "greatest event" in the musical season of the Hungarian capital. "Stravinsky's latest works," he added, "which he calls neoclassical and which really do resemble the music of Bach's time, seemed dry to me initially, but they were greatly enriched for me after his concert in Pest."[70] These public words of praise concealed a more ambivalent private reaction. Writing to Bartók's mother three days after Stravinsky's concert, Ditta Pásztory, the composer's second wife, conveyed the intensity of the mixed emotions Stravinsky's music elicited in the Bartók household:

> Monday was the Stravinsky concert.—Now I know quite exactly what the new direction is. Imagine, mama, for yourself such a music, in which there is absolutely no room for feelings, in which you can find no part that causes tears to come to your eyes. You know, *bare rhythm*, bare hammering, bare some-kind-of-timbre. I can say that the whole thing, as it is, really carries one away. Stravinsky is a magnificent genius, and we very, very much enjoyed the evening, truly one gets caught up in his miraculously beautifully timbred *machine music*, music of pulsating rhythm—but if Béla would make such music, then I would not be able to relate to Béla the artist as I do and always will. Because this music is not my homeland, mine is Béla's music, where there are also plenty of tone colors and pulsating rhythms, but where feelings also live and are, and which has *soul*.[71]

Pásztory's account sounds intensely personal; there is no reason to doubt its sincerity. At the same time, her letter is a nearly perfect summary of what had become a commonplace critical assessment of Stravinsky's music in Hungary. Aladár Tóth had not only expressed the essence of Pásztory's reaction a number of times, he even used many of the same phrases. Specifically, in his review of the Philharmonic's performance of *Pulcinella* four months earlier, he had used the expression "carried away" exactly as would Pásztory—to explain the attraction of Stravinsky's music while giving that attraction a negative spin. Drawing a parallel between Stravinsky and Liszt, Tóth had written:

> A fire burns in [Stravinsky and Liszt], but it is a cold fire . . . they lack lyric poetry, the honest, deep lyric. . . . Therefore, although they conquer, they dazzle, they *carry one away,* they can not completely persuade one. There is another strange, almost tragic-comical similarity between [Stravinsky and Liszt's] artistic fate: those musical innovations and revolutionary achievements for which they fought so bravely . . . find deeper, truer poetical expression elsewhere. Next to Franz Liszt appeared Richard Wagner, next to Igor Stravinsky appears the deep, poetic figure of Béla Bartók.[72]

Several other Hungarian reviewers echoed Tóth's formulation, itself a variant of Molnár's. None was more negative than that of the reactionary critic Izor Béldi, notorious for having called for aspirin after the premiere of Bartók's Second Suite.[73] Béldi's criticism of Stravinsky may have been ringing in Pásztory's ears when she put down expressions such as "bare rhythm," "machine music," and "no room for feelings" to describe her sense that Stravinsky's music lacked "soul." Compare Pásztory's choice of words with Béldi's description: "[Stravinsky's] playing was *bare rhythm,* without color, spirit, or *soul.* It is possible that by the time our earth cools and there is ice on the equator, at that time this will be considered music too. But as long as *feeling and spirit* live in man, as long as feelings and passions find a home in our hearts, this *mechanical* clattering, this rhythmical but colorless ticking, this mixing of tones without melody or harmony cannot be considered music."[74] Béldi's review appeared in the widely read *Pesti Hírlap* two days before Ditta penned her letter.

Antal Molnár, Ditta Pásztory, and Aladár Tóth all agreed that Bartók's music combined the profundity of Beethoven ("soul") with the fashionable modernity of Stravinsky's neoclassicism. In 1925 and early 1926 they wrote about Bartók's music as if this combination of qualities had already been achieved. In fact, Bartók would only begin to confront Stravinsky's neoclassical style in earnest a few months later.

Expression in the Time of Objectivity: Bartók's First Piano Concerto

In the three years preceding the fateful Stravinsky concert Bartók had virtually retired from composition. During this time he had written only one work, a folk-song arrangement entitled *Falun* (Village Scenes, 1924) and had never written anything comparable to Stravinsky's Piano Concerto in mood and scope. Bartók had been relying on his now woefully outdated Rhapsody, op. 1, for engagements with orchestra for over twenty years. He badly needed a piano concerto of his own, and Stravinsky's concert in Budapest made this need even more urgent.[75] When he began to compose again shortly after hearing Stravinsky, the effect of a long absence from composition left Bartók unsure of how to begin a piano concerto. Reporting on his progress to his wife during his summer vacation devoted to composition he wrote:

> The problem is that I haven't been able to begin precisely the most important thing, the piano concerto. . . . Somehow now after not composing for a long time I've been like a person who after a very-very long time of lying in bed motionless finally tries to use his arms and legs and stands [but can only] take one or two steps. . . . I too have slowly-slowly been getting used to movement: although this way I've only been able to shake [a few] piano pieces out of myself. But this is already something. Because, to be frank, I have recently felt so stupid, so dazed, so empty-headed that I have truly doubted whether I am able to write anything new at all anymore. All the tangled chaos that the musical periodicals vomit thick and fast about the music of today has come to weigh heavily on me: the watchwords, linear, horizontal, vertical, objective, impersonal, polyphonic, homophonic, tonal, polytonal, atonal, and the rest; even if one does not concern oneself with all of it, one still becomes quite dazed when they shout it in one's ears so much. Actually it is best not to read anything, to just write without any regard for slogans. Of course, all this hub-bub would have run off me without making any effect if there had been continuity in [my] work.[76]

Although Bartók never lost his distinctive musical voice, some of the works he began to compose in the summer of 1926 do mark a change that show him moving closer to neoclassicism as practiced by Stravinsky. Bartók himself acknowledged this stylistic shift in 1930 when he summarized his development for the German musicologist Edwin von der Nüll: "In my youth my ideal for what was beautiful was not so much Bach's or Mozart's creations as those of Beethoven. Recently this has changed to a certain extent; in the past few years I have been very occupied with music preceding Bach, and I believe that traces of this are revealed in the [First] Piano Concerto and the Nine Little Piano Pieces."[77] Although Bartók states that the change in his style was due to the influence of composers preceding Bach, his interest in music untainted by the "excesses of the nineteenth century" was directly connected to modern musical fashion.

The circumstances of the genesis of Bartók's First Piano Concerto suggest that it may be read as a musical analogy to Ditta's impassioned, if ambiva-

EXAMPLE 52. Stravinsky, Concerto for Piano and Winds, introduction, mm. 1–4

lent, reaction to Stravinsky's concert. Although the concerto bears the imprint of Stravinsky in both detail and mood, Bartók gives new shape and meaning to what he borrowed. In the First Piano Concerto, Hungarian attitudes about serious music, and Beethoven's legacy in particular, are mixed with Stravinskyan echoes and hints of Debussy, Schoenberg, and, as Bartók observed, composers before Bach. The result is a work richly layered with evocations of folk music alongside eighteenth-, nineteenth-, and twentieth-century musical topoi: a work difficult to classify and, finally, too difficult to be very warmly received in European and American concert halls in the late 1920s and early '30s. An examination of three points of intersection between the first movements of Bartók's and Stravinsky's concertos (their introductions, primary themes, and culminating climaxes) reveals some telling similarities, which in turn cast their differences in a more meaningful relief.

Stravinsky and Bartók both begin their concertos by evoking the conventions of another musical genre. The dotted rhythms of Stravinsky's Largo introduction to the main Allegro of the movement recall the tradition of the French Baroque overture, which Stravinsky projects through an odd prism of Gabriellian brass orchestration and a dirgelike theme reminiscent of the funeral march of Chopin's B-Minor Sonata (example 52). The Baroque implications of Stravinsky's dotted rhythms were not lost on Aladár Tóth, who commented that "[Stravinsky] cut a noble, festive robe for himself from Händel's punctuated rhythms."[78] In A minor, the introduction establishes the key of the Allegro. For orchestra alone, the music metaphorically paves the way for the entrance of the king, the soloist—in this case, Stravinsky himself.

Given the strong effect of Stravinsky's concerto on Bartók and the rarity of slow introductions in concertos generally, it hardly seems coincidental that Bartók also chose to begin his concerto with an introduction set off from the main Allegro by its slower tempo and contrasting mood (example 53). Indeed, Bartók's introduction may be seen to challenge its predecessor

EXAMPLE 53. Bartók, Piano Concerto No. 1, introduction

(continued)

EXAMPLE 53 *(continued)*

by taking Stravinsky's idea of "objective" orchestration one step further. As in Stravinsky's work, strings are absent and brass emphasized, but here the prominent role for the percussion, including the percussive use of the piano, lends a brutal edge to Stravinsky's brittle game. Comparison of the opening bars of the Allegro sections of each work makes Bartók's inspiration more explicit: both passages begin with a long series of repeated As that require an outstretched hand position that invites percussive attacks. The rhythm of the accompaniments to the passages is identical; Bartók is quoting or at least alluding here to his rival's work (example 54).

But if Bartók seems to have been inspired by Stravinsky's instrumentation, use of rhythm, choice of pitch, and the opening gambit of an introduction, his introduction has roots in a very different tradition. As he had in *The Wooden Prince*, in the First Piano Concerto Bartók continues the Beethovenian tradition of the "creation" opening by gradually building a distinct shape from amorphous material. By relying on this topos, he instills the expectation that his concerto will carry the profound weight of other works in this tradition such as Beethoven's Ninth Symphony, *Das*

EXAMPLE 54. Bartók and Stravinsky Piano Concertos, comparison of primary themes (Bartók continues example 53)

Rheingold, and Mahler's First Symphony. In short, whereas Stravinsky's orientation is Gallic, Bartók's is Germanic; while Stravinsky's Allegro cockily contradicts the pomposity of the preceding music, Bartók's Allegro organically continues the process begun in bar 1.

"Creation" openings typically begin with long pedal points that provide a backdrop for metaphorical birth: the crystallization of the musical material. Bartók continues this tradition in his First Piano Concerto, but with a modernist twist. Instead of one continuous pedal, he employs two (B and A) set to sharply contrasting rhythms. The two pitches dissonantly contradict each other as they are literally drummed out on the timpani and in the lowest, percussive depths of the solo piano. In alternation with this increasingly energetic rhythmic exchange, Bartók presents the elements of music one by one. First rhythm: the pounding of the single pitches on the timpani and piano. Then harmony: a lone, stark chord in the brass. And finally melody: a primitive, *Rite of Spring*–like tune with a restricted range of a perfect fourth that appears in several orchestrations before the percussive energy of the dual pedals bursts into full bloom and launches the vital first theme of the Allegro.[79]

As well as using the dual pedals of the introduction to begin an organic process of thematic development, Bartók uses them to generate at least two other crucial aspects of the movement. They give rise to the harmonic structure of the exposition and form the basis of the harmonic conflict that resolves only at the movement's culmination point. The diagram below illustrates the harmonic structure of the exposition, which consists of two main parts:

EXPOSITION PART 1

Section	Intro.	1st Theme Group	Transition 1	2nd Theme Group	Transition 2
Measure Nos.	(1–37)	(38–65)	(66–93)	(94–112)	(113–30)
Pedal	A/B		B		
Tonal Area		→ D		→ E	

EXPOSITION PART 2

Section	1st Theme Group	Transition 3	2nd Theme Group
Measure Nos.	(131–42)	(152–62)	(152–62)
Tonal Area	F→(F♯)		G

In the first part (mm. 38–130) Bartók states the primary and secondary theme groups in D and E, respectively. In the second, shorter part (mm. 131–

EXAMPLE 55. Tonal structure of Bartók's Piano Concerto No. 1, movement 1

a. Reduction of the introduction and exposition: A–B, the pedals of the introduction; D–E, the tonal areas of the first part of the exposition; and F/F♯–G, the tonal areas of the second part of the exposition

b. D-Dorian scale with unstable third degree compared with the concerto's primary theme

62) he restates music from the first part transposed up a minor third, beginning a second statement of the primary theme in F (m. 131) and recalling material from the secondary theme group in G (mm. 152–62). The whole step separating the tonal areas of the primary and secondary themes grows directly out of the whole-step relationship between the dual pedals of the introduction. Bartók makes the generative power of A and B explicit by using them as dominant pedals that resolve respectively to the tonal areas of the primary and secondary themes. In the last bars of the introduction (mm. 30–37) he raises the A pedal in the solo piano three octaves, where it functions as the dominant of the primary theme on D. (The tonal orientation of the primary theme is clearest in the melodic cadence to D at the end of the theme proper [m. 49].) Similarly, the B pedal reemerges in a higher octave during the transition to the secondary theme group (m. 82); its resolution to E at measure 94 marks the arrival of the tonal area of the secondary theme group (the secondary theme proper begins at measure 101). A significant additional detail in the tonal structure of the exposition is that over the course of the second part Bartók shifts from F to F♯ when restating the primary theme (the shift is clearest at the melodic cadence to F♯ at m. 142). In summary, Bartók builds the introduction and exposition on what may seen as literally three successive generations of dyads: A–B, the pedals of the introduction; D–E, the tonal areas of the first part of the exposition; and F/F♯–G, the tonal areas of the second part of the exposition (example 55a). One of the beauties of this structure is that taken together these tonal areas imply a D-Dorian scale with an unstable third degree: D–E–F/F♯–G–A–B. This is precisely the mode of the melody of the primary theme and a mode characteristic of Hungarian folk

music (example 55b). This type of integration of folk music on multiple levels continues to connect Bartók directly to a Central European organicist tradition even while under the ostensible influence of neoclassicism.

An important aspect of tonal structure for understanding the drama of the movement's culmination point is that the exposition does not establish the primacy of any one tonal center. As the "key" of the primary theme, D might seem to be the tonal center of the movement, but it is the victorious arrival on E at measure 94 that has the weight of a structural downbeat. Because Bartók's construction of the exposition does not conform to the key relationships of traditional *Formenlehre,* there is no accepted a priori model by which to determine which tonal center will emerge as the final, governing "key" of the movement. Although the "competition" between D and E has its roots in the initial superimposition of A and B in the introduction, Bartók saves the direct confrontation of D and E for the recapitulation.

Bartók creates the first such confrontation at the point where, by analogy to the exposition, the B pedal at the end of the transition should resolve to E (reh. no. 45). That resolution does occur in the upper voices as expected, but a deceptive move to D in the bass contradicts it (example 56). This precipitates a crisis. Instead of a resolution to the material of the secondary theme group that had occurred in the analogous place in the exposition, the orchestra explodes into a stormy, octatonically inflected G minor (G–A–Bb–C–Db–[Eb/D♯]–E–F♯) while the solo piano pounds out dissonant tone clusters. The storm clears momentarily when Bartók completes the octatonic collection with a resolution to a statement of the second theme proper on D♯ (reh. no. 46), but it is an uneasy, temporary compromise, literally a "middle ground" in the battle between D and E.

The conclusive confrontation between D and E occurs in a more diatonic context (reh. no. 50) that produces the movement's culmination point (example 57) and the definitive assertion of E as its ultimate tonal center. Already in the nine bars preceding the climactic passage, beginning at reh. no. 49, Bartók strengthens E as a tonal center by dovetailing a $\hat{1}$–$\hat{4}$–$\hat{5}$–$\hat{1}$ melodic progression with an E-major scale. When the upper voices reach their expected melodic arrival on E, the composer appears to contradict the resolution with another deceptive move to D in the bass at reh. no. 50. The passage that now ensues features all the main pitch centers of the exposition and the dual pedals of the introduction: the low D in the trombone and bassoon and the high E in the woodwinds frame an alternation between B and A in the horns, answered one quarter note later by the second trumpet in a canon by inversion that alternates F and G. A manuscript draft of the concerto shows the superimposition of all the functional pitches even more

EXAMPLE 56. Bartók, Piano Concerto No. 1, movement 1, pedal tone B resolves to E in upper voices and D in bass (reh. no. 45) followed by second theme on D♯ (reh. no. 46)

(continued)

EXAMPLE 56 *(continued)*

EXAMPLE 57. Bartók, Piano Concerto No. 1, movement 1, buildup (reh. no. 49) to conclusive confrontation between D and E (reh. no. 50)

(continued)

EXAMPLE 57 (continued)

explicitly by bringing the F in immediately on the first beat of the bar instead of following a quarter rest.[80]

For the actual climax at reh. no. 50, Bartók reverts to a creation metaphor, bringing back the pitches B and A, the dual pedals of the introduction, and giving them a new melodic function. Beginning with a simple alternation in the horns, the two pitches gradually expand into a pentatonic protomelody that finally erupts into a full-throated tenor-range tune.[81] The modality of this tune (E Dorian with a strong pentatonic component), its Hungarian *short*-long rhythms (especially the cadential formula ♪♪ ♩), its descending profile, and its $\hat{5}$–$\hat{4}$–$\hat{1}$ melodic cadence all betray its debt to old-style Hungarian folk song.[82] Concomitant with the cathartic eruption of the tune (8 after reh. no. 50), Bartók brings the harmony to a brilliant C major, arising out of the downward resolution of the dissonant D in the bass. Having excised D from the accompaniment at the beginning of the folk-song-like melody, Bartók affirms E as the ultimate tonal goal of the movement and demonstrates how B and A relate to that goal through peasant music with the tune's climactic $\hat{5}$–$\hat{4}$–$\hat{1}$ (B–A–E) folk cadence.

As we have already seen in the Rhapsody for Piano (chapter 2), Bartók uses the culmination point of the first movement of the First Piano Concerto to bring a latent potential for Hungarian sentiment to fruition. Unlike the analogous point in the Rhapsody, however, the culmination point of the Piano Concerto conforms to a twentieth-century (i.e., Bartókian) notion of Hungarian music based on peasant song. The way he generates

EXAMPLE 58. Stravinsky, Concerto for Piano and Winds, movement 1, "Largo del principio," reh. no. 45

the culminating tune out of the seemingly abstract tonal plan of the introduction and exposition in fact may be seen as analogous to his analysis of folk music, only proceeding in reverse. Rather than breaking down a peasant melody into its constituent elements, he builds a folklike melody of his own invention from the pitches that form the primary building blocks of the movement. The result is all the more powerful for its artificiality. The culminating tune at reh. no. 50 owes a great deal of its cathartic power to its composed quality, which enables the tune to function at once as harmonic resolution and as an emblem of folk song with far greater efficiency than any field-collected relic.

To effect a climactic point of arrival at the end of the first movement of the *Concerto for Piano and Winds*, Stravinsky had also returned to materials from the introduction. Following in the tradition of the French overture, Stravinsky's climactic *Largo del principo* brings back the music and tempo of the opening pompous slow march, now intensified by the inclusion of added layers of rhythmic activity in the solo piano (example 58). The result is a rigid metrical matrix of deftly interlocking rhythms that emphasizes the mechanical aspect of the music, dividing the bars of $\frac{2}{4}$ into quarter notes in the orchestra and quarter-note triplets in the piano's left hand while supporting each large division of the bar with its own subdivision, sixteenth notes in the dotted melody in the orchestra and sextuplets in the piano right hand.[83] Stravinsky's climactic return revels in rhythmic counterpoint, while Bartók's celebrates a seemingly rough-hewn melody—human song, Bartók (or Tóth) might have said, as opposed to musical clockwork.

The clarity of this distinction between Bartók's and Stravinsky's styles evaporates, however, if we broaden the scope of our comparison to include the actual conclusions of the two movements. Just as Bartók retreated from the expressive, folk-oriented music representing the embrace of the Prince and Princess in *The Wooden Prince*, the culmination point of the first movement of the First Piano Concerto gives way to a contrasting coda. As if embarrassed by the frank expressivity of a climax, which Bartók even goes so far as to indulge with a *poco ritardando* that nods in the direction of Romantic performance practice, after the $\hat{5}-\hat{4}-\hat{1}$ melodic cadence he abruptly breaks off the high-tenor, human quality of the "old-style" song of the trombones. The texture now shifts to a ticking eighth-note accompaniment in the strings that paves the way for the piano's entrance *(marcato)* in a "music-box" register. The neatly interlocking stretto that follows, based on the second theme, is capped by symmetrically unfolding scales in piano and orchestra (example 59).

Thus, despite the antithetical orientation of their climaxes, the first movements of Stravinsky's and Bartók's concertos end on the same "objective" note. But, as in the final scenes of *The Firebird* and *The Rite of Spring*, Stravinsky's climactic and closing gestures are one and the same, whereas Bartók continues to separate and even oppose these two events, just as he had done in *The Miraculous Mandarin*, *The Wooden Prince*, and the Rhapsody, op. 1.

In the First Piano Concerto the relationship between the culmination point and the coda of the first movement suggests something far more complex than did the relationship between the coda and the culmination point in the Rhapsody for Piano. Instead of reflecting Bartók's early unquestioning acceptance of national tropes, the culmination point (like that of *The Wooden Prince*) can now be seen as an expression of Bartók's belief in peasant music as the essence of *magyarság*. The ensuing gesture of alienation, however, that calls the expression of the preceding passage into question, shows the composer caught between two aesthetic ideals: a traditionally Romantic ideal symbolized by the outpouring of emotion at the culmination point, and a fashionably modernist ideal of "objectivity" represented by the mechanistic conclusion. That tension between modernity and tradition had already found expression in the introduction, where the brutality of the

EXAMPLE 59. Bartók, Piano Concerto No. 1, movement 1, concluding stretto, reh. no. 51 to end

(continued)

EXAMPLE 59 *(continued)*

percussive gestures had masked the debt to the nineteenth-century tradition of "creation" openings. This peculiar mix seems to have been born of the double weight of the Hungarian ideals of "grandness," "emotional expression," profundity, and synthesis coupled with Bartók's obligation to meet the challenge of fashionable European modernism as embodied by Stravinsky. Although the notion of the culmination point is useful for combining musical analysis with historically informed interpretation, it should also be recognized as an emblem of deep-seated Hungarian tradition. This tradition bridges the two-decade gap separating Bartók's Rhapsody for Piano and First Piano Concerto, quite belying all the radical changes in musical fashion and Bartók's own nationalist orientation that had transpired between 1905 and 1926. The highly concentrated evocation of Hungarian peasant music in the brief culmination point of the first movement of the First Piano Concerto thus provided Bartók with a characteristically Hungarian refuge for expression in the time of objectivity.

CRITICAL RECEPTION

Predictably, both Antal Molnár and Aladár Tóth claimed that Bartók's First Piano Concerto represented a new "classicism" that rose above neoclassical fashion. For them Bartók succeeded in challenging the neoclassical Stravinsky while staying true to the Hungarian belief in music's "soul," in its moral obligation to be uplifting and profound, and in its debt to the Beethovenian tradition. Molnár, in terms that recall the theme of *The Miraculous Mandarin*, took Bartók's development of the primitive melody in the introduction of the concerto as a human element, which in his words created "absolute value out of the indifferent mood of the time: the eternal soul of primitive man."[84]

In his review of the first Budapest performance of Bartók's concerto on 19 March 1928 Tóth also interpreted the primitive quality of the concerto as central to the work's classicism. Once again defending Bartók against Stravinsky as if Stravinsky's performance of the Concerto for Piano and Winds had preceded Bartók's performance of his own concerto by two weeks rather than by two years, Tóth declared:

> What remained in the "neoclassical" Stravinsky of the barbaric Asian quality of *The Rite of Spring?* Virtually nothing: Stravinsky's barbarism was nothing more than a moveable stage set that he left out of his music the closer he came to the filtered concentration of French neoclassicism. The more "classical" Bartók is, however, the more concentrated, the more complicated, the more differentiated, . . . the more elemental, the more "barbaric," all the more "Asia."

Words like "barbaric" and "Asia," plugged repeatedly throughout the review, signal the usual nationalistic stance, connecting Bartók's music and the ancient Magyar tribes. Tóth makes the connection explicit in his peroration:

> What amazing power there is in the music of this small [tribe of] people that has been knocked from the east to the west! It produced a Ferenc Liszt. . . . It produced a Zoltán Kodály. . . . And then [it produced] Béla Bartók, who led us back to the ancient homeland, whose music brings alive the ancient pagan creed with which we once rested in Asia's breast.[85]

Such rhetoric, Tóth hoped, would shame Hungarians out of their "overestimation" of Stravinsky vis-à-vis their own national treasure, for Bartók's First Piano Concerto was a nearly perfect embodiment of the critic's criteria for a new Hungarian music that would help foster the new Hungary of his dreams. It reflected an outlook that was modern and enlightened, open to and informed by greater-European culture, yet uniquely Hungarian in its synthesis of modernity with ancient peasant music and the Central European belief in the humanly expressive imperative for art.

Controlled Response: Bartók's Second Piano Concerto

However perfectly Bartók's First Piano Concerto fit Tóth's and Molnár's standards for new Hungarian music, their defense of it faced some formidable difficulties. Despite Bartók's twenty-odd performances of the concerto in the space of five years, the work never achieved more than a succès d'estime. What Bartók's Hungarian apologists considered great depth, an impressive melding of modern style and traditional Hungarian values, was frequently taken for simple confusion. In contrast to the genuine enthusiasm with which they had greeted Stravinsky's concerto two years earlier, the Budapest audience received Bartók's with perfunctory applause. According to Emil Haraszti of *Budapesti Hírlap:* "The public of tonight's Bartók premiere was perplexed. They did not understand the piece, they chided it, belittled it, mocked it, . . . even those who believed in it, with few exceptions, voiced only banal commonplaces. . . . Béla Bartók's Piano Concerto is one of the composer's less successful works."[86]

The reaction of the Hungarian audience was not unique. The concerto had a lukewarm reception throughout Europe. As a Dutch critic suggested after its performance in Amsterdam, the problem may have been the concerto's odd mix of topoi. Bartók's combination of Stravinskyan style with Romantic rhetoric, the very thing Bartók's Hungarian champions greeted with such enthusiasm, proved to be an obstacle to the work's international success: "We cannot condemn the audience in its judgment. Béla Bartók is a serious thinker and exceptional composer, but his reach is different than—we do not want to say beyond—his grasp. In his Piano Concerto he made use of lessons from Stravinsky's *Rite of Spring*, indeed from *Petrushka* as well, but his mentality is different; his tools are not in agreement with his temperament, which is still Romantic. So there is a gulf between the mode of expression and the content, for this reason the piece is not convincing."[87]

The First Piano Concerto had not successfully met the challenge posed by Stravinsky, and Bartók knew it. Its rhythmic complexity was notoriously difficult for orchestras, which frequently led to mediocre performances. (A letter to Bartók from the general music director in Freiburg suggests that on at least one occasion a conductor resorted to rebarring some of the tricky meter changes in the first movement.)[88] Bartók implicitly admitted the work's failure with orchestras and audiences by dropping it from his repertoire as soon as the Second Piano Concerto was ready for performance in 1933. In 1939 he explicitly acknowledged that the First Concerto was "a bit difficult—one might even say very difficult!—as much for the orchestra as for the audience." He went on to explain, "That is why some years later (1930–31) while writing my Second Concerto, I wanted to produce a piece which would contrast with the first: a work which would be less bristling with difficulties for the orchestra and whose thematic material would be more pleasing."[89] As is often the case with composers' pronouncements about their own works, what Bartók left unsaid about the relationship between the two concertos appears to be at least as significant as what he did say. In his Second Piano Concerto Bartók again confronted Stravinsky, this time more explicitly and with greater control than he did while navigating Stravinsky's turbulent wake in 1926.

The allusions to Stravinsky in Bartók's Second Piano Concerto mark a new stage in Bartók's relationship to his more fashionable contemporary. Several of these allusions are so direct as to qualify as near quotations. They must be regarded as intentional, and with this comes a sense of measured purpose vis-à-vis Stravinsky that was absent from the First Concerto. In his Second Piano Concerto Bartók shows virtuoso skill in transforming material, assimilating gestures borrowed directly from Stravinsky's "Russian works" into music that melds the structures of Hungarian folk music with the "neoclassical" Stravinsky's percussive linearity.

In the first movement of the First Piano Concerto Bartók had given a particularly large role to the wind instruments. In the first movement of the Second Piano Concerto he omits the strings altogether; the reference to Stravinsky is so obvious that it must have been apparent even to a listener who knew only the title of Stravinsky's Concerto for Piano and Winds. Two other evocations, one from the *Firebird,* the other from *Petrushka,* are similarly obvious examples of modeling (example 60a–d). The opening trumpet motto of the Second Piano Concerto shares its first six notes with the theme of the last scene of *The Firebird* ("By the Gate," see example 42, p. 131), and the opening theme in the piano closely follows the voicing, range, rhythm, and melodic shape of the opening piano solo of the "Danse russe" from *Petrushka.*[90] The evocation of the "Danse russe" even extends to Bartók's *piano espressivo* horn solo at "Un poco tranquillo" (m. 124), the color and mood of which recalls the expressive clarinet and English horn solos at the similarly marked *Poco meno (tranquillo)* passage in *Petrushka* (7 before reh. no. 43).

Bartók seems to have heard *Petrushka* first in Paris in 1922 when he heard excerpts played on a Pleyela player piano.[91] Following this occasion he had numerous opportunities to hear it before he began work on the Second Concerto. He heard it at Stravinsky's concert in Budapest in 1926 and may have seen it staged at the Hungarian Opera in the years 1926–28. He is also almost certain to have heard it while on tour in the United States in December 1927 when Fritz Reiner conducted it in Cincinnati on a program in which Bartók appeared as soloist.[92] His special affection for the work is

EXAMPLE 60. Stravinsky as a model for Bartók's Piano Concerto No. 2

a. Opening six notes of "By the Gate" used in *The Firebird*

b. Bartók, Piano Concerto No. 2, opening motto

c. *Petrushka,* "Danse russe"

d. Bartók, Piano Concerto No. 2, movement 1, entrance of solo piano, mm. 4–5

also reflected by the fact that in 1928 a recording of it was among the first gramophone records he bought for himself and his wife Ditta Pásztory, with whom he played the four-hand reduction of the score.[93]

The rhythm and melodic profile of the motto reminiscent of *The Firebird* with which Bartók opens the Second Piano Concerto are not distinctively Hungarian. Nor does it have its original Russian profile; ending it on the highest note, Bartók neutralizes the Dorian mode of the Russian folk melody that Stravinsky incorporated into *The Firebird*. In other words, Bartók's opening fanfare is stripped of any strong national character. As László Somfai has observed, at the climactic stretto directly preceding the cadenza (mm. 211–16) in the recapitulation of the first movement Bartók transforms the motto's nationally neutral profile into a specifically

EXAMPLE 61. Bartók, Piano Concerto No. 2, movement 1, opening motto and its transformation in the recapitulation

Hungarian statement (example 61).[94] Here he uses the retrograde inversion of the motto, which gives it a more natural dome shape and allows it to end with a traditional stepwise descent. Although the original form of the motto served as an effective opening, the retrograde inversion at once functions naturally as a closing gesture and has a melodic profile more typical of Hungarian folk song. Bartók's transformation of the motto from an opening to a closing gesture involves more than a purely mechanical construction of the retrograde inversion. Bartók diverges from the strict retrograde of the original rhythm by tripling the length of what has become the final note. The result is a cadential *short*-long figure that strongly asserts the Hungarian quality of this version of the motto. Bartók's addition of an accent to the short note of the *short*-long pair leaves no doubt as to the national implications of the transformation. Indeed, Bartók himself seems to have acknowledged that this passage had special meaning when, describing his compositional methods to Denijs Dille in 1937, he emphasized that "It is not just a game when I invert the theme in my Second Piano Concerto."[95] In the next sentence, as if to justify his sincerity, Bartók brings up folk music as an inspiration for thematic transformation, stating that the "extreme variety that is characteristic of Hungarian folk songs is similar to what I am trying to do."

Following the "straight" inversion of themes in the first part of the recapitulation (mm. 180–211), a series of more emphatic statements of the retrograde inversion of the motto appear in the orchestral tutti preceding the cadenza (mm. 211–221). This section provides at once a climactic arrival and reveals the Hungarian potential of the musical materials.[96] Unlike such culmination points in Bartók's earlier works, however, this one is rather lacking in expressive human character. Instead, the composer uses the retrograde inversion of the motto to set in motion a neatly interlocking stretto (mm. 211–16) that fits the spirit of the self-consciously Bachian counterpoint that pervades the movement (see especially the invention-like figuration in the solo piano: mm. 63–67 and 145–71). Continuing in this vein Bartók turns the last six notes of the retrograde inversion of the motto into the subject of a series of rising imitative entrances leading to a cadence on a

EXAMPLE 62. Bartók, Piano Concerto No. 2, movement 1, the four-line "new style" Hungarian folk-song structure of the solo piano theme

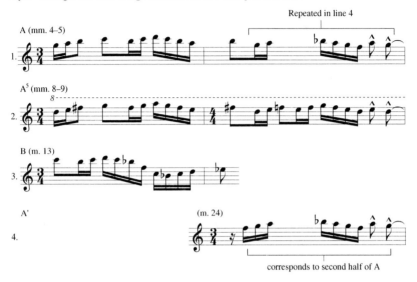

chord that, like a traditional cadential six-four chord preceding the cadenza in an eighteenth-century concerto, contains a perfect fourth as its lowest interval (mm. 218–21).

Although this version of the motto is clearly modeled on Hungarian folk music, Bartók's tight contrapuntal treatment of it throughout the recapitulation never allows for the hint of *espressivo* that had so tellingly betrayed his Romantic temperament in the analogous point in the First Concerto. Thus, while he transforms Stravinsky's Russian motive into an expression of *magyarság*, the nature of that expression, unusually for Bartók, remains bound to a Stravinskyan "neoclassical" aesthetic.[97]

In the reference to Stravinsky's "Danse russe" beginning in m. 4, Bartók maintains the light, busy character of the original, but again finds a way to give an originally Russian gesture a Hungarian twist. Rather than transforming the shape of the musical line, he uses it as the basis of a four-line structure AA⁵BA' (A⁵ = A transposed up a fifth) that is typical of what he labeled "new-style" Hungarian folk songs (example 62).[98] Bartók shows his usual aversion to exact repetition by foreshortening the final statement of A.

Whereas in the First Piano Concerto Bartók seems to have resisted Stravinsky's style while adopting some of his gestures, in the Second Piano Concerto he appears to be in total control. The references to Stravinsky are overt, allowing Bartók to show his mastery in bringing them into a Hungarian orbit. At the same time, however, he seems to have given in to the new Stravinskyan "objectivity." Whereas critics had often heard similarities between the First Concerto and *The Rite of Spring*, the Second Concerto more often elicited comparisons to the Bachian style of Stravinsky's Concerto for Piano and Winds.

In the light spirit of the opening of *Petrushka*, Bartók begins the first movement of the Second Concerto as if in medias res, avoiding the "creation" opening of the First Concerto, and with it the burden of symphonic expectations. The lean, contrapuntal style dominated by winds and the ticking eighth-note pulse that drives the first movement of the Second Concerto might seem a capitulation to the Stravinskyan aesthetic, and yet the concerto's connection to Hungarian folk music is no less explicit. With its cool exterior, however, the movement is less an embodiment of Molnár's "new classicism" than an example of the dehumanized neoclassicism that Hungarian critics had disparagingly referred to as "fashionable" before Bartók had put his own stamp on the style.

THE HUNGARIAN RECEPTION
OF THE SECOND PIANO CONCERTO

The lack of personal expression in the first movement of Bartók's Second Piano Concerto might seem to make it an unlikely embodiment of the new Hungarian music that Molnár and Tóth had projected on the basis of Bartók's earlier work. Happily their allegiance to Bartók outweighed allegiance to their theories. This time, the composer also pleased a wider audience, beginning with the premiere in Frankfurt on 23 January 1933, and even including Vienna, where Bartók performed it with the young musicians of the newly formed Budapesti Hangverseny Zenekar (Budapest Concert Orchestra), under the baton of Otto Klemperer.[99]

The first Budapest performance of the Second Concerto took place on 2 June 1933. Because in 1931 Bartók had become so discouraged by his reception at home that he had withdrawn from performing his own works in Budapest, Lajos (Louis) Kentner (1905–87) took Bartók's place as piano soloist.[100] Kentner's performance of a work Bartók had written as a vehicle for himself became another occasion for Tóth to rail against the composer's neglect in Hungary. One of the notable features of Tóth's polemic is that in this review of Bartók's most Stravinskyan work, he never mentions Stravinsky. Instead, he insisted, "Béla Bartók has shown that our people 'became cultured' not only under the 'beneficial influence' of the West, but also [from] the culture they brought with themselves, and which is pregnant with a future."[101] For Tóth, Bartók was also a political symbol, providing a model of progressive Hungarian leadership among the countries of the region:

How strange that when Hungarian politicians are daydreaming about a Hungary that would lead the countries of the Danube basin, they do not notice that Bartók has already created this in terms of the spiritual empire of culture and art. Bartók, who was scorned by stupid, limited minds for looking beyond the music of his people and collecting and using Romanian and Slovakian folk music, just as he collected and absorbed into his art the music of the Arabs as well!—Indeed, can a nation do anything more glorious than to work for other people, to represent, to summarize in its own culture an entire human community?[102]

Finally, Tóth claimed for Bartók a world stature precisely because he was "a Hungarian who could learn from the West what 'high culture' is, and who could learn among the peasants of his own nation what 'deep culture' is."[103] As Tóth seems to have realized instinctively, it was precisely in this work, in which Bartók leaned most heavily on Stravinsky, that Stravinsky was no longer a threat to his Hungarian rival's international reputation.

Just as the Second Piano Concerto marked a turning point for Hungarian criticism of Bartók vis-à-vis Stravinsky, so was it a turning point for Bartók. While composing the work, Bartók found a way to justify his music as "objective" despite his belief in the fundamentally expressive nature of music. In a lecture he gave in Budapest on 10 March 1931 he declared, "Peasant music contains everything that more recently they like to call 'objectivity' and what I would call the absence of sentimentality."[104] Of course, Bartók's new "objectivity" also implied increased reliance on abstract compositional techniques like inversions and retrogrades, which the composer justified as creating thematic variety similar to that of folk music.[105] Such techniques had less to do with folk music than they did with an increasing reliance on techniques of thematic transformation on the part of some modern composers whom Bartók felt called upon to emulate. And yet his more frequent reliance on academic techniques coincided with a new level of abstraction in his approach to folk music, exemplified by his construction of the opening theme in the Second Piano Concerto on the model of a four-line new-style Hungarian folk song (AA^5BA). This level of abstraction gave Bartók the freedom to incorporate a wide range of modern materials while maintaining the close connection to folk music on which he relied both for inspiration and for the justification of his work.

· · ·

Except in connection with Béla and Ditta Bartók's performances of Stravinsky's Concerto for Two Solo Pianos toward the end of the decade, Stravinsky's name practically disappeared from Bartók's interviews and correspondence during the 1930s.[106] In February 1943 Bartók gave a series of lectures at Harvard University, where Stravinsky had been Norton Lecturer a few years earlier.[107] In his lectures Bartók confirmed his retreat from the position he had held in the late 1920s. By this time he was no longer parroting Tóth's polemical labeling of Stravinsky as a "revolutionary," as merely a groundbreaker who had paved the way for Bartók's own "summarizing" synthesis.[108] Instead he put Stravinsky into the category of composers whose works are "decidedly the outcome of evolution. In the succession of their compositions," Bartók continued, "there is no abrupt turning away from previous devices and no abolition of almost all the means used by preceding composers. What we will see is a gradual change, leading from the patterns and means of their predecessors, to a style and means of expression of their own."[109] In the seventeen years since Stravinsky's Budapest performance of his Concerto for Piano and Winds, Bartók had gained some perspective on Stravinsky. By this time he owned or otherwise knew a large number of Stravinsky's works (table 3). Although he still used Stravinsky to explain his own music, he no longer relied on the clichés of press coverage about Stravinsky's work.

Greater familiarity with Stravinsky's music as well as his new willingness to endorse a neoclassical stance allowed Bartók to consider both himself and Stravinsky as representatives of a similar artistic "evolution." He now justified his own music by comparing it to that of his celebrated contemporary and compared Stravinsky's assimilation of elements of seventeenth- and eighteenth-century music with his own incorporation of elements from folk music:

> When I once met Stravinsky in Paris, he told me that he thinks he has the right to incorporate into his music any music he believes to be fit or appropriate for his purposes. This belief reminds us of Molière's saying: "Je prends mon bien où je le trouve." With this conviction, Stravinsky turned to the music of bygone times, to the so-called classical music of the seventeenth and eighteenth centuries, for a new starting point. This start again shows pure evolutionary principles and is by no means revolutionary in concept.
>
> The opinion of some people that Stravinsky's neoclassical style is based on Bach, Handel, and other composers of their time is a rather superficial one. As a matter of fact, he turns only to the material of that period, to the patterns used by Bach, Handel, and others. Stravinsky uses this material in his own way, arranging and transforming it according to his own individual spirit, thus creating works of a new, individual style.[110]

This recollection appears to invoke Stravinsky's practice as a justification for Bartók's own reliance on folk music. But it might also be read as the Hungarian composer's apologia for his debt to Stravinsky. That debt was not

TABLE 3. Works of Stravinsky's Known to Bartók by the Time of the Harvard Lectures (1943)

Much of the data for this table is taken from Vera Lampert, "Zeitgenössische Musik in Bartóks Notensammlung," *DocB* 5, 164–65.

1. *Stravinsky Masterpieces: Selected Compositions for Piano Solo* (arr.) (E. B. Marks Music, 1941). Contents: *Petrushka* ("Chez Petroushka," "Danse de la foire," "Danse russe"); *Pastorale;* Etude (F♯ major), op. 7, no. 4; *Rossignol* ("Chant du rossignol"); *L'histoire du soldat* ("The Devil's Dance"); *Le chant du rossignol* ("Marche chinoise"); *Le sacre du printemps* ("Danse des adolescents"); *L'oiseau de feu* ("Jeux des princesses," "Supplications," "Ronde des princesses," "Danse infernale," "Berceuse and finale").

2. *Chant du rossignol* (score, 1921)

3. Cinq pièces faciles pour piano à quatre mains (Bartók performed this in 1930)

4. Concerto en Ré (arr. violin and piano, 1931)

5. Concerto for Piano and Winds

6. Concerto per due pianoforti soli (played by Bartók in 1939 and 1940)

7. *Feu d'artifice* (mentioned in Harvard Lectures, *BBE*, 359)

8. *L'histoire du soldat* (full score and the arrangement by the composer for clarinet, violin, and piano). In 1923 Bartók intended to play the trio arrangement of *L'histoire* with Zoltán Székely in Budapest, but Székely was unable to make the arranged date. (Claude Kenneson, *Székely and Bartók: The Story of a Friendship* [Portland: Amadeus, 1994], 60)

9. *Trois histoires pour enfants*

10. Étude for pianola (reported to Aladár Tóth that he heard this in Paris in 1922 on a Pleyela player piano).

11. *Les noces* (score)

12. Octet (see Harvard Lectures, *BBE*, 360)

13. *Petrushka* (full score and arrangement for piano)

14. *Piano-Rag-Music*

15. *Pribaoutki*

16. *Quatre chants russes*

17. *Rag-time*

18. *Renard* (full score and piano-vocal score)

19. *Le rossignol* (piano-vocal score)

20. *Le sacre du printemps* (full score and arrangement for piano four hands)

21. *Suite de Pulcinella* (see Harvard Lectures, *BBE*, 360)

22. Symphonies d'instruments à vent (arranged for piano)

limited to the few references to Stravinsky's music in Bartók's scores. More important, by challenging traditional Hungarian musical values both in music and in rhetoric, Stravinsky provided an impetus for Bartók and a small circle of Hungarian critics to articulate and refine a specifically Hungarian view of musical modernism.

Highly cultured musicians and thinkers such as Aladár Tóth, Antal Molnár, Bartók, and Kodály never believed that Hungarian art music could or should be insulated from Western European traditions. For them, the quality of a Hungarian work was less bound to traditional notions of *magyarság* than to a Hungarian composer's ability to synthesize native and foreign elements. Tóth and Molnár saw the potential for a universally valid new "classicism" in Bartók's openness to inspiration from many sources and in his ability to imbue his works with a sense of moral responsibility. Since in Hungary the notion of eternal value had become inextricably bound to an ancient past preserved in peasant music, progressive critics saw Bartók's music as a guide to national self-awareness, a means of uplifting Hungarian culture by teaching it to know itself.

The obstacles to the realization of Tóth's vision were many, and music was but one small factor in a very large sociopolitical mechanism that shaped Hungarian national consciousness in the years following the First World War. In Bartók's works, and especially in *The Miraculous Mandarin* and the first two piano concertos, we can see how thoroughly Hungarian was Bartók's practice of transforming ideas borrowed from abroad. Viewed from this perspective, there is something especially poignant about Bartók's increasing alienation from Hungarian society in the years following the premiere of the First Piano Concerto. It shows that, despite the theoretically perfect model for a progressive, modern Hungary that his compositions seemed to provide, Bartók and his apologists misjudged the very audience they presumed to know best. By turning one element of Hungary's historical backwardness—its intact peasant culture—into a path to modernity and liberalism, Bartók and his champions showed ingenuity and idealism. Nevertheless, in the late 1920s and early 1930s few Hungarians were persuaded to replace a notion of musical *magyarság* that combined "Gypsy bands," recitals of visiting opera stars, and the latest sensation in operetta with what Aladár Tóth argued was the real thing: Kodály's folk-song arrangements and Bartók's compositions.

FIVE

Tradition Transcribed

The Rhapsody for Violin No. 1,
the Politics of Folk-Music Research,
and the Artifice of Authenticity

The truest poetry is the most feigning
SHAKESPEARE, *As You Like It* (3.3.20)

Much of the music discussed in the previous chapter relies on elements of Hungarian folk music (modes, structures, rhythms) that Bartók habitually abstracted in his original compositions. The First Rhapsody for violin and piano (1928; arranged for violin and orchestra, 1929) reflects a somewhat different type of relationship to folk music. Its sources are instrumental melodies as opposed to folk songs; the melodies were mainly collected from Romanians as opposed to Hungarians; and, most important, he not only takes inspiration from their general characteristics, but actually quotes them. More precisely, the Rhapsody consists of tunes collected from village fiddlers in rural Transylvania that Bartók arranged in a manner suitable for concert performance. Such a work embodies two levels of transcription: first the notation of the original tunes, and then their arrangement as a piece of "art music."

With a few exceptions (e.g., Improvisations on Hungarian Peasant Songs) Bartók's concert arrangements of folk music tend to be among his most accessible works. Many of them are also pedagogical in nature. He originally intended them as a popularizing branch of his folk-music research. In the preface to their early folk-music publication *Hungarian Folk Songs* for voice and piano (1906), Bartók and Kodály described two ways of publishing folk songs, each with its own purpose: comprehensive dictionaries of folk songs for scientific analysis, and transcriptions of what they saw as the most beautiful songs with added accompaniments for the enjoyment of the general public.[1] The fact that the First Rhapsody for Violin differs from many of Bartók's arrangements of folk music in that it makes considerable technical demands on the performer reflects the relative virtuosity of instrumental dance music itself. The virtuosity of the First Rhapsody also suggests a connection between Bartók's arrangement of peasant dances and the Lisztian tradition of the Hungarian rhapsody. A popular showpiece, the First Rhapsody fulfills Bartók's original goal of generating enthusiasm for folk music among a wide audience and stands in contrast to the abstract complexity of "original" compositions like the Fourth String Quartet, written the same year.

As Bartók and Kodály emphasized, the accompaniment added to the folk tunes should be more than a neutral background for the melody; it should provide the melody with, as Kodály put it, "a proper musical attire . . . [that] must attempt to make up for the lost meadow and village."[2] In other words, Bartók and Kodály understood the act of transcription to be one of transplantation that challenges the arranger to re-create the feeling of the original environment with composerly additions. Thus, in Bartók's view, folk-music arrangements required much the same creativity as original composition.

Yet transcription is also appropriation. At the very least, notation and arrangement of peasant music appropriates an artifact from a rural oral tradition for an urban literate one. When a composer of a different nationality from the original peasant performer makes the transcription, he may be seen as committing cultural theft. This distinction is especially relevant in the case of the First Rhapsody because the majority of the tunes Bartók used were collected from Romanian peasants.[3]

Hungarian Composer

One of the most important documents pertaining to the issue of cultural appropriation is Bartók's letter to the Romanian writer Octavian Beu on 10 January 1931. In it Bartók gives a detailed response to a draft of a lecture Beu was preparing about him for the Romanian Radio. The date of Bartók's letter suggests that the radio program may have been intended as a fiftieth-birthday tribute to the composer, whose Hungarian birthplace (Nagyszentmiklós, or Sînnicolau Mare in Romanian) had become part of Romania with the border changes imposed by the Treaty of Trianon in 1920. Apparently Beu himself had engaged in an appropriation of his own by referring to Bartók as a Romanian composer *(compositorul român)*. It is unclear to what extent this characterization was designed to pave the way for a positive Romanian reception of Bartók's music. Beu seems to have touched a sensitive nerve, however, because Bartók reacted at some length, beginning with a vigorous defense of his Hungarian identity and the Hungarian nature of his work:

> [Re:] *"compositorul român."* My opinion is the following: I consider myself a Hungarian composer. Because some of my original works contain Rumanian folk music or melodies inspired by Rumanian folk music is just as little reason for calling me a Rumanian composer as it would be to regard Brahms, Schubert, and Debussy as Hungarian or Spanish composers because they have used Hungarian- or Spanish-style themes as the basis for original compositions.—You or other scholars—in my opinion—would be better served by ignoring these labels and confining yourself to remarking that "here and there, in this or that work, there are themes of Rumanian inspiration."—If your notion were correct, I could be called a "Slovak composer" with the same justification, and then I would be a composer of three nationalities!

Bartók went on to comment on the potential political interpretation of his use of the folk music of various peoples:

> As I'm being so frank, I should like to give you some idea of what I think about all this:
> My compositional work, just because it arises from three types of sources (Hungarian, Rumanian, Slovakian), might be regarded as the embodiment of the very concept of integrity [i.e., irredentism] so much emphasized in Hungary today. Of course, I do not write this for you to make it public; you will yourself beware of doing so, for such ideas are not for the Rumanian press. I only mention it as a possible point of view that I encountered about 10 years ago when I was attacked in the most violent manner by our chauvinists as a musical Scotus Viator.[4] My own idea, however—of which I have been fully conscious since I found myself as a composer—is the brotherhood of peoples, brotherhood in spite of all wars and conflicts. I try—to the best of my ability—to serve this idea in my music; therefore I don't reject any influence, be it Slovakian, Rumanian, Arabic or from any other source.[5]

Since the "concept of integrity" to which Bartók refers appears to be the post-Trianon revisionist idea that argued for the reestablishment of the unity of the Carpathian Basin under Hungarian leadership,[6] it is strange that he associates it with an attack on him by Hungarian chauvinists who had accused him of working to undermine Hungarian culture by studying Romanian music in Transylvania. These two contradictory perceptions of Bartók's work seem to have been united in his mind by the fact that they were both overtly political and crudely nationalistic. In contrast, by describing the mix of folk sources in his music as the embodiment of a Herderian or even Beethovenian vision of brotherhood ("alle Menschen werden Brüder") Bartók suggests that the integrity with which he himself associated his music represented a higher, more universal ideal than that expressed by national politics. Indeed, the phrase "brotherhood of peoples" has come to symbolize the idealism and humanity of Bartók's work—both in his compositions and in his approach to folk music.

Despite Bartók's emphasis on the brotherhood of peoples, he concludes his response to Beu by reaffirming the fundamentally Hungarian nature of his work: "Owing to my—let us say geographical—position it is the Hungarian source that is nearest to me, and therefore the Hungarian influence is the strongest. Whether my style—notwithstanding its various sources—has a Hungarian character or not (and that is the point)—is for others to judge, not for me. For my own part, I certainly feel that it has. For character and milieu must somehow harmonize with each other." Bartók's apparent inability to articulate the precise nature of his Hungarian orientation may reflect his reluctance to delve into a politically sensitive area. Because of the direct adaptation of specific tunes in his folk-music arrangements, Bartók seems to be more sensitive about the potential political interpretation of his treatment of his sources in these works than in the case of his more abstract "original" compositions. Evidence for this comes later in the same letter to Beu, when Bartók declines to provide a specific concordance between the melodies he uses in the two violin Rhapsodies and the nationalities of their origin.[7]

Bartók's letter thus challenges us with an implicit question: What makes Bartók's arrangement of non-Hungarian tunes characteristically Hungarian? The First Rhapsody for Violin, with its Romanian tunes, is an ideal piece with which to explore this question, so important to Bartók's self-identity as a composer. Because his involvement with Romanian folk music made Bartók vulnerable to attacks by both Hungarians and Romanians, the context necessary for interpreting the Rhapsody includes the political implications of his folk-music research and the controversies surrounding it. In short, a historically informed interpretation of the Rhapsody must take into consideration the subtleties of Bartók's peculiar blend of national pride and openness to many cultures at a time and place in which political conflicts encouraged a crudely reductive discourse about nationality and culture.

Folk Music and Purity

There is a tension in much of Bartók's writing between his desire to conduct folk-music research in a scientifically objective manner and his personal taste as a composer. It comes across most strikingly in Bartók's frequent use of the adjective "pure" in relation to folk music; for although Bartók was interested in the folk music of many cultures, he did not consider all types of folk music equally valuable. To Beu he explained that it was not nationality that made folk music a potential source for his compositions but its quality of being "clean, fresh, and healthy."[8] Indeed, although Bartók did not always express his notion of purity clearly, it seems that his governing principle was not nationality or ethnicity but musical style. Specifically, his insistence on purity reflected his objection to the influence of urban popular music on peasant music. He justified his dislike of popular music, which he variously labeled as "pseudo-folk" music, "urban folk music," or "the folk music of the educated classes in the city (that is, the popular art song),"[9] on the basis that it was a mixed or heterogeneous style. What disturbed him the most was the identification of these "amateur, pseudo-folk melodies with true peasant music." In Bartók's words, "The composers of the former usually possess a certain musical culture imported from the city, but more often than not they are amateurs, and their melodies are a combination of hackneyed city music and a certain exotic variation of their own folk music. As a result, despite the fact that they retain some traces of exoticism, such melodies are nevertheless much too vulgar to be of any essential value. And true folk music is always distinguished by absolute purity of style."[10]

Bartók's assessment of popular music as "vulgar" reflects a modernist aesthetic that equated stylistic purity with quality. It hardly appears coincidental that the folk music he singled out as most valuable or interesting (e.g., pentatonic old-style Hungarian melodies, the Romanian *hora lunga* with its lack of rigid structure, Dalmatian epics with parallel dissonances, and Bulgarian dance tunes in asymmetrical meters) were those types that could be used to justify his own modernist compositional tendencies.

Bartók's insistence that "genuine folk music" or "peasant music" (the latter a term he frequently but inconsistently used to describe the type of folk music he valued) was "pure" and thus homogeneous in style reflected his aesthetic judgment, but it also echoed Romantic views of the folk and folk creativity.[11] Bartók reasoned that the spontaneous creations of the peasants were of a stylistic homogeneity that reflected the peasant community. Thus, in his view, urban popular music or any music that was the conscious creation of an individual could not claim the same authenticity of communal expression:

> Genuine folk music, in its broader sense, contains melodies—those popular both now and in the past among the peasantry inhabiting a given geographical region—that are a spontaneous expression of the people's musical instinct.

In its more restricted sense, folk music is a separate type of melodic creativity that, by reason of its being a part of the peasant environment, reflects a certain uniform emotional pattern and has its own specific style. Even the simplest melodies, if they are not widespread among the peasantry and are sung only by individuals from that class, cannot be considered examples of folk music. Such music also does not encompass various patriotic songs, since these are learned only in school and are never a spontaneous expression of the peasants' collective musical instinct.[12]

Bartók saw the education of peasants as detrimental to the preservation of folk music because it encouraged them to imitate the higher classes and removed them from the natural state in which he felt that they instinctively expressed something of the essence of their community in music. Bartók's "neoclassical" observation that folk music was objective stemmed from his belief that it embodied the unconscious expression of a relatively large, primitive community, and as such was insulated from the subjective whim of the individual. This does not mean that he did not value variant renditions of tunes by individual peasants. Quite the contrary, he maintained that individual variation was a sign of the vitality of folk music, which in part explains the extraordinary amount of detail he included in his transcriptions intended for scientific use. At the same time he considered as representative of communal expression only those melodies whose basic structures corresponded to melodic types that he had determined through analysis of a very large number of melodies—hence Bartók's stipulation that a single melody, no matter how simple, could not constitute folk music. To put it differently, he believed that only when numerous individual performances converged into a homogeneous style did that style reflect the unique essence of a community.

COMPARATIVE FOLK-MUSIC RESEARCH

Bartók's opinion of the relative value of different types of folk music may have been elite and subjective, but it was not based on ethnic purity. Nor need the subjectivity of his personal taste imply that his scholarly conclusions about the age and purity of various repertories relied on quixotic or biased interpretations of his data. Still, his focus on disputed territories like Transylvania made his ethnographic work the subject of numerous attacks. With significant Romanian and Hungarian settlements, Transylvania was claimed both by Hungary, to which it had belonged since the Middle Ages, and by Romania, to which it was annexed after the conclusion of the First World War. Not surprisingly, the political tension between Hungary and Romania in the years surrounding Trianon made inevitable the insertion of discussions about the relative age of the folk music of Hungarians and Romanians into the more urgent discussion about the legitimacy of each nation's claim to Transylvania.

One of the conclusions that grew out of Bartók's work with Transylvanian materials was that the type of melody and style of performance associated with the "old-style" Hungarian folk songs had been brought to the Carpathian Basin by Magyar tribes around 896.[13] "Old-style" melodies were found most frequently among the Székely, a Hungarian people of Transylvania, but also in widely separated Hungarian communities throughout greater Hungary as well as among the Csángó, a Hungarian-speaking people of Moldavia who have preserved some of the oldest Hungarian folk traditions. Bartók believed it was highly unlikely that these communities, many of them very isolated, would have had communication with each other in their present locations. He therefore concluded that the "old-style" melodies represented a musical remnant of the culture that had belonged to the Magyars before they settled in East Central Europe. The fact that some of the folk songs of the Finno-Ugric Cheremiss people of the central-Volga region were similar to the "old-style" Hungarian melodies further strengthened Bartók's hypothesis that this musical style had its origins in territories that Hungarians had occupied before their European settlement. In asserting the ancient Asiatic roots of the old-style Hungarian melodies Bartók did for a time believe that these melodies expressed a Finno-Ugric essence. When it was discovered that the Cheremiss language revealed the influence of the Turks and northern Tatars, however, he revised his belief and hypothesized instead that the similarities between the Cheremiss and Hungarian materials could be traced to a common Turco-Tatar influence.[14] This revision did not, however, alter his belief about the presettlement age of the "old-style" folk song.

The question of the provenance of the "old-style" melodies was particularly sensitive politically because melodies of this category were also found in some Romanian peasant communities in Transylvania. Since there was no evidence of "old-style" melodies in Transylvanian regions in which Romanian villages appeared to be completely isolated from cultural interchange with the neighboring Hungarian population, Bartók concluded that Hungarians had indeed brought the "old-style" melodies to the region.[15] Because the Romanian melodies that corresponded to the "old-style" Hungarian melodies were a small fraction of the Romanian repertoire as a whole, Bartók by no means believed that all Romanian music of Transylvania exhibited a Hungarian influence. Nor did he believe that Hungarian folk music in general was older than Romanian folk music. He considered the Romanian *hora lunga* melodies, for instance, to be very ancient. In fine, given the data available to him and the existing state of comparative folklore, there is no reason to doubt that Bartók was making his hypotheses in a scientifically responsible manner.

His scientific rigor did not, however, prevent Bartók from taking particular pride in Hungarian folk culture. He stated in his essay "Hungarian Folk Music and the Folk Music of Neighboring Peoples" (1934) that his discovery of specifically Hungarian musical styles was a triumphant refutation of the disparaging assumption that "the Hungarian village possessed no genuine characteristic music, and that the existing music was borrowed from the Slavs or Romanians." His comparative research "attempted to refute these theses with the greatest possible objectivity."[16] This essay, originally published as a pamphlet of the series *Népszerű zenefüzetek* (Popular Music Notebooks), seems to have been intended for a more general readership than that of the specialized musical or anthropological journals in which Bartók usually published articles on folk music. The body of the essay is a detailed, dense description of the folk music of the peoples of the Carpathian Basin. The conclusion, however, printed in boldface (in italics below), cuts to the chase. Expressing pride in the strength and integrity of Hungarian folk music, it appears to lend support to the prospect that scientific research might legitimately serve political ends. Beginning with a declaration of objectivity, Bartók states:

> I would have published the results of my research even if they had not been in our favor. It is only more pleasant to establish undeniably that the obtained results could hardly have been more favorable. It is possible that future research may modify a few of my findings. But I am fully convinced that I have not been mistaken insofar as the main points of the problem are concerned. And they can be summarized, in my opinion, as follows: *The old and new melodies of the Hungarian villages constitute a specifically Hungarian spiritual treasure that we have not borrowed from our present-day neighbors; on the contrary, it is we who have given it to them.*[17]

That Bartók knew that his almost childish pride had potentially serious political implications is also suggested by an earlier passage in the essay, in which he deftly encourages his readers to use his findings for political purposes. Trying to find answers to the questions of why the music of some Romanian regions is so diverse, or why certain Romanian regions have intimate musical relationships with neighboring Hungarian regions while others "stubbornly seclude themselves behind their frontiers," he speculates:

> Would not all this have some relationship with the time and circumstances surrounding the settlement of this or that people? By means of the findings gained through folklore research, would we not be able to restore certain

questionable issues or support certain arguments? Or, furthermore, if it is a matter of questions already resolved, would not these musical findings confirm the result? Although I cannot answer these questions, I bring them forward to demonstrate that comparative folklore research is not an abstract and useless branch of science, as perhaps thought by many people, but is able to collaborate perfectly with the other, more practical scientific branches and even exert an influence on the solution of problems which are of more interest to the public at large.[18]

Although coyly unspecific about the nature of "certain questions" and "problems" that would hold the interest of the public at large, Bartók knew that his words would be read in the context of interwar Hungary's political grievances. His hints were more than sufficient to evoke that subtext and suggest a specific political interpretation of his scientific findings.

Why does Bartók flirt so explicitly with politics here, while, as his letter to Beu implies, he more often kept aloof from such concerns? We have no definitive answer, but the date of this essay suggests that he may have sought to attract official support for his project of preparing a large collection of Hungarian folk songs for publication. Long-awaited approval for Bartók's transfer from his position as professor of piano at the Music Academy to one of folk-music researcher at the Academy of Sciences, both state-funded institutions, came in June 1934, approximately three months after the publication of his pamphlet.[19] These events also coincided with a new government initiative to support Hungarian culture known as the "New Spiritual Front" (*Új szellemi front*) instigated by Prime Minister Gyula Gömbös (1886–1936). The timing of these events suggests that, "objective research" notwithstanding, Bartók was well aware of the political implications of his work. He could not have been surprised to find himself a target of attack from political chauvinists in both Hungary and Romania.

ATTACKS FROM THE EAST, MISUNDERSTANDING AT HOME

For Bartók, collecting folk music required a thick skin. Not only were conditions often harsh, but the peasants were suspicious of anyone in city clothes. They suspected a hoax—"perhaps another tax, this one on music."[20] But the suspicions Bartók encountered in the countryside were refreshing in comparison with the disapproval or indifference with which his folk-music research tended to be greeted by musicians in Budapest. (Bartók and Kodály's 1906 edition of *Hungarian Folk Songs*, printed at their own expense and intended to generate popular enthusiasm for their work, took thirty years to sell out a modest first printing of five hundred copies.)[21] More scientific publications of his folk-music research often led to more direct criticism. The fraught year 1914 witnessed the first of what would become a series of public censures from Hungarians and Romanians alike.

Despite the support for his work by the Romanian Academy of Sciences, which published Bartók's *Cântece populare românești din comitatul bihor (Ungaria)* (Romanian Folk Songs from the Bihar District [Hungary]) in 1913, he noted that a review of the volume in the Romanian ethnographical journal *Sezătoarea* (Society) branded it a work of "no value whatsoever." In his response to the review, Bartók repudiated what he saw as "the charge behind every line of the critic, namely, that the collector has erroneously notated the melodies,"[22] by explaining in detail the method of collection of the songs and the reasoning behind his notation. Left unmentioned, however, was the more significant charge of cultural imperialism. In the estimation of the critic, Bartók's notations represented "Hungarianized" versions of Romanian melodies. It is important to note that in his defense Bartók avoided discussion of the many reciprocal influences in the music of the various peoples of the ethnically heterogeneous region. Instead he simply reported the statistical prevalence of dotted rhythms: "The reviewer thinks that, in all probability, the rhythms ♫♩ or ♫♩ are Hungarian peculiarities; but he is mistaken, because to a large extent they can be met with in Slovakian folk music too. Furthermore, ninety percent of the Maramureș [another Transylvanian region] people's melodies are in the same 'dance rhythm.'"[23] Behind the neutral statistic, however, lurked Bartók's belief, stated in "Hungarian Folk Music and the Folk Music of Neighboring People," that melodies with dotted rhythm among the Slovaks were borrowings from the repertory of Hungarian "new-style" melodies.[24]

As would remain the case after World War I, Hungarians were also suspicious of Bartók's keen interest in what was then Hungary's largest ethnic minority. Although no written account of the criticism has come to light, we know from Bartók's discussion of it in 1920 that the 1914 publication of another study, "A Hunyadi román nép zenedialektusa" (The Dialect of the Folk Music of the Romanians of Hunedoara) in the Hungarian journal *Ethnographia*, prompted an attack on the composer at a meeting of the Hungarian Ethnographic Society in February 1914.[25] Apparently the society blamed Bartók for working in the service of Romanian interests, the opposite transgression from the one his Romanian critics had noted in the Bihar collection.

Before the First World War, any opposition Bartók encountered to his research in comparative folk music was confined to scientific forums in accordance with the limited appeal of the work. After the war, however, Bartók's research (even in the case of an exact translation of a prewar article) led to attacks in the popular press. On 19 May 1920, in the heated atmosphere that prevailed on the eve of the Treaty of Trianon (4 June 1920), Bartók was confronted with an editorial in *Nemzeti Újság* (National News) entitled "Bartók Béla az oláh kultúra szolgálatában" (Béla Bartók in the Service of Romanian Culture) signed by a Dr. Elemér Sereghy.[26] Two days later a defense of Bartók's work appeared in the newspaper *Új Nemzedék* (New Generation), this one signed anonymously by "a teacher of the Music Academy."[27] Two more attacks followed: Dr. Sereghy reiterated his position in *Új Nemzedék* on 23 May; and on 25 May the violinist and composer Jenő Hubay, who had recently been appointed director of the Music Academy following the change in administration concomitant with the ousting of the short-lived communist regime, added the weight of his official prestige to the attack. Bartók, invoking his right under Hungarian law to a published response, refuted the attacks on 26 May.[28] The press coverage of the affair ended two days later with an article that, much to Bartók's relief, included a statement of support for him by the Hungarian Geographical Society, which had convened specially to discuss the matter, and a communication from Director Hubay slightly softening his position.[29]

The immediate excuse for turning what had been considered by some to be a misguided interest in one of Hungary's minority populations in the prewar period into accusations tantamount to cultural treason was the March 1920 publication of Bartók's "Der Musikdialekt der Rumänen von Hunyad" in the *Zeitschrift für Musikwissenschaft*. This was a translation of the article from *Ethnographia* that had already caused a fuss within the Ethnographic Society in 1914. The angle the attacks now took declared Bartók's study unscientific in its acknowledgment of the integrity of Romanian music in Transylvania. This was again a misinterpretation of the study, which dealt only with Romanian villages in one small section of Transylvania, but its publication on the eve of the Treaty of Trianon was taken as proof of a lack of patriotism.

Bartók, like virtually all Hungarians and most neutral observers, opposed the extremity of the measures imposed by the treaty. Ignoring the political motivation of the attack, Bartók refuted Sereghy's and Hubay's assertion that he considered the counties in which he conducted research to be 100 percent culturally Romanian:

> My article deals with the area of a musical dialect, not a cultural one. It should be understood that Ugocsa is intended to refer to the eight Romanian-inhabited villages there, Maramureș to that part of it inhabited by Romanians, and so forth. It is a sheer impossibility in such a short article to deliberately impart otherwise well-known statistical data on language areas.

Similarly, refuting the statement that "[Bartók] intends to trace back all our Transylvanian tunes to Romanian origin," the composer simply refers to the facts presented in his article:

> My article reads: "We also have to mention a third area of musical dialect: the area of the 'Hungarian type' adjacent to the Székely [Transylvanian Hungarian] territory, which shows strong Székely influence . . ." (a further assertion of the cultural superiority of the Székely, that is, Hungarians, in relation to the Romanians).

Nor is this the only time that Bartók refers to Hungarian cultural superiority in the course of his self-defense. Regarding the allegedly unpatriotic timing of the article, he points out its prior publication in Hungary, but then proceeds to counter Hubay's and Sereghy's ultranationalism with a rhetoric that almost equals theirs in chauvinism:

> As to the charge that the publication of the article abroad "is now extremely untimely, nay, unfortunate," I declare that my opinion is diametrically opposed. Its publication now is downright desirable, because it makes evident the cultural superiority of the Hungarians. I cite the following from my article: "From among the peoples of our country (that is, Hungary) the Romanians are the ones who have conserved in a relatively intact form the ancient condition of the folk music." Anyone who is not completely illiterate in the science of ethnography knows that the survival of such "ancient conditions" is possible only on a low cultural level. The article also makes it quite plain that not a single Romanian has appeared who is suitable for the systematic study of Romanian folk music: a Hungarian had to undertake this scientific research, which is extremely important from the Hungarian viewpoint.—Is this not proof of our cultural superiority?[30]

In all of Bartók's mature writings this is the only point at which he yields so crudely to the rhetoric of his opponents. It is therefore significant to note that the distinction he makes between Romanian cultural areas and musical dialects, and, more importantly, the idea that his research in itself demonstrates Hungarian superiority, are both taken over almost verbatim from the anonymous article that was published in his defense on 21 May:

> The third and most serious accusation is that Bartók declares that Máramaros [Hungarian spelling of Maramureş], Ugocsa, etc., are Romanian cultural territories. I have Bartók's article in hand and he did not say this. . . . He speaks about music dialect and nothing else. . . .
>
> The fact that folk music is collected in Transylvania while it is not collected in Romania only proves our cultural superiority, so well, that I would like to present this data to the Peace Conference [Trianon].[31]

Bartók's decision to publish the article in the *Zeitschrift für Musik-wissenschaft* may have had something to do with his dissatisfaction with Hungary, but not at all in the sense imagined by his attackers. In the academic year 1919–20 Bartók was on leave from the Music Academy and was devoting the greater part of his energies to folk-music research. With practically no prospects for receiving support for publication in postwar Hungary even for his Hungarian material, he seriously considered removing his whole project to neutral and more affluent ground, to Germany or even to the United States (although the latter seems to have been more a joking speculation than a real consideration at the time). In hopes of finding a research position, he traveled to Berlin in March 1920 to meet with Erich von Hornbostel (1877–1935), a pioneer in ethnomusicology and director of the Berlin Phonogramm-Archiv.[32] Severely disappointed that Hornbostel had no position for him, Bartók ultimately decided to remain in Hungary in part because the Hungarian Academy of Sciences would not grant him permission to transport the recordings of folk music in their possession to Germany. He still harbored hopes, moreover, of being able to continue collecting expeditions in regions east of Hungary.[33]

Although the German trip did not result in a post for Bartók, it did secure for him the benefit of several high-paying (by Hungarian standards) commissions for articles on folk music.[34] If the German publication of the article that caused the uproar in Budapest served an agenda beyond that of "pure science," it appears to have been Bartók's attempt to forge connections with an international musicological community that he hoped would lend material support to his folk-music publications. Making these connections and finding this support were his main preoccupations during his year of leave from teaching.

In the decade following the explosion of unwanted publicity at the end of May 1920, Bartók's folk-music activities generated more neglect than debate in the Hungarian and Romanian press. Despite the cessation of hostilities over the greater part of the 1920s, there is reason to believe that Bartók was far from sanguine about his position and prospects. Evidence of his unease is his decision sometime between 1922 and 1924 to discontinue his practice of including information in his own published compositions regarding the provenance of the melodies used in his folk-music arrangements. Although Romanian attacks on Bartók had abated since 1914, Bartók was right to be discreet. His situation vis-à-vis Romania became increasingly untenable beginning in 1931.

The immediate occasion for the renewal of political intrigue from Romania was Bartók's fiftieth birthday (25 March 1931). At the instigation of Radu Urlateanu, a Romanian conductor who led an orchestra in Temesvár/Timişoara, a formerly Hungarian city, the Romanian Society of Composers agreed to a celebration consisting of three concerts and a dedication of a plaque on the house where Bartók was born. The concerts were to take place in Bucharest, Temesvár/Timişoara, and Arad—the last two being the Romanian cities closest to Bartók's birthplace. The Romanian Society of Composers requested Bartók's participation in the concerts and his presence at the dedication. Bartók responded to the request by gladly accepting participation in the first two of the concerts—a prior engagement forced him to decline the third—but asked that there be no dedication, because, in his words, "I don't like the idea of people being forced to contribute money to a memorial plaque."[35] After receiving assurances that the expense was minimal and that the money had already been collected, Bartók agreed to attend the dedication on the condition that the plaque be written in Hungarian as well as Romanian. Following this communication the planned concerts were first postponed a month, apparently without explanation, and later canceled by default—the Romanians simply never sent Bartók or his agent more details.[36] No more mention seems to have been made regarding the dedication ceremony.

The Hungarian press, characteristically trying to push the subtlety of Bartók's position into the stark black and white of aggressive nationalism, reported incorrectly that he had agreed to participate in the dedication ceremony only on the condition that "they erect a Hungarian-language plaque in place of the planned Romanian one."[37] Apparently Bartók's constant caution was justified in regard not only to the Romanian press but to the Hungarian as well.

There was even a third group that exploited Bartók for its political purposes. Many Hungarians in Transylvania were especially keen on representing Bartók as a quasi "high priest" of Hungarian ethnic purity. Despite the fact that Bartók's recital in Kolozsvár/Cluj on 15 December 1933 included his *Román népi táncok* (Romanian Folk Dances), the review of it in the Hungarian-language *Ellenzék* (Opposition) traced Bartók's compositional achievements exclusively to his interest in pure Hungarian folk music: "The arrangement of pure Hungarian folk music begins with Bartók and this beginning immediately rises to the purest artistic heights. . . . The classically pure performance, like the value of the works performed, deeply affected the audience's understanding."[38] Of the "works performed" the reviewer omitted to list *Romanian Folk Dances*.

The particularly sensitive position Bartók and his music occupied in Transylvania becomes especially clear in a sequel to the 1931 "birth-house affair" at the end of February 1934. This event is especially notable for demonstrating the contrast between Bartók's treatment in Bucharest and in Transylvania. The primary motivation for his trip to Romania at this time was an opportunity to study a collection of some thirty-five hundred folk songs from pre-Trianon Romania housed at the headquarters of the Society for Romanian Composers in Bucharest. In addition to what Bartók describes as six days of "round-the-clock study,"[39] he played a highly publicized and warmly received recital, broadcast live on Romanian Radio, and gave a lecture in French on the influence of peasant music on modern music. His cordial reception in Bucharest included a front-page newspaper article that not only emphasized Bartók's stature as a scientist but also his political neutrality: "[Bartók is] a serious scholar who acknowledges that the sons of other races besides his own also have a culture that is worth studying with great intensity. This is fortunate and it has special importance for the life of our country's minority [Hungarians] that such steps are being taken by the Hungarians when the Saxons from Germany are being commanded to avoid any rapprochement."[40] Following the visit to Bucharest, Bartók was again to have traveled to Nagyszentmiklós/Sînnicolau Mare for the dedication of a plaque to be attached to his birthplace, this time in celebration of his twenty-five years of research of Romanian folk music. The following day he was scheduled to perform with the orchestra in Temesvár/Timişoara. As in 1931, plans for these events were initiated by the conductor Radu Urleteanu and were canceled under suspicious circumstances.

The "official explanation" for the cancellation (termed "postponement") was the "resignation of Urleteanu and many members of his orchestra."[41] In fact, Urleteanu had been fired after having led a performance of Kodály's *Psalmus hungaricus* earlier that month. The same members of the Transylvanian section of the Romanian Society of Composers responsible for firing Urleteanu managed to cancel all events related to Bartók in Transylvania. Although it is unclear precisely what the composer knew of the specifics, he clearly understood that the change in plans was the result of chauvinistic political intrigue.[42] It is unlikely, however, that he knew the details of Urleteanu's fate. Following his dismissal, Urleteanu committed suicide after having been stripped of his passport in the process of applying for emigration to the Soviet Union.[43]

Considering the increasing tension between Romania and Hungary in the years before World War II, it is hardly surprising that the next attack on Bartók, again spearheaded by a Transylvanian Romanian, surpassed earlier ones in its overt political motivation. When Bartók arrived in Temesvár/Timişoara for a recital with violinist Ede Zathureczky on 2 May 1936, he was greeted with a flurry of unwanted publicity including newspaper reports of demonstrations against him and an article in *Frucea*, a Romanian art journal, demanding that he publicly declare "whether or not he is a friend of Romanian folk music before stepping onto the stage at his upcoming concert."[44]

The material used against Bartók in Temesvár/Timişoara in late April and early May was drawn from a February 1936 article by Corlian Petranu, a professor of art history in Kolozsvár/Cluj.[45] Petranu claimed that although Bartók's prewar publications had been neutral, those following the war were made explicitly in the interest of irredentist revisionism with the specific aim of reclaiming Transylvania. Among Petranu's examples of the composer's revisionist stance was "Der Musikdialekt der Rumänen von Hunyad"—the same study that had already been used against him by Hungarians in 1914 and 1920. Petranu's article required no reading between the lines. What had been a political subtext in the Romanian critique of Bartók in 1914 was now brought to center stage, while he was promoted from inept researcher to an agent of official Hungarian policy: "In Hungary scientific truth is not an end in itself, but it must serve as a redeemer of old [pre-Trianon] Hungary. Bartók could not resist this political pressure, and it is very typical that he discovered Hungarian influence on Romanian music [only] after 1918. . . . In his publications, revisionist Bartók does not ask overtly for the reannexation of Transylvania to Hungary, but by emphasizing Hungarian elements in Romanian folk music he provides weapons for revisionism."[46]

Although Petranu's article included an easily refuted attack on Bartók's scientific method, what is most important for our present purposes is that by painting Bartók as an accomplice of official Hungarian irredentism, Petranu misrepresented the status and symbolic function of the composer's work in Hungary. For although the amateur folk-music activities of the paramilitary *cserkész* (Hungarian Boy Scouts) would indeed take on an aggressive nationalist function starting in 1939, in 1936 Bartók's and Kodály's folk-music research was still associated with a liberal, progressive stance and had not yet been co-opted to serve ultranationalist aims.[47]

FOLK-MUSIC RESEARCH IN HUNGARY

In Hungary, folk-music research, along with Bartók, its most famous practitioner, was still associated with a liberal and progressive intellectual movement that represented the political antithesis of the Horthy government's policies. At the time of Petranu's article (1936) the music that served the interests of irredentism was not peasant music but *magyar nóta*, the music of coffee-house "Gypsy orchestras," the style of which had represented Hungarian nationalism since the early nineteenth century. The association of "Gypsy music" and irredentism is made explicit in the words of Emil Haraszti, a music critic for whom Bartók had a low regard: "Today we have a far greater need for Gypsy music than ever because the Gypsy is the agitator and soldier of Hungarian irredentism. . . . On the four corners of the earth the Hungarian sigh weeps on the Gypsy's dry wood [violin] and the Hungarian heart beats in his music. Just now [by accepting peasant music] should we deny the world of Hungarianness?"[48] Although, as will be shown in the next chapter, Bartók did take an accessible turn that rebuilt bridges with *verbunkos* in the second half of the 1930s, Haraszti's fear that peasant music might supplant "Gypsy music" did not reflect the reality of Hungarian musical life.

For Hungarians at all familiar with Bartók's folk-music activity, the main issue was not Bartók's legitimizing Hungary's claim to Transylvania, but his elitism vis-à-vis Hungarian popular music. In his promotion of peasant music they saw a desire to deny them the *magyar nóta*, and with it a piece of Hungary's noble heritage and imperial past. The perceived dual threat of peasant music and modernism to the *magyar nóta* can be seen in a response to a radio program on the Hungarian folk song that Bartók broadcast in 1933. A writer for *Rádió Újság* (Radio News) complained: "Why, when he searches for the origin of the *magyar nóta* does Béla Bartók conduct research with the folk of [peasant] origin and why not with the descendants of the old noble families. . . . Bartók does a bad thing by claiming his disfigured fragments [of folk song] to be ancient *magyar nóta* and by introducing them abroad, especially in his ultramodern arrangements."[49] Peasant music, at least in association with Bartók, meant musical modernism, which in turn was associated with political liberalism in Hungary between the two world wars. The so-called Greguss affair bears further witness to these associations.

Bartók was awarded the Greguss Prize on 29 December 1935 by the Kisfaludy Society, a literary society constituted largely of men of aristocratic heritage that gave awards in several areas of creativity every six years. The previous three compositions chosen for the music award demonstrate the society's conservative bent: Bartók's former attacker Jenő Hubay's Symphony, 1917; Árpád Szendy's *Helikon Suite*, 1923; and Ernő Dohnányi's *Ruralia hungarica*, 1929. In 1935 the members of the society reached back thirty years to find a composition of Bartók's that was conservative enough for their tastes—the First Suite for Orchestra (1905), a work without a trace of peasant music. Bartók's letter refusing the award expresses offense at the society's tacit censure of the last three decades of his composing activity. The refusal was published on 3 January 1936 in *Népszava* (People's Word), the newspaper of the Social Democrats. Bartók's caustic closing lines express both a wounded pride and the extent of the divide he saw between his mission and the values of the society: "And lastly I take the liberty of declaring that I do not wish to accept the Greguss Medal, neither at this time, nor in the future, neither during my lifetime, nor after my death."[50] Bartók's perception of the gulf between his work and the ideals of the Kisfaludy Society seems to have been justified not only by the Greguss affair but also by a speech given on 11 November 1935 by István Karácsonyi, one of the society's members:

> Since the death of Wagner and Liszt we do not see anywhere a genius who, with the magic of his genius, would produce something new, epoch-making and enduring. It seems that the art of music has also become obsessed with technique. Where the role of the heart and soul is essential, there it is evident that the man of today is cold, spiritually lacking and conceited. . . . Modern composers, who without soul and heart already long ago left the true path of music with atonality, that is, with the musical denial of God, they arrived at musical Bolshevism. One must look on the convinced moderns with pity because they are disturbed. The cheaters who want to make everything Bolshevist, who call it progress when they destroy everything that we call progress over the centuries, these people must be mercilessly struck down and made harmless. The former into an insane asylum, the cheaters into prison, but neither should be allowed into a concert hall or theater.[51]

For the time being, then, Hungarians within Hungary's borders took Bartók's interest in folk music to be emblematic of his modernity, not of a desire to revert to a pre–World War I status quo.

The First Rhapsody: Withheld Sources

The First Rhapsody is a perfect example of how Bartók, a believer in "pure sources," incorporated elements of Romanian and Hungarian folk styles, the peasant variant of the Gypsy *verbunkos,* and the cimbalom, an urbanized folk instrument, to create a virtuoso art-music evocation of an intact, homogeneous peasant culture. The most politically charged part of this mixture was Bartók's emphasis on the Hungarian elements of the original Romanian tunes. No wonder he had become unwilling to specify his sources.

A chronological examination of all of Bartók's folk-music transcriptions and arrangements (table 4) demonstrates that through the publication of

TABLE 4. Bartók's Folk-Music Transcriptions and Arrangements

Date/Publication	Title	Forces	Source Information Given	Observations
1904/1905 *Magyar Lant* (Hungarian Lute)	*Székely Folk Song*	Voice and piano	Year and place of collection at end of song	Rhythmic changes; prelude and postlude added
1904–5/1906 Bartók and Kodály's private subscription release; series planned	*Hungarian Folk Songs* (I)	Voice and piano	Name of collector, place of collection; notes on performance; notes on individual songs	Introductory essay by Kodály explaining educational function of volume; piano follows melodies exactly
1906–7/unpub.[a]	*Hungarian Folk Songs* (II)			No. 2 = no. 3 of *Twenty Hungarian Folk Songs*; no. 3 = no. 8 of *Eight Hungarian Folk Songs*; no. 5 = *For Children* II, no. 28; no. 10 = *For Children* I, no. 17
c. 1907/unpub.[a]	*Two Hungarian Folk Songs*	Voice and piano		Melody of no. 1 used for no. 1 of *Transylvanian Folk Songs for Men's Chorus*; no. 2 reproduced in *DocB* 4, 145–47
1907/unpub.[a]	*From Gyergyó*	Recorder and piano		
1907/1910, Rozsnyai Károly	*Three Hungarian Folk Songs from Csík*	Piano solo	Footnotes indicate place of collection, performer, and instrument	Arrangement of *From Gyergyó*; ornaments written out in introduction
c. 1907/unpub.[a]	*Four Slovak Folk Songs*	Voice and piano	Folk text written over or under melody	No. 1 = *For Children* III, no. 11; no. 3 = *For Children* IV, no. 43
1908/1909, Rozsnyai Károly	*Fourteen Bagatelles*, op. 6, nos. 4 and 5	Piano solo		

Date/Publisher	Title	Medium	Description	Notes
1908/1908, Rozsnyai Károly	Ten Easy Pieces, nos. 6 and 8	Piano solo	Titles give names of songs and identify them as folk songs	Pedagogical
1908–10/1910, 1912, Rozsnyai Károly	For Children	Piano solo	Notes indicate place of collection, words, type of song; for Slovak songs (vol. 2), texts are given in Slovak, German, and Hungarian	Pedagogical; no. 1 shows different phrasing for piano version and original folk song
1908–10/1912, Rozsnyai Károly	Seven Sketches, op. 9b/5	Piano solo	Title gives type of song; footnote gives place of collection	
c. 1909/unpub.[a]	Two Romanian Folk Songs	4-part women's chorus		
1910/1928, Universal	Four Old Hungarian Folk Songs	Men's chorus	Title page indicates region in which songs were collected	
c. 1912/unpub.[a]	Nine Romanian Folk Songs	Voice and piano		
1913/1913, Rózsavölgyi	Piano Method (nos. 44, 68, 95, 115, and 116)	Piano solo	Footnotes indicate folk songs except for no. 115, which is of ambiguous origin	Method = *First Term* 44 = 7 68 = 10 95 = 13 115 = 16 116 = 15
1913/1929, Rózsavölgyi	First Term at the Piano (nos. 7, 10, 13, 15, 16)	Piano solo	Title suggests that piece is of folk origin	See concordance above

(continued)

TABLE 4 *(continued)*

Date/ Publication	Title	Forces	Source Information Given	Observations
1915/1918, Universal	*Romanian Christmas Songs* (Colindas)	Piano solo	Index at beginning of volume prints original songs (music and text) and lists place of collection	Appendix includes arrangements for concert performance
1915/1918, Universal	*Romanian Folk Dances*	Piano solo	Titles give names of dances in German, Hungarian, and Romanian; footnote indicates place of collection	No. 4 is a fast dance in the folk original
1915/1919, Rózsavölgyi	*Sonatina*	Piano solo	Footnote indicates type of song, place of collection, and publication in Bartók's collections	Mvt. 1 collected from bagpiper, Mvts. 2 and 3 from violinist
1916?/unpub.[a]	Slovak Folk Song	Voice and piano		
c. 1916/1924, Universal	*Four Slovak Folk Songs*	Chorus and piano	After title page, lists title in Slovak and Hungarian and place of collection	Text in Hungarian
1907, 1917/1922, Universal	*Eight Hungarian Folk Songs*	Voice and piano	None	
1917/1918, Universal	Slovak Folk Songs	4-part men's chorus	None	
1914, 1918/1920, Universal	*Fifteen Hungarian Peasant Songs*	Piano solo	Index at beginning of volume prints songs (texts and music), place, and year of collection	

Date & Publisher	Title	Medium	Indication of folk origin	Comments
1914, 1918/1942, Boosey & Hawkes	*Three Hungarian Folk Tunes*	Piano solo		Originally intended as part of *Fifteen Hungarian Peasant Songs*
1920/1922, Universal	*Improvisations on Hungarian Peasant Songs*	Piano solo	In front of volume, index indicates songs (music and text), place, and year of collection	
1924/1927, Universal	*Village Scenes*	Voice and piano	None	Arrangement of three mvts. for 4 or 8 women's voices and orch., 1926
1916, 1927/1930, Universal	*Three Rondos on Folk Tunes*	Piano solo	None	Based on Slovak songs
1928/1929, Universal	Rhapsody No. 1	Violin and piano/orch.	Subtitled *Folk Dances*	Based on Romanian and Hungarian violin tunes
1928/1929, Universal	Rhapsody No. 2	Violin and piano/orch.	Subtitled *Folk Dances*	Based on Romanian, Hungarian, and Ruthenian violin tunes
1929/1932, Universal	*Twenty Hungarian Folk Songs*	Voice and piano	Title is only indication of folk origin	
1930/1932, Universal	*Hungarian Folk Songs*	Chorus	Title is only indication of folk origin	
1931/1933, Universal	*Fourty-four Duos*	2 violins	Introduction states that all but two pieces are based on peasant melodies	Seven pieces of this set published by Schott in 1932
1932/1938, Magyar Kórus	*Székely Folk Songs*	6-part men's chorus	Title is only indication of folk origin	
1926, 1932–39/1940, Boosey & Hawkes	*Mikrokosmos*	Piano solo	Titles of nos. 74, 95, 112, and 127 are only indication of folk origin	

a "Unpub." indicates that the work was unpublished during Bartók's lifetime.

Four Slovak Folk Songs in 1924, Bartók consistently documented the precise folk sources of his melodies. The practice began with his first folk-song arrangement, a Romantic setting of "Piros Alma" (Red Apple) published by the journal *Magyar Lant* (Hungarian Lute) in 1905 and continued in publications by all of Bartók's publishers through 1924: Rozsnyai, Rózsavölgyi, and Universal Edition. In each case Bartók listed source information such as the date and location of the collection much as he did in his folk-music collections. Indeed, Bartók and Kodály considered their folk-music arrangements different from their scholarly collections only in that they were not comprehensive and included accompaniments necessary to "dress up" the tunes for city audiences. "As for the authenticity of the melodies," Bartók and Kodály declared, "the songs of the popular edition should not be second to those of the [scholarly] one."[52] Like the Ph.D. that lends weight to Kodály's signature at the end of the preface to *Hungarian Folk Songs* (1906), Bartók's folk-music arrangements proudly display their badges of authenticity until the 1927 publication of *Village Scenes*.

The publication of both violin Rhapsodies with no more hint of their origins than that provided by the generic subtitle *Folk Dances* was thus a deliberate withholding on Bartók's part. When asked directly by Beu about the sources for the violin Rhapsodies, Bartók answered: "The two Rhapsodies contain folk melodies from various sources. I intentionally did not indicate any source here [in a previous letter], so I restrict myself to saying to you that No. 1 uses Romanian and Hungarian melodies, No. 2 Romanian, Hungarian, and Ruthenian."[53] It is clear from this comment that even when Bartók provided information regarding the folk sources for the Rhapsodies in response to direct questioning, he withheld concordances between specific tunes and the regions of their origin. A detailed examination of the first theme of the First Rhapsody suggests reasons for Bartók's reticence.

NATIONAL AMBIGUITY: THE THEME OF THE FIRST RHAPSODY

Bartók collected the tune he used to open the First Rhapsody from a twenty-two-year-old Romanian violinist in the Romanian-speaking village Râpa-de-Lus (Mures County, Transylvania) in March 1914.[54] The location of the collection is especially important to mention here, because Mures County ("Maros-Torda" in Hungarian) is a bastion of the Székelys, a Hungarian people whose traditions were especially well preserved at the time of Bartók's collecting. His conclusion in his comparative research that Székely music influenced the music of Romanians living in adjacent areas was one of the most controversial aspects of that research. In his study of Romanian instrumental music, Bartók lists the tune that serves as the main theme of the first part of the First Rhapsody as a "De ciuit," which he reports was described to him as a "calling to the dance."[55] This description suggests why he may have chosen the tune to open the series of dance melodies that make up the Rhapsody.

Yet the description also intimates a connection to the early recruiting function of the Hungarian *verbunkos*. Bartók described this tune as belonging to a set of melodies closely related to the "Hungarian *verbunkos* type."[56] This particular "De ciuit" is in fact a veritable textbook example of Bartók's category "(b) 1, 'heroic' melodies in $\frac{2}{4}$ time":

> The $\frac{2}{4}$-time melodies have a rather rugged rhythm as a result of the frequent use of ♫♫ patterns, instead of even sixteenth-note values, which give a marchlike "heroic" character to the pieces. As a compensation, longer values, as for instance ♩ or ♩, frequently occur at the end of melody sections. Groups made of thirty-second notes (♫♫) are occasionally substituted for pairs of sixteenth notes. . . . All this involves a comparatively slow tempo of about ♩ = 80. The scales have a minor third degree, sometimes augmented second intervals like Bb¹–C♯², and a sixth degree that may be major or minor.[57]

While Bartók allows that melodies conforming to this type may have originated from Ukrainian Kolomejka dance melodies, he goes on to suggest that the "presence of numerous rhythmic and melodic turns of Western European nineteenth-century style" point to another possible derivation, the *verbunkos*.[58] "Many melodies of the 'heroic' type are probably of Hungarian origin," Bartók asserts.[59]

The classification of the tune leads us to suspect that Bartók chose it specifically to tap into a Hungarian tradition. Indeed, a comparison of the tune collected in 1914 with the version used in Bartók's First Rhapsody confirms this suspicion. This comparison suggests that his usual "dressing up" of the melodies was not confined to "adding suitable accompaniments"—as Bartók and Kodály had claimed in 1906—but sometimes extended to alterations of the tunes themselves. Significantly, these alterations are intimately related to Bartók's understanding of the origin of the tunes. (Example 63 below details differences between the two versions of the melody.)[60]

The greatest change that Bartók makes in his arrangement of the "De ciuit" melody is to its tempo, which he slows down from ♩ = 80 to ♪ = 104 (♩ = 52). (This change is not likely to have been inspired by a variant rendition of the tune since he specifically includes the "De ciuit" in a class of dances with very little variation in tempo from village to village.)[61] Concomitantly with slowing the tempo, Bartók shifts the main beat from the quarter note to the eighth note by changing the meter from $\frac{2}{4}$ to $\frac{4}{8}$, a meter typical of the notated *verbunkos*. The alterations in tempo and meter serve to lend weight to the dotted rhythms and heighten the melody's "marchlike, 'heroic character.'"[62] In sum, Bartók's changes make the tune better fit his description of the "'heroic' type" and thus highlight its Hungarian *verbunkos* characteristics.[63]

Several rhythms and ornaments found only in Bartók's arrangement of the "De ciuit" tune complement the changes to meter and tempo. These include the accented pairs of a thirty-second note and a double-dotted-eighth note that begin the third and fourth lines of the tune (mm. 9 and 13) and the accented thirty-second-note triplet figure at the end of the first line (m. 4). The former is a tightening and regularization of the sixteenth-note dotted-eighth-note figure that occurs only once in the original (m. 13).[64] A similar tightening and exaggeration of this type of typically Hungarian *short*-long figure occurs on beat 1 of measure 11; a related transformation of an even sixteenth-note pattern into a dotted pattern occurs on the last eighth of the same measure. Although none of the resulting rhythmic figures are unknown in Romanian folk music, they are all typical of the Hungarian style as it was presented in nineteenth-century Hungarian art music.

The accented ornament in measure 4, however, has no basis in Romanian folk music. Again, this type of "hiccupped" pickup, described in Géza Molnár's book on Hungarian rhythm, is a typical *verbunkos* gesture. The identification of this figure with the *verbunkos* can be seen especially clearly if we compare the return of the melody at the end of the first part of the Rhapsody with a well-known *verbunkos* tune used by Kodály in his *Háry János* (1927) (see example 71b and c, p. 240).

Thus, Bartók's changes to the original folk melody emphasize the Hungarian quality of a tune of supposedly Hungarian origin but rendered by a Romanian musician in a Romanian-language area. In other words, in his setting of the melody Bartók returns the tune to its hypothetical roots in the Hungarian *verbunkos*.

In the context of post-Trianon tensions it is easy to see how Bartók, a Hungarian, could have been accused of musico-political aggression because of his reclamation of a tune preserved by generations of Romanian peasants, and thus how his arrangement of the tune could be interpreted as musical irredentism. This potential charge might well be one reason Bartók chose to withhold the concordance between the Rhapsodies' tunes and the regions of their origins from the Romanian Octavian Beu. Such reasoning is, however, dangerously incomplete, for it accepts the dialectical extremes of innocence and guilt imagined by Bartók's attackers, who reduced subtle theories of folk music to crude nationalistic extremes. Following a line of reasoning that directly translates Bartók's scientific or artistic endeavors into categories of political right and wrong means accepting notions of ethnic and musical purity that were antithetical to Bartók's own conception of folk music and its relationship to his original compositions.

PEASANT MUSIC ON STAGE

While many of the adaptations of the violin tunes for inclusion in the First Rhapsody point to Bartók's intention to "Magyarize" them, nearly all of the changes also can be understood in a musico-dramatic context, taking into account the difference between observing a folk custom on the concert stage and observing it on location. The one is by definition artificial and foreign to the other, for the stage is a place where the authentic and "natural" often looks dull and artificial. Conversely, "reality" can be conjured up on stage only through the illusions wrought by artifice, which distance the object of depiction from its natural state and thus render it fit for the stage. Bartók and Kodály had already recognized this much in 1906 when they stated that folk songs needed to be "dressed up" when taken out of their natural environment. In his review of both Rhapsodies for Violin, Hungarian composer and music critic Sándor Jemnitz (1890–1963) makes a similar observation: "These reconstructions [of peasant dance music] differ greatly from their original models in that they depart from the realm of absolute music and enter the realm of musical depiction: they give to the music the picture of the musicians and their surroundings—the original models have no need for this. The original models are already in place, thus they can sing freely, they do not have to illustrate anything to anyone."[65]

Bartók's ability to convey a peasant style owes a great deal not only to his knowledge of individual folk tunes and styles, but also to his general knowledge of folk traditions and his practice of making alterations to the tunes that enhanced their idiomatic typicality. Bartók's treatment of the multiple stops in the "De ciuit" melody in the violin part of the First Rhapsody (example 63) illustrates this practice. As he had written, "One tone of the comparatively frequent double stops is generally played on an open string. . . . Double stops, stopped deliberately on two strings of which neither is open, are comparatively rare."[66] In his arrangement of the "De ciuit" all multiple stops but the last one engage at least one open string. But of the eighteen places in which Bartók calls for playing on more than one string simultaneously, sixteen of them occur in places where there was in fact no multiple stop in the informant's rendition. This is consistent with a number of Bartók's adjustments of the original tune, because they exaggerate its

EXAMPLE 63. Comparison of "De ciuit" as notated in *Rumanian Folk Music*, Vol. 1 (melody No. 232) and arranged in the Rhapsody for Violin No. 1

Numbers indicate changes in the Rhapsody: (1) Slower tempo, in $\frac{4}{8}$; (2) Added double stops and grace notes; (3) Altered rhythm; (4) Added "folk" ornament; (5) Altered rhythm; (6) Added quadruple stop; (7) Deleted grace note; (8) Altered rhythm; (9) Added multiple stops; (10) Deleted grace note; (11) Introduction of dotted rhythms; (12) Note omitted; (13) Trill omitted; (14) Grace note omitted; (15) Double dotting of rhythm and omitted thirty-second notes; (16) Introduction of dotted rhythm; (17) Added multiple stops; (18) Double dotting of rhythm; (19) Added grace notes; (20) Added double stop and introduction of dotted rhythm

EXAMPLE 63 *(continued)*

rough, "folklike" quality. The execution of the multiple stops in his version is at the same time made more feasible than it would have been in the original because of his choice of tempo, itself an exaggeration of the original melody's relatively slow pulse. The irony of this example, however, is that the particular Romanian fiddler who played the tune for Bartók did not use open strings in either of the two double stops in his actual performance. In his transcription of the first of these double stops (octave Gs in m. 8) Bartók changes the lower note to an A, which engages the rougher sound of the open A string and results in the interval of a minor seventh, a central feature of his modern style ever since the famous last chord of the second movement of the Second Suite. In his transcription of the second of the original double stops, at the end, Bartók retains the original G. Thus, of the eighteen multiple stops in his version of the melody, the last is the least "folklike" according to his definition, but it is in fact the only one that actually conforms to the playing of the informant.

EXAMPLE 64. Comparison of "Cuiesdeanca" as notated in *Rumanian Folk Music,* Vol. 1 (No. 226) and arranged in the Rhapsody for Violin No. 1

A similar treatment of double stops to enhance the folk effect of the music by exaggeration occurs in Bartók's arrangement of the tune that serves as the basis for the last dance of the second part of the Rhapsody (example 64). In this setting Bartók transposes the tune down a perfect fourth to begin on E. The motivation for the transposition appears to be that it allows him to introduce a drone on the open E string. Again the result is an exaggeration of the melody's original spirit, a vigor bordering on hysteria used to accompany a dance called *joc feciorese* (dance for teenage boys), a name that suggests in turn a dance likely to have been used in recruiting.[67]

The transposition of the *joc feciorese* is a rare instance of a change of key that serves to enhance the "folk effect" of a melody. Many of Bartók's other transpositions of tunes seem to be born out of the difference between the practice of folk music and the requirements of art music. Of the six melodies that make up the First Rhapsody, only two, the opening "De ciuit" (in G) and the first tune of the fast section (in D), were collected by Bartók in keys other than A.[68] Therefore, he needed to transpose some of the tunes into keys rarely encountered in this folk tradition to achieve a tonal balance suitable for art music. The resulting settings at times require great virtuosity and imagination from the performer so as to give an illusion of folk simplicity.

A case in point is the opening tune of the second, faster part of the Rhapsody, the *friss.* In D major, the tonality of the original tune, it sits quite

EXAMPLE 65. "Judecata"

a. In D major, *Rumanian Folk Music,* Vol. 1 (No. 404)

b. In E major, from Rhapsody for Violin No. 1, with Joseph Szigeti's "folk-fiddler" fingering

c. In E major, with what Szigeti calls "citified" fingering

easily in first position on the A and E strings with three string crossings (example 65a). Although the tune is hardly virtuosic, in E-major transposition its performance involves several shifts and half positions uncommon in peasant fiddling (example 65c gives what violinist Joseph Szigeti regarded as a typical interpretation).[69] The idea of a typical "folk" realization of the tune in E major in the register given is, however, an oxymoron because this key is practically unknown in this folk repertoire. Joseph Szigeti, who premiered the First Rhapsody and to whom Bartók dedicated the work, comments on the problem in some detail: "Béla Bartók was in wholehearted agreement with me when I showed him that the dance theme of the second part ('Friss') of his first Rhapsody should be played mostly on two strings [example 65b], in order to bring out the 'folk-fiddler' quality of the tune, instead of with the normal, comfortable fingering [example 65c], which makes of it something citified, lacking in precisely the character he was aiming for and which is implicit in the whole movement."[70]

Although Szigeti's interpretation of the passage does manage to engage the genuine folk effect of the open string on the majority of the tune's As, the most remarkable feature of his suggested fingering is its extraordinary complexity. Szigeti's interpretation requires string crossings on every successive pitch save one, and demands decidedly unfolklike contortions including a counterintuitive jump to the lower G string in the midst of a scalar ascent (F♯ of beat 1). Yet Szigeti claims that in the hands of a master, "the unprejudiced listener will barely notice what contortions [are] necessary to play it my way because it will sound so right, so inevitable."[71]

Indeed, in his review of Szigeti's performance of the First Rhapsody in Budapest on 22 November 1929, Aladár Tóth supports Szigeti's claim when he states that "how Szigeti found this unprecedented ancient style of interpretation in this concert is a miracle of intuition."[72] Tóth's praise of the naturalness of Szigeti's interpretation is in fact a response to consummate modern technique. Just as Bartók makes peasant music suitable for the stage in the Rhapsodies by distancing the melodies from their folk models, animating these tunes in performance requires the ability to conjure an imaginary peasant performance through the contortions of virtuoso artifice. For Bartók, then, successful concert arrangement was far more than a transcription. A series of peasant dances for violin and piano or orchestra had to be transported far enough from their roots so as to create an illusion of a peasant ritual brilliant enough not to fade under the spotlight of the modern concert stage.

CIMBALOM AS SYMBOL

Bartók's decision in 1928 to turn to Transylvanian fiddle tunes he had collected before the First World War in his two Rhapsodies for Violin may have been inspired by Kodály's use of Transylvanian instrumental music in his popular *Dances of Marosszék* (1923?–27).[73] Likewise, Bartók's inclusion of a cimbalom in the orchestration of the First Rhapsody may owe a debt to Kodály's use of the instrument in *Háry János* (1926). Although only a small detail of orchestration, the cimbalom was taken as an important sign of the authentic peasant roots of the First Rhapsody by critics at Joseph Szigeti's first performance of Bartók's work in Hungary on 22 November 1929.[74] Paradoxically, this cimbalom was the innovation of the same Vencel József Schunda who invented the modern *tárogató* discussed in chapter 3. In the early 1870s Schunda transformed the traditional diatonic, dulcimer-like *kiscimbalom* (little cimbalom) into an instrument with four legs, a damper pedal, and an expanded, now chromatic, range (D–e³).[75] Schunda's cimbalom was a wildly popular instrument with a newfound orchestral viability stemming not only from the added chromatic strings and extended range, but also from the increased volume provided by an expanded sound box and from the steel strings as well as the damper pedal that allows for quick, clean changes of harmony—all innovations borrowed from the piano, a distant relative of the cimbalom with more urban savvy.[76]

Like the Wagner tuba, developed approximately two decades earlier, the invention of the modern cimbalom may have been inspired by an opera composer. Looking for nationalistic colors to add to his orchestral palette, Ferenc Erkel included a cimbalom in the pit for his opera *Bánk bán* in 1861. Within two decades Schunda's version of the instrument had become not only a staple of Erkel's orchestra, but a mainstay of urban Gypsy ensembles and a common parlor instrument. The legitimacy of the cimbalom as subject for serious "classical" study was officially recognized in 1890 with the establishment of a chair for cimbalom instruction at the Nemzeti Zenede, Budapest's oldest music conservatory.[77] At the same time, the cimbalom, initially imported to the city from the countryside, gradually spread back into rural areas, now in the urbanized form developed by Schunda for bourgeois entertainment. Despite its folk roots, Bartók includes it in the "art instrument" section of his 1924 dictionary entry "Instruments of Hungary."[78]

By incorporating the cimbalom in the orchestration of the First Rhapsody, Bartók takes advantage of the richness of the instrument's checkered genealogy. Although the cimbalom virtuoso Aladár Rácz (1886–1958) had inspired Stravinsky to write for the instrument in *Renard* (1915–16) and *Ragtime* (1917–18) before Bartók and Kodály turned to it in the 1920s, in 1929 Budapest critics accepted Bartók's use of the instrument variously as an authentic peasant artifact or a "Gypsy instrument."[79] Bartók's cimbalom part, some of which Aladár Rácz found unplayable, combines traditional accompanimental figures with a few innovative *pizzicati* that lend a mild modernist touch.[80] Indeed, Bartók could use the cimbalom in performance of the transformed fiddle tunes precisely because it had already been transformed into an art instrument in the course of its own analogous journey from field to stage. Without the innovations of an instrument maker drawn to Budapest at the time of Hungary's first major industrial expansion, the cimbalom would never have been able to play the key changes of Bartók's First Rhapsody (key changes, we should remember, that had little to do with the original fiddle tunes).

A part of the traditional role of the cimbalom is to partake in a continuo-like chordal accompaniment. The accompanying rhythm of the opening bars of the First Rhapsody is Bartók's orchestral realization of *esztam*, a traditional accompaniment used by both Gypsy and peasant musicians (see chapter 1).[81] His integration of the cimbalom into the orchestra with the aid of Schunda's innovations was thus a continuation of a Hungarian tradition; as the history of the cimbalom demonstrates, however, this was not a tradition of purity, but one of importation and change.

. . .

In choosing a group of Transylvanian fiddle tunes for his First Rhapsody for violin, Bartók believed he was tapping into the collective, ancient spirit of a diverse folk. This implication was not lost on Aladár Tóth, who wrote:

> [Bartók] selects melodies for a bouquet out of the flourishing of the folk music of the various ethnicities of old Hungary, he picks rhythmic and melodic flowers grown out of different temperaments and lets them blossom freely on the tone of the violin; but the orchestra—in which the cimbalom also plays a part—puts this blossoming into a miraculously deep perspective by quoting every single mysterious element of natural life in its ancient roots. The orchestra not only provides a congenial surrounding for the melodies, not only encircles the melodies' lives, but allows the melodies to burst forth.[82]

Tóth paints Bartók's work as a reincarnation of an idyllic pre-Trianon Hungary, in which Bartók's setting of the melodies allows a mixed bouquet of "interwoven" melodies (read: cultures) to burst into life. Central to this description is the word "ancient," which suggests that the origins of Bartók's work lie in a mythical paradise of the distant past—a time when the "mysterious element[s] of natural life" were an instinctive part of human expression.

When Bartók wrote to Octavian Beu that the sources for his peasant melodies must be "clean, fresh and healthy," the composer was referring to the purity vouchsafed by isolation from what he saw as the corruption of the city. In Bartók's view, isolated rural communities were places where healthy cultural interaction between different ethnic groups could take place. Indeed, as he acknowledged, for a culture to be healthy it needed foreign stimulus, but it also needed to be strong enough to absorb foreign elements into a unique and uniform style.[83] Similarly Bartók believed that his own style remained distinct (and distinctively Hungarian) no matter what the ethnic or regional sources of his melodies.[84] One of the distinctively Hungarian aspects of his work was his desire to unify music of different cultures in a Rhapsody—the traditional Hungarian art-music form par excellence—much as the peasants of the Carpathian Basin had lived together in harmony in the days of greater Hungary. Bartók seems to achieve a similar effect in his *Dance Suite* (1923), a series of dances the themes of which are inspired by various folk traditions (Arab, Hungarian, Romanian), and are tied together with a ritornello of Hungarian character.[85]

While definitive statistics such as the age of a peasant performer, and the date and place of the collection of a melody, were the stuff of science about which Bartók was willing to write extensively in his scholarly publications, he seems to have treated the creative act as sacred and fragile, open neither to defense nor to discussion. If his music draws extensively on the fruits of his research, in his compositions, unlike his scientific endeavors, the goal was not scientific accuracy but artistic transcendence—always a vulnerable position. In the case of the First Rhapsody for Violin, as Aladár Tóth's review implied, transcendence stemmed from the evocation of a mythical past through an artifice applied to authentic artifacts. As enduring as these melodies must have been in folk use, their arrangement in the Rhapsody strips them of their isolation, of their natural preservative. By withholding a concordance between the melodies of his Rhapsodies for Violin and the regions of their origin, Bartók the composer was forestalling potentially destructive discussion of a fragile artistic vision at least as much as Bartók the folklorist was avoiding a politically explosive debate.

Still, by studying peasant music, Bartók was indeed seeking purity—a place free of the corruption of modern life in which aesthetic discussions often replaced artistic expression. These are the longings of a sophisticated urbanite; the concept of an escape to rural values would have been meaningless to a villager. For Bartók the study of peasant music and peasant life created a vision that lent him strength to withstand the political storms that surrounded his work. This vision provided him with a quiet, well-insulated space in which he could compose. As much as the First Rhapsody is a transcription of a multiethnic bouquet of Transylvanian dances that recaptures an idyllic brotherhood of peasant cultures in old Hungary, it is also a representation of how tenaciously Bartók defended that vision in his artistic imagination. Rational discussion would expose the gap between art and science and thereby burst the utopian bubble, which, though inspired by village ritual, comes to life on stage only through the artifice of compositional fantasy.

SIX

Tradition Restored

The Violin Concerto, Verbunkos, and Hungary on the Eve of World War II

Except for the Sixth String Quartet, with its *Mesto* spreading ever more cancerously with every recurrence and finally engulfing the whole last movement, Bartók's last European works (Divertimento, *Contrasts,* and the Violin Concerto) are notoriously difficult to relate to the political tensions in Hungary at the time of their composition. Of these works, the Violin Concerto is especially perplexing, for its lush lyricism seems to clash most oddly with the forebodingly late date at the end of the score: 31 December 1938. In his discussion of the work, György Kroó includes a description of the increasing unease in Hungary preceding the Second World War and Bartók's agitation in the face of Nazi expansion. Finding no direct connection between the mood of the Violin Concerto and the tenor of the time, Kroó resorts to dispensing with the disjunction by simply attributing it to "unknown laws between life and art, man and artist."[1]

Halsey Stevens, addressing interpretation on a far more local level, comes to nearly the opposite conclusion. Hearing caustic sarcasm in the orchestral outbursts following the "twelve-tone" phrases of the second theme area of the first movement (mm. 92–95), he reads this theme as direct criticism of Schoenberg's dodecaphonic style.[2]

Like most opposites, Kroó's and Stevens's interpretations share a common assumption: for there to be a connection between a composition and a given context, the work must address that context specifically and directly. Kroó, taking the significant context to be the Nazification of Central Europe, which literally brought Germany to Hungary's borders with the Anschluss in April 1938, and focusing on what he takes to be the spirit of the work as a whole, perceives no such connection; Stevens, taking advanced compositional techniques of the 1930s as the significant context and focusing on a few startling moments, finds one. Neither position can be disproved; neither does justice to the complexity of the work. Although Hungary was undeniably a place of extreme political tension in the late 1930s and Bartók was well aware of Schoenberg's compositional practices, neither critic allows for a multivalent, flexible, or indirect manifestation of his chosen context in the composer's work. Furthermore, though Bartók's letters from this time reveal him to be highly disturbed by the spread of National Socialism, we must not forget that these documents were private, written to confidantes, whereas the Violin Concerto is a large-scale, commissioned work in one of the most public genres. To argue persuasively for a connection between aspects of the musical style of the Violin Concerto and the relevant political and musical contexts of its time while trivializing neither work nor context requires a delicate balancing of general mood and specific circumstance, public and private. Most of all it demands a good hard look at Bartók's position in Hungary in the years 1937 and 1938 and a sufficiently contextualized notion of what might constitute his artistic response to it.

To put events surrounding the composition of the Violin Concerto in perspective, our account begins after the work's completion at a time of political tension in Hungary that Bartók anticipated, but never personally experienced. We then turn back to the early 1930s to work toward an understanding of Bartók's relationship to the conditions in the later part of the decade before relating these to musical details of the composition.

Getting Out

In the spring of 1941 Hungarian prime minister Count Pál Teleki faced a difficult decision: he could either offer aid to the Germans in their planned invasion of Yugoslavia, or withhold it and risk an almost certain German invasion of Hungary. Teleki was no liberal. Having been the leading champion of the infamous *numerus clausus*, the 1920 legislation that limited Jewish admission to Hungarian universities, and an instrumental supporter of other anti-Jewish regulations, Teleki had robust anti-Semitic credentials.[3] Despite a domestic policy congenial to the Germans, Teleki was known as an "Anglophile," the unofficial designation for politicians in favor of official neutrality for Hungary.[4] The profundity of Teleki's dilemma, his helplessness in the face of the contradiction between his hopes for a nonaligned Hungary and the realities that now confronted him, is best conveyed by his reaction: he escaped responsibility for the decision by putting a bullet through his head.

Bartók's political sympathies were far more liberal than Teleki's; his departure for the United States on 12 October 1940 was a more timely and infinitely less violent exit than the prime minister's suicide several months later. Yet, that even a man with Teleki's anti-Semitic credentials would share Bartók's sense that abdication was the only moral response to Hungary's increasing attraction to the magnet of radical National Socialism illustrates the tension of the political atmosphere. It was becoming increasingly clear that neutrality was no longer an option.

Teleki's and Bartók's respective departures were tacit admissions that the gap between the various positions they embodied and the current political reality was, at least for the foreseeable future, unbridgeable. To acknowledge that Bartók's decision to leave Hungary represented a cul-de-sac on the road of negotiation is, however, to imply that he had indeed been negotiating until that time. Until Bartók left Hungary for good in 1940, that is, he must have been finding a way to reconcile his ideals with official policies. For as Hitler's radical brand of fascism swept Germany and began to hold sway in Hungary, compromise became a fact of life, a matter of survival. Lucky were those who, like Bartók, found a way to produce valuable art through the end of the decade. Luckier still, Bartók was well enough connected outside Hungary to be able to leave when the time came, and, unlike Prime Minister Teleki, politically unimportant enough to arrange for a peaceful exit.

Negotiating with Germany

One of the best examples of Bartók's complicated negotiations of the 1930s can be seen in his professional relationship to Germany. Because he performed there for the last time exactly one week before Hitler assumed the chancellorship on 30 January 1933, Bartók has often been credited with having "boycotted" Hitler's Germany.[5] This interpretation has its roots in the composer's own words. In the program note for his Second Piano Concerto that he supplied to neutral Switzerland's La Radio in Lausanne (17 February 1939), Bartók proudly announced the date of his last appearance in Germany: "The first performance of the [Second Piano Concerto] took place in Frankfurt on 23 January 1933; the radio orchestra was conducted by Hans Rosbaud and I played the piano solo. (This was my last appearance in Germany.)"[6] The parenthesis accentuates like a stage whisper—calling attention to the phrase while acknowledging its peripheral relationship to the subject of the program note proper. But, while by 1939 Bartók's absence from the roll call of artists performing in Germany was a source of pride, recent research by János Breuer has helped clarify the fact that for several years between 1933 and 1938 it had been a source of recurrent frustration.[7]

Thus, describing Bartók's absence from the concert stages of the Third Reich as a boycott ascribes to him an intention that contemporary documents do not corroborate.

Between April 1935 and July 1938 Bartók was invited to play in Germany no fewer than ten times. Eight of these invitations involved a perpetually postponed tour, which, among a number of other appearances, was always to have included performances of the Second Piano Concerto with the Berlin Philharmonic.[8] That Bartók was initially neither an unwilling recipient of German overtures nor ignorant of the intrusion of new German politics into artistic affairs is suggested by a draft, dated 4 February 1935, of a letter he wrote to officials of the Reichsmusikkammer in response to their inquiry about his availability and repertoire for playing with the Berlin Philharmonic in the spring of 1935. Bartók recommends his Second Piano Concerto because he had "already played the Rhapsody op. 1 under Bruno Walter and the First Piano Concerto under Erich Kleiber in Berlin."[9] Significantly, in revising the draft Bartók saw fit to cross out the names of both of these conductors—by then much publicized refugees from Hitler's Germany.

Having played the Second Piano Concerto with Otto Klemperer in Vienna shortly after Klemperer's dismissal from the Opera in Berlin in 1933, Bartók must have known of the circumstances forcing Jews out of Germany. Still, with its abundance of orchestras and modern music festivals, Germany had provided by far the largest market for Bartók's music from the record-breaking 1925–26 season of fifty performances of *Dance Suite* through the 1932–33 season. Additionally, Germany would have been a convenient stop on the way to many of Bartók's other concert destinations, especially the Netherlands, Belgium, and England. Although the number of performances of Bartók's music in Germany dropped significantly after Hitler came to power, with at least forty-seven performances of his music between 1933 and 1942 (including thirteen performances of *Music for Strings, Percussion, and Celesta*), Germany remained a significant forum for Bartók's music.[10]

Still, it should be stressed that if before the Anschluss Bartók remained interested in performing and having his works performed in Germany, it was not a goal he would pursue at any price. As early as 4 April 1934, Universal Edition, Bartók's publisher and concert manager for his German concerts, requested proof of his non-Jewish origin. The letter includes a transcription of a communication from Universal Edition's representative in Berlin:

> [T]he Department of Race has stated that Bartók is not Aryan. This claim must be examined. It is of greatest importance that this be clarified here. I ask you to arrange for Bartók's papers to be obtained and that I be provided with

copies of them. Bartók is again a subject of interest to conductors, and every false rumor must be decisively opposed.

A member of Universal Edition's Vienna office continued in more conciliatory, but no less chilling terms:

> We know your position in these matters, and it is far from our intention to ask you on purely business grounds to take a position that you might absolutely not accept. The new German terminology is not concerned with whether one is Aryan (which is not at all to be found in Hungary), but above all, whether or not he is of Jewish origin. Several of our composers were inclined, in order to facilitate further performances in Germany, to provide this type of proof in which they supplied copies of their baptismal certificates and the marriage certificates of their parents and grandparents. We give these facts to you without any commentary and consider ourselves to be obliged only to notify you, and we must leave it to your own judgment whether or not you will provide us with the necessary papers for forwarding to Berlin.[11]

As the tone of the letter from Universal's Vienna office anticipates, Bartók had no intention of complying with their request. In his words: "I would not dream of sending certificates of baptism to Germany even if I had them at hand."[12] Bartók's refusal to cooperate with his publisher in the face of German pressure, a position he would take again in 1938, shows that when asked to make a moral compromise, he was indeed willing to take a risky stand.[13]

In many of Bartók's dealings with German organizations in the half-dozen years before the Anschluss, however, the choices between moral rights and wrongs were not so clearly articulated. As a non-Jewish citizen of a country officially friendly to Germany, Bartók's lack of cooperation in the documentation of his racial background was apparently overlooked in light of his nationality. Thus, he could occupy a moral high ground vis-à-vis Germany while continuing to enjoy performances and plan tours there.

And yet uncertainty as to Bartók's proper status in Germany appears to be the most likely explanation for the constant on-again/off-again that resulted in the ultimate cancellation or indefinite postponement of all ten of his invitations to Germany beginning in 1935. In light of the fact that the evidence we have indicates that he was willing to accept all the invitations except the last, which arrived after the Anschluss,[14] there seems to have been ambivalence toward him on the part of some German administrators. This might explain Furtwängler's decision to cancel performances of the orchestration of *Hungarian Peasant Songs* from the Berlin Philharmonic's tour of England in January 1936.[15] A report by Bartók from 3 February 1937 further strengthens the notion that German arts administrators were confused about how to handle him: "I was to travel to Berlin in April. . . . But now—after two years of negotiations and lots of delays—those Nazis have again postponed the concert, [this time] to the beginning of June (if not *ad graecas calendas*): there must be a lot of confusion there, they themselves don't even know what they want."[16]

THE RADIO AFFAIR

A clearer example of mixing money and politics was the so-called Radio affair. In early October 1937, Bartók, in a private communication to officials of the Hungarian Radio, forbade them from sharing his broadcasts with the German or Italian Radios. This information was leaked to the Hungarian press, and in a clumsy attempt at political damage control, Endre Hlatky, artistic director of the Radio, tried to deny the obvious: "Do not think even for a minute that Bartók was led to take this step for political reasons. Everyone who knows the world-famous composer and pianist knows that it has always been his principle that art and politics cannot be combined."[17] Bartók's own response to the news coverage was considerably shrewder in its careful, detached wording that appears to focus entirely on fact:

> I see with sorrow that this matter has become public, because I consider this matter to be a private one concerning only me and the Radio company. But if it has already become public then I am forced to explain why I asked the Hungarian Radio not to offer my performances to the German and Italian Radios. The reason for this is simply that I never appeared as a performer on either the Italian Radio or that of the Third Reich, indeed these two radio companies never asked me to perform. I do not consider it to be fair that these two radio companies would just receive my performances for the Hungarian Radio for free. I must emphasize specially that I am talking only about giving my performances, this does not apply to my works, because I naturally cannot get involved in that, that is an entirely different matter.[18]

In fact, Bartók had been scheduled to give a broadcast recital in Berlin in April 1937, and the cancellation of this engagement may have accounted in part for his attitude toward the German Radio.[19] Similarly, Bartók was furious over Germany's decision to stop paying rental fees for orchestral parts obtained from Universal Edition, which came to his attention early in 1937 when he received a biannual financial statement.[20] He was similarly outraged in March 1938 when a change in German copyright law reclassified his works employing folk music as arrangements instead of original compositions.[21]

Despite Bartók's growing hostility to German policies, he repeatedly tried to avoid having his opinions publicized. This is shown again in late

March 1938 when, in the heated political atmosphere directly following the Anschluss, two Hungarian papers reopened the affair of his Radio ban from the preceding fall. Now, in response to an article reporting the ban published in the January 1938 issue of *Die Musik*,[22] several Hungarian papers ran to the composer's "defense" by reiterating the "apolitical" motivation for his action.[23] Dismayed that the affair was attracting publicity once again, Bartók responded with another carefully worded letter to the editor:

> [It has] come to my attention that in one of your issues of last week they returned to an affair of mine that we could rightly consider closed with my published response in the November *Pesti Napló*. Now they have again published my statement with the mistaken addition that I made it for or sent it to the German officials. I would be very much obliged to you for your publication of the fact that to this date, that is until the twenty-seventh of March 1938, I have never made any kind of statement for the German officials, I did not send them anything of the kind. . . . Whose interest can it be in to continually stir up this matter?[24]

As Bartók seems to have been aware, any report of an action as politically charged as his negotiations with the Hungarian Radio was potentially dangerous. In a climate in which "Anglophile" was the term used to describe neutrality, accounts of Bartók's actions as apolitical were likely and perhaps even intended to be read as implying the exact opposite.

Bartók's two communications to the Hungarian papers regarding the Radio ban are finely tuned pieces of writing designed to defuse as much as possible the political content of his stance. Although his reluctance to have his views publicized was in part due to the potential dangers of offending the Germans and the pro-German sympathizers in Hungary, Bartók may have also wanted to avoid too close an association with various anti-German factions in Hungary. Articles focusing on his opposition to Germany were probably disturbing for Bartók more because of their domestic implications than their potential for destroying what little relationship he had with institutions in the Third Reich. In Hungary, opposition to Germany was a common characteristic of many factions, from the extreme right of the fascist Turanians—who saw the Magyars (not the Germans) as the true master race—to the far left, the communists. Publicity that painted him as an outspoken opponent of Germany would have thrust Bartók into a position of prominence that might have led to co-option by any number of political camps. As we will see in the next section, this did happen once; but in general, whatever his privately held convictions, the composer wanted no such public role.

By the time he wrote his program note for the Lausanne performance of his Second Piano Concerto in 1939, Bartók had a right to be proud not to have played in Germany since Hitler's rise to power. Although it may not imply a lack of desire to perform there or an unwillingness to associate with the cultural institutions of the Third Reich, the fact does testify to Bartók's skill as a negotiator. He understood the importance of ambiguity in a time of increasing political polarization.

Hungary and the Politics of Withdrawal

Even as Bartók was banning the Hungarian Radio from sharing his broadcasts with the German and Italian Radios, he was enjoying the kind of recognition at home that had eluded him since his short-lived period of favor with the Hungarian Opera following the premiere of *The Wooden Prince*. To appreciate Bartók's position in Hungary by 1937, we must briefly trace it from its low point earlier in the decade.

Perhaps the best evidence for Bartók's sense of rejection by Hungary are the events surrounding his fiftieth birthday on 25 March 1931. While the French Embassy conveyed its government's respect for his work by awarding him the Legion of Honor, the Hungarian government let the occasion pass in stony silence.[25] The Hungarian Opera, however, did offer a greeting of sorts—two days after Bartók's birthday it canceled what was to have been the Hungarian premiere of *The Miraculous Mandarin*.[26] Sándor (Alexander) Jemnitz, one of his most vocal Hungarian apologists, summed up the odd relationship between Bartók and Hungary with a messianic metaphor in a birthday tribute to the composer, comparing him with the despised and rejected Jesus. In Jemnitz's view Bartók was the neglected Messiah of Hungarian music, castigated because he refused to mine the ever-popular vein of irredentist clichés that formed the bulwark of Hungarian nationalism between the two world wars.[27] As proof of the injustice of Bartók's neglect at home Jemnitz went on to cite the composer's high reputation abroad. Although not without some truth, the disparity between the international and domestic appreciation of Bartók was consistently and productively exaggerated by his defenders in the Hungarian press.[28] Ironically, Bartók's reputation abroad rested to a certain extent on his status as Hungary's foremost composer, while in Hungary his reputation (not to be mistaken for popularity) rested on his status as Hungary's only composer to be widely recognized in elite musical circles abroad.

Although not one for public display, Bartók communicated his sense of alienation from Hungary on a number of occasions. In April 1934 he wryly summed up his relationship to the government and the leaders of Hungary's musical life in a letter to Walter Frey (1898–1985), a Swiss pianist who was seeking Bartók's help in arranging concerts in Hungary: "I unfortunately have no influence [in Hungary]: my relations with the Opera are very bad, with Hubay [director of the Academy of Music] utterly bad, with Dohnányi [conductor of the Philharmonic Society] very chilly, with the government quite bad, and I am just on the verge of having a quarrel with the Radio, though we have never been on particularly friendly terms."[29]

Bartók's reaction to his neglect in Hungary was to withdraw from public appearances in Budapest. He stopped giving concerts there altogether between 1930 and 1934 and did not take part in performances of his own compositions from 1930 to 1937. Writing to Joseph Szigeti, who wanted to include one of his compositions in a joint recital in 1935, Bartók explains the reason for his boycott of Budapest—acknowledging that it was due to the psychological effect of the poor or indifferent reception he experienced there rather than an objectively better reception abroad:

> I do not play, I cannot play, my own works in Budapest. There are a thousand and one reasons for this. I would prefer not to play them anywhere, just as I am fed up with the whole business of giving concerts. I am sick and tired of it. But the trouble is I need money. For this reason I am compelled to undertake as much of the profession—always alien to me—as I can bear. Of course, neither is there any sense in my playing my own works abroad, but I do it regardless of how people behave toward us [me]. I have nothing to do with them. But in Budapest I expect something different from what I receive—and I am not able to endure this in any other way than by withdrawing completely.[30]

For Bartók, withdrawal meant not only a retreat from the Budapest concert stage, but immersion in the solitary world of folk-music research. Beginning in the fall of 1934, Bartók's desire for seclusion was aided by his new position at the Academy of Sciences where he transcribed and classified a large collection of field recordings of Hungarian folk music.

There is considerable irony in Bartók's escape from the bright lights of Budapest's public stages to the dark isolation of the folk-music studio at the Academy of Sciences. A good part of his desire to withdraw stemmed from distaste for a government and public unsympathetic to modern art and suspicious of his broad interest in folk music of many ethnicities. Yet, as suggested in chapter 5, it may have been in part the nationalist, irredentist tendencies of this government—looking for justification of Hungary as the purest, most ancient culture in central Europe—that led to the allocation of funds for folk-related research and made it financially feasible for Bartók to withdraw into folk music.

And yet Bartók's seclusion at the Academy of Sciences did not amount to the envisioned withdrawal from public life in Hungary. Although one might logically expect his isolation to have increased throughout the decade as the Hungarian government drifted even closer to the increasingly radical manifestations of National Socialism in Germany, in fact something nearer to the opposite occurred.

Appreciation at Home

An important goal of the New Spiritual Front, the cultural initiative begun by Prime Minister Gömbös in 1934, seems to have been to gain the support of the intelligentsia, specifically a prominent group known as the Folk Writers *(Népi írók)*. The unifying characteristic of the Folk Writers was their focus on Hungarian village life as a medium for social criticism. Although the group was potentially a dangerous source of opposition to the government, it shared the government's aggressively nationalistic stance. Like Bartók, they believed in a conception of the nation rooted in its peasantry, but the composer tended to remain aloof from the Folk Writers as he did from most organizations and movements originating in a generation younger than his own.[31]

Bartók's transfer to the Academy of Sciences had already reflected an increase in government support of peasant culture; under Gömbös, support of Bartók gradually expanded beyond the sphere of ethnographic research. The first sign was the Opera's 1935 revival of *The Wooden Prince* following sixteen years of conspicuous neglect. This production, with choreography informed by Hungarian peasant dances, reflected an informal transition between Hungarian institutional support of Bartók the folklorist and support of Bartók the composer.[32] In a repeat of the sequence of events in 1917 and 1918, in 1936 the Opera added a revival of *Bluebeard's Castle*, last performed in Hungary in January 1919, to continued performances of *The Wooden Prince*.

The balm of these encouraging signs did not immediately heal the deep wounds inflicted earlier in the decade. Sándor Jemnitz's review of the London BBC Orchestra's performance of Bartók's *Four Pieces for Orchestra* on 24 April 1936 rehearses the theme of unjust neglect as if nothing had changed since the birthday "tribute" five years before:

> In every country the BBC puts the works of representative significant composers of the places it will be touring on its program and in this way expresses its respect for the contemporary music of that country. But the group obvi-

ously was mistaken when it performed Bartók's *Four Pieces for Orchestra*, which was introduced on one of the Philharmonic Society's concerts in 1922 and has never been heard [here] since. . . . How could they even have suspected that it would not have been performed here for fourteen years?! . . . This kind of situation glaringly illuminates the complete absurdity of our musical life. . . . It is, in the last analysis, an untenable situation that precisely those works that established the world fame of Hungary's musical life in other countries are completely unknown here.[33]

Bartók seems to have agreed, for, in the fall of 1936, when he received the immense honor of being the first musician elected to membership in the Hungarian Academy of Sciences (not to be confused with his 1934 appointment, which merely made him an employee of the academy), he chose to use the occasion of his inaugural address to lodge a thinly veiled complaint at his exclusion from Hungarian concert life. Using Liszt as his surrogate, he accused Hungary of neglecting the most interesting works of its most famous composer.[34] But if his elevation to membership in the Academy of Sciences was not enough to mollify him immediately, it would not be long before the results of Gömbös's policies could no longer be ignored either by Bartók himself or by his advocates.

Only a year after Sándor Jemnitz had complained so bitterly of Bartók's neglect in Hungary, Aladár Tóth reported: "We have perhaps never felt the power of Bartók's music to be so redeeming, so liberating as this year, when our great composer's works have been performed by ever greater numbers of our singers and musicians. Our pleasure is especially joyous because the majority of the new works are for our youth, our children."[35] The year to which Tóth refers was the 1936–37 concert season, which, in addition to *Bluebeard* and *The Wooden Prince* at the Opera, had also seen a celebration of Bartók's orchestral music at the Vigadó, Pest's fanciest concert hall. The orchestral program was entirely made up of revivals: *Two Pictures*, First Suite for Orchestra, the Rhapsody, op. 1, for Piano and Orchestra, and most significantly *Cantata profana*, the Hungarian premiere of which had come less than two years before. For practically the first time, Bartók's works were not just receiving obligatory Hungarian premieres, but showed signs of actually entering the repertoire. The specific occasion for Tóth's glowing report, however, was no gala event at the Vigadó or Opera, but an amateur choral festival of Bartók's music in Kecskemét at which the composer himself introduced several selections from the still incomplete *Mikrokosmos*.

Kecskemét, a small city an hour-and-a-half by train from Budapest, was Kodály's birthplace and, not coincidentally, a place of significance for the Hungarian choral movement. Beginning in the early 1930s, community choruses, especially youth choruses, were the lifeblood of Kodály's crusade for Hungarian music education—a manifestation of nationalism that united many otherwise opposed political camps.[36] In part because Kodály was the guiding spirit of the chorus movement, a large part of their repertoire consisted of arrangements of folk songs; the movement thus acquired a loose association with the Folk Writers. Like the work of the Folk Writers, these choruses were seen as a bridge between city and peasant culture, and they too had begun to thrive in the atmosphere cultivated by Gömbös's New Spiritual Front.

On 7 May 1937, two weeks after the Bartók Festival in Kecskemét, the composer ended his eight-year boycott of the Budapest stage when he again played selections from the *Mikrokosmos* at a concert of his works by several of Budapest's youth choruses. Bartók's description of the concert shows his high spirits at this time:

> At the concert on May 7th I really did play some pieces from the *Mikrokosmos*. However, at this particular concert they were not so important as the children's choruses. It was a great experience for me when—at the rehearsal—I heard for the first time my little choruses coming from the lips of these children. I shall never forget this impression of the freshness and gaiety of the little ones' voices. There is something in the natural way these children from the suburban schools produce their voices that reminds one of the unspoiled sound of peasant singing.[37]

Perhaps the most telling sign of Bartók's newfound success, bordering for the first time in his life on actual popularity in Hungary, was neither his own private enthusiasm nor the optimistic reviews of critics who had long rallied behind him, but the response to a vicious attack hurled at him from the pages of *Magyar Kultúra* (Hungarian Culture), a conservative Catholic paper.[38] Bartók's attacker, a Jesuit priest, charged him and Kodály with corrupting Hungary's youth with their modernistic arrangements of folk music. That Bartók was now considered threatening enough to warrant a full-throttled attack from a priest with close ties to the government testifies both to the scale of the composer's public prominence and to the factionalization of Hungarian politics at this time. Moreover, in response to the attack, Bartók and Kodály received a veritable flood of defense in no fewer than six different papers.[39] Considering Bartók's tendency to withdraw in the face of domestic criticism, that he continued to perform his works and maintain a public presence in Budapest at this time suggests that he now felt solidly supported and appreciated at home.

This atmosphere of success led to what for Bartók was a very rare act: his participation in a concert with explicitly political overtones. The concert of

Bartók's and Kodály's choral compositions organized by a group of Folk Writers calling themselves the *Magyar Múzsa* (Hungarian Muse) at the Music Academy on 13 November 1937 was intended to celebrate the success of a petition that had been introduced in Parliament ten days before.[40] At issue had been the imprisonment of Géza Féja and Imre Kovács, two village researchers *(falu kutatók)* whose arrests were widely regarded as an illegal abuse of power. The call for Féja and Kovács's release had the support of a wide spectrum of left-wing and moderate contingents. Owing in large part to its basis in folk music, Bartók and Kodály's choral music was seen as a rallying point to bring these diverse groups together in concerted action.

A concert of Bartók's and Kodály's music did not necessarily imply the composers' personal involvement or political endorsement. Bartók's reluctance openly to associate his music with particular political causes was so well known that he was reportedly almost not even invited to participate.[41] But, having signed the petition submitted to Parliament (something Kodály could not be persuaded to do), Bartók unexpectedly did agree to lend his prestige to the event with a performance of his *Fifteen Hungarian Peasant Songs* (nos. 6–15).

Although the concert was supported by a number of groups, the most vocal were the communist members of the *Márciusi front* (March Front).[42] For them, Bartók's appearance was a publicist's dream-come-true, and they played up his participation for all it was worth by publishing an article entitled "Bartók for the People" in their official organ *Gondolat* (Thought). In the volume, which was distributed during the concert and presented to Bartók on stage after his performance, the composer was touted as a fearless leader of the Hungarian masses: "[Bartók] the genius researcher of Hungarian folk song could not remain silent when he saw that prison threatened those researching the misery of the Hungarian folk. . . . Until now he served this cause only with his music, but now he signals with his personal appearance how much he considers it his own. . . . Bartók's signature on the freedom-manifesto [Parliamentary petition] of the Hungarian writers is the most comforting act of the last months. When they heard about it on a cold, stormy day, the Hungarian masses felt gratitude and pride."[43]

Considering Bartók's general allergy to political publicity, it seems unlikely that he would have appeared on this occasion had he been fully aware of what lay in store. Bence Szabolcsi (1899–1973), a critic close to Bartók and Kodály, took this view of Bartók's position in his review, significantly the only report by a musician that even acknowledges the concert's political implications.[44] Furiously trying to throw water on the partisan flames (fanned by *Gondolat*) that were threatening to consume Bartók, Szabolcsi declared:

It is a fatal mistake to believe that one can fulfill the command of [Bartók's and Kodály's] art by accepting any kind of political program. Everyday politics is at once too general and too narrow for Bartók and Kodály. To be a people, to grow into a unified nation, to rise into a free country . . . all these things take priority in the requirements of Bartók's and Kodály's credo; but beyond all this their command requires greatness, freedom, independent opposition to the world of slavery—a consciousness, a bravery that exists nowhere in the world at this time except in them.[45]

However anomalous Bartók's participation on 13 November may have been, it indicates both how far he had come from his withdrawal in the face of indifference earlier in the decade and the extent of his new desire to maintain public visibility in Hungary. Bartók also chose this moment to resume concertizing in Hungary with the Rhapsody, op. 1, his old standby in the long out-of-date Hungarian national style of the nineteenth century. Now that Bartók had evidence of sympathy and support from a greater number of Hungarians, he seems to have been moved to return the favor by adopting a more congenial manner in communicating with them. It is not so surprising, then, that under these conditions Bartók's compositional style should also have become more warmly accessible than it had been since the First World War.

Negotiation in Music: The Violin Concerto

Although its orchestration was not finished until 31 December 1938, the Violin Concerto was a conception of the 1936–37 season and the very embodiment of the lush new style that emerged during Bartók's period of reconciliation with the Hungarian public.[46] Written for Hungarian violinist Zoltán Székely (1903–2001), its manner suggests that Bartók intended the work to communicate a special meaning to domestic audiences. Although the concerto was performed in Budapest in 1944, the war prevented Bartók and Székely from participating in its Hungarian premiere. The world premiere took place in Holland, where Székely gave four highly successful performances of the Violin Concerto in 1939 and 1940. Reviewing the premiere, Dutch critics immediately recognized a softening in tone compared with Bartók's works of the preceding decades.[47] The change is hard to miss as the harp's B-major triads—seemingly designed, as one critic put it, to "put the audience in a good mood"—announce it at the very outset.[48]

Although the Dutch critics at the premiere acknowledged the Violin Concerto's immediate success with the audience, they were made uneasy by its accessibility. The critic of Amsterdam's *De Telegraaf* sums up the dichotomy: "The whole thing strives to please: sharp rhythms or sharp dissonances were relatively undisturbing and frequently created a good impression. 'Even I liked it'—audience members commented during the intermission. Nine times out of ten this kind of pleasing is the sign of the composer's weakness."[49] Although some critics apparently accused Bartók of "dumbing down" his style and avoiding the difficult sonorities they took to be prerequisites for a modern masterpiece, behind the congenial surface of the Violin Concerto the composer had woven a complex web of motivic relations and topical allusions that can be interpreted on many levels. It is precisely in Bartók's manipulation of a highly referential, hence multivalent, musical language in the Violin Concerto that one sees a musical analogy to his use of ambiguous rhetoric to navigate politically stormy seas.

MOTIVIC UNITY AND TOPICAL ALLUSION

Bartók generates a sense of tightly controlled internal reference in the Violin Concerto through motivic unity on several planes. The opening bass line of the first movement contains a motivic kernel that generates much of the material of the movement (example 66, mm. 3–6). On the most direct level, the opening bass line returns as the theme that preoccupies the first part of the development section (mm. 115–137). This commonly noted recurrence points to several conspicuous connections between the opening bass line and the melody of the primary theme. Initially, the bass line articulates the harmony $B-A^7$ under an internal pedal on B; the same progression (now over a more conventional pedal in the bass) also serves as the harmonization of the first phrase of the primary theme. The third beat of the opening melody echoes this initial modal-harmonic move from tonic to flat seventh, which reverberates in several other places as well, including the beginning of the development (transposed as F–E♭, m. 116) and the transition following the primary theme in both the exposition and recapitulation (mm. 22 and 220). In its farthest-reaching manifestation it defines the tonal areas of the primary and secondary themes (B and A, respectively). Shorn of the sixteenth-note pickups that were added to the score as an afterthought, the concerto's opening phrase is clearly an embellishment of the bass line that introduces it (example 66, mm. 3–6 and 7–8).[50]

Somewhat less obvious is the connection between the opening bass line and the third, contrasting phrase of the primary theme. Here Bartók takes the bass's pattern—down a fourth, up a minor third, down a fourth—and uses it as the structural frame for the melodic phrase (compare the first note

EXAMPLE 66. Violin Concerto, movement 1, primary theme, mm. 1–22

(continued)

EXAMPLE 66 *(continued)*

in each measure of the B section in example 66 with the upper voice of the abstract in example 67). Thus the third section of the primary theme is a melodic elaboration of the harmonic progression that underlies the first section. The care with which Bartók has worked out this connection looks even more impressive when we observe that the circle-of-fifths bass line of the third phrase of the theme (G–C–F–B♭) provides just those pitches needed to expand the notes of the first phrase (B Dorian with an added major third:

EXAMPLE 67. Violin Concerto, movement 1, reduction of section B of primary theme (cf. example 66, mm. 15–18)

EXAMPLE 68. B-Dorian scale with D/D♯ unstable third degree from the first phrase of the primary theme melody; the four-note, circle-of-fifths pentatonic bass line from the third phrase of the primary theme; and the twelve-tone combination of the two

B–C♯–D/D♯–E–F♯–G♯–A) into a complete twelve-note chromatic collection (example 68).

As one has a right to expect with Bartók, these modal and motivic observations can be meaningfully connected with folk music. The Dorian scale of the opening phrase with its unstable third degree (represented as D/D♯) is a characteristic mode of "new-style" Hungarian folk song, while the bass line of the third phrase, being a subset of a pentatonic collection, refers to the characteristic mode of "old-style" Hungarian folk song. When the two are interleaved, the result is a kind of modal chromaticism, or, in the loosest sense of the term, a folk-based "dodecaphony," reflected again in the twelve-note phrases of the second theme that have excited much critical comment (mm. 73–91).[51]

Yet another connection between the primary theme and Hungarian folk music lies in its particular four-phrase structure that echoes the same common quatrain structure (AA⁵BA) of the "new-style" melodies that Bartók also used in the Second Piano Concerto (cf. example 62). Unlike the folk songs that fit this description, this second phrase is not exactly A⁵, that is, the first phrase literally transposed up a fifth. The second phrase begins on the fifth degree (example 66, m. 11), but like a tonal answer retains B as the tonal center in preparation for the arrival on the dominant, F♯, at the end of the phrase (m. 14). The chromatically deceptive resolution of the F♯ to a G¹³ chord postpones the return to B by opening up the contrasting harmonic sphere of the third phrase with its circle-of-fifths progression, the bass line (down a fifth, up a fourth, down a fifth) now expanding all the intervals of the opening bass line (down a fourth, up a minor third, down a fourth) by a major second (mm. 15–18). The sequence ends on a B♭ pedal that is quickly reinterpreted as A♯, the leading tone, which asserts its traditional function to return the harmony to its starting point (mm. 21–22).

The fourth phrase of the opening quatrain departs from the folk model, referring to the melody of the opening phrase only through the typically Hungarian palindromic dotted rhythm or "choriamb" of its first bar (♩ ♪♪♩). Bartók then applies this rhythmic pattern to a descending sequence of perfect fourths joined by half steps (known in the American analytic literature as Z cells), elided at the very end with a folklike $\hat{5}$–$\hat{4}$–$\hat{1}$ melodic cadence that joins the bass in harmonic closure on B (m. 22).[52]

The transformation of three notes of the chromatic Z cell ($\hat{5}$–#$\hat{4}$–$\hat{1}$) into a diatonic ($\hat{5}$–$\hat{4}$–$\hat{1}$) cadence emblematic of Eastern European peasant music over a leading-tone pedal is emblematic of Bartók's deft negotiation between three musical worlds: the structures and modal inflections of peasant music, the late-nineteenth-century harmony of his early idol Richard Strauss, and the modernistic utopia of abstractly symmetrical intervallic constructions. None of the elements of this mix were new to Bartók's music in 1937, nor was the idea of synthesizing them; what was new was the tonal clarity and inviting accessibility of the aural surface.

Especially in contrast to much of his music from the previous decade, Bartók's works of the late 1930s tend toward a Romantic tone unexpectedly reminiscent of nineteenth-century Hungarian national music. The composer's move toward a more accessible style accorded with a general European retreat from the extremes of postwar modernism. In Bartók's case it was also the result of a reawakened interest in the instrumental traditions of *verbunkos*, which he fused seamlessly with elements derived from peasant song in a manner that smoothed over the jagged dissonances so characteristic of his music in the 1920s.

It is especially significant that several of Bartók's final European works (*Contrasts*, Sixth String Quartet, and the Violin Concerto) contain explicit references to the gestures of the *verbunkos*.[53] These are the first clear examples of *verbunkos* elements in Bartók's work since the Violin Rhapsodies of 1928. To find an unambiguous example of *verbunkos* in Bartók's oeuvre that is neither an actual folk-music arrangement (as are the Violin Rhapsodies) nor a parody (as in *The Wooden Prince*) we must go all the way back to works that preceded his discovery of peasant music and that employ the Hungarian national style that Bartók began to reject in 1907. Before considering the wider implications of the *verbunkos* in the late 1930s, let us take a closer look at the portion of the Violin Concerto we have already considered from some other points of view.

As Bartók implied by writing "Tempo di verbunkos" in the solo violin part he copied out for a rehearsal with Zoltán Székely, tempo and accompaniment convey the spirit of the *verbunkos* in the Violin Concerto even before the soloist's entrance (figure 4). The harp's steady, medium-fast, quarter-note opening accompaniment in $\frac{4}{4}$ time may be traced to *dűvő*, a common accompanimental pattern for Hungarian dances discussed in chapter 1. The most pertinent characteristic of *dűvő* for the present discussion is the way it articulates a steady stream of more or less even pulses into pairs with an accent on the second note of each. A comparison between the *dűvő* accompaniment in a traditional village ensemble and the opening of Bartók's Second Rhapsody shows how the opening of the Violin Concerto is indebted both to the traditional *dűvő* and to Bartók's earlier attempt at realizing it.

Example 69 shows a transcription of a performance by a four-member band of village Gypsy musicians with a *dűvő* pattern in the second violin *(kontra)* and contrabass *(nagybőgő)*. Example 70 shows the opening of the Second Rhapsody (also written for Székely), in which Bartók gives a similar accompanimental pattern to the harp, a common substitute for the cimbalom in Hungarian orchestral music. To arrive at the opening of the Violin Concerto requires one more layer of abstraction (one might say urbanization), namely, the removal of the accents from beats 2 and 4 from the steady quarter notes in the harp. The beauty of this further abstraction of the accompaniment, befitting the Violin Concerto, which unlike the Rhapsody does not quote folk melodies, is that it opens the music to a wider range of associations. The uninflected strumming of the harp might suggest the introduction to a bardic rendition of a tale. It also recalls the exoticism of Rimsky-Korsakov's *Sheherazade*, the best-known pairing of harp and solo violin in the repertoire.[54] The slightly percussive effect of the harp's playing even and detached quarter notes, four to a bar, might also vaguely recall the four timpani strokes that open Beethoven's Violin Concerto. Although such multivalent readings of the work certainly increase its potential richness, and although a desire not to limit its interpretation may lie behind Bartók's decision not to include "tempo di verbunkos" in the final score, it is nevertheless the *verbunkos* topic that resonates most strongly at the outset of the work.

In addition to the harp in lieu of cimbalom, there are several other details in the opening bars of the Violin Concerto that evoke the *verbunkos* tradition. The space-opening effect of a tonic pedal in the horn (doubled in the

FIGURE 4. Violin Concerto, solo violin part with the performance indication "tempo di verbunkos" written out by Bartók for a rehearsal with Zoltán Székély. (Violin Concerto No. 2 © 1941 by Hawkes & Son [London] Ltd. Copyright Renewed. Reprinted by permission of Boosey & Hawkes, Inc. Used by kind permission of Peter Bartók and Gábor Vásárhelyi.)

EXAMPLE 69. Csárdás as played by a four-member band in Szatmárökörító, Transylvania. Collected by György Martin and Bálint Sárosi in 1968 (Bálint Sárosi, *Hangszerek a magyar néphagyományban* [Budapest: Planétás Kiadó, 1998], 207).

EXAMPLE 70. Rhapsody for Violin No. 2, mm. 1–4

harp) conveys a pastoral tone and may have been inspired by simple *düvő* accompaniments in which the *kontra* or *brácsa* sometimes uses one of its open strings as a drone.[55] Another detail of orchestration, the clarinet as the first instrument to begin a countermelody, echoes a larger *verbunkos* ensemble (violin, clarinet, *brácsa/kontra*, bass, and cimbalom—the ensemble roughly approximated in *Contrasts*, the only work in which Bartók uses the term *verbunkos* in the published score).[56] Finally, the hiccupped or interrupted pickup to the second phrase (m. 10) is a *verbunkos* cliché, with familiar precedents in Gyula Káldy's late-nineteenth-century arrangements of Hungarian tunes, Kodály's opera *Háry János* (1926), and Bartók's own First Rhapsody, but not characteristic of peasant fiddling (example 71a–c).[57]

Once one is alert to the presence of *verbunkos* elements in the first movement of the Violin Concerto, one hardly knows where nineteenth-

EXAMPLE 71. "Hiccupped" pickup

a. Gyula Káldy's arrangement of the "Rákóczi dal"

b. Kodály, *Háry János* (Intermezzo), m. 1

c. Bartók, Rhapsody for Violin No. 1, 1 before reh. no. 12

century Hungarian national elements leave off and other related elements—"new-style" Hungarian peasant song and instrumental folk music,
for example—begin. Which of the so-called *verbunkos* gestures are derived
from "authentic" peasant culture—to return to Bartók's earlier writings—
and which from what he had heretofore considered the "corrupt" imitations of urban Gypsy bands or nineteenth-century Hungarian composers?
The question of origin is complicated both by the mixed roots of *verbunkos*
itself and by the abstract nature of Bartók's adaptation of the tradition in
composition as rich and complex as the Violin Concerto. What significant
conceptual gap remains between an accessible and highly Romantic work
like Bartók's Violin Concerto and the best works of his nineteenth-century
Hungarian predecessors, whose Hungarian idiom relied on the popular
style of "Gypsy bands"? Is there a crucial difference between Bartók's late
music and that of Ferenc Erkel, whose Hungarian musical style Bartók
repudiated after his discovery of peasant music?

EXAMPLE 72. Ferenc Erkel, *Bánk bán*, the climactic phrase of Bánk and Melinda's act 2 duet (cf. example 66, mm. 15–18)

BÁNK BÁN REVISITED

A comparison of a musical high point from Erkel's influential opera *Bánk bán* and the climactic third phrase of the primary theme of Bartók's Violin Concerto sheds some light on these questions (cf. example 72 and example 66, mm. 15–22).[58] The passage from *Bánk bán* is the climax of the duet between Melinda and Bánk from the opera's second act, discussed in chapter 2. This highly expressive Hungarian-style music, quoted in example 72 from the opera's prelude (where it forms the middle section), is first sung by Melinda in the first finale to act 1. It serves as the opera's most potent musical reminiscence motif.

Bartók's and Erkel's passages have a number of similarities: both are in quadruple meter, both begin with a pickup of an ascending run to the highest note of a four-bar phrase a major sixth above the bass, and both four-bar phrases are divided into two nearly identical subphrases, each tied off with a characteristically Hungarian front-accented, *short*-long dotted rhythm applied to a descending perfect fourth. The first two bars of each are accompanied by fifth-related harmonic progressions. In each, the initial four-bar phrase is answered by another that brings the melody to rest on a lower tonic; and both capture the unstable third and sixth scale degrees of much folk music by using both major and minor versions of these scale degrees.

There are also some conspicuous differences. Where Erkel returns to D (now D minor, iv) in bar 3 and then moves the harmony down a major second to a C-major chord (bIII) in measure 4, for example, Bartók continues his circle-of-fifths progression all the way through the phrase. Yet both harmonic choices can be heard as syntheses of the composers' indigenous sources of inspiration. Bartók's circle-of-fifths progression, as we have observed, is a four-note subset of a pentatonic set, the backbone of the "old-style" Hungarian folk songs. By the same token Erkel's move to bIII (C major) in the context of A major might be seen as a harmonic expression of the variable or unstable third scale degree in Hungarian folk melodies.

Other differences between these two passages include Bartók's avoidance of repeated dotted figures (as in Erkel's m. 1) and the interval of an augmented second (as in Erkel's m. 3), both being *verbunkos* clichés associated with "Gypsy music" but not typical of Hungarian folk song. Furthermore, the flats and sharps used to reflect the unstable degrees of folk music in Erkel's example are separated from each other by a caesura and modal contrast between parallel phrases. Put another way, Erkel's representation of the unstable scale degrees of folk music coincides with the color changes of major-minor mixtures common in the art music of the time. By contrast, Bartók's dual scale degrees sometimes occur together in a single harmony—a widespread harmonic characteristic of the art music of *his* time. Erkel's and Bartók's phrases, separated by over seventy years, both exemplify syntheses of standard Western European harmonic practice (fairly conservatively in both cases) with the composers' respective preferences in Hungarian national style.

Although Bartók's notion of Hungarian style was greatly influenced by his work with peasants in the countryside, whereas Erkel's notion came primarily from the popular Hungarian idioms of his day, many of the folk features from which they drew inspiration are indistinguishable when integrated into original compositions. Many of the Hungarianisms in Erkel's and Bartók's music appear in both what Bartók regarded as "authentic" and "corrupt" repertoires (rural *verbunkos* of Transylvanian fiddlers versus urban popular music). The difference between their styles is less a reflection of differing relationships to folk music than the result of the different (but in both cases Western-oriented) trainings they received some sixty-five years apart.

A FINAL CULMINATION POINT

Erkel, as a young opera conductor in Kolozsvár (now Cluj, Romania), learned the craft of operatic composition primarily from the examples of Rossini, Donizetti, Bellini, Meyerbeer, and early Verdi. Bartók, as a student at the Music Academy, grew to musical maturity on a diet of Beethoven, Brahms, Liszt, and, later, Strauss. Given this training it is no surprise that he cared passionately about the organic unity of his music. We have already seen this in the relationship between the opening bass line and the primary theme of the first movement of the Violin Concerto. When the third phrase of the primary theme returns as the "culmination point" of the movement, the multivalent connections are even more potent.

A culmination point (so named by Somfai) is a carefully planned moment designed to summarize and surpass all that has come before. Although Bartók restates material from the A section of the primary theme a total of five times in the course of the movement (mm. 43, 51, 115, 194, 213), in each of these thematic recalls he adjusts the trajectory of the phrase so as to avoid arriving at a restatement of the B section. Rather, he holds that music in reserve for the emotional climax, which occurs in the coda after the cadenza (example 73). The melody of the B section now begins a major second higher than on its first appearance, and the circle-of-fifths sequence is now extended so that the bass line encompasses a full pentatonic collection. Thus, as at the analogous culmination point of the first movement of the First Piano Concerto (discussed in chapter 4), Bartók completes a crucial element of "old-style" Hungarian folk song that had been incomplete in the passage's first incarnation.

Beginning the sequence a major second higher not only lends more brilliance and passion to the solo violin, but also allows Bartók to avoid ending on the Bb/A♯ leading tone in the bass. He saves the harmonically significant use of the leading tone until measure 363 and reserves its appearance in the bass until the final five bars of the movement. The structurally prominent pitches of the culmination point's melody are so calculated as specifically — and uniquely — to exclude that crucial note (example 74).

In addition to nearly supersaturating the passage in terms of pitch content, Bartók also concentrates the thematic content of the culmination point by reuniting the music of the B section of the primary theme with that of the A section. This time, however, he superimposes the two phrases by using music from the A section as a countermelody to the high-flying B section in

EXAMPLE 73. Violin Concerto, "culmination point," movement 1, mm. 354–60

EXAMPLE 74. Violin Concerto, reduction of "culmination point"

the solo violin. Since the melodic outline of B takes its shape from the opening bass line, the movement's thematic kernel, and since the bass line of the B section is an intervallic transformation of the same material, the culmination point embodies three simultaneous statements of the same basic shape. At the very moment when Bartók finally realizes the pentatonic ("old-style") implications of the bass line, he also changes the role of the harp. The harp, which had initially grounded the articulation of the *verbunkos* topic in *dűvő*, now emphasizes the unabashed Romantic passion of the culmination point with glissandi that accentuate the highest and structurally most important notes of the solo violin. Freed from the role of providing a rhythmically steady harmonic accompaniment—unleashed, so to speak, from its *dűvő* foundation—the harp indulges in its most sensual and romantic cliché. The ascending sweeps in the solo violin and harp now epitomize the phrase, symbolizing Bartók's newfound (or newly refound) inclination to appeal directly and unabashedly to sentimental emotion. Thus, even as the composer builds the culmination point on an "objective" element of peasant music (the "old-style" pentatonicism of the bass), he revels in the Romantic sentimentality of the national tradition of nineteenth-century Hungarian art music. This synthesis moves beyond the standard combination of peasant music and art music to embody several layers of Hungarian tradition, both within "peasant music" and within "art music."

Although Bartók spent most of his life campaigning for peasant music and against the legitimacy of "urban folk music," a number of the gestures in his original compositions inevitably overlap with those of composers whose models were "Gypsy bands." Thus while peasant music was of great psychological, philosophical, and musical importance to Bartók, neither peasant music as such nor his impressive ability to synthesize art and folk traditions suffices to define the difference between Bartók and his Hungarian predecessors. Rather, the difference, and it is indeed a profound one, lies in his fidelity to those characteristics serious musicians have come to value so highly in the works of the first generation of modernist composers: subtlety

and complexity. Bartók's music stands apart from that of his Hungarian predecessors less because of its greater fidelity to authentic folklore than because
it asserts more elite standards of craftsmanship, originality, and modernity.

Gaining Distance

In 1937, in direct response to the racism inherent in growing ultranationalism, Bartók finally admitted in print that rigid distinctions between various
folk styles are generally the fabrication of aggressive nationalists. In an
essay titled "Folk-Song Research and Nationalism," he wrote:

> It cannot be denied that the impulse to begin folk-song research . . . is attrib-
> utable to the awakening of national feeling. The discovery of the values of
> folklore and folk music excited the national pride, and . . . the members of each
> nation were convinced that the possession of such treasures was their only
> and particular privilege. . . . But soon these nations encountered some disap-
> pointments. . . . [I]t was impossible to avoid coming into contact now and then
> with some aspect of the neighboring nation's cultural treasure. And so the
> trouble began. The offended national sentiment had to defend itself somehow,
> and—offended by the fact that the neighboring nation was also in possession
> of the treasure that up to that time had been considered ancient, original
> national property—did so by claiming priority. . . . It is regrettable that the
> ideological tensions of our time further the spread of morbid one-sidedness
> instead of promoting an unbiased view. . . . Even if musical folklore is very
> indebted to nationalism, today's ultranationalism does it such harm as many
> times exceeds its benefits.[59]

In 1942, in an article titled "Race Purity in Music," Bartók put virtually the
same idea even more strongly: "There is much talk these days, mostly for
political reasons, about the purity and impurity of the human race, the usual
implication being that purity of race should be preserved, even by means of
prohibitive laws." He goes on to declare that the wealth of folk music in
Eastern Europe is due to a "continuous give and take of melodies, a constant
crossing and recrossing that persisted for centuries. . . . The situation of folk
music in Eastern Europe may be summed up thus: as a result of uninter-
rupted reciprocal influence upon the folk music of these peoples there are an
immense variety and wealth of melodies and melodic types. The 'racial
impurity' finally attained is definitely beneficial."[60]

Bartók's agenda in these two writings differs considerably from that in
"Our Folk Music and the Folk Music of Neighboring Peoples," written when
he was hoping to withdraw into the cloistered world of the Academy of

Sciences in 1934. The writings from the late 1930s and early 1940s reflect his chastened desire to break down barriers rather than construct them. As we have already seen in reference to his Hungarian performances of his own works, by 1937 the composer was also more interested in fostering communication with his Hungarian audience than he had been earlier in the decade. Bartók's resurrection and elevation of the *verbunkos* tradition in his original compositions was perhaps the most significant and productive result of his new status at home. But it confronts us with a paradox. For even as Bartók was reacting against ultranationalism with a flexible notion of the productive intercourse between various folk cultures, by evoking the *verbunkos* he returned in part to the musical style that had represented a chauvinistic brand of Hungarian nationalism at the turn of the century.

To note this much prompts further speculation. In the face of Germany's growing influence over Hungary and from the distance of more than three decades, might Bartók have harked back to the days of his early *verbunkos*-inspired works so as to reinvoke their anti-Austrian associations? More specifically, could the passage in the Violin Concerto that I have compared to *Bánk bán* have been intended to recall one of the main themes in that opera—namely, the corrupting force of Western Europeans in Hungary's government? Despite Bartók's earlier rejection of his youthful *verbunkos* style along with the chauvinism that it once implied, memory may have rendered idyllic what had been thought outgrown and spurned.

Thus nostalgia might explain Bartók's late reembrace of the *verbunkos*. And yet, in interpreting the Violin Concerto, I counsel caution. Focusing one-sidedly on one or another stylistic association—be it the twelve-tone row of the second theme or the *verbunkos* topic of the first—can lead us into the same trap that snared Halsey Stevens and György Kroó: that of unintentionally trivializing the work by expecting it to correspond simply and directly to its historical context or, in the absence of such an obvious connection, denying that such a relationship exists at all. Monochromatic interpretation can only fail to do justice to the rich network of associations so crucial to Bartók's late style. In the Violin Concerto Bartók reached out to the Hungarian public in a manner they would have understood. As in the works of Liszt, motivic transformation, thematic recall, and topical allusion guarantee the work a certain semiotic intensity; but without any hint of a program provided by the composer, what the work communicates must remain above all a musical experience, its precise meaning eluding paraphrase.

Describing Bartók's almost pathological reluctance to communicate emotion in words, Kodály said in a memorial tribute: "Happy are those who could help him in removing the barbed-wire fence he raised around himself in self-defense."[61] The precise extent to which Bartók's careful reticence, especially when it came to the meaning of his own creative work, was the product of his innate personality, and the extent to which it was conditioned by the tensions of his time, are things we will never know. But, given that he lived under circumstances in which barbed wire was hardly a neutral metaphor for artistic isolation, we can be thankful for his ability to withdraw. In his self-imposed isolation, Bartók found a space for expressive complexity at a time too often beset with crudely reductive polarization.

Tradition Achieved

At the first orchestral concert in Budapest to have been devoted exclusively to Bartók's works (10 December 1936) Aladár Tóth detected a change in the attitude of the audience:

> The biggest, epoch-making achievement of Thursday's Bartók concert is that Bartók's voice was understood by the portion of the Hungarian middle class whose politics, education, societal upbringing, and "social" taste had until now artificially kept it away from the truly life-providing geniuses of living *mag-yarság*—from Ady, Babits, Móricz, Kodály, and most importantly . . . from Bartók. . . . This program not only included Bartók's "more easily understood" youthful works . . . but the *Two Pictures* and Bartók's "most revolutionary," most difficult, dense masterwork, the *Cantata profana.* And lo! the first hearing of this masterwork immediately, deeply and completely captivated Hungarian ears and hearts that had been nurtured for so long only by Gypsy music, [*magyar*] *nóták*, and hit tunes from operettas. [62]

Bartók, Tóth seemed to say, was finding a place within a notion of the nation that was embraced not only by a select group of artists and intellectuals, but also by a greater segment of the Hungarian middle class. The softening of Bartók's style that coincided with his achieving a greater degree of recognition at home would be received with suspicion in Western Europe as early as 1940 and would open him to the specific charge of compromise after the Second World War. To those unaware of the Hungarian context for Bartók's work, the composer's rapprochement with the society he had struggled against for so many years could indeed sound like a retreat from the ideals that had secured a place for him in the highest echelon of modernist composers. Inside Hungary, however, the notion of compromise in connection with Bartók's life and work was unthinkable in the late 1930s. Bartók's decision to leave Hungary for the United States in 1940 was indeed definitive proof of uncompromising moral integrity—a final act of withdrawal from the society that had given him reason to withdraw so many times before.

In his review of Bartók and Ditta Pásztory's farewell concert to a sold-out house at the Music Academy on 8 October 1940, Sándor Jemnitz wisely put aside conventional topics of music criticism, such as the quality of the playing or the value of Bartók's compositions. Instead he addressed the question, "What does it mean that a great master *lives among us* . . ." He concluded: "This is not the time for details, when with tearful eyes we bid farewell to the whole thing—to Béla Bartók living among us. Those who ardently applauded him took a stand next to these symbols: the crystalline purity of human and artistic character."[63] Had Aladár Tóth not already fled to Sweden to protect his Jewish wife from the increasingly oppressive anti-Semitic policies in Hungary, he might have expressed the symbolism of Bartók's last appearance in Hungary even more eloquently. Although Jemnitz's review is an extreme case befitting an extreme circumstance, it reflects the fact that ever since *Kossuth*, Bartók's reception in Hungary had been governed as much by what he was seen to represent as it was by the sound of his music.

It is grimly ironic that Bartók's late-found peace with Hungary, the spiritual homecoming reflected so intensely in the Violin Concerto, should have come so soon before his physical departure.[64] Grimmer still was the fact that the interest in folk music that he had done so much to make part of the national discourse had by 1940 been enlisted in the propaganda war that supported Hungarian irredentism and helped propel Hungary into World War II.[65] In the past, Bartók had coped with rejection or indifference at home by withdrawing to the sanctuary provided by folk-music research. By 1940, however, his symbolic power had become too great to allow him the anonymity he would have needed to survive in an aggressively hostile environment.

Despite his many successes and failures throughout Europe and the United States, only in Hungary was Bartók's position so deeply and consistently tied to questions of national identity often considered beyond the scope of abstract artistic expression. It is a testimony both to the strength of his artistic vision and to Hungary's need for symbols of *magyarság* that Bartók, who for much of his life challenged his country's self-image, should have become, in the eyes of his countrymen, a reflection of it as well.

Notes

The following abbreviations are used throughout the notes:

BBCsaL   *Bartók Béla családi levelei* (Béla Bartók's Family Letters), ed.
Béla Bartók, Jr., and Adrienne Gombocz-Konkoly (Budapest:
Zeneműkiadó, 1981)

BBE   *Béla Bartók Essays*, ed. Benjamin Suchoff (New York: St. Martin's
Press, 1976; reprint ed. Lincoln: University of Nebraska Press, 1994)

BBÍ/1   *Bartók Béla írásai* (Béla Bartók's Writings), vol. 1: *Bartók Béla
önmagáról, műveiről, az új magyar zenéről, műzene és népzene
viszonyáról* (Béla Bartók on His Life, His Works, the New
Hungarian Music, the Relationship of Art Music and Folk Music),
ed. Tibor Tallián (Budapest: Zeneműkiadó, 1989)

BBL   *Béla Bartók Letters*, ed. János Demény (London and Budapest: Faber
and Faber and Corvina, 1971)

BBLev   *Bartók Béla levelei* (Béla Bartók's Letters), ed. János Demény
(Budapest: Zeneműkiadó, 1976)

BBÖÍ   *Bartók Béla összegyűjtött írásai* (Béla Bartók's Collected Writings),
ed. András Szőllősy (Budapest: Zeneműkiadó, 1966)

DocB 1–4 *Documenta Bartókiana*, ed. Denijs Dille, vols. 1–4 (Budapest:
Akadémiai Kiadó; Mainz: Schott's Söhne, 1964–70)

DocB 5–6 *Documenta Bartókiana*, ed. László Somfai, vols. 5–6 (Budapest:
Akadémiai Kiadó; Mainz: Schott's Söhne, 1977–81)

Zt 3   *Zenetudományi tanulmányok 3: Liszt Ferenc és Bartók Béla
emlékére* (Studies in Musicology 3: In Memory of Franz Liszt and
Béla Bartók), ed. Bence Szabolcsi and Dénes Bartha (Budapest:
Akadémiai Kiadó, 1955)

Zt 7   *Zenetudományi tanulmányok 7: Bartók Béla 1914–1926; Liszt
Ferenc hagyatéka* (Studies in Musicology 7: Béla Bartók 1914–
1926; Franz Liszt's Legacy), ed. Bence Szabolcsi and Dénes Bartha
(Budapest: Akadémiai Kiadó, 1959)

Zt 10   Zenetudományi tanulmányok 10: Bartók Béla emlékére (Studies in
         Musicology 10: In Memory of Béla Bartók), ed. Bence Szabolcsi and
         Dénes Bartha (Budapest: Akadémiai Kiadó, 1962)

INTRODUCTION

The epigraphs are from Benedict Anderson, *Imagined Communities: Reflections on the Origin and Spread of Nationalism*, rev. ed. (New York: Verso, 1991), 204, and Béla Bartók, "The Influence of Peasant Music on Modern Music [1931]," *BBE*, 340.

1. For Debussy's comments about these composers see *Debussy on Music: The Critical Writings of the Great French Composer*, collected and introduced by François Lesure, trans. and ed. Richard Langham Smith (Ithaca, NY: Cornell University Press, 1977). For Janáček's relationship to Dvořák and Smetana see Michael Beckerman, "In Search of Czechness in Music," *19th-Century Music*, 10, no. 1 (1986): 61–73 (especially 66–67).

2. Anderson, *Imagined Communities*, 204.

3. Personal communication, February 2003.

4. Hans Kohn, "Western and Eastern Nationalisms," in *Nationalism*, ed. John Hutchinson and Anthony D. Smith (Oxford: Oxford University Press, 1994), 164.

5. Anthony D. Smith, *National Identity* (London: Penguin Books, 1991), viii.

6. John Lukacs describes Munkácsy's funeral in *Budapest 1900: A Historical Portrait of a City and Its Culture* (New York: Grove Weidenfeld, 1988), 3–4. Susan Gal describes Bartók's reburial in "Bartók's Funeral: Representations of Europe in Hungarian Political Rhetoric," *American Ethnologist* 18: 440–58. Rákóczi's return is documented in the October 1906 issues of the *Vasárnapi Újság* (Sunday Newspaper).

7. See István Hargittai, "Some Experiences beyond Chemistry of the 2004 Nobel Prize in Chemistry," www.crookedtimber.org/archives/002639.html (accessed 22 November 2004).

8. Judit Frigyesi, "Béla Bartók and the Concept of Nation and *Volk* in Modern Hungary," *Musical Quarterly* 78, no. 2 (1994): 255–87; and Peter Sugar, "Nationalism in Eastern Europe," in *Nationalism*, ed. John Hutchinson and Anthony D. Smith (Oxford: Oxford University Press, 1994), 171–77.

9. Bartók uses the phrase "brotherhood of peoples" in a letter to the Romanian writer, diplomat, and music historian Octavian Beu, 10 January 1931, *BBL*, 201. (See my discussion of this letter in ch. 5.)

10. In an excellent essay on Bartók's nationalism David Cooper reaches a similar conclusion when he characterizes Bartók's compositions as a reconstruction of Hungarian nationalism. See "Béla Bartók and the Question of Race Purity in Music," in *Musical Constructions of Nationalism: Essays on the History and Ideology of European Musical Culture 1800–1945*, ed. Harry White and Michael Murphy (Cork: Cork University Press, 2001), 16–32.

11. Art historian Clement Greenberg characterizes this kind of chauvinism in "Self-Hatred and Jewish Chauvinism: Some Reflections on 'Positive Jewishness,'" *Commentary* (November 1950), reprinted in *Clement Greenberg: The Collected Essays and Criticism*, ed. John O'Brian (Chicago: University of Chicago Press, 1993), vol. 3, 48.

12. Ernest Gellner, *Nations and Nationalism* (Ithaca, NY: Cornell University Press, 1983), 57.

13. See Richard Taruskin, *Stravinsky and the Russian Traditions* (Berkeley: University of California Press, 1996), 502–18.

14. The earliest scholarly suggestion that peasant music and "Gypsy music" might not be mutually exclusive categories I am aware of was made in 1994 by Frigyesi in "Béla Bartók and the Concept of Nation and *Volk* in Modern Hungary," 277.

15. For a discussion of the prevalence of the saying in Hungary see Klára Móricz, "'From Pure Sources Only': Bartók and the Modernist Quest for Purity," *International Journal of Musicology* 9 (2000): 247–70.

CHAPTER ONE

The epigraph is from Béla Bartók, "The Relation of Folk Song to the Development of the Art Music of Our Time," *The Sackbut*, 2, no. 1 (June 1921). Reprinted in *BBE*, 326.

1. Lynn Hooker discusses writings on Hungarian music that predate Bartók's in "Modernism Meets Nationalism: Béla Bartók and the Musical Life of Pre–World War I Hungary" (Ph.D. diss., University of Chicago, 2001), 48–102, especially 59–68.

2. Gyula Szekfű, ed., *Mi a magyar?* (Budapest: Magyar Szemle Társaság, 1939; reprint 1992).

3. All the contributors were or became members of the Hungarian Academy of Sciences. Besides Szekfű and Kodály they were Mihály Babits (1883–1941), a writer associated with the literary journal *Nyugat* (West); Lajos Bartucz (1885–1966), anthropologist; Sándor Eckhardt (1890–1969), linguist; Gyula Farkas (1894–1958), literary historian and director of the Hungarian Academy of Sciences; Tibor Gerevich (1882–1954), art historian; Dezső Kerecsényi (1898–1945), literary historian; László Ravasz (1882–1975), theologian; Károly Viski (1882–1945), geographer; Béla Zolnai (1890–1969), linguist; and Miklós Zsirai (1892–1955), linguist.

4. *Mi a Magyar?* 417. The Votyaks and Cheremiss are Finno-Ugric peoples of the Volga region; the Nogay-Tartars are Turkish-Tartar people of the Caucasus. Kodály mentions these peoples to evoke the Magyars' Asian roots.

5. Andrew C. Janos, *The Politics of Backwardness in Hungary: 1825–1945* (Princeton: Princeton University Press, 1982), 28.

6. The exact moment of Bartók's recognition of the pentatonicism of the "old-style" songs appears to be documented in the notation of the pentatonic scale just below his notation of two folk songs in the sketchbook he took to Transylvania in 1907. *Béla Bartók: Black Pocket-Book*, facsimile with commentary by László Somfai (Budapest: Editio Musica, 1987), XII and 1^v.

7. *Auróra* (Dawn) 1, no. 3 (1911): 126–8. Reprinted in *BBI/1*, 99–101. In English in *BBE*, 301–3.

8. See Judit Frigyesi, "The Verbunkos and Bartók's Modern Style: The Case of Bluebeard's Castle," in *Bartók Perspectives: Man, Composer, and Ethnomusicologist*, ed. Elliott Antokoletz, Victoria Fischer, and Benjamin Suchoff (Oxford: Oxford University Press, 2000), 140–51; Hooker, "Folksong and Hungary's Musical Avant-Garde" and "Writing Hungarian Music: Motive, Genre, Spirit," in "Modernism Meets Nationalism"; and David E. Schneider, "Peasant Music or Gypsy Music: The Implications of *Dűvő* for Bartók's Polemics," *International Journal of Musicology* 9 (2000): 141–68.

9. Bartók appears to be referring to Géza Molnár (1870–1933), author of the book *A magyar zene elmélete* (The Theory of Hungarian Music) (Budapest: Pesti Könyvnyomda-Rt., 1904). Géza Molnár taught a course on Hungarian music at the Music Academy from 1900. Bartók could have also had in mind Molnár's predecessor Gyula Káldy (1838–1901), who taught a course at the Music Academy entitled "Characteristics of Hungarian Music" (A magyar zene sajátságai, 1894–1900). Géza Molnár's rhythmic theories are the subject of Hooker, "Modernism Meets Nationalism," ch. 4. In the margin of Bartók's copy of Molnár's book (Budapest Bartók Archives, BH 421) Bartók notes: "We *won't* invent Hungarian effects first *in theory!*"

10. Bartók's identification of Bohemian native Anton Csermák (1774–1822), János Palotási (born Pecsenyánszki; 1821–78), and Márk Rózsavölgyi (born Rosenthal; 1789?–1848) as foreigners appears designed to appeal to nationalist bigotry. Csermák had been accepted as leading figure in Hungarian musical life in his lifetime, and although Rózsavölgyi and Palotási were of Jewish and Polish descent, respectively, both were natives of Hungary. The other composers mentioned are János Bihari ((1764–1827) and János Lavotta (1764–1820).

11. *Auróra* 1, no. 3 (1911): 126–28. Translation adapted from *BBE*, 301.

12. Evidence of the prestige of *Auróra* is Béla Balázs's letter to György Lukács in late January 1911: "There's a new journal here that you may have seen, 'Auróra.' It has started off as a more high class, more elite enterprise than the rest." *Balázs Béla levelei Lukács Györgyhöz* (Béla Balázs's Letters to György Lukács) (Budapest: MTA Filozófiai Intézet, 1982), 44. Quoted in *BBÍ/1*, 101.

13. For a list of publications see *BBE*, 530.

14. László Dobszay, "A 'Rákóczi'-dallamkör" (The "Rákóczi"-Melody Type), in *Magyar zenetörténet* (History of Hungarian Music), 2nd enlarged ed., *Jelenlévő múlt* (Present Past) (Budapest: Planétás Kiadó, 1998), 183–90; Bálint Sárosi, *Folk Music: Hungarian Musical Idiom*, trans. Maria Steiner (Budapest: Corvina, 1986), 104. For the Hungarian style's international acceptance see Jonathan Bellman, *The Style Hongrois in the Music of Western Europe* (Boston: Northeastern University Press, 1993).

15. Dobszay, *Magyar zenetörténet*, 183.

16. Béla Bartók, "Race Purity In Music," *Modern Music* 19, nos. 3–4 (1942): 153–55, in *BBE*, 31–32.

17. Although Vincze's melody lacks the Phrygian second characteristic of seventeenth- and early-eighteenth-century Rákóczi-type melodies, by beginning on the fifth degree in melodic minor, it evokes that melody type. For discussion of Bartók's transformation of Zsigmond Vincze's tune see Klára Móricz, "From Pure Sources Only."

18. Dobszay traced the first appearance of this new type of melody in the *Apponyi-MS* (1730). See Dobszay, *Magyar zenetörténet*, 266–67. See Béla Bartók, "Hungarian Folk Music and the Folk Music of Neighboring Peoples," in *Béla Bartók: Studies in Ethnomusicology*, ed. Benjamin Suchoff (Lincoln: University of Nebraska Press, 1997), 187–88.

19. Géza Papp, "Die Quellen der 'Verbunkos-Musik': Ein bibliographischer Versuch," *Studia musicologica* 21 (1979): 152–217; 24 (1982): 35–97; 26 (1984): 59–132; 32 (1990): 55–224; "Hungarian Dances (1784–1810)," in *Musicalia Danubiana*

7, ed. Géza Papp (Budapest: MTA Zenetudományi Intézet, 1986); *A verbunkos kéziratos emlékei: Tematikus jegyzék* (Manuscript Sources of Verbunkos: Thematic Catalog) (Budapest: MTA Zenetudományi Intézet, 1999).

20. About the *verbunkos* see Bence Szabolcsi and Géza Papp, "Verbunkos," in *Brockhaus-Riemann zenei lexikon*, ed. Carl Dalhaus and Hans Heinrich Eggebrecht, Hungarian edition by Antal Boronkay (Budapest: Zeneműkiadó, 1983–85), vol. 3, 592–94; Sárosi, *Gypsy Music*, 85–119, and *Folk Music: Hungarian Musical Idiom*, trans. Maria Steiner (Budapest: Corvina, 1986), 52, 54, 57–58, 73, 81, 159–62; Miklós Rakos, ed., *Magyar Nóták Veszprém Vármegyéből: 136 Verbunkos táncdarab 1823–1832 mellyek fortepianóra alkalmaztattak Ruzitska Ignátz által Veszprémben* (Hungarian Songs from Veszprém County: 136 *Verbunkos* Dances 1823–1832 Arranged for Piano by Ignátz Ruzitska in Veszprém County), (1823–1832; reprint, with commentary by Miklós Rakos, Budapest: Kiadja a szerző [published by the editor], 1994), 42–43; *Hungarian Dances 1784–1810*, ed. Géza Papp, Musicalia Danubiana 7 (Budapest: MTA Zenetudományi Intézet, 1986), 23–36; and Dobszay, *Magyar zenetörténet*, 183–90 and 264–75. I thank Ferenc Sebő and Lujza Tari for a number of communications on the topic. For discussion of the military reforms of 1715 see Peter F. Sugar, ed., *A History of Hungary* (Bloomington: Indiana University Press, 1990), 140–42.

21. See Ernő Pesovár, "Verbunk," in *Néptánc kislexikon* (Concise Dictionary of Folk Dance), ed. Lajos Lelkes (Budapest: Planétás Kiadó, 1996), 177–78.

22. Although the *csárdás* came into vogue as a society dance in the 1830s, and, as a couple's dance, differed significantly from the men's dances referred to as *verbunkos*, the musical accompaniments for the two dances are largely indistinguishable. Regional traditions vary as to which tunes carry the designation *verbunkos* and which *csárdás*. I am indebted to László Kelemen, Ferenc Sebő, and István Pávai for discussing this point with me.

23. I am grateful to Lujza Tari for sharing her view of the characteristic order of movements in *verbunkos* with me. For a more complete range of movement designations and arrangements see Papp, *A verbunkos kéziratos emlékei*.

24. Dobszay, *Magyar zenetörténet*, 276.

25. "Barbunc" is the title of a dance tune collected by Bartók in a Romanian village in Transylvania in 1914. See Bartók, *Rumanian Folk Music 1*, ed. Benjamin Suchoff (The Hague: Martinus Nijhoff, 1967), 416 (no. 511).

26. For a discussion of *verbunkos* elements in the music of non-Hungarian composers see Bellman, *The* Style Hongrois *in the Music of Western Europe*.

27. Gergely Czuczor, "A' magyar tánczról" (About Hungarian Dance), *Atheneum* 1 (1843): 109–19. My translation largely follows that in Sárosi, *Gypsy Music*, 87–88.

28. See Rakos, *Magyar Nóták Veszprém Vármegyéből*, nos. 2, 26, 44, 84.

29. For more characteristics see Bellman, *The* Style Hongrois *in the Music of Western Europe*, 91–130.

30. "Hungary: II, 2," *The New Grove Dictionary of Music and Musicians*, 2nd ed. (London: Macmillan, 2000), online. Bálint Sárosi, "Magyar nóta," in Dalhaus and Eggebrecht, *Brockhaus-Riemann zenei lexikon 2*, 466–67.

31. A census from 1782 reported 1,582 professional Gypsy musicians in Hungary. Presumably the number grew significantly over the course of the nineteenth century; Dobszay, *Magyar zenetörténet*, 232. For the date of the Gypsies' admission

to Hungarian towns see "Hungary I, 3," in *New Grove Dictionary of Music and Musicians,* 2nd ed., online.

32. For Bartók's ideas about the use of the term "Gypsy music" see "Gypsy Music or Hungarian Music?" *BBE,* 206. János Bihari and Pista Dankó (1858–1903) are the two best-known Romany musicians who composed music in the "Gypsy" style. "Gypsy folk music" is one of the few categories of folk music in Hungary in which Bartók and Kodály appear to have had little interest. The few examples of it they did collect (all songs) have been published in Rudolf Víg, "Gypsy Folk Songs from the Béla Bartók and Zoltán Kodály Collections," *Studia musicologica* 16, nos. 1–4 (1974): 89–131.

33. Lynn Hooker describes the debates that followed the publication of this work in detail in "Modernism Meets Nationalism," ch. 2, especially pp. 59–71. As Hooker observes, Liszt's argument does occasionally distinguish the performance practice of Gypsies from musical material, but Hungarian musicians were offended by the privileged position accorded Gypsies in Liszt's work. Ibid., 64–65.

34. *BBE,* 206.

35. Ibid., 207.

36. For discussion of his dissatisfaction with the Hungarian reception of his music in the early 1930s see ch. 6, pp. 225–27.

37. Bartók, "Gypsy Music or Hungarian Music?" *BBE,* 222, 206.

38. Although it is not unusual for someone to sing the tune that serves as the basis for elaboration in Gypsy music and there are some styles of Gypsy performance that feature vocalists, it is clear from Bartók's writings that these are not the performance practices with which he was concerned when discussing "Gypsy music."

39. Bartók's use of the phrase "szöveges népies műdalok" (texted folklike art songs) appears to be his scientifically accurate way of describing *magyar nóta.*

40. Béla Bartók, "Cigányzene? Magyar zene (Magyar népdalok a német zeneműpiacon)" (Gypsy Music? Hungarian Music? [Hungarian Folk Songs on the German Music Market]), lecture given at the forty-third annual meeting of the Hungarian Ethnographical Society (1931), in *BBÖI,* 638–39. A different translation appears in *BBE,* 221–22.

41. Béla Bartók, "A hangszeres zene folklórja Magyarországon" (The Folklore of Instrumental Music in Hungary), *Zeneközlöny* (Music Gazette) (1911), reprinted in *BBÖI,* 60. A different translation appears in *BBE,* 240.

42. See Judit Frigyesi, *Béla Bartók and Turn-of-the-Century Budapest* (Berkeley: University of California Press, 1998), 59–60.

43. Bartók, "Gypsy Music or Hungarian Music?" *BBE,* 201.

44. Julius (Gyula) Káldy, *A History of Hungarian Music* (London: William Reeves, 1902; reprint, New York: Haskell House, 1969), 17–18. Cited in Bellman, *The Style Hongrois in the Music of Western Europe,* 57.

45. For a discussion of the suite as a favorite Hungarian genre see Tibor Tallián, " 'Um 1900 nachweisbar': Skizze zu einem Gruppenbild mit Musikern," *Studia musicologica* 24, nos. 3–4 (1982): 500–501.

46. "Dohnányi Ernő," *Esti Újság* (8 January 1903): 1.

47. "One cannot speak in dialect for an entire evening." Zoltán Kodály, "Béla Bartók the Folklorist," in Kodály, *The Selected Writings of Zoltán Kodály,* trans. Lili Halápy and Fred Macnicol (London: Boosey and Hawkes, 1974), 102.

48. János Arany's poem "Rodostó" takes its title from the place in Turkey where Ferenc Rákóczi II lived in exile after his failed revolution against the Habsburgs (1703–11). An opera by this title is the last work of Géza Zichy's *Rákóczi Trilogy* (1912).

49. *BBCsaL*, 70. My translation is adapted from Judit Frigyesi, "Béla Bartók and Hungarian Nationalism: The Development of Bartók's Social and Political Ideas at the Turn of the Century" (Ph.D. diss., University of Pennsylvania, 1989), 232.

50. Bartók mentions the article in a letter to his mother, 9 January 1903, in *BBLev*, 34.

51. Bartók's letter to his mother, 12 November 1902, in *BBCsaL*, 74.

52. Bartók alludes to the fact that the most renowned cellist in Hungary at the time was the Prague native David Popper (1843–1913), a German-speaking Jewish professor of cello at the Music Academy.

53. Koessler was one of the professors who spoke German with his students. Bartók's letter to his mother, 12 November 1902, in *BBCsaL*, 74–75, emphasis added.

CHAPTER 2

The epigraph is from *BBL*, 29.

1. Éva Somogyi, "The Age of Neoabsolutism, 1849–1867," in Sugar, *A History of Hungary*, 235.

2. Lukacs, *Budapest 1900*, 118.

3. Géza Jeszenszky, "Hungary through World War I and the End of the Dual Monarchy," in Sugar, *A History of Hungary*, 267–81.

4. For a discussion of these paintings see Júlia Szabó, *Paintings in Nineteenth Century Hungary*, trans. Ilona Patay, trans. revised by Elizabeth West (Budapest: Corvina, 1985), 296–98. Franz Liszt had commemorated the executions at Arad in "Funérailles," the seventh piece of *Harmonies poétiques et religieuses* (1853).

5. Béla Csuka, *Kilenc évtized a magyar zeneművészet szolgálatában: A Filharmóniai Társaság emlékkönyve 90 éves jubileuma alkalmából* (Nine Decades in the Service of Hungarian Musical Art: Memorial Album of the Philharmonic Society on the Occasion of Its Ninetieth Anniversary) (Budapest: Filharmóniai Társaság, 1943).

6. Lukacs, *Budapest 1900*, 120.

7. Szabó, *Painting in Nineteenth Century Hungary*, 306.

8. David Cooper, "Bartók's Orchestral Music and the Modern World," in *The Cambridge Companion to Bartók*, ed. Amanda Bayley (Cambridge: Cambridge University Press, 2001). I extend my thanks to Cooper for sharing with me his discussion of "Est" in his unpublished paper "Bartók and the Encoding of Hungarian National Identity."

9. Between January and April 1903 Bartók also composed the first two movements of Four Piano Pieces, BB27, portions of the first and third movements of a sonata for violin and piano, BB28, and two settings of Kálmán Harsányi's "Est" (Evening), one for voice and piano, BB29, one for male choir, BB30.

10. "Dohnányi Ernő," *Esti Újság* (8 January 1903): 1.

11. Bartók's letter to his mother, 9 January 1903, in *BBLev*, 34. A somewhat different translation appears in *BBL*, 20.

12. László Vikárius argues that Dohnányi's symphony affected five early works

of Bartók's: the *Andante* for Violin and Piano, the Symphony in E♭, *Kossuth*, the Rhapsody, op. 1, and the Suite for Large Orchestra no. 1. See *Modell és inspiráció Bartók zenei gondolkodásában* (Model and Inspiration in Bartók's Musical Thought) (Pécs: Jelenkor 1999), 82–86, 89–90, 94, and 154.

13. See Bartók's letter to his mother, 29 October 1902, in *BBCsaL*, 72.

14. Alan Walker, *Franz Liszt: The Final Years, 1861–1886* (Ithaca, NY: Cornell University Press, 1996), 289.

15. "Színház és Művészet: Dohnányi Ernő" (Theater and Art: Ernő Dohnányi), *Pesti Napló* (8 January 1903): 10.

16. "Dohnányi Ernő," *Esti Újság* (8 January 1903): 1.

17. Ibid.

18. For discussion of the relationship between *Kossuth* and Strauss's symphonic poems see Frigyesi, "Béla Bartók and Hungarian Nationalism," 117–21; Günter Weiss-Aigner, "Youthful Orchestral Works," in *The Bartók Companion*, ed. Malcolm Gillies (London: Faber and Faber, 1993), 445–46; Cooper, "Bartók's Orchestral Music and the Modern World," 46; György Kroó, *A Guide to Bartók*, trans. Ruth Pataki and Mária Steiner, trans. rev. Elisabeth West (Budapest: Corvina, 1974), 11–14.

19. In autobiographical sketches from 1918, 1921, and 1923 Bartók singles out Dohnányi's Piano Quintet, op. 1, as an important early influence. *DocB* 2, 113–24.

20. At *Kossuth*'s premiere critic István Kereszty noted the "well-known Hungarian rhythm everywhere (with the exception of the minor-mode distortion of the *Gott erhalte*)." *Zenelap* (Music Journal) (15 January 1904), in *DocB* 1, 51.

21. Bartók's program note for *Kossuth* was originally published in *Zeneközlöny* (11 January 1904): 82–87, reprinted in *BBÖI*, 767–73, and translated into English by Judit Frigyesi, "Béla Bartók and Hungarian Nationalism," 270–77. My outline is a modification of Frigyesi's translation based on the original Hungarian. An abridged English version of the text was published in the program for the performance on 18 February 1904 in Manchester (see *BBE*, 399–403).

22. An arrangement of the Funeral March for piano was the only part of *Kossuth* published during Bartók's lifetime (Budapest: Rozsnyai Károly, 1910).

23. Molnár was removed from the faculty in the years 1919–25. See Hooker, "Modernism Meets Nationalism," 168.

24. Ibid., 160–61.

25. Molnár, *A magyar zene elmélete*, 88–89. Translated differently in Hooker, "Modernism Meets Nationalism," 175.

26. In 1910 a competition for a new orchestral work in the Hungarian style sponsored by the music publisher Rózsavölgyi included symphonic poems but not symphonies in a list of suggested genres. See Hooker, "Modernism Meets Nationalism," 181–82.

27. Aurél Kern, *Budapesti Hírlap* (Budapest News) (14 January 1904), quoted in *DocB* 1 (1964), 32–33.

28. Frigyesi, "Béla Bartók and Hungarian Nationalism," 122.

29. Frigyesi argues that sections nine and ten fulfill a recapitulatory function and that the structure of *Kossuth* is a sonata/rhapsody hybrid. Ibid., 123–26.

30. Antal Csermák's string quartet *Az intézet[t] veszedelem vagy Haza szeretete* (Threatening Danger or Love of the Fatherland; 1809) is an exceptional early attempt at program music in the Hungarian style. Unlike *Kossuth*, however, *Az*

intézet[t] veszedelem is made up of numerous short movements and does not fit the *lassú-friss* pattern of the Hungarian rhapsody.

31. Kálmán Harsányi, *Költemények* (Poems) (Budapest, 1903 [no publisher's imprint]), 23–24. Bartók's setting of "Est" for solo voice and piano is probably earlier than the entirely different setting of the poem he made for eight-part male choir finished in April 1903. See László Somfai, notes to *Bartók Early Works and Rarities* (Hungaroton CD 31909), 6–7.

32. The Hungarian text has been reprinted in *DocB* 1, 92.

33. Denis Dille, "Bemerkungen zum programm der symphonischen Dichtung 'Kossuth' und zur Aufführung dieser Komposition," in *DocB* 1, 94.

34. Four of Liszt's *Seven Hungarian Historical Portraits* for piano (1870–85) were funereal ("István Széchenyi," "László Teleki," "Sándor Petőfi," and "Mihály Mosonyi"). Other examples of Hungarian funeral music include Ferenc Erkel: *A halálnak éjszakája, gyászdal* (The Night of Death, Dirge, c. 1856); János Bihari: *Requiem fia halálára* (Requiem to the Death of His Son, 1821); Mihály Mosonyi: *Gyászhangok Széchenyi István halálára* (Funeral Music on the Death of István Széchenyi, 1860); Antal Siposs: *Szondy gyászdala* (Szondy's Dirge, 1895); Victor Langer: *Gyászhangok Deák Ferencz halálára* (Funeral Music for the Death of Ferencz Deák, 1876); Endre Kovács: *Szentpétery Zsigmond gyász emléke* (Mourning Memory of Zsigmond Szentpéteri, 1850s); Károly Doppler: *Gyász-Induló Lendvai Márton temetése alkalmára* (Funeral March on the Occasion of the Funeral of Márton Lendvai, 1858); Károly Borsch: *Örökgyász Gróf Széchenyi István emlékére* (Eternal Mourning in Memory of Count István Széchenyi, 1860); Pista Dankó: *A Magyar nemzet gyászdala* (Dirge of the Hungarian Nation, 1890s?); János Kirch: *Emlék Egressy Beni sírkövére* (To the Tombstone of Béni Egressy, 1851?); Károly Agghazy: *Gyászhangok II.Rákóczi Ferenc Fejedelem emlékére*, op. 37 (Funeral Music in Memory of Prince Ferenc Rákóczi II, 1905); Ödön Mihalovich, *Gyászhangok Erzsébet királyné emlékére* (Funeral Music in Memory of Queen Elisabeth, 1899); Franz Doppler, *Magyar és Gyász-zene* Bánk-bán cz. drámához (Hungarian and Funeral Music for *Bánk bán*, n.d.).

35. László Somfai, "'Per finire': Some Aspects of the Finale in Bartók's Cyclic Form," *Studia musicologica* 11, nos. 1–4 (1969); 391–408. Klára Móricz discusses similar problems in the finale of the Concerto for Orchestra in "Operating on a Fetus: Sketch Studies and Their Relevance to the Interpretation of the Finale of Bartók's Concerto for Orchestra," *Studia musicologica* 36, nos. 3–4 (1995): 461–76.

36. The Rhapsody, op. 1, (hereafter Rhapsody) exists in three versions: for piano solo (1904), for piano and orchestra (1905), and for two pianos (1914). The first slow section of the version for solo piano has also been published separately (Rózsavölgyi, 1908). Although some aspects of the present discussion apply to all of the versions, I refer here to the version for solo piano completed in November 1904 and published by Rózsavölgyi (Budapest, 1923), Zeneműkiadó (Budapest, 1950), and reprinted in Dover's *Piano Music of Béla Bartók*, series 1, ed. Benjamin Suchoff (New York, 1981), 39–65.

37. Bösendorfer concert grand pianos, Bartók's instrument of choice, in fact extend a major third lower, to F_0.

38. László Somfai, "A Characteristic Culmination Point in Bartók's Instrumental Forms," in *International Musicological Conference in Commemoration of Béla*

Bartók 1971, ed. József Ujfalussy and János Breuer (Budapest: Editio Musica, 1972), 53–64. In this article Somfai is primarily concerned with Bartók's later works. The earliest work of Bartók's he discusses is *The Wooden Prince* (1914–16).

39. For a discussion of Bartók's use of the *tenuto* mark see László Somfai, "Nineteenth-Century Ideas Developed in Bartók's Piano Notation in the Years 1907–14," *19th-Century Music* 11, no. 1 (1987): 81.

40. Of Liszt's nineteen Hungarian Rhapsodies only two, numbers 5 and 12, have references to the *lassú* openings near the end of the *friss,* and in all cases the references are very brief. Of these only no. 5 changes mode, from C♯ minor to C♯ Phrygian, and this reference lasts only one bar. The return in no. 12 is *sotto voce* and does not constitute a "culmination point."

41. László Vikárius considers both Liszt's *Hungarian Fantasy* and *Spanish Rhapsody* to have influenced Bartók in the composition of the Rhapsody. Vikárius documents Bartók's attendance at the "Hungarian Evening," a concert in celebration of the fiftieth anniversary of the Philharmonic Society at which Dohnányi was soloist in the *Hungarian Fantasy.* See *Modell és inspiráció,* 80. The fact that even in the first version for solo piano Bartók's Rhapsody has symphonic proportions suggests that he was already planning its orchestration in 1904. Bartók competed in the 1905 Rubinstein competition in Paris with the version for piano and orchestra.

42. In nineteenth-century Hungary, the terms rhapsody and fantasy (*ábránd*) were often used interchangeably. See Mária Ekhardt, "Magyar fantázia, ábránd, rapszódia a XIX. század zongoramuzsikájában" 1–2 (Hungarian Fantasy and Rhapsody in the Piano Music of the 19th Century), *Magyar Zene* 34, no. 2 (1983): 120–44, and 35, no. 4 (1984): 346–66.

43. Somfai, "A Characteristic Culmination Point."

44. Bartók's letter to his mother, 12 June 1903, in *BBCsal,* 104.

45. *BBL,* 32.

46. *BBCsaL,* 110–111 (emphasis added). My translation is adapted from that in *BBL,* 29–31.

47. Frigyesi, "Béla Bartók and Hungarian Nationalism," 96–98.

48. Bartók's father created a gentry title for himself, Szuhafői (von Szuhafő). See Tibor Tallián, *Béla Bartók: The Man and His Work,* trans. Gyula Gulyás (Budapest, 1988), 9. See also Denijs Dille, *Bartók Béla családfája* (Béla Bartók's Family Tree), trans. Dóra F. Csanak (Budapest: Balassi Kiadó, 1996), 59–63.

49. *BBCsaL,* 77–78.

50. Bartók's letter to Irmy Jurkovics, 15 August 1905, in *BBL,* 50.

51. Concerning József Lukács's support of Bartók see Kenneth Chambers, *Béla Bartók* (London: Phaidon, 1995), 137.

52. Zoltán Kodály, "Confession: A Lecture Given to the *Nyugat* Circle of Friends," in *The Selected Writings of Zoltán Kodály,* 210. Quoted in Frigyesi, "Béla Bartók and Hungarian Nationalism," 45.

53. Bartók's letter to his mother, 18 June 1903, in *BBCsaL,* 106. My translation follows that in Tallián, *Béla Bartók,* 33.

54. Quoted in Lukacs, *Budapest 1900,* 128.

55. Pongrácz Kacsóh, "Bartók Béla," *Zenevilág* 5, no. 3, 17–18. Reprinted in János Demény, "Zeitgenössische Kritiken über die Erstaufführungen der Kossuth-Symphonie von Béla Bartók," *DocB* 1, 58 (emphasis added).

56. That Bartók knew *Bánk bán* hardly needs proof as Bartók was a student of Ferenc Erkel's son László in Pozsony, and the opera has been a staple of the Hungarian Opera's repertoire since the 1890s. We do know, however, that Bartók specifically studied the opera. See Denis Dille, *Thematisches Verzeichnis der Jugendwerke Béla Bartóks 1890–1904* (Budapest: Akadémiai Kiadó, 1974), 233.

57. Zoltán Kodály, "Béla Bartók the Man," in Kodály, *The Selected Writings of Zoltán Kodály*, 99.

58. A critical edition of *Bánk bán* is now in progress under the editorship of Tibor Tallián. The edition I cite is the piano vocal score published by Rózsavölgyi (plate number R. & Co. 2792), c. 1900. This is likely to be the same edition Bartók knew. The designation "first finale to act 1" is used because the end of the first act could occur at the end of this number but could also be placed after the next ensemble, the so-called second finale to act 1.

59. *A History of Hungarian Literature*, ed. Tibor Klaniczay (Budapest: Corvina, 1982), 175–76.

60. Reported in the review by Tivadar Lándor, "Kossuth-szimfónia," *Pesti Napló* 55, no. 14 (14 January 1904): 13–14, reprinted in *DocB* 1, 45.

61. Bartók to his mother, 8 September 1903, *BBL*, 29. Letters expressing similar nationalistic sentiments are concentrated in the years 1900–1903. For more examples in English see *BBL*, 18, 22, 29–32; in Hungarian see *BBCsaL*, 26–30, 40, 44, 47–49, 74, 77–78, 80, 99–100, 104, 113.

62. For reviews of Strauss see *Zenelap* 9, nos. 7–8 (15 March 1897): 9 (*Till Eulenspiegels lustige Streiche*); *Zenelap* 12, no. 31 (15 December 1898): 6 (*Don Juan*); *Budapesti Hírlap* 47, no. 12 (16 February 1905): 12 (*Symphonia Domestica*); *Pesti Hírlap* (16 February 1905): 6 (*Symphonia Domestica*); *Az Újság* (The News) (16 February 1905) (*Symphonia Domestica*). While none of these reviews is mainly positive, most of the negative criticism reflects a sense that Strauss's music was not as great as the foreign press reports had said. All the reviews show great respect for Strauss's composing technique and his skill as an orchestrator. No review calls him excessively modern.

63. See especially the reviews in: *Magyarország* (Hungary) in *DocB* 1, 31–32; *Egyetértés* (Agreement), especially the last paragraph, in *DocB* 1, 34–35; and *Ország-Világ* (Country-World) in *DocB* 1, 55–57. A rare, largely negative review appeared in *Az Újság* in *DocB* 1, 48.

64. See Lajos Bartucz, "Hungarian Man, Species, Race," published in Gyula Szekfű's *Mi a magyar?* (What Is Hungarian?) (Budapest: Magyar Szemle Társaság, 1939; reprint, Budapest: Helikon Kft, 1992), quoted in Móricz, "From Pure Sources Only."

65. *Magyar Hírlap* (17 November 1909), quoted in *Zt* 3, 347.

66. *Pressburger Presse* (5 November 1906), ibid., 312.

67. Frigyesi, "Béla Bartók and the Concept of Nation and *Volk* in Modern Hungary."

CHAPTER 3

1. The seven movements of *Nine Little Piano Pieces* were "3 párbeszéd" (3 Dialogues), "Csörgő tánc" (Tambourine), "Menuetto," "Dal" (Air), "Marcia delle bestie," "Preludio—all'Ungherese." The program also included the Five Songs, op. 16, and the Eight Hungarian Folk Songs sung by Mária Basilides. See *Zt* 7, 417.

2. Reviews of the concert reprinted in *Zt* 7, 417–24. "Az éjszaka zenéje" was initially referred to as "Hangverseny éjjel" (Nocturnal Concert) at Bartók's radio concert (3 December 1926). László Somfai, notes for *Béla Bartók Complete Edition* (Hungaroton), Piano Works 8 (1969), 1.

3. Other solo piano works of his own that Bartók performed with similar frequency in the late 1920s were *Allegro Barbaro* (1911), "Medvetánc" (Bear Dance, 1908), and "Este a Székelyeknél" (Evening in Transylvania, 1908).

4. My reading of "Az éjszaka zenéje" as composed of fundamental mythical symbols follows a tradition of Hungarian criticism of the work initiated by Aladár Tóth's review of the premiere (*Zt* 7, 423) and continued by József Ujfalussy in *Béla Bartók*, trans. Ruth Pataki (Budapest: Corvina, 1971; Hungarian original 1964), 232–36; Tallián in *Béla Bartók*, 144; and László Somfai in "Analytical Notes on Bartók's Piano Year of 1926," *Studia musicologica* 26, nos. 1–4 (1984): 5–6.

5. "Bartók Béla szerzői estje" (Concert of Béla Bartók's Works), *Pesti Napló* (10 December 1926), reprinted in *Zt* 7, 423.

6. "Új Bartók-művek bemutató előadása" (Premiere of New Bartók Works), *Pesti Napló* (22 March 1929), reprinted in *Zt* 10, 330. My translation is partially adapted from the excerpts translated by Erzsébet Marosszéki in *Arion 13*, *Bartók és a szavak* (Bartók and Words), ed. György Somlyó (Budapest: Corvina, 1982), 206–7 (emphasis added). By using the word *muzsika* as opposed to *zene* in his construction of the phrase "music of the night," Tóth manages to avoid directly quoting the title "Az éjszaka zenéje."

7. Márta Ziegler's account is translated into English in *Bartók Remembered*, ed. Malcolm Gillies (London: Faber and Faber, 1990), 25. Four other accounts appear in *Így láttuk Bartókot* (As We Saw Bartók), 2nd ed., ed. Ferenc Bónis (Budapest: Püski, 1995): Béla Bartók, Jr., 54; Magdolna Emil Oláh, 64; Pál Voit, 72; Albert Koós, 126. Bartók's niece, Mrs. Pál Voit (née Éva Oláh Tóth), described Bartók's interest and knowledge about insects and remembered sitting outside on clear summer nights with Bartók at Szőllős puszta in "Recollections of Béla Bartók," trans. Peter Laki, in *Bartók and His World*, ed. Peter Laki (Princeton: Princeton University Press, 1995), 243–44. See also Peter Bartók, *My Father* (Homosassa: Bartók Records, 2002), 161–64.

8. Éva Forgács has made a similar point about American versus Hungarian artistic representations of the city: "Instead of the future-bound optimism of New York, there was in Budapest a past-bound melancholy and nostalgia." "Avant-Garde and Conservatism in the Budapest Art World: 1910–1932," in *Budapest and New York: Studies in Metropolitan Transformation, 1870–1930*, ed. Thomas Bender and Carl E. Schorske (New York: Russell Sage Foundation, 1994), 310.

9. *Petőfi Sándor összes költeményei* (Sándor Petőfi's Complete Poems), vol. 1 (Budapest: Szépirodalmi Könyvkiadó, 1966), 109.

10. Mosonyi published his *Pusztai élet* under his birth name Michael Brand. He changed his name to the Hungarian Mihály Mosonyi two years later in 1859. *Mosonyi Mihály: Zongoraművek* (Mihály Mosonyi: Works for Piano), ed. István Kassai (Budapest: Akkord Music Publishers, 1997), 71.

11. Mosonyi also depicts the *furulya* in "Kis furulyás" (Little Piper) from *Magyar gyermekvilág* (Hungarian Children's World) for piano (1859).

12. In addition to Mosonyi's *Pusztai élet*, the second part of Ferenc (Franz)

Doppler's overture to his opera *Die beiden Husaren* (1853) provides an important precedent for the soloistic use of flute and piccolo in a pastoral mode.

13. *Mosonyi Mihály: Zongoraművek*, 71.

14. *Pester Lloyd* (23 November 1909), by A.B., in *Zt 3*, 349; *Magyarország* (23 November 1909), by M.A., ibid., 350.

15. F♯ minor is also a "natural" key for the bass clarinet in A, which reads the key of F♯ minor with no flats or sharps. The Boosey and Hawkes score of the Second Suite (B. & H. 16160) specifies bass clarinet in B♭ because the instrument pitched in A fell out of use shortly after World War I. Peter Bartók and Nelson Dellamaggiore have prepared an edition of the score that reinstates the bass clarinet in A, which accords with Bartók's own manuscript (Boosey and Hawkes, corr. ed., 2000). The tradition of using the bass clarinet in scenes of darkness and death goes back at least to Donizetti's *Dom Sébastien* (1843).

16. Bálint Sárosi, *Folk Music: Hungarian Musical Idiom*, 132.

17. Eszter Fontana, "Tárogató," in *New Grove II*, online. For late-eighteenth-century texts mentioning the *tárogató* see Bence Szabolcsi and Mária Domokos, "Rákóczi-induló" (Rákóczi-March), in Boronkay, *Brockhaus-Riemann zenei lexikon*, vol. 3, 179.

18. The expression "régi nagy idők" was a cliché applied to many events in Hungarian history and is especially common in connection with the *kuruc* period. Here I quote from the preface to *Wágner A. Károly módszeres tárogató iskolája* (Károly A. Wágner's Methodical *tárogató* Tutor) (Budapest: Wágner A. Károly, 1915). Bálint Sárosi gives 1830 as the end of the active use of the *tárogató* in *Folk Music: Hungarian Musical Idiom*, 132.

19. Zoltán Falvy, "Tárogató as a Regional Instrument," *Studia musicologica* 38, nos. 3–4 (1997): 361–70.

20. Schunda began to make a prototype of his *tárogató* in 1894. No data remain about Stowasser's first experiments. In 1897 Stowasser submitted a patent for his version of the *tárogató* several days ahead of Schunda. Each claimed each other's instrument to be a copy of his own. Ibid.

21. The most common *tárogató* was the instrument pitched in B♭ with a range A♭–b♭^{1}. Lower-pitched instruments were also produced in the keys of A♭ and E♭.

22. See Lynn Hooker, "The Political and Cultural Climate in Hungary at the Turn of the Twentieth Century," in Bayley, *The Cambridge Companion to Bartók*, 11.

23. Preface to *Wágner A. Károly módszeres tárogató iskolája* (emphasis in original).

24. Richter also used the *tárogató* in a Bayreuth production of *Tristan* in 1904. Falvy, "Tárogató as a Regional Instrument," 370.

25. The three operas in Zichy's *Rákóczi Trilogy* and the dates of their premieres are 1. *Ferenc Rákóczi II.* (1909); 2. *Nemo* (1905); 3. *Rodostó* (1912).

26. Albert Siklós, *Hangszereléstan elméleti és gyakorlati alapon* (Study of Orchestration on a Theoretical and Practical Basis), vol. 1 (Budapest: Rozsnyai Károly, 1909), 207–9.

27. L.D.T., "Színház és zene: Hatodik filharmoniai hangverseny" (Theater and Music: The Sixth Concert of the Philharmonic), *Pesti Hírlap* (8 January 1903): 5.

28. A.L., "Színház. Zene: A filharmónikusok," *Magyar Nemzet* (8 January 1903): 6 (emphasis added).

29. The Rákóczi March, an amalgamation of motives from the "Rákóczi nóta," military signals from the *kuruc* period, and Hungarian dance music (*verbunkos*), may have been composed by János Bihari. The march was first orchestrated (1809?) by Miklós Scholl, leader of a military band in Eszterháza. Ferenc Erkel's arrangement for piano *Emlékül Liszt Ferenczre, Rákóczi indulója* (Souvenir for Franz Liszt, Rákóczi's March) (1840) was made after hearing Liszt's rendition (later included in the Hungarian Rhapsody no. 15). Berlioz's orchestration of the march (1846) is based on Erkel's version. See Szabolcsi and Domokos, "Rákóczi-induló." Bartók played what may have been his own four-hand arrangement of the Rákóczi March in May 1896 at millennial celebrations in Pozsony. See Dille, *Thematisches Verzeichnis der Jugendwerke Béla Bartóks, 1890–1904*, 23, 187. Liszt used the "Rákóczi nóta" in his *Ungarisches Königslied* (1883). See Walker, *Franz Liszt*, vol. 3, 410.

30. Two examples of the "original "Rákóczi Nóta" with the phrase "mint azt a Rákóczi korban tárogatón fújták" (as it was played on the *tárogató* in Rákóczi's time) appear in János Stowasser, Jr., *Elméleti és gyakorlati tárogató iskola* (Theoretical and Practical *Tárogató* Tutor) (Budapest: J. Stowasser, c. 1900), 27; and in Gyula Káldy, *Schätze der alten ungarischen Musik (1672–1833): Weisen und Lieder aus den Zeiten von Thököly und Rákóczi* (Budapest: Rózsavölgyi, 1895), 3. The designation "original" served to distinguish that version of the tune from Transylvanian and Ruthenian variants.

31. Szendy won the Greguss Prize in 1917 for his *Helikon Suite*. Bartók performed movements 5–10 of Szendy's *Aforizmák magyar népdalok fölött zongorára* (Aphorisms on Hungarian Folk Songs for Piano) on the 12 March 1910 Hungarian Festival Concert in Paris and also possessed scores to his "Rhapsodie hongoise" for Piano and String Quartet in C Major. See Vikárius, *Modell és inspiráció*, 81.

32. The score of Szendy's *Hat magyar zeneköltemény* published by Károly Rozsnai (Budapest) is, like many Hungarian scores of the time, undated. Press reports of the 1909 premiere of Szendy's arrangement of the work for orchestra indicate, however, that the original version for piano was in circulation for some time before 1909. This information combined with the plate number (R.K. 131) suggests that "Tárogató hangzik . . ." dates from between 1900 and 1908.

33. "Szendy Árpád: Magyar poémák" (Árpád Szendy: Hungarian Poems), *Zeneközlöny* 7, no. 10 (6 March 1909): 124. This article was printed anonymously but may have been by Szendy as it was common for the guides to new Hungarian works in *Zeneközlöny* to have been written by their composers. The reviewer's comment that the *tárogató* is difficult to handle may be a reference to the instrument's slippery intonation. This, however, did not prevent amateurs from taking up the instrument.

34. L.D.T., "Színház és zene: Kilencedik filharmoniai hangverseny" (Theater and Music: Ninth Philharmonic Concert," *Pesti Hírlap* (9 March 1909): 8.

35. "Magyar poémák," *Zenelap* 23, no. 5 (March 1909): 5.

36. *BBL*, 105.

37. "The Folk Songs of Hungary," *Pro Musica* (New York), reprinted in *BBE*, 334–35.

38. In his 1909 program note for the Second Suite, Bartók also singled out the final chord of the third movement but did not relate it to folk music. Instead he called it "in reality nothing but the simultaneous sounding of the notes of the much

repeated motive." "Bartók: II. suite. Op. 4," *Zeneközlöny* 8, no. 7 (20 November 1909), in *BBÍ/1*, 59. The first evidence of the "old-style" melodies making a direct impact on Bartók's original composition is the pentatonic theme of the fourth movement of the Second Suite, written some two years after the third movement and after his trip to Transylvania in 1907.

39. Carl Dahlhaus, *Nineteenth-Century Music*, trans. J. Bradford Robinson (Berkeley: University of California Press, 1989), 307.

40. Ernő Lendvai, *Bartók dramaturgiája* (Bartók's Dramaturgy) (Budapest: Akkord, 1993): 44–47, 86, and 113. Lendvai first discussed the acoustic scale in *Bartók stílusa* (Bartók's Style) (Budapest: Zeneműkiadó, 1955), 30.

41. Excerpts from Weiner's incidental music were first performed in Budapest in February 1914. Bartók began work on *The Wooden Prince* in April 1914. Weiner's arrangement of the music as the *Csongor és Tünde* Suite was first performed in Dresden and shortly afterwards in Budapest on 4 February 1916, some six months before the premiere of *The Wooden Prince*. The first production of the stage play with Weiner's incidental music took place on 6 December 1916. Although we have no proof of Bartók's having known Weiner's "Night," it is hard to imagine that he would not have been aware of a major new composition by a composer whom he held in high regard. László Vikárius has argued convincingly that hearing Weiner's First String Quartet inspired Bartók to begin his own first essay in that genre. Bartók promoted Weiner's work by playing his Präludium, Nocturne, and Scherzo, op. 7, on the second concert of the New Hungarian Music Society (12 December 1911). See Vikárius, *Modell és inspiráció*, 109, 172–73.

42. Five Songs, op. 15, was completed in 1916. Despite several plans to perform and publish these songs in various configurations they remained unpublished and unperformed in Bartók's lifetime. Bartók's reluctance to pursue their publication may have stemmed both from the mediocre quality of the texts, written by two teenage girls he befriended while collecting folk songs, and from his desire to conceal a possible romantic relationship with one of them. See László Somfai's essay in the booklet to accompany *Bartók Complete Edition: Vocal Works*, Hungaroton Classic, HCD 31906–08, 14–15. Ujfalussy remarks on the similarity of "Itt lent a völgyben" and "Az éjszaka zenéje" in *Béla Bartók*, 235.

43. Béla Bartók, "The Folk Songs of Hungary" (1928), *BBE*, 338; "The Influence of Folk Music on the Art Music of Today" (1920), *BBE*, 318; "The Relation of Folk Song to the Development of the Art Music of Our Time" (1921), *BBE*, 321; "What Is Folk Music?" (1931), *BBE*, 6.

44. In a letter to his mother 12 November 1902 Bartók reports: "Today I took the slow movement [of the Symphony in Eb] to Koessler who said: 'In the *Adagio* there has to be love; in this movement, however, there is nothing that speaks of love. This is a problem.' . . . Koessler is a very harsh judge when it comes to *adagio*-s. He likes to say: In order to write an *adagio*, one has to have life experience (what?! probably love and what goes with it: wonder, infatuation, pain, etc.). . . . By the way he doesn't consider Dohnányi's *adagio*-s perfect either. (Neither do I!)." *BBCsaL*, 75.

45. The original version of *Ruralia hungarica*, op. 32a for piano (1923), consists of seven pieces. The orchestral version, op. 32b (1924), includes only five. The movement in question is the third piece of op. 32a and the first of op. 32b.

46. The Kisfaludy Society was a literary society that counted a high percentage

of aristocrats among its members. It granted the Greguss Prize (somewhat analogous to the Pulitzer Prize in the United States) in several literary and artistic areas on a rotating basis, which meant that an award in composition occurred every six years. *Ruralia Hungarica* won the Greguss Prize in 1929, the first year after its completion in which the prize was awarded in music. Árpád Szendy won the prize for his *Helikon Suite* in 1923, and Bartók was awarded the prize in 1935 for his First Suite for Large Orchestra (1905). Offended that the Society had snubbed him for so long and then recognized him for a work completed three decades before, Bartók publicly refused the award.

CHAPTER 4

1. Sugar, *A History of Hungary*, 293.
2. "Hiszek egy Istenben/Hiszek egy hazában/Hiszek egy Isteni örök igazságban/ Hiszek egy Magyarország feltámadásában/Csonka Magyarország nem ország/Egész Magyarország mennyország."
3. In Boronkay, *Brockhaus-Riemann zenei lexikon*, vol. 3, 532.
4. Bartók's oft-repeated notion that a composer should learn folk music so well that he can use its idioms as if it were "his mother tongue" is, in fact, a paraphrase of Tóth writing about Kodály in *Nyugat* (July 1920). See *BBÍ/1*, 111.
5. "Operaházi kilátások" (Perspectives on the Opera House), *Nyugat* (16 September 1921). Reprinted in *Zenei írások a* Nyugatban (Musical Writings in the *Nyugat*), ed. János Breuer (Budapest: Zeneműkiadó, 1978), 186, 188.
6. "Jegyzetek a filharmonikusok idei műsorához" (Notes on This Year's Philharmonic Program), *Nyugat* (1 March 1923); reprinted in *Zenei írások a* Nyugatban, 196, 198.
7. Aladár Tóth, "A magyar zenekritika feladatai" (The Tasks of the Hungarian Music Critic), *Nyugat* (1 October 1925); reprinted in *Zenei írások a* Nyugatban, 15–16.
8. *A Magyar Királyi Operaház évkönyve "1928–1929"* (The Yearbook of the Royal Hungarian Opera House "1928–1929") (Budapest: A Magyar Királyi Operaház Igazgatósága, 1928?), 17; and *The Art of Dance in Hungary*, ed. Edit Kapossi and Ernő Pesovár, trans. Lili Halápy et al. (Budapest: Corvina, 1985), 118.
9. Stravinsky, 27 September 1945, upon hearing of Bartók's death. Reported in Vera Stravinsky and Robert Craft, *Stravinsky in Pictures and Documents* (New York: Faber and Faber, 1978), 648; reprinted in Gillies, *Bartók Remembered*, 223.
10. Igor Stravinsky and Robert Craft, *Conversations with Igor Stravinsky* (London: Faber and Faber, 1959; reprint, Berkeley: University of California Press, 1980), 74.
11. Richard Taruskin makes this argument in "Russian Folk Melodies in the *Rite of Spring*," *Journal of the American Musicological Society* 33, no. 3 (1980): 501–43; "Stravinsky and the Traditions: Why the Memory Hole," *Opus* 3 (1983): 10–17; and *Stravinsky and the Russian Traditions*, esp. pp. 8 and 14.
12. In an interview with Stravinsky by János Fóthy (*Pesti Hírlap*, 14 March 1926, 10), Stravinsky mentions having been in Budapest in 1912, but states that he knew of Bartók primarily through reports in the international press.
13. For information pertaining to Bartók's meeting Stravinsky in Paris see Bartók's letters to his mother on 10 and 15 April 1922 in *BBCsaL*, 330–31, and *BBL*, 160, respectively; and Aladár Tóth, "Bartók külföldi útja" (Bartók's Foreign Tour),

Nyugat 15, no. 12 (1922): 830–33; translated by David E. Schneider and Klára Móricz in Laki, *Bartók and His World*, 282–89.

14. Aladár Tóth, "A magyar zenekritika feladatai," *Nyugat* (1 October 1925), in *Zenei írások a Nyugatban*, 21.

15. Géza Vilmos Zágon, "Kubizmus a zenében" (Cubism in Music), *Zeneközlöny* (15 October 1913), quoted in János Breuer, "A Magyarországi Stravinsky-kultusz nyomában" (In Search of the Stravinsky-Cult in Hungary), in *Bartók és Kodály: Tanulmányok századunk magyar zenetörténetéhez* (Bartók and Kodály: Studies of Our Century's Hungarian Music History) (Budapest: Magvető Könyvkiadó, 1978), 307–8.

16. In *The Sackbut* 1, no. 7 (1920): 302, Cecil Gray argued vigorously against the facile equation of Bartók and Stravinsky made by Leigh Henry in *Musical Opinion* earlier that year.

17. The Népopera opened in 1911. The original opera house of the Népopera is now the Erkel Theatre, a second venue for the Hungarian Opera.

18. Tibor Tallián, "Das holzgeschnitzte Hauptwerk," *Studia musicologica* 37, no. 1 (1996): 54.

19. Breuer, "A magyarországi Stravinsky-kultusz nyomában," 307.

20. Ibid., 315. From 3 May 1911 to 21 May 1920 Bartók lived in quasi self-exile in Rákoskeresztúr outside Budapest and rarely went into the city except to teach.

21. Ibid., 307.

22. Bartók's letter to Philip Heseltine, 24 November 1920, in *DocB* 5 (1977), 140.

23. Béla Balázs, *Napló 1903–1914* (Diary 1903–1914) (Budapest: Magvető Könyvkiadó, 1982), 526–75. In early 1912 an extensive article on the Ballets Russes entitled "A ballett reneszánsza" (Ballet's Renaissance) appeared in *Auróra* (nos. 14–15: 339–42), the progressive literary magazine in which Bartók had published "On Hungarian Music" and with which Balázs was associated.

24. Eric Walter White, *Stravinsky: The Composer and His Works* (Berkeley: University of California Press, 1979), 182–89; and Richard Taruskin, "Chernomor to Kashchei: Harmonic Sorcery; or, Stravinsky's 'Angle,'" *Journal of the American Musicological Society* 38, no. 1 (1985): 72–142.

25. For a brief summary of Bartók's use of "pure" and "corrupt" Hungarian styles in *Bluebeard's Castle* see my review of Carl Leafstedt's *Inside* Bluebeard's Castle, *MLA Notes* 58, no. 2 (2001): 359–60.

26. The clarinet became a regular member of Hungarian Gypsy ensembles in the 1840s. See Sárosi, *Folk Music: Hungarian Musical Idiom*, 130–31.

27. Taruskin, *Stravinsky and the Russian Traditions*, 632.

28. According to Roy Howat, Bartók described the opening of the Sonata for Two Pianos and Percussion in terms of creation archetypes. See "Masterworks (II): *Sonata for Two Pianos and Percussion*," in Gillies, *The Bartók Companion*, 317. György Kroó has also recognized that movements beginning with creation metaphors are a recurring type in Bartók's oeuvre (Kroó, *A Guide to Bartók*, 193). See also László Vikárius, "'Per introdurre': A bartóki bevezetés megformálásának problematikája" ("Per introdurre": A Contribution to the Problem of Constructing Introductions in Bartók's Music), *Magyar zene* 35, no. 2 (1994): 190–203.

29. *Pester Lloyd* (13 May 1917), in *Zt* 7, 46.

30. *Zenei Szemle* (Temesvár/Timişoara) 1, no. 4 (1917): 128–29, in *Zt* 7, 34.

31. The production of *The Wooden Prince* was nearly sabotaged by recalcitrant orchestra members and a director who abandoned it midway through the rehearsal schedule.

32. *Színházi Élet* (25 December 1918), reproduced in Breuer, *Bartók és Kodály*, 49.

33. Márta Ziegler's recollection dates from 1966 and is translated in Gillies, *Bartók Remembered*, 23. Kodály also reported that Bartók played *The Rite of Spring* for Bánffy, but says it was during the rehearsals for *The Wooden Prince* (*DocB* 3, 93). See Breuer, *Bartók és Kodály*, 402.

34. Bartók, "Arnold Schönbergs Musik in Ungarn," *Musikblätter des Anbruch* 11, no. 20 (1920): 647–48, in *BBE*, 468. *The Rite of Spring* was first performed in Hungary on 17 February 1929 by the Philharmonic conducted by Ernő Dohnányi.

35. Arisztid Valkó, "Adatok Bartók színpadi műveihez" (Documents Relating to Bartók's Stage Works), *Magyar zene* 18 (1977): 433–39, cited in Vera Lampert, "*The Miraculous Mandarin:* Melchior Lengyel, His Pantomime, and His Connections to Béla Bartók," in Laki, *Bartók and His World*, 170.

36. "Bartók Béla elmondja a Lengyel-Bartók-opera meséjét" (Béla Bartók Relates the Story of the Lengyel-Bartók Opera), *Színházi Élet* 8, no. 12 (1919), 25, in *Beszélgetések Bartókkal: Interjúk, nyilatkozatok 1911–1945* (Conversations with Bartók: Interviews, Communiqués 1911–1945), ed. András Wilheim (Budapest: Kijárat Kiadó, 2000), 14.

37. Elza Galafrés, *Lives . . . Loves . . . Losses* (Vancouver: Versatile, 1973), 236–37.

38. The identity of the first two men is confused here. The first is "the Old Gallant," the second "the Youth."

39. Wilheim, *Beszélgetések Bartókkal*, 14.

40. Márta Ziegler's letter to Bartók's mother, 14 May 1919, in *BBCsaL*, 295. Elza Galafrés, soon to be Dohnáni's second wife, was his lover at the time.

41. Béla Bartók, Jr., *Apám életének krónikája* (Chronicle of My Father's Life) (Budapest: Zeneműkiadó, 1981), 162–63.

42. Éva Forgács, "Avant-Garde and Conservatism in the Budapest Art World: 1910–1932," in Bender and Schorske, *Budapest and New York*, 309–31, especially 310 and 317.

43. In the second movement of the Suite, op. 14 (1916), Bartók occasionally writes in parallel seconds, but this is not an example of a harmonization of a folklike melody.

44. Taruskin, *Stravinsky and the Russian Traditions*, 951–54.

45. Ibid.; and John Vinton, "The Case of *The Miraculous Mandarin*," *Musical Quarterly* 50, no. 1 (1964): 1–17, especially 8–12.

46. In his book *Modell és inspiráció* László Vikárius relates Bartók's frequent use of the minor third to his early fascination with Richard Strauss's *Salome* (186–91). The interval's sexual connotation is hard to miss in *The Miraculous Mandarin*.

47. The young student is also sympathetically portrayed by Bartók, but his appearance is very brief. Shortening the scene in which he appears was one of Bartók's most significant revisions of the original score. See Vinton, "The Case of *The Miraculous Mandarin*," *Musical Quarterly* 50, no. 1 (1964): 4.

48. See Carl Leafstedt, "The Stage Works: Portraits of Loneliness," in Bayley, *The Cambridge Companion to Bartók*, 75.

49. *DocB* 5, 140; original in French.

50. *BBE*, 325–26.

51. "Now, almost all the motives (for instance, of *Sacre*) seem to be Russian peasant music motives or their excellent imitations. And the harmonies into which they are inserted are marvelously suitable for the creation of a kind of apotheosis of the Russian rural music. But, despite the quite incredible novelty displayed throughout, the aforementioned bases as original starting points remain recognizable. Even the origin of the rough-grained, brittle, and jerky musical structure, backed by ostinatos, which is so completely different from any structural proceeding of the past, may be sought in the short-breathed Russian peasant motives." Bartók, "Harvard Lectures" (1943), in *BBE*, 360.

52. Bartók's letter to Philip Heseltine, 7 February 1921, in *DocB* 5, 141 (emphasis added); original in English. Bartók's interest in the Dutch-born English composer Bernard van Dieren (1887–1936) had been sparked by Heseltine's enthusiastic reviews of his music in *The Sackbut*. If Bartók ever did get to know van Dieren's music we have no record that it was more interesting to him than the rest of the lot.

53. Breuer, "A magyarországi Stravinsky-kultusz nyomában," 309.

54. "Budapest Welcomes Dohnanyi's Return," *DocB* 5, 112. Originally in *Musical Courier* (14 July 1921).

55. "The Influence of Folk Music on the Art Music of Today," *BBE*, 317–18. Originally in *Melos* (16 October 1920).

56. Bartók seems to have suspected that the melodies Stravinsky used in *Pribaoutki* were folk songs, but lacking proof he cautiously described them as "folk-like." It seems Bartók's suspicions were well founded at least in the case of the first song, "Kornilo," the folk source of which Richard Taruskin has identified. See *Stravinsky and the Russian Traditions*, 1167–68.

57. See Bartók's letters of 10 and 15 April 1922, *BBCsaL*, 330–32.

58. "Bartók külföldi útja" (see n. 13 above). The cited passage is on p. 286.

59. Letter to Ernst Latzko, 16 December 1924, in *BBL*, 312.

60. Dezső Kosztolányi, "Bartók Béla megjelenése az európai zeneéletben" (Béla Bartók's Appearance in the Musical Life of Europe), *Pesti Hírlap* (31 May 1925): 38. Translated in Laki, *Bartók and His World*, 152.

61. Ibid.

62. My summary of Molnár's position is taken from "Újabb zenemozgalmak" (Newer Movements in Music), ch. 4 of *Az új zene. A zeneművészet legujabb irányának ismertetése kultúretikai megvilágításban* (The New Music: Introduction to the Newest Trends of Music in Light of Cultural Ethics) (Budapest: Révai, 1925), 96–110.

63. Ibid., 204.

64. *Zenei Szemle* 9 (1926–27): 77.

65. "Bartók Béla nyilatkozata a 'progresszív zenei alkotásokról'" (Béla Bartók's Proclamation about 'Progressive Musical Works'), ed. László Somfai, *Magyar zene* 16, no. 2 (1975): 115.

66. François Gachot, "Stravinsky," *Nyugat* (16 March 1926), in *Zenei írások a Nyugatban*, 320–27; Jenő Feiks, "Igor Stravinsky," *Pesti Napló* (14 March 1926); and János Fóthy, "Stravinsky Budapesten: beszélgetés a Tűzmadár zeneszerzőjével" (Stravinsky in Budapest: A Conversation with the Composer of the Firebird), *Pesti Hírlap* (14 March 1926), in Breuer, *Bartók és Kodály*, 317–20.

67. Jenő Szenkár conducted the Philharmonic in *Pulcinella* on 23 November 1925. Szenkár conducted the premiere of *The Miraculous Mandarin* on 27 November 1926 in Cologne.

68. "Sztravinsky-est" (An Evening of Stravinsky's Music), *Pesti Napló* (16 March 1926): 15.

69. Ibid., 14–15.

70. "Beszélgetés Bartók Bélával" (Conversation with Béla Bartók), interview in *Kassai Napló* (Kassa Journal) (23 April 1926): 4, in Wilheim, *Beszélgetések Bartókkal*, 74.

71. Ditta Pásztory's letter to Bartók's mother, Mrs. Paula Voit Bartók, 18 March 1926, in *BBCsaL*, 375. Emphasis added to highlight phrases or words similar to those in the contemporary published reviews of Stravinsky's concert.

72. Aladár Tóth, "Modern szerzők a hangversenyteremben" (Modern Compositions in the Concert Hall), *Nyugat* (1 December 1925), in Breuer, *Zenei írások a Nyugatban*, 296. Emphasis added to highlight a point of intersection with Pásztory's letter.

73. Peter Laki, "The Gallows and the Altar: Poetic Criticism and Critical Poetry about Bartók in Hungary," in Laki, *Bartók and His World*, 82–83.

74. Izor Béldi, "Casals és Stravinsky" (Casals and Stravinsky), *Pesti Hírlap* (16 March 1926): 13–14. Emphasis added to highlight phrases or words that overlap with Pásztory's letter.

75. Bartók reported needing to write a piano concerto as early as November 1925. See Károly Kristóf, "A jazz-zene analógiája a cigányzenének" (Jazz Music's Analogy to Gypsy Music), *Ma Este* (Tonight) 3/45 (12 November 1925). Reprinted in Wilheim, *Beszélgetések Bartók Bélával*, 63.

76. Bartók's letter to his wife Ditta Pásztory, 21 June 1926, in *BBCsaL*, 381. Part of my translation follows that in Tallián, *Béla Bartók: The Man and His Work*, 140.

77. Bartók to Edwin von der Nüll, quoted in Edwin von der Nüll, *Béla Bartók, Ein Beitrag zur Morphologie der neuen Musik* (Halle: Mitteldeutsche Verlags-Aktien-Gesellschaft, 1930), 108. In 1926 and 1927 Bartók made several transcriptions of seventeenth- and early-eighteenth-century Italian keyboard music.

78. Aladár Tóth, "Sztravinsky-est" (An Evening of Stravinsky's Music), *Pesti Napló* (16 March 1926): 14–15.

79. For a discussion of the motivic interrelationships of the themes of the first movement of the First Piano Concerto see Frigyesi, *Béla Bartók and Turn-of-the-Century Budapest*, 135–38.

80. Budapest Bartók Archives manuscript 58PPS1, 15.

81. Somfai discusses the Hungarian quality of this theme and its relationship to passages in the brass at reh. nos. 11 and 18 in "Analytical Notes on Bartók's Piano Year 1926." He first wrote about it in "A Characteristic Culmination Point," 59–61.

82. Bartók lists these characteristics of the "old-style" Hungarian melodies in many of his discussions of Hungarian folk music. The best summary is in his 1934 essay "Hungarian Folk Music and the Folk Music of Neighboring Peoples," translated in Suchoff, *Béla Bartók: Studies in Ethnomusicology*, 174–75. Bartók describes how pitches not belonging to the pentatonic set may occur in "old-style" songs in his 1921 essay "Hungarian Folk Music," *BBE*, 61.

83. My interpretation of this passage of Stravinsky's concerto is indebted to

Richard Taruskin's "The Pastness of the Present and the Presentness of the Past," in *Authenticity and Early Music*, ed. Nicholas Kenyon (Oxford: Oxford University Press, 1988), 137–210. Reprinted in *Text and Act: Essays on Music and Performance* (New York: Oxford University Press, 1995), 90–154.

84. "Béla Bartók: Piano Concerto—On the Occasion of its Premiere 1 July 1927," *Melos* 6, no. 6 (1927): 256–57, in *Zt 10*, 218.

85. "Bartók Béla zongoraversenyműve a hétfői filharmonikus hangversenyen" (Béla Bartók's Piano Concerto on Monday's Philharmonic Concert), *Pesti Napló* (20 March 1928), in *Zt 10*, 270–71.

86. "Bartók bemutató" (Bartók Premiere), *Budapesti Hírlap* (20 March 1928), in *Zt 10*, 272.

87. *Nieuwe Rotterdamische Courant* (9 November 1928), in *Zt 10*, 291.

88. Letter to Bartók from the general music director of the city of Freiburg, 21 November 1930. "Zu Ihrem Klavierkonzert ist hier ein gespieltes Material eingetroffen, die Partitur ist aber noch nicht benützt worden. In dieser sind einige Takte zusammengezogen. . . . Z[um] Beispiel: $\frac{5}{8}$ and $\frac{3}{8}$ sind in verschiedenen Orchesterstimmen zu zweimal $\frac{2}{4}$ Takte verändert!" Budapest Bartók Archives, MTA 74.

89. "Analyse du Deuxième Concerto pour Piano et Orchestre de Béla Bartók par son Auteur," *La Radio* (Lausanne) (17 February 1939), in *BBE*, 419.

90. Although the reference/quotation is obvious to anyone familiar with *The Firebird*, the first published reference to the connection between the two works appears in Ferenc Bónis, "Quotations in Bartók's Music," *Studia musicologica* 5, nos. 1–4 (1963): 377. The similarity between *Petrushka* and Bartók's Second Piano Concerto was immediately observed by at least one critic, Edwin von der Nüll, who wrote about it in 1933. See Vikárius, *Modell és inspiráció*, 144, n. 162.

91. Aladár Tóth, "Bartók's Foreign Tour," in Laki, *Bartók and His World*, 287.

92. Bartók performed the Rhapsody, op. 1. Vikárius, *Modell és inspiráció*, 145.

93. Bartók and Ditta's playing the four-hand arrangement of *Petrushka* was reported to me by Denijs Dille in a personal conversation in May 1993. Ditta reports on the recording of *Petrushka* in a letter to Bartók's mother on 25 December 1928, in *BBCsaL*, 459.

94. László Somfai, "Statikai tervezés és formai dramaturgia a 2. zongoraversenyben" (Static Planning and Formal Dramaturgy in the Second Piano Concerto), in Somfai, *Tizennyolc Bartók-tanulmány* (Eighteen Bartók Studies) (Budapest: Zeneműkiadó, 1981), 200–205.

95. Interview with Denijs Dille, *La Sirène* (Brussels) 1, no. 1 (1937): 3–6. In Wilheim, *Beszélgetések Bartókkal*, 181.

96. Somfai discusses Bartók's strategy of retrograde inversion in "Classicism as Bartók Conceptualized It in His Classical Period 1926–1937," in *Die klassizistische Moderne in der Music des 20. Jahrhunderts*, ed. Hermann Danuser (Basel: Paul Sacher Stiftung, 1997), 137–38.

97. Somfai argues that "the triumphant 'singing' Hungarian-style" version of the motto theme in the coda (mm. 295–307) retains "Romantic" associations. The point is valid, but this final moment does not erase the overall mechanistic "neoclassical" effect of the movement (ibid.).

98. "Old-" and "new-style" Hungarian folk songs are Bartók's own categories.

See Béla Bartók, *The Hungarian Folk Song*, ed. Benjamin Suchoff (Albany: State University of New York Press, 1981), especially 37–38 and 51–52. The relationship between the opening of the Second Piano Concerto and the four-line structure of Hungarian folk song is described by László Somfai in "Statikai tervezés és formai dramaturgia a 2. zongoraversenyben," 201. A similar observation has been made independently by Peter Petersen, *Die Tonalität im Instrumentalschaffen von Béla Bartók* (Hamburg: Karl Dieter Wagner, 1971), 147–53.

99. Reviews quoted in *Zt 10*, 448–49.

100. *Művelt Nép* (Cultured Folk) 6, no. 39 (1955): 5, in *Zt 10*, 445.

101. "Bartók Béla és új zongoraversenyműve" (Béla Bartók and His New Piano Concerto), *Pesti Napló* (4 June 1933), in *Zt 10*, 443.

102. Ibid.

103. Ibid.

104. "A parasztzene hatása az újabb műzenére" (The Influence of Peasant Music on the Art Music of Today), *BBÖI*, 674. The text quoted is part of the version of this essay given as a lecture in Budapest on 10 March 1931 and originally published 10 May 1931 in *Új Idők* (New Times).

105. Interview with Denijs Dille (1937), in Wilheim, *Beszélgetések Bartókkal*, 181.

106. For references to Stravinsky after 1932 see *BBLev*, 621, 634, 641 (all concerning the Concerto for Two Pianos); on 1 May 1933, Bartók notes Stravinsky's absence at an international music festival in Florence; *BBCsaL*, 537. Bartók brings up Stravinsky in an interview after 1932 only once: see Wilheim, *Beszélgetések Bartókkal*, 137.

107. For details of Bartók's Harvard residency see Vera Lampert, "Bartók at Harvard University as Witnessed in Unpublished Archival Documents," *Studia musicologica* 35, nos. 1–3 (1993–94): 113–54.

108. "Bartók Béla nyilatkozata a progresszív zenei alkotásokról," *Magyar zene* 16, no. 2 (1975): 115.

109. Bartók, "Harvard Lectures," in *BBE*, 358–59.

110. Ibid., 360.

CHAPTER 5

1. Béla Bartók and Zoltán Kodály, *Hungarian Folk Songs* (facsimile edition), ed. Denijs Dille (Budapest: Zeneműkiadó, 1970), 1. The preface was written by Kodály but signed by both Kodály and Bartók. Approximately half of Bartók's folk-music arrangements (at least 156 of the 313 folk melodies) constitute works that are explicitly pedagogical. *Ten Easy Pieces* includes arrangements of two folk songs, *44 Duos* contains 42, *Mikrokosmos* contains 4, *For Children* contains 85, *First Term at the Piano* contains 3. A number of Bartók's other folk-music arrangements are also technically simple and appropriate for children.

2. Ibid.

3. The folk-music sources of the First Rhapsody for violin are listed in Lampert, *Bartók népdalfeldolgozásainak forrásjegyzéke*, 113–16. Of the six tunes in the Rhapsody, four were collected from Romanian peasants in Romanian villages (nos. 1, 3, 4, and 6) and two from Gypsies (nos. 2 and 5). The name of the performer of the second melody, János Balog, suggests he was Hungarian-speaking. No name was indicated for the performer of the fifth melody.

4. Scotus Viator (Scottish Traveler) is an allusion to the Scottish historian of central and southeastern Europe R. W. Seton-Watson (1879–1951), who advocated independence for the national minorities of greater Hungary (although he did not support the draconian terms of the Treaty of Trianon). See Hugh Seton-Watson, "R. W. Seton-Watson and the Trianon Settlement," in *Essays on World War I: Total War and Peacemaking, A Case Study on Trianon,* ed. Béla K. Király, Peter Pastor, and Ivan Sanders (New York: Brooklyn College Press, 1982). Digitalized by Ferenc Jakab, Istvan Lippai, and Andrew L. Simon, 1997 (www.hungarian-history.hu/lib/tria/tria02.htm).

5. Bartók's letter to Octavian Beu, 10 January 1931, in *BBL,* 200–201.

6. Ignác Romsics, *Magyarország története a XX. században* (The History of Hungary in the Twentieth Century) (Budapest: Osiris, 2000), 237.

7. *BBL,* 202–3.

8. *BBL,* 201.

9. These quotes are taken, respectively, from Bartók, "Hungarian Folk Music" (1929), in *BBE,* 3; Bartók, "What Is Folk Music?" (1931), in *BBE,* 5; and Bartók, "Hungarian Folk Music" (1935), in *Béla Bartók: Studies in Ethnomusicology,* 163.

10. Ibid.

11. Bartók first seems to have begun using the term "peasant music" in the introduction to his article "A Biskra-vidéki arabok népzenéje" (Arab Folk Music from Biskra), *Szimfónia* (1917) no. 1, 12–13; translated into English (with a date of 1920 referring to the German translation of the article in *Zeitschrift der Musikwissenschaft*) in *Béla Bartók: Studies in Ethnomusicology,* 29. I am grateful to László Vikárius for calling this to my attention.

12. Bartók, "Hungarian Folk Music" (1929), *BBE,* 3.

13. Bartók's description of "old-style" melodies may be summarized with the following four characteristics:

1. A general adherence to the following pentatonic scale, which Bartók characterized as an "archaic scale, anhemitonic-pentatonic, of Asiatic origin: G–Bb–C–D–F–G".

2. An isometric four-section melodic structure corresponding to four isometric lines of text.

3. A descending structure in which the first part of the melody moves in the upper part of the octave, and the last part in the lower part of the octave.

4. Three kinds of rhythms: parlando (free rhythm), invariable dance rhythm, and dotted rhythm metrically adjusted to the text.

(Definition adapted from "Hungarian Folk Music and the Folk Music of Neighboring Peoples," in *Béla Bartók: Studies in Ethnomusicology,* 174–75.)

14. Ibid., 191.

15. Bartók's hypothesis was further supported by the fact that the "old-style" songs found in Romanian communities were only used with text lines of eight syllables, whereas a greater variety of "old-style" melodies were found in Hungarian villages. Because the repertoire of Romanian folk songs that did not exhibit similarities to the Hungarian melodies were also made up exclusively of eight-syllable lines, Bartók reasoned that Romanians had adopted only those Hungarian melodies that fit a preexisting poetic scheme. A basic premise of Bartók's work was that the greater the variation among the individual melodies that constituted a homoge-

neous category, the more actively that category participated in the life of the community. Thus, the greater variety of "old-style" melodies known to Hungarians proved for Bartók that these melodies had historically constituted a more important part of the Hungarian folk repertoire than they did of the Romanian. Ibid., 190–91.

16. Bartók, "Népzenénk és a szomszéd népek zenéje" (Hungarian Folk Music and the Folk Music of Neighboring People), in *Népszerű zenefüzetek* (Popular Music Notebooks), no. 3, ed. Antal Molnár, reprinted in *BBÖI*, 403–61. My translation is based on that in *Béla Bartók: Studies in Ethnomusicology*, 199.

17. This passage was originally intended to be the conclusion of the essay and is dated 15 January 1934. The publication includes a postscript dated March 1934 based on Bartók's just-completed research in Bucharest that, he implies, further strengthens his findings regarding the unique qualities of Hungarian folk music.

18. Ibid., 197.

19. On 29 July 1934 Bartók described the details of his transfer to the Academy of Sciences in a letter to Ernő Dohnányi, new director of the Music Academy. See *BBLev*, 482–83. The letter makes clear that Bartók was already aware in June that the transfer would take place. The administration of the Music Academy received official word of it only in the middle of July.

The pamphlet contains no month of publication. Bartók dated the main text 15 January 1934. The short postscript dated March 1934 suggests that most of the text had already been typeset by then. It is thus likely that the pamphlet appeared in March or April 1934. The date of the postscript is included in *BBÖI*, 429.

20. Several of Bartók's accounts of collecting folk music include statements such as this. See, for example, "What Is Folk Music?" (1931) in *BBE*, 4; and "The Peasant Music of Hungary" (1931), in *Béla Bartók: Studies in Ethnomusicology*, 139.

21. Tallián, *Béla Bartók: The Man and His Work*, 58.

22. Bartók, "Reply to Jenő Hubay" (1920), in *BBE*, 200.

23. Ibid., 199.

24. Bartók, "Hungarian Folk Music and the Folk Music of the Neighboring Peoples," 180.

25. Bartók, "Reply to Jenő Hubay," in *BBE*, 201.

26. The use of the word *oláh* (Wallachian) to describe Romanians has a somewhat pejorative edge. In Bartók's scientific writings he always uses the more neutral term *román* (Romanian).

All of the articles described in this section are included in *BBÖI*, 861–64, except Bartók's "Válasz Hubay Jenő nyilatkozatára" (Reply to Jenő Hubay's announcement), which is on pp. 617–18. Elemér Sereghy is identified as a teacher in the Conservatory in Budapest's eighth district in "'Van ott egyéb furcsaság is'—mondja Bartók Béla" ("There Are Also Some Strange Things There"—Says Béla Bartók), *Ma Este* 1, no. 15 (1923): 3, reprinted in *Beszélgetések Bartókkal*, 44.

27. *BBÖI*, 863. In Sereghy's next article he assumes this defense was written by Kodály.

28. Hubay's article appeared in *Szózat* (Declaration) (25 May 1920). Bartók's response was published in the same publication the next day.

29. On the society's support for him, see Bartók's letter to Géza Révész, 22 August 1920, in *BBLev*, 260. Hubay's communication was published in *Szózat* (28 May 1920).

30. Bartók, "Reply to Jenő Hubay." My translation largely follows that in *BBE*, 201–2.

31. In *Új Nemzedék* (21 May 1920), reprinted in *BBÖI*, 863.

32. Bartók's letter to his wife Márta Ziegler, 4 March 1920, in *BBCsaL*, 303–4.

33. Bartók's letter to Ioan Buşiţia, 30 March 1920, in *BBLev*, 259.

34. Bartók mentions the commissions from *Melos*, which was offering him fifty marks per page, and *Musical Courier* (not identified by name) in the same letter to his wife (see n. 32 above).

35. Bartók's letter to Constantin Brailoiu, 22 February 1931, in *BBLev*, 402–3.

36. Bartók's letter to Constantin Brailoiu, 23 March 1931, in *BBLev*, 407.

37. *Az Est* (20 March 1931), in *Zt 10*, 400.

38. "Bartók Béla Hangversenye" (Béla Bartók's Concert), *Ellenzék* (17 December 1933), in *Zt 10*, 460.

39. Bartók's letter to Ditta Pásztory, 20 February 1934, in *BBCsaL*, 541.

40. Neamul Românesc in "Miért és kinek az intézkedésére maradt el a temesvári és nagyszentmiklósi Bartók-ünnepély?" (Why and by Whose Order Was the Bartók-Celebration in Temesvár and Nagyszentmiklós Canceled?), *Brassói Lapok* (2 March 1934), in *Zt 10*, 474.

41. Ibid., 475.

42. According to a letter written to his wife on 20 February 1934 (*BBCsaL*, 541) Bartók wrote about the affair in detail to Kodály. This letter is unavailable to me.

43. Reported by Júlia Székely (*Zt 10*, 469) and confirmed in András Benkő, "Romániában megjelent Bartók-interjúk" (Bartók Interviews Published in Romania), in *Bartók-Dolgozatok 1981* (Bartók Studies 1981), ed. Ferenc László (Bucharest: Kriterion, 1982), 346.

44. Reported in *Temesvári Hírlap* (29 April 1936), in *Zt 10*, 542.

45. "D. Béla Bartók si muzica româneasca" (Dr. Béla Bartók and Romanian Music), *Grând Românesc* (February 1936): 120–25. Reprinted in Hungarian in *BBÖI*, 878–81.

46. Ibid., 878.

47. Eric Hirsch, "Pure Sources, Pure Souls: Folk Nationalism and Folk Music in Hungary in the 1930s" (Ph.D. diss., University of California at Berkeley, 1995), 73–84.

48. "Cigányzene—paraszt zene—hivatalos zene" (Gypsy Music—Peasant Music—Official Music), *Budapesti Hírlap* (1 May 1929), in *Zt 10*, 341.

49. *Zt 10*, 439–40.

50. Bartók's letter to the Kisfaludy Society, 29 December 1935 (see *BBL*, 245, 419).

51. Published as "Schubertről" (About Schubert), *A kis akadémia könyvtára* 22, no. 38–39 (January 1936): 1, in *Zt 10*, 514.

52. Béla Bartók and Zoltán Kodály, *Hungarian Folk Songs*, 1.

53. Bartók's letter to Beu, 10 January 1931, in *BBL*, 202. Vera Lampert's identification of the tunes confirms Bartók's statement of their origin. See Lampert, *Bartók népdalfeldolgozásainak forrásjegyzéke*, 113–22.

54. Béla Bartók, *Rumanian Folk Music*, vol. 1, ed. Benjamin Suchoff, with a foreword by Victor Bator (The Hague: M. Nijhoff, 1967), 221.

55. Ibid., 41.

56. Ibid., 49.

57. Ibid., 48.

58. Ibid., 49–50.

59. Ibid., 57. Here it is important to note that Bartók indeed included all melodies he collected in Romanian-speaking villages in *Rumanian Folk Music;* that is, he did not discriminate according to style. Therefore if a melody had characteristics traditionally considered to be Hungarian, as is the case with a number of melodies Bartók used in his two violin rhapsodies, he nevertheless labeled them Romanian.

60. The folk tune in example 63 is based on the one in *Rumanian Folk Music,* vol. 1, 221. I have also consulted the original *támlap* (the folk-music collector's notation sheet) and the recording on M.F. 3544, the Edison cylinder Bartók made of the performance.

61. Bartók, *Rumanian Folk Music,* 33.

62. Ibid., 48.

63. Bartók's description of the "heroic" melodies is ibid., 48–50.

64. An analogous change also exists in the first theme of the Second Rhapsody.

65. "The Philharmonic Society's Third Concert," *Népszava* (26 November 1929), in *Zt 10,* 360–61.

66. Bartók, *Rumanian Folk Music,* 17.

67. Ibid., 218 (no. 226). I gratefully acknowledge the assistance of Gabriella Dudas for her help in translating the Romanian dance titles.

68. The manuscript sources for the First Rhapsody (Budapest Bartók Archives no. 61VPS1) show that Bartók had originally included a seventh dance. The tune for this dance (no. 376a in *Rumanian Folk Music*) was also collected by Bartók in the key of A.

69. Joseph Szigeti, *Szigeti on the Violin* (New York: Praeger, 1969), 185.

70. Ibid.

71. Ibid.

72. "Szigeti Concert with a Bartók Premiere," *Pesti Napló* (24 November 1929), in *Zt 10,* 355.

73. Marosszék is a Hungarian region in Transylvania. The dance tunes Kodály used in his composition were not collected in Marosszék, but belong to a folk-music type associated with the region. János Breuer, *A Guide to Kodály,* trans. Maria Steiner (Budapest: Corvina, 1990), 117.

74. Reviews in *Zt 10,* 355–57.

75. "Cimbalom," in Boronkay, *Brockhaus-Riemann zenei lexikon,* vol. 1, 334.

76. Schunda's firm manufactured over ten thousand cimbaloms between 1874 and 1921. Several other companies also produced pianofied cimbaloms in Budapest during this same period.

77. Now the Béla Bartók Conservatory.

78. Bartók's article appeared in *A Dictionary of Modern Music and Musicians,* ed. Hugh P. Allen, Granville Bantock, Edward J. Dent, Henry J. Wood, and A. Eaglefield-Hull (London: J. M. Dent & Sons, 1924), 243–44.

79. Aladár Tóth and István Péterfi treat it as an authentic folk instrument, Emil Haraszti as a Gypsy instrument. Szigeti also sees the cimbalom as an indication of the "folk quality" Bartók intends to capture.

80. György Kroó, *Rácz Aladár* (Budapest: Zeneműkiadó, 1979), 78.

81. Although the existence of players of the traditional cimbalom is documented in Hungarian lands before the eighteenth century, its strongest association was with "Gypsy ensembles," who are likely to have adopted the cimbalom from Jewish musicians who came to Hungary from Bohemia in the first half of the eighteenth century. Paul M. Gifford, *The Hammered Dulcimer: A History* (Lanham, MD: Scarecrow Press, 2001), 112–13.

82. "Szigeti-koncert Bartók-bemutatóval" (Szigeti Concert with a Bartók Premiere), *Pesti Napló* (24 November 1929), in *Zt 10*, 355–56.

83. The summary of Bartók's view of folk music in this paragraph is based on his views expressed in the essay on folklore most nearly contemporaneous with the First Rhapsody for Violin: "Hungarian Folk Music" (1929), in *BBE*, 3–4.

84. Bartók's letter to Octavian Beu, 10 January 1931, in *BBL*, 201.

85. Bartók describes the national quality of the sections of *Dance Suite* as follows: "No. 1 partly Arab; No. 2 Hungarian; No. 3 alternation of Hungarian, Romanian, and Arab; No. 4 Arab; No. 5 too primitive to assign a national character; *ritornello* Hungarian." See letter to Octavian Beu, ibid., 202. Bartók originally also wrote a Slovak movement, which he omitted from the final version of the work. See László Somfai, *Béla Bartók: Compositions, Concepts and Autograph Sources* (Berkeley: University of California Press, 1996), 17–18, 190; Ferenc Bónis, *Béla Bartók's Dance Suite*, trans. Nicholas Bodoczky (Budapest: Balassi, 1998), 27–31.

CHAPTER 6

1. György Kroó, *A Guide to Bartók*, 204.

2. Halsey Stevens, *The Life and Music of Béla Bartók* (New York: Oxford University Press, 1964), 248. According to Yehudi Menuhin, Bartók said, "I wanted to show Schoenberg that one can use all twelve tones and still remain tonal." Quoted in Gillies, *Bartók Remembered*, 185. While good-humored compositional criticism of Schoenberg is in keeping with Bartók's penchant for inside jokes, it hardly captures the deeper essence of the Violin Concerto.

3. In addition to the *numerus clausus*, in 1939 Teleki introduced the "second Jewish law," which cut Jewish occupational quotas from 20 to 6 percent in the professions and to 12 percent of the payroll of salaried employees in business. See Andrew Janos, *The Politics of Backwardness in Hungary: 1825–1945* (Princeton: Princeton University Press, 1982), 302; Raul Hilberg, *The Destruction of the European Jews* (Chicago: Quadrangle, 1960), 511–13; and Ezra Mendelsohn, *The Jews of East Central Europe between the World Wars* (Bloomington: Indiana University Press, 1983), 118–24.

4. Following the Munich agreement of 30 September 1938, Germany returned to Hungary a portion of the territory ceded to Czechoslovakia in the Treaty of Trianon. Like the majority of Hungarians, Teleki supported the Munich agreement.

5. For example, János Demény claims that "after his concert in Germany at the beginning of 1933, Bartók severed all connections to that 'pestilent' country." In *Zt 10*, 451.

6. Translation taken from *BBE*, 423.

7. In an interview for the *Dagens Nyheter* (Stockholm) (17 April 1934) Bartók mentions that invitations to play in Germany have stopped since the beginning of the Third Reich because they consider him a cultural Bolshevik. At this time Bartók appears to be offended rather then proud. Reprinted in Károly Kristóf, *Beszélgetések*

Bartók Bélával (Conversations with Béla Bartók) (Budapest: Zeneműkiadó, 1957), 143. Breuer has published his finding in "Bartók a Harmadik Birodalomban" (Bartók in the Third Reich), *Muzsika* 10 (1995): 9–12.

8. Ibid., 9.

9. Budapest Bartók Archives, no. BH II/67.

10. Breuer, "Bartók a Harmadik Birodalomban," 10.

11. In *DocB* 3, 170; original in German.

12. Quoted in Kroó, *A Guide to Bartók*, 174.

13. For documentation of Bartók's 1938 refusal see his letter to Annie Müller-Widmann, 13 April 1938, in *BBL*, 267.

14. Breuer, "Bartók a Harmadik Birodalomban," 11.

15. Ibid., 10.

16. Letter to Sándor Albrecht, 3 February 1937, in *BBL*, 545–46.

17. "Bartók Béla nem engedi meg, hogy előadói szerepléseit a Rádió Német- és Olaszországnak közvetítse" (Bartók Does Not Allow His Performances to Be Broadcast on German and Italian Radio), *Pesti Napló* (10 October 1937), in *Zt 10*, 627.

18. Ibid., 627–28.

19. Two letters from Bartók's manager André Schulhof mention the possibility of Bartók playing on German Radio: 16 July 1936 and 7 December 1936 (Budapest Bartók Archives, nos. BH 1374 and BH 1378).

20. Breuer, "Bartók a Harmadik Birodalomban," 11.

21. Somfai, "Eine Erklärung Bartóks aus dem Jahre 1938," *DocB* 4, 148–52.

22. "Rundfunk," *Die Musik* 30, no. 4 (1938): 287.

23. "Mi igaz abból, hogy Bartók nem engedélyezte műveinek közvetítését az olasz és német rádiók számára?" (What Is True about Bartók Not Allowing His Works to Be Broadcast on Italian and German Radio?), *A Zene* (16 March 1938): 187, in *Zt 10*, 662–63; and "Bartók Béla megmagyarázza rádiótilalmát" (Béla Bartók Explains His Radio Boycott), *Az Est* (22 March 1938), in *Zt 10*, 663.

24. *Az Est* (27 March 1938), in *Zt 10*, 663. In the first sentence of the quotation Bartók remembers incorrectly. He wrote the letter in question to *Pesti Napló* on 10 October 1937, not in November.

25. The official silence may have itself been a reaction to Bartók's failure to appear at a ceremony in February at which Admiral Miklós Horthy, the Hungarian Regent, would have bestowed a minor award on him. The Corvin Award was instituted by Horthy in recognition of Hungary's greatest minds. Twelve major and sixty minor awards were to have been awarded. Jenő Hubay and Ernő Dohnányi received major awards, and Bartók was slated for a minor award. See Andor Földes, "My First Meeting with Bartók," *Etude* 73, no. 3 (March 1955): 12, in Gillies, *Bartók Remembered*, 79–80. A brief article about the incident reports that Bartók had gone to London. There is no evidence to support this.·See "Bartók nélkül" (Without Bartók), *Az Est* (23 February 1931), reprinted in Károly Kristóf, *Beszélgetések Bartók Bélával*, 70.

26. The official reason for the cancellation of *The Miraculous Mandarin* was the illness of Karola Szalay, who was to have danced the Girl. Contemporary press reports widely portrayed this as a convenient, perhaps trumped-up excuse. Although the precise circumstances are unclear, according to some reports Bartók was so annoyed by the quality of the production that he asked for the postponement of the premiere—a request the Opera appears to have been only too pleased to honor. See

reports in *Az Est* (24, 26, 27, 28 March 1931), reprinted in Kristóf, *Beszélgetések Bartók Bélával*, 74–79; in *Pesti Napló* (29 March 1931); and *Délibáb* (Mirage) (4 April 1931), in *Zt 10*, 395–96.

27. Alexander Jemnitz, "Béla Bartók," trans. Theodore Baker, *Musical Quarterly* (1933): 260–62. This tribute was originally published as "Béla Bartók, eine west-östliche Geburtstagsbetrachtung," *Musikblätter des Anbruch* 12, no. 4 (1931): 77–82. A preliminary version of the article was published on Bartók's fiftieth birthday as "Bartók Béla és Magyarország" (Béla Bartók and Hungary), *Népszava* (People's Word) (25 March 1931), in *Zt 10*, 398–99.

28. See the fiftieth-birthday tributes reprinted in *Zt 10*, 396–400, especially "Hogyan ünneplik Bartók Bélát külföldön és hogyan nálunk!" (How They Celebrate Béla Bartók Abroad and at Home!), *Az Est* (28 March 1931). Making a reference to the cancellation of *The Miraculous Mandarin* the article concludes: "On this day abroad they publicly celebrate the spirit of the Hungarian genius, here they not only remain silent about him, they also silence him and his music."

29. Bartók's letter to Walter Frey, 28 April 1934, in *BBL*, 479.

30. Bartók's letter to Joseph Szigeti, 10 August 1935, in *BBLev*, 506. In place of his own sonata Bartók suggests substituting Ravel's Sonata for Violin and Piano. The frequently noted reference to the opening of the second movement of Ravel's sonata, "Blues," in the opening of the first movement of *Contrasts* (written for Szigeti and Benny Goodman) was first described by Ferenc Bónis in "Quotations in Bartók's Music," *Studia musicologica* 5, nos. 1–4 (1963): 373.

31. Bartók showed no interest in collaborating with the great poet Attila József (1905–1937), who wanted Bartók to set his poetry and planned a biography of the composer. (József and Bartók's wife Ditta Pásztory were both patients of a psychiatrist through whom the poet attempted to establish contact with Bartók. I am grateful to László Somfai for this information.) Bartók also resisted close association with the circle surrounding the avant-garde magazine *Ma* (Today, 1916–25).

32. By the mid-1930s peasant dances had begun to influence some of the choreography at the Hungarian Opera, whose dancers were learning the style in part from the newly formed, tourist-oriented folk ensembles known as *Gyöngyös bokréta* (Pearly Bouquet), another beneficiary of Gömbös's governmental subventions. For documentation of the choreography of the Hungarian Opera's 1935 production of *The Wooden Prince* see Aladár Tóth, "A Fából faragott királyfi: Bartók táncjátéka az Operaházban" (The Wooden Prince: Bartók's Pantomime at the Opera), *Pesti Napló* (31 January 1935), in *Zt 10*, 496–97.

33. Sándor Jemnitz, "B.B.C.," *Népszava* (25 April 1936), in *Zt 10*, 541.

34. The lecture was published as "Liszt-Problémák" (Liszt Problems), in *Nyugat* (March 1936): 171–79, in *BBE*, 501–10.

35. Aladár Tóth, "Bartók új műveinek bemutatása az Éneklő Ifjúság hangversenyén" (Premiere of New Bartók Compositions at the Concert of the Singing Youth), *Pesti Napló* (8 May 1937), in *Zt 10*, 611–12.

36. For Kodály's defense of choral education as a bulwark of Hungarian music education see "Magyarság a zenében" (Hungarianness in Music), in *Mi a magyar?* 413–14.

37. Bartók's letter to Mrs. Müller-Widmann, 24 May 1937, in *BBL*, 257.

38. Béla Bangha, "Tollheggyel" (With the Tip of a Pen), *Magyar Kultúra* 24, nos.

13–14 (1937): 47, in *Zt 10*, 315. In response to articles in Bartók's and Kodály's defense the attack was elaborated in *Magyar Kultúra* 24, nos. 15–16 (1937): 94–95, in *Zt 10*, 621–24.

39. They include *Magyar Hírlap* (18 July); *Magyarország* (15 July); *Pesti Napló* (18 July); *Magyarság* (16 July); *Népszava* (15 July); and *Az Est* (16 July), in *Zt 10*, 615–21.

40. Konrád Salamon, "Bartók és a Márciusi Front" (Bartók and the March Front), *Forrás* 13, no. 3 (1981): 40–43.

41. Ibid., 42.

42. The March Front took its name from the unsuccessful Hungarian revolution begun on 15 March 1848.

43. Original in György Bálint, "Bartók a népért" (Bartók for the People), *Gondolat* 2, no. 8 (1936): 345–46. Quoted in Konrád Salamon, "Bartók és a Márciusi Front," *Forrás* 13, no. 3 (1981): 41.

44. Szabolcsi studied composition with Kodály. In 1942 Bartók wrote the entry on Szabolcsi for *The Universal Jewish Encyclopedia;* see *BBE*, 519–20. János Demény's inclusion of Hungarian reviews of Bartók's concerts in *Zt 10* is quite comprehensive. It is therefore odd that he included only one account of Bartók's participation in the "Magyar Múzsa" concert, an innocuous one by Dezső Szabó in *Szabó Dezső újabb művei*, nos. 34–35 (December 1937–January 1938), in *Zt 10*, 632. That Demény omitted Szabolcsi's review of the concert and that Szabolcsi was one of the editors of the volume in which Demény's study appeared suggests the subject was politically charged.

45. Szabolcsi's review in *Magyar Dal* (Hungarian Song), nos. 7–9 (October–December 1937).

46. For a discussion of the manuscript evidence that implies that at least the first and second movements of the Violin Concerto are primarily products of 1936–37 see László Somfai, "Három vázlat 1936/37-ból a Hegedűversenyhez" (Three Sketches for the Violin Concerto from 1936 and '37), in *Tizennyolc Bartóktanulmány*, 104–16.

47. Bartók's compositions familiar to Dutch critics at this time included the first two piano concertos, *Music for Strings, Percussion, and Celesta*, the Fourth and Fifth String Quartets, and the two sonatas for violin and piano.

48. L. M. G. Arntzenius, *De Telegraaf* (24 March 1939), in *Zt 10*, 699.

49. Ibid. This view was shared in reviews by Herman Rutters for the *Algemeen Handelsblad* (24 March 1939), and Lou van Strien for the *Nieuwe Rotterdamsche Courant* (24 March 1939), in *Zt 10*, 699–701.

50. Manuscripts of the Violin Concerto in the Budapest Bartók Archives show that Bartók originally conceived of the theme beginning on the first beat of the bar with no pickup. In June 1990 Zoltán Székely told me that Bartók decided to add the pickups shortly before the work's premiere when Vilmos Palotai, cellist of the New Hungarian String Quartet, asked him why he had omitted the pickups in the first statement of the theme although they served to reintroduce the theme at the recapitulation (mm. 212–13). Bartók's original conception may have taken its inspiration from Hungarian folk song, which reflects the first-syllable accent pattern of the Hungarian language by avoiding voiced pickups. Clearly, in making this revision Bartók showed more concern for practical matters of performance than for a rigidly

conceived authenticity. Székely encouraged Bartók to make the change, claiming that it allowed him to lend a more singing cantabile to the whole phrase.

51. László Somfai uses manuscript sources to demonstrate that Bartók's original idea was for a ten-note theme, which he later transformed into the twelve-note theme. See Somfai, *Béla Bartók*, 158–63.

52. Leo Treitler first used the designation "Z group" to refer to two conjunct ascending or descending fourths joined by a half step in the same direction as the leaps, in "Harmonic Procedure in the Fourth Quartet of Béla Bartók," *Journal of Music Theory* (November 1959): 292–98. The term "Z cell" has subsequently been widely adopted among American music theorists. For an introduction to Bartók's use of the Z cell see Elliott Antokoletz, *The Music of Béla Bartók* (Berkeley: University of California Press, 1984), especially 71–72.

53. The opening motive of the "Marcia" episode in the second movement of the Sixth String Quartet is identical to the beginning of the theme in the first movement of *Contrasts,* explicitly entitled "Verbunkos."

54. Although Bartók's knowledge of the standard orchestral repertoire hardly needs proof, the presence of *Sheherazade* on the concerts of the Budapest Philharmonic Society suggests that the work was as well known in Hungary as in most other European countries. For information regarding its performance in Hungary see Béla Csuka, *Kilenc évtized a magyar zeneművészet szolgálatában*, 193.

55. For examples of this see Bartók, *Rumanian Folk Music,* vol. 1, nos. 426 (pp. 366–67) and 493b (pp. 408–9).

56. Bartók originally conceived of *Contrasts* as a rhapsody. Its first movement, entitled "Verbunkos (Recruiting Dance)," serves the function of a *lassú;* its last movement, "Sebes (Fast Dance)," serves the function of a *friss.* The middle movement, "Pihenő (Relaxation)," which Bartók added after completing the outer movements, has no place in the standard Hungarian-rhapsody form.

57. Ferenc Bónis points to the connection between Kodály's Intermezzo from *Háry János* and Bartók's First Rhapsody in "Bartók és a verbunkos" (Bartók and the *Verbunkos*), in *Hódolat Bartóknak és Kodálynak* (Budapest: Püski, 1992), 27–29.

58. Ernő Lendvai mentions the similarity of the shape of Melinda's music at the end of act 1 of *Bánk bán* and the third phrase of the primary theme of Bartók's Violin Concerto in *The Workshop of Bartók and Kodály* (Budapest: Editio Musica, 1983), 438.

59. *BBE,* 25.

60. Bartók, "Race Purity in Music" (1942), in *BBE,* 29, 30–31.

61. "Béla Bartók the Man" (1946), in *The Selected Writings of Zoltán Kodály,* 101.

62. Aladár Tóth, "A népművelési Bizottság Bartók-estje" (The Bartók Concert of the Committee for Adult Education), *Pesti Napló* (11 December 1936), in *Zt 10,* 581.

63. Sándor Jemnitz, "Bartók Béla és B. Pásztory Ditta" (Béla Bartók and Ditta Pásztory B[artók]), *Népszava,* in *Zt 10,* 726.

64. Although it is clear from the preparations that Bartók made for his trip to the United States that he expected to stay there for a significant amount of time, his departure from Hungary was officially billed as a foreign tour. He did not enter the United States as an immigrant.

65. Eric Hirsch, "Pure Sources, Pure Souls: Folk Nationalism and Folk Music in Hungary in the 1930s," 1–8 and 62–73.

Bibliography

See also the sources cited in the list of abbreviations (pp. 251–52).

PRIMARY LITERATURE

A. L. "Színház. Zene: A filharmónikusok." *Magyar Nemzet* (8 January 1903): 6.

Balázs, Béla. *Balázs Béla levelei Lukács Györgyhöz* (Béla Balázs's Letters to György Lukács). Edited by Julia Lenkei. Budapest: MTA Filozófiai Intézet, 1982.

———. *Napló 1903–1914* (Diary 1903–1914). Budapest: Magvető Könyvkiadó, 1982.

Bartók, Béla. "Bartók Béla nyilatkozata a 'progresszív zenei alkotásokról' " (Béla Bartók's Proclamation about Progressive Musical Works). Edited by László Somfai. *Magyar zene* 16, no. 2 (1975): 115–16.

———. *Bartók breviárium. Levelek—írások—dokumentumok* (Bartók Breviary: Letters, Writings, Documents). Edited by József Ujfalussy and Vera Lampert. Budapest: Zeneműkiadó, 1980.

———. *The Hungarian Folk Song*. Edited by Benjamin Suchoff. Albany: State University of New York Press, 1981.

———. *A magyar népdal* (The Hungarian Folk Song). Bartók Béla írásai 5 (The Writings of Béla Bartók, 5). Edited by Dorit Révész. Budapest: Editio Musica, 1990.

———. *Rumanian Folk Music*. Volume 1. Edited by Benjamin Suchoff. With a foreword by Victor Bator. The Hague: M. Nijhoff, 1967.

———. *Volksmusik der Rumänen von Maramures*. Ethnomusikologische Schriften Faksimile-Nachdrücke II. Edited by Denijs Dille. Mainz: Schott's Söhne, 1966.

Bartók, Béla, and Zoltán Kodály. *Hungarian Folksongs for Voice with Piano*. Translated by Ilona L. Lukács. Reprint of the original manuscript with commentaries by Denijs Dille. Budapest: Editio Musica, 1970.

Béldi, Izor. "Casals és Stravinsky" (Casals and Stravinsky). *Pesti Hírlap*, 16 March 1926.

Benkő, András. *Bartók Béla romániai hangversenyei (1922–1936)* (Béla Bartók's Concerts in Romania [1922–1936]). Bucharest: Kriterion, 1970.

———. "Romániában megjelent Bartók-interjúk"(Bartók Interviews Published in

Romania). In *Bartók-dolgozatok 1981* (Bartók Studies 1981), 272–361. Bucharest: Kriterion, 1982.

Bónis, Ferenc, ed. *Így láttuk Bartókot* (As We Saw Bartók). 2nd ed. Budapest: Püski, 1995.

———. *Selected Writing of Zoltán Kodály.* Budapest: Zeneműkiadó, 1964.

———. *Tóth Aladár válogatott zenekritikái 1934–1939* (Aladár Tóth's Selected Music Reviews). Budapest: Zeneműkiadó, 1968.

Breuer, János, ed. *Zenei írások a* Nyugatban (Musical Writings in the *Nyugat*). Budapest: Zeneműkiadó, 1978.

Csuka, Béla. *Kilenc évtized a magyar zeneművészet szolgálatában: A Filharmóniai Társaság emlékkönyve 90 éves jubileuma alkalmából* (Nine Decades in the Service of Hungarian Musical Art: Memorial Album of the Philharmonic Society on the Occasion of Its Ninetieth Anniversary). Budapest: Filharmóniai Társaság, 1943.

Czuczor, Gergely. "A' magyar tánczról" (About Hungarian Dance). *Athenaeum* 1 (1843): 109–19.

Debussy, Claude. *Debussy on Music: The Critical Writings of the Great French Composer.* Collected and introduced by François Lesure. Translated and edited by Richard Langham Smith. Ithaca, NY: Cornell University Press, 1977.

Dille, Denijs. *Bartók Béla családfája* (Béla Bartók's Family Tree). Translated by Dóra F. Csanak. Budapest: Balassa, 1994.

———. *Thematischer Verzeichnis der Jugendwerke Béla Bartóks, 1890–1904.* Budapest: Akadémiai Kiadó, 1974.

Fábian, László. "Stravinsky." *Zenei Szemle* 11 (1926–27): 77–81.

Fóthy, János. "Stravinsky Budapesten: beszélgetés a Tűzmadár zeneszerzőjével" (Stravinsky in Budapest: A Conversation with the Composer of the Firebird). *Pesti Hírlap*, 14 March 1926.

Harsányi, Kálmán. *Költemények* (Poems). Budapest, 1903 (no publisher's imprint).

Huber, Sándor, ed. *Magyar zenei ereklyék: A régi magyar zene kincseiből 1672–1838* (Hungarian Musical Relics: From the Treasures of Old Hungarian Music 1672–1838). Budapest: Rozsnyai Károly, n.d. Reprinted as *Musica antiqua Hungarica* No. 1. Budapest: Tradeorg Kft., 1991.

Káldy, Gyula (Julius). *Schätze der alten ungarischen Musik (1672–1833): Weisen und Lieder aus den Zeiten von Thököly und Rákóczi.* Budapest: Rózsavölgyi & Co., 1895.

Kassai, István, ed. *Mosonyi Mihály: Zongoraművek* (Mihály Mosonyi: Works for Piano). Budapest: Akkord Music Publishers, 1997.

Kodály, Zoltán. *Folk Music of Hungary.* Revised and enlarged by Lajos Vargyas. Budapest: Corvina, 1960.

———. *The Selected Writings of Zoltán Kodály.* Translated by Lili Halápy and Fred Macnicol. London: Boosey & Hawkes, 1974.

———. *Visszatekintés 1–2. Összegyűjtött írások, beszédek, nyilatkozatok* (Looking Back: Collected Writings, Speeches, and Declarations, Vols. 1–2). Edited by Ferenc Bónis. Budapest: Zeneműkiadó, 1982.

———. *Visszatekintés. Hátrahagyott írások, beszédek, nyilatkozatok.* Volume 3 (Looking Back: Writings, Speeches, and Declarations Left Behind). Edited by Ferenc Bónis. Budapest: Zeneműkiadó, 1989.

Kristóf, Károly. *Beszélgetések Bartók Bélával* (Conversations with Béla Bartók). Budapest: Zeneműkiadó, 1957.

L.D.T. "Színház és zene: Hatodik filharmoniai hangverseny" (Theater and Music: The Sixth Concert of the Philharmonic). *Pesti Hírlap*, 8 January 1903, 5.

———. "Színház és zene: Kilencedik filharmoniai hangverseny" (Theater and Music: Ninth Philharmonic Concert). *Pesti Hírlap*, 9 March 1909, 8.

Legkedveltebb csárdás tánczok gyűjteménye (Collection of Favorite Csárdás Dances). Budapest: Rózsavölgyi és Társa, n.d. Reprint as *Musica antiqua Hungarica* No. 2. Budapest: Polifon Zeneműkiadó, 1993.

A Magyar Királyi Operaház évkönyve "1928–1929" (Yearbook of the Hungarian Royal Opera "1928–1929"). Budapest: A Magyar Királyi Operaház Igazgatósága, [1928?].

Molnár, Antal. *Az új zene: A zeneművészet legújabb irányának ismertetése kultúretikai megvilágításban* (The New Music: Introduction to the Newest Trends of Music in Light of Cultural Ethics). Budapest: Révai, 1925.

———. *Bartók művészete emlékezésekkel a művész életére* (Bartók's Art: With Memories of the Life of the Artist). Budapest: Rózsavölgyi, n.d.

Molnár, Géza. *A magyar zene elmélete* (The Theory of Hungarian Music). Budapest: Pesti Könyvnyomda-Rt., 1904.

Papp, Géza, ed. *Hungarian Dances 1784–1810*. Musicalia Danubiana 7. Budapest: MTA Zenetudományi Intézet, 1986.

Rakos, Miklós, ed. *Magyar Nóták Veszprém Vármegyéből: 136 Verbunkos táncdarab 1823–1832 mellyek fortepianóra alkalmaztattak Ruzitska Ignátz által Veszprémben* (Hungarian Songs from Veszprém County: 136 *Verbunkos* Dances 1823–1832 Arranged for Piano by Ignátz Ruzitska in Veszprém County). Budapest: Kiadja a szerző (published by the editor), 1994.

Révai kislexikona. (Révai's Concise Encyclopedia). Edited by Elemér Csekei Varjú. Budapest: Révai Irodalmi Intézet, 1936.

Siklós, Albert. *Hangszereléstan elméleti és gyakorlati alapon (Study of Orchestration on a Theoretical and Practical Basis)*. Volume 1. Budapest: Rozsnyai Károly, 1909.

Somfai, László, ed. *Béla Bartók: Black Pocket-Book*. Facsimile with commentary by László Somfai. Budapest: Editio Musica, 1987.

Stowasser, János, Jr. *Elméleti és gyakorlati tárogató iskola* (Theoretical and Practical *Tárogató* Tutor). Budapest: J. Stowasser, c. 1900.

Suchoff, Benjamin, ed. *Béla Bartók: Studies in Ethnomusicology*. Lincoln: University of Nebraska Press, 1997.

Szabolcsi, Bence, and Aladár Tóth, eds. *Zenei lexicon* (Musical Encyclopedia). Volumes 1–2. Budapest: Győző Andor, 1930, 1931.

Szekfű, Gyula, ed. *Mi a magyar?* (What Is Hungarian?) Budapest: Magyar Szemle Társaság, 1939. Reprint, Budapest: Helikon Kft, 1992.

"Szendy Árpád: Magyar poémák" (Árpád Szendy: Hungarian Poems). *Zeneközlöny* 7, no. 10 (6 March 1909): 124.

"Sztravinsky-est" (An Evening of Stravinsky's Music). *Pesti Napló*, 16 March 1926, 14–15.

Tóth, Aladár. "Modern szerzők a hangversenyteremben" (Modern Composers in the Concert Hall). *Nyugat*, 1 December 1925.

Tóth, Dénes. *A magyar népszínmű zenei kialakulása* (The Musical Development of Hungarian Folk Drama). Budapest: Sárkány-Nyomda Részvénytársaság, 1930.

Vasárnapi Újság (Sunday Newspaper). October 1906.

Wágner, A. Károly. *Wágner A. Károly módszeres tárogató iskolája* (Károly A. Wágner's Methodical *Tárogató* Tutor). Budapest: A. Károly Wágner, 1915.

Wilheim, András, ed. *Beszélgetések Bartókkal: Interjúk, nyilatkozatok 1911–1945* (Conversations with Bartók: Interviews, Communiqués 1911–1945). Budapest: Kijárat Kiadó, 2000.

SECONDARY LITERATURE

Abbate, Carolyn. "*Tristan* in the Composition of *Pelléas.*" *19th-Century Music* 5, no. 2 (1981): 117–41.

Allen, Hugh P., Granville Bantock, Edward J. Dent, Henry J. Wood, and A. Eaglefield-Hull, eds. *A Dictionary of Modern Music and Musicians*. London: J. M. Dent & Sons, 1924.

Anderson, Benedict. *Imagined Communities*. Revised ed. London: Verso, 1991.

Antokoletz, Elliott. *The Music of Béla Bartók*. Berkeley: University of California Press, 1984.

Antokoletz, Elliott, Victoria Fisher, and Benjamin Suchoff, eds. *Bartók Perspectives: Man, Composer, and Ethnomusicologist*. New York: Oxford University Press, 2000.

Bartók, Béla, Jr. *Apám életének krónikája* (Chronicle of My Father's Life). Budapest: Zeneműkiadó, 1981.

Bartók, Peter. *My Father*. Homosassa: Bartók Records, 2002.

Bayley, Amanda, ed. *The Cambridge Companion to Bartók*. Cambridge: Cambridge University Press, 2001.

Beckerman, Michael. "In Search of Czechness in Music." *19th-Century Music*, 10, no. 1 (1986): 61–73.

Bellman, Jonathan. *The Style Hongrois in the Music of Western Europe*. Boston: Northeastern University Press, 1993.

———. "Toward a Lexicon for the *Style hongrois.*" *Journal of Musicology* 9, no. 2 (1991): 214–37.

Bender, Thomas, and Carl E. Schorske, eds. *Budapest and New York: Studies in Metropolitan Transformation, 1870–1930*. New York: Russell Sage Foundation, 1994.

Bónis, Ferenc. *Béla Bartók's Dance Suite*. Translated by Nicholas Bodoczky. Budapest: Balassi, 1998.

———, ed. *Erkel Ferencről és koráról* (Ferenc Erkel and His Time). Budapest: Püski, 1995.

———. *Hódolat Bartóknak és Kodálynak* (Homage to Bartók and Kodály). Budapest: Püski, 1992.

———. *Mozarttól Bartókig* (From Mozart to Bartók). Budapest: Püski, 2000.

———. "Quotations in Bartók's Music." *Studia musicologica* 5, nos. 1–4 (1963): 355–82.

Boronkay, Antal, ed. *Brockhaus-Riemann zenei lexikon* (Brockhaus-Riemann Musical Encyclopedia). Edited by Carl Dahlhaus and Hans Heinrich Eggebrecht. Hungarian version. Budapest: Zeneműkiadó, 1983–85.

Breuer, János. "Bartók a Harmadik Birodalomban" (Bartók in the Third Reich). *Muzsika* 10 (1995): 9–12.

———. *Bartók és Kodály. Tanulmányok századunk magyar zenetörténetéhez* (Bartók and Kodály: Studies of Our Century's Hungarian Music History). Budapest: Magvető Könyvkiadó, 1978.

———. *A Guide to Kodály.* Translated by Maria Steiner. Budapest: Corvina, 1990.

Chambers, Kenneth. *Béla Bartók.* London: Phaidon, 1995.

Crow, Todd, ed. *Bartók Studies.* Detroit: Information Coordinators, 1976.

Dahlhaus, Carl. *Nineteenth-Century Music.* Translated by J. Bradford Robinson. Berkeley: University of California Press, 1989.

Demény, János. "Bartók Béla művészi kibontakozásának évei: Találkozás a népzenével (1906–1914)" (The Years of Béla Bartók's Artistic Development: Encounter with Folk Music [1906–1914]). In *Zt* 3, 286–459.

———. "Bartók Béla művészi kibontakozásának évei. II. rész: Bartók Béla megjelenése az europai zeneéletben (1914–1926)" (The Years of Béla Bartók's Artistic Development. Part 2: Béla Bartók's Appearance in European Musical Life [1914–1926]). In *Zt* 7, 5–426.

———. "Bartók Béla pályája delelőjén—teremtő évek—Világhódító alkotások (1927–1940)" (Béla Bartók at the Height of His Career—Creative Years—World-Conquering Works [1927–1940]). In *Zt* 10, 189–727.

———. "Bartók Béla tanulóévei és romantikus korszaka" (Béla Bartók's Student Years and Romantic Period). In *Zt* 2, 323–487.

Dés, Mihály, ed. *A százéves Operaház válogatott iratai* (Selected Documents of the Hundred-Year-Old Opera House). Budapest: Magyar Színházi Intézet, 1984.

Dille, Denijs. *Bartók Béla családfája* (Béla Bartók's Family Tree). Translated by Dóra F. Csanak. Budapest: Balassi, 1996.

Dobszay, László. *Magyar zenetörténet* (History of Hungarian Music). 2nd exp. ed. *Jelenlévő múlt* (Present Past). Budapest: Planétás Kiadó, 1998.

Ekhardt, Mária. "Magyar fantázia, ábránd, rapszódia a XIX század zongoramuzsikájában" 1–2 (Hungarian Fantasy and Rhapsody in the Piano Music of the 19th Century). *Magyar zene* 34, no. 2 (1983): 120–44, and 35, no. 4 (1984): 346–66.

Falvy, Zoltán. "*Tárogató* as a Regional Instrument." *Studia musicologica* 38, nos. 3–4 (1997): 361–70.

Frigyesi, Judit. "Béla Bartók and Hungarian Nationalism: The Development of Bartók's Social and Political Ideas at the Turn of the Century." Ph.D. dissertation, University of Pennsylvania, 1989.

———. "Béla Bartók and the Concept of Nation and *Volk* in Modern Hungary." *Musical Quarterly* 78, no. 2 (1994): 255–87.

———. *Béla Bartók and Turn-of-the-Century Budapest.* Berkeley: University of California Press, 1998.

Gal, Susan. "Bartók's Funeral: Representations of Europe in Hungarian Political Rhetoric." *American Ethnologist* 18 (1991): 440–58.

Galafrés, Elza. *Lives . . . Loves . . . Losses.* Vancouver: Versatile, 1973.

Gellner, Ernest. *Nations and Nationalism.* Ithaca, NY: Cornell University Press, 1983.

Gifford, Paul M. *The Hammered Dulcimer: A History.* Lanham, MD: Scarecrow Press, 2001.

Gillies, Malcolm, ed. *The Bartók Companion*. Portland: Amadeus Press, 1993.

———. *Bartók in Britain*. Oxford: Clarendon Press, 1989.

———. *Bartók Remembered*. London: Faber and Faber, 1990.

Gluck, Mary. *George Lukács and His Generation*. Cambridge, MA: Harvard University Press, 1985.

Gray, Cecil. *A Survey of Contemporary Music*. London: Oxford University Press, 1927.

Greenberg, Clement. *Clement Greenberg: The Collected Essays and Criticism*. Volume 3. Edited by John O'Brian. Chicago: University of Chicago Press, 1993.

Hargittai, István. "Some Experiences beyond Chemistry of the 2004 Nobel Prize in Chemistry." www.crookedtimber.org/archives/002639.html (accessed 22 November 2004).

Held, Joseph. *The Columbia History of Eastern Europe in the Twentieth Century*. New York: Columbia University Press, 1992.

Hilberg, Raul. *The Destruction of the European Jews*. Chicago: Quadrangle, 1960.

Hinton, Steven. "The Idea of Gebrauchsmusik: A Study of Musical Aesthetics in the Weimar Republic 1919–1933 with Particular Reference to the Works of Paul Hindemith." Outstanding Dissertations in Music From British Universities. New York: Garland Publishing, 1989.

Hirsch, Eric. "Pure Sources, Pure Souls: Folk Nationalism and Folk Music in Hungary in the 1930s." Ph.D. dissertation, University of California at Berkeley, 1995.

Hooker, Lynn. "Modernism Meets Nationalism: Béla Bartók and the Musical Life of Pre–World War I Hungary." Ph.D. dissertation, University of Chicago, 2001.

Hutchinson, John, and Anthony D. Smith, eds. *Nationalism*. Oxford: Oxford University Press, 1994.

Janos, Andrew C. *The Politics of Backwardness in Hungary: 1825–1945*. Princeton: Princeton University Press, 1982.

John, Nicholas, ed. *The Stage Works of Béla Bartók. Opera Guide*. London: John Calder and Riverrun Press, 1991.

Káldy, Julius (Gyula). *A History of Hungarian Music*. London: William Reeves, 1902; reprinted, New York: Haskell House, 1969.

Kapossi, Edit, and Ernő Pesovár, eds. *The Art of Dance in Hungary*. Translated by Lili Halápy et al. Budapest: Corvina, 1985.

Katz, Derek. "'A pen filled only with my own passion': Leoš Janáček and the Grand Operatic Traditions." Ph.D. dissertation, University of California at Santa Barbara, 2000.

Kenneson, Claude. *Székely and Bartók: The Story of a Friendship*. Portland: Amadeus Press, 1994.

Klaniczay, Tibor, ed. *A History of Hungarian Literature*. Budapest: Corvina, 1982.

Kodály, Zoltán, ed. *Studia Memoriae Belae Bartók Sacra*. Budapest: Akadémiai kiadó, 1958.

Konrád, Salamon. "Bartók és a Márciusi Front" (Bartók and the March Front). *Forrás* 13, no. 3 (March 1981): 40–43.

Kroó, György. *A Guide to Bartók*. Translated by Ruth Pataki and Mária Steiner. Translation revised by Elisabeth West. Budapest: Corvina, 1974.

———. *Rácz Aladár*. Budapest: Zeneműkiadó, 1979.

Kürti, László. *The Remote Borderland: Transylvania in the Hungarian Imagination.* Albany: State University of New York Press, 2001.

Laki, Peter, ed. *Bartók and His World.* Princeton: Princeton University Press, 1995.

Lampert, Vera. "Bartók at Harvard University as Witnessed in Unpublished Archival Documents." *Studia musicologica* 35, nos. 1–3 (1993–94): 113–54.

———. *Bartók népdalfeldolgozásainak forrásjegyzéke* (Catalog of Sources for Bartók's Folk-Song Arrangements). Budapest: Zeneműkiadó, 1980.

———. "Zeitgenössische Musik in Bartóks Notensammlung." In *Documenta Bartókiana* 5, 142–68. Budapest: Akadémiai kiadó, 1977.

László, Ferenc. *Bartók Béla. Tanulmányok és tanulságok* (Béla Bartók: Studies and Conclusions). Bucharest: Kriterion, 1980.

———, ed. *Bartók-dolgozatok* (Bartók Studies). Bucharest: Kriterion, 1974.

———, ed. *Bartók-dolgozatok 1981* (Bartók Studies 1981). Bucharest: Kriterion, 1982.

Legány, Dezső. *A Magyar zene krónikája* (Chronicle of Hungarian Music). Budapest: Zeneműkiadó, 1962.

Lelkes, Lajos, ed. *Néptánc kislexikon* (Concise Dictionary of Folk Dance). Budapest: Planétás Kiadó, 1996.

Lendvai, Ernő. *Bartók dramaturgiája* (Bartók's Dramaturgy). Budapest: Akkord, 1993.

———. *Bartók stílusa* (Bartók's Style). Budapest: Zeneműkiadó, 1955.

———. *The Workshop of Bartók and Kodály.* Budapest: Editio Musica, 1983.

Lukacs, John. *Budapest 1900: A Historical Portrait of a City and Its Culture.* New York: Grove Weidenfeld, 1988.

Macartney, C. A. *A History of Hungary 1929–1945.* New York: Frederick A. Praeger, 1957.

Martin, György. *Hungarian Folk Dances.* Translated by Rudolf Fischer. Budapest: Corvina, 1974.

———, ed. *Magyar néptánchagyományok* (Hungarian Folk Dance Traditions). Budapest: Planétás Kiadó, 1995.

———. *Magyar tánctípusok és táncdialektusok* (Hungarian Dance Types and Dance Dialects). Budapest: Népművelési Propaganda Iroda, 1970.

Martin, György, and András Takács. *Mátyusföldi népi táncok* (Folk Dances of Mátyusföld). Budapest: Gondolat, 1981.

Mendelsohn, Ezra. *The Jews of East Central Europe between the World Wars.* Bloomington: Indiana University Press, 1983.

Messing, Scott. *Neoclassicism in Music.* Ann Arbor, MI: UMI Research Press, 1988.

Moreux, Serge. *Bartók.* Translated by G. S. Fraser and Erik de Mauny. Introduction by Arthur Honegger. London: Harvill Press, 1953.

Móricz, Klára. "'From Pure Sources Only': Bartók and the Modernist Quest for Purity." *International Journal of Musicology* 9 (2000): 247–70.

———. "Operating on a Fetus: Sketch Studies and Their Relevance to the Interpretation of the Finale of Bartók's Concerto for Orchestra." *Studia musicologica* 36, nos. 3–4 (1995): 461–76.

Németh, Amadé. *Ferenc Erkel: sein Leben und Wirken.* Budapest: Corvina, 1979.

Nüll, Edwin von der. *Béla Bartók, Ein Beitrag zur Morphologie der neuen Musik.* Halle: Mitteldeutsche Verlags-Aktien-Gesellschaft, 1930.

Paksa, Katalin. *Magyar népzenekutatás a 19. században* (Hungarian Folk-Music Research in the Nineteenth Century). Budapest: MTA Zenetudományi Intézet, 1988.

Papp, Géza. "Hungarian Dances (1784–1810)." In *Musicalia Danubiana 7*, ed. Géza Papp. Budapest: MTA Zenetudományi Intézet, 1986.

———. "Die Quellen der 'Verbunkos-Musik': Ein bibliographischer Versuch." *Studia musicologica* 21 (1979): 152–217; 24 (1982): 35–97; 26 (1984): 59–132; 32 (1990): 55–224.

———. *A verbunkos kéziratos emlékei: Tematikus jegyzék* (Manuscript Sources of *Verbunkos:* Thematic Catalog). Budapest: MTA Zenetudományi Intézet, 1999.

Petersen, Peter. *Die Tonalität im Instrumentalschaffen von Béla Bartók.* Hamburg: Karl Dieter Wagner, 1971.

Petőfi, Sándor. *Petőfi Sándor összes költeményei* (Sándor Petőfi's Complete Poems). Volume 1. Budapest: Szépirodalmi könyvkiadó, 1966.

Ránki, György, ed. *Bartók and Kodály Revisited.* Budapest: Akadémiai Kiadó, 1987.

Réthei, Marián Prikkel. *A magyarság táncai* (Hungarian Dances). Budapest: Studium, 1924.

Romsics, Ignác. *Magyarország története a XX. században* (History of Hungary in the Twentieth Century). Budapest: Osiris, 2000.

Rosenstein, Léonie. *Nadia Boulanger: A Life in Music.* New York: W. W. Norton, 1982.

Sárosi, Bálint. *Folk Music: Hungarian Musical Idiom.* Translated by Maria Steiner. Budapest: Corvina, 1986.

———. *Gypsy Music.* Translated by Fred Macnicol. Budapest: Corvina, 1978.

Schneider, David E. "Peasant Music or Gypsy Music: The Implications of *Düvő* for Bartók's Polemics." *International Journal of Musicology* 9 (20): 141–68.

———. Review of Carl Leafstedt's *Inside Bluebeard's Castle, MLA Notes* 58, no. 2 (Dec. 2001): 359–60.

Sebő, Ferenc. *Népzenei olvasókönyv* (A Folk-Music Reader). Budapest: Planétás Kiadó, 1990.

Seton-Watson, Hugh. "R. W. Seton-Watson and the Trianon Settlement." In *Essays on World War I: Total War and Peacemaking, A Case Study on Trianon.* Edited by Béla K. Király, Peter Pastor, and Ivan Sanders. New York: Brooklyn College Press, 1982. Digitalized by Ferenc Jakab, Istvan Lippai, and Andrew L. Simon, 1997 (www.hungarian-history.hu/lib/tria/tria02.htm).

Smith, Anthony D. *National Identity.* London: Penguin Books, 1991.

Somfai, László. "Analytical Notes on Bartók's Piano Year 1926." *Studia musicologica* 26, nos. 1–4 (1984): 57–58.

———. *Béla Bartók: Composition, Concepts, and Autograph Sources.* Berkeley: University of California Press, 1996.

———. *Booklet to Accompany "Bartók Complete Edition: Vocal Works."* Hungaroton Classic, HCD 31906–08.

———. "A Characteristic Culmination Point in Bartók's Instrumental Forms." In *International Musicological Conference in Commemoration of Béla Bartók 1971*, ed. József Ujfalussy and János Breuer, 53–64. Budapest: Editio Musica, 1972.

———. "Classicism as Bartók Conceptualized It in His Classical Period 1926–1937."

In *Die klassizistische Moderne in der Music des 20. Jahrhunderts*, ed. Hermann Danuser, 123–41. Basel: Paul Sacher Stiftung, 1997.

———. "Nineteenth-Century Ideas Developed in Bartók's Piano Notation in the Years 1907–14." *19th-Century Music* 11, no. 1 (1987): 73–91.

———. *Notes for Béla Bartók Complete Edition.* Hungaroton, Piano Works 8 (1969).

———. "'Per finire': Some Aspects of the Finale in Bartók's Cyclic Form." *Studia musicologica* 11, nos. 1–4 (1969): 391–408.

———. *Tizennyolc Bartók-tanulmány* (Eighteen Bartók Studies). Budapest: Zeneműkiadó, 1981.

Somlyó, György, ed. *Arion 13: Bartók és a szavak* (Bartók and Words). Budapest: Corvina, 1982.

Stravinsky, Igor, and Robert Craft. *Conversations with Igor Stravinsky.* London: Faber and Faber, 1959.

Stravinsky, Vera, and Robert Craft. *Stravinsky in Pictures and Documents.* New York: Simon & Schuster, 1978.

Suchoff, Benjamin. "The Impact of Italian Baroque Music on Bartók's Music." In *Bartók and Kodály Revisited*, ed. György Ránki, 183–98. Budapest: Akadémiai Kiadó, 1987.

Sugar, Peter F., ed. *A History of Hungary.* Bloomington: Indiana University Press, 1990.

———. "Nationalism in Eastern Europe." In *Nationalism*, ed. John Hutchinson and Anthony D. Smith, 171–77. Oxford: Oxford University Press, 1994.

Szabó, Júlia. *Paintings in Nineteenth Century Hungary.* Translated by Ilona Patay. Revised by Elizabeth West. Budapest: Corvina, 1985.

Szabolcsi, Bence. *A Concise History of Hungarian Music.* 2nd ed. Translated by Sára Karig and Fred Macnicol. Budapest: Corvina, 1974.

Szigeti, Joseph. *Szigeti on the Violin.* New York: Frederick A. Praeger, 1969.

———. *With Strings Attached: Reminiscences and Reflections.* New York: Alfred A. Knopf, 1967.

Tallián, Tibor. *Béla Bartók: The Man and His Work.* Translated by Gyula Gulyás. Budapest, 1988. Originally published as *Bartók Béla: Szemtöl szemben* (Béla Bartók: Face to Face). Budapest: Gondolat, 1981.

———. "Das holzgeschnitzte Hauptwerk." *Studia musicologica* 37, no. 1 (1996): 54–67.

———. "'Um 1900 nachweisbar': Skizze zu einem Gruppenbild mit Musikern." *Studia musicologica* 24, nos. 3–4 (1982): 497–503.

Taruskin, Richard. "Back to Whom? Neoclassicism as Ideology." *19th-Century Music* 16 (1993): 286–302.

———. "Chernomor to Kashchei: Harmonic Sorcery; or, Stravinsky's 'Angle.'" *Journal of the American Musicological Society* 38, no. 1 (1985): 72–142.

———. "The Dark Side of Modern Music." *New Republic* (2 September 1988): 28–34.

———. "The Pastness of the Present and the Presentness of the Past." In *Authenticity and Early Music*, ed. Nicholas Kenyon, 137–210. Oxford: Oxford University Press, 1988. Reprinted in *Text and Act: Essays on Music and Performance* (New York: Oxford University Press, 1995), 90–154.

———. "Revising Revision." *Journal of the American Musicological Society* 46 (1993): 114–38.

———. "Russian Folk Melodies in the *Rite of Spring.*" *Journal of the American Musicological Society* 33, no. 3 (1980): 501–43.

———. *Stravinsky and the Russian Traditions.* 2 vols. Berkeley: University of California Press, 1996.

———. "Stravinsky and the Traditions: Why the Memory Hole." *Opus* 3 (1983): 10–17.

Treitler, Leo. "Harmonic Procedure in the Fourth Quartet of Béla Bartók." *Journal of Music Theory* (November 1959): 292–98.

Ujfalussy, József. *Béla Bartók.* Translated by Ruth Pataki. Budapest: Corvina, 1971.

Valkó, Arisztid. "Adatok Bartók színpadi műveihez" (Documents Relating to Bartók's Stage Works). *Magyar zene* 18 (1977): 433–39.

Vázsonyi, Bálint. *Dohnányi Ernő.* 2nd ed. Budapest: Nap, 2002.

Víg, Rudolf. "Gypsy Folk Songs from the Béla Bartók and Zoltán Kodály Collections." *Studia musicologica* 16, nos. 1–4 (1974): 89–131.

Vikárius, László. *Modell és inspiráció Bartók zenei gondolkodásában* (Model and Inspiration in Bartók's Musical Thought). Pécs: Jelenkor, 1999.

———. "'Per introdurre': A bartóki bevezetés megformálásának problematikája" ("Per introdurre": A Contribution to the Problem of Constructing Introductions in Bartók's Music). *Magyar zene* 35, no. 2 (1994): 190–203.

Vinton, John. "The Case of *The Miraculous Mandarin.*" *Musical Quarterly* 50, no. 1 (1964): 1–17.

Walker, Alan. *Franz Liszt: The Final Years, 1861–1886.* Ithaca, NY: Cornell University Press, 1996.

White, Eric Walter. *Stravinsky: The Composer and His Works.* Berkeley: University of California Press, 1979.

White, Harry, and Michael Murphy, eds. *Musical Constructions of Nationalism: Essays on the History and Ideology of European Musical Culture 1800–1945.* Cork: Cork University Press, 2001.

Index

Italic page numbers refer to figures and examples (or their captions) and tables.

"Scena della Puszta." *See* Suite for Orchestra No. 2, Andante

Scherzo (Buttykay), *40*

Scherzo for Orchestra (Kun), *40*

Schiller, Johann, 152

Schleier der Pierrette, Der [The Veil of Pierrette] (Dohnányi), 134

Schmidt, Gusztáv. *See* Szerémi, Gusztáv

Schoenberg, Arnold, 1, 124, 152, 158, 219, 277n2

Schubert, Franz, 186

Schunda, Wenzel Josef, 97, 99, 214, 215, 263n20

Scottish music, 7

Second Suite for String Orchestra (Bloch), *40*

Second Symphony "Salambo" (Buttykay), 41

Serbs, 35, 69

Sereghy, Elemér, 194, 195

Serenade (Rieger), *40*

Serenade for Strings (Herzfeld), *40*

Serenade for Strings (Major), *40*

Serenade for Strings (Szerémi), 41

Serenade No. 2 for Orchestra (Mannheimer), *39*

Sezătoarea [Society] (Romanian ethnographical journal), 193

Sheherazade (Rimsky-Korsakov), 237, 281n54

short-long rhythm, 21, 22, 208; in Erkel's *Bánk bán*, 241–42; Molnár's theory and, 52, 53; musical depiction of nature and, 118; in Piano Concerto No. 1, 168; in Piano Concerto No. 2, 177; in Rhapsody, op. 1, 60, 62–63, 77; in "Scena della puszta," 94

short-*long*-short rhythm, 49, 51, 52

Siklós, Albert, 41, 100

Siposs, Antal, *88*

Six, Les ("The Six"), 150

Six Hungarian Dances for String Quartet, No. 3 (Csermák), *23*

Slavs, 120, 191

Slovakia and Slovaks, 4, 35, 69, 120, 193

Slovakian music, 14

slow-fast-slow pattern, 20

Social Democrats, 201

sombrero de tres picos, El (Falla), 124

Somfai, László, 58, 63, 176, 243, 270n81

Sonata for Piano (Stravinsky), 126

Soviet Union, 198

Steiger, Lajos, 39

Stevens, Halsey, 218, 247

Stocker, István, 39

Stowasser, János, 97, 263n20

Strauss, Richard, 45, 53, 78, 150, 261n62; Music Academy and, 243; Romanticism and, 151; *Salome*, 135, 268n46; symphonic poems, 54, 55

Stravinsky, Igor, 1, 122, 215; Budapest reception of, 124, 125; as challenge to Bartók, 125–26; concert in Budapest, 153–56, 157–58, 181; folk music and, 147–49; modernism and, 172; neoclassical style, 117, 122, 147, 156, 157, 181; "objectivity" and, 150, 151–52, 160, 179; Philharmonic program and, 124; "Russian period," 5; works known to Bartók, *182*

Stravinsky Masterpieces: Selected Compositions for Piano Solo, 182

Stróbl, Alajos, 37

style hongrois (Hungarian style), 18, 53, 129

Suite (Rékai), 41

Suite de ballet (Pischinger), 41

Suite de ballet in Hungarian style (Erkel), *40*

Suite de Pulcinella (Stravinsky), 154, 155, *182*

Suite for Orchestra No. 2, Andante ("Scena della Puszta") (Bartók), 6, *89*, 119, 156, 211, 263n15; folk music and, 264–65n38; pastorale and, 94–96, *95*, 109–10, *110*; *tárogató* in, 100, 101, 106–8, 118

Suite in D Major for String Orchestra (Bloch), *40*

Suite romantique (Gyula), *40*

swineherd melodies *(kanász-nóták)*, 15, *16*

Switzerland, 220

Symphonic poem (Bartay), *39*

symphonic poems, 53, 54, 70, 258n26

symphonies, 30, 31

Symphonies d'instruments à vent (Stravinsky), *182*

Symphony in B♭ Major (Hubay), *39*

Symphony in C Minor (Ábrányi), 41

Symphony in C Minor (Mihalovich), 41

Symphony in C♯ Minor (Buttykay), *40*

Symphony in D Minor (Dohnányi), 30, 41–42, 53, 101, 102–3, *103*; Bartók's criticism of, 117; as model for *Kossuth*, 45–49, *46*, *49–51*, *51*; pastoral origins of

Text:	10/13 Aldus
Display:	Aldus
Compositor:	BookMatters, Berkeley
Music engraver:	Mansfield Music-Graphics
Indexer:	Alexander Trotter
Printer/Binder:	Odyssey Press